Chinese Chicago

ASIAN AMERICA
A series edited by Gordon H. Chang

The increasing size and diversity of the Asian American population, its growing significance in American society and culture, and the expanded appreciation, both popular and scholarly, of the importance of Asian Americans in the country's present and past—all these developments have converged to stimulate wide interest in scholarly work on topics related to the Asian American experience. The general recognition of the pivotal role that race and ethnicity have played in American life, and in relations between the United States and other countries, has also fostered the heightened attention.

Although Asian Americans were a subject of serious inquiry in the late nineteenth and early twentieth centuries, they were subsequently ignored by the mainstream scholarly community for several decades. In recent years, however, this neglect has ended, with an increasing number of writers examining a good many aspects of Asian American life and culture. Moreover, many students of American society are recognizing that the study of issues related to Asian America speaks to, and may be essential for, many current discussions on the part of the informed public and various scholarly communities.

The Stanford series on Asian America seeks to address these interests. The series will include works from the humanities and social sciences, including history, anthropology, political science, American studies, law, literary criticism, sociology, and interdisciplinary and policy studies.

A full list of titles in the Asian America series can be found online at www.sup.org/asianamerica

Chinese Chicago

RACE, TRANSNATIONAL MIGRATION,
AND COMMUNITY SINCE 1870

Huping Ling

STANFORD UNIVERSITY PRESS

STANFORD, CALIFORNIA

Stanford University Press
Stanford, California

Printed in the United States of America on acid-free, archival-quality
paper

Library of Congress Cataloging-in-Publication Data
Ling, Huping, 1956– author.
  Chinese Chicago: race, transnational migration, and community since
1870 / Huping Ling.
      pages cm. — (Asian America)
  Includes bibliographical references and index.
  ISBN 978-0-8047-7558-8 (cloth : alk. paper) — ISBN 978-0-8047-7559-5
(pbk. : alk. paper)
  1. Chinese Americans—Illinois—Chicago—History—19th century.
  2. Chinese Americans—Illinois—Chicago—History—20th century.
  3. Chicago (Ill.)—Emigration and immigration—Social aspects.
  4. Chicago (Ill.)—History—1875– 5. Transnationalism. I. Title.
II. Series: Asian America.
  F548.9.C5L56 2012
  305.8951'073077311—dc22

                              2011014089

Typeset by Bruce Lundquist in 11/14 Adobe Garamond

To Paul C. P. Siu
whose work inspired this book

Contents

Illustrations

Maps

Tables

Acknowledgments

The idea of writing a book on Chinese Chicago first emerged over twenty years ago, when I encountered Paul C. P. Siu's *The Chinese Laundryman* while working on my doctoral dissertation. Thirteen years ago, when I was writing *Chinese St. Louis: From Enclave to Cultural Community*, I felt that a comprehensive volume on Chinese in Chicago would be very helpful in making known the importance of Chinese communities in the Midwest. Research and data collection for this project have taken me to archives, libraries, museums, and community sites on both sides of the transnational migration. During this long journey, in both time and mileage, many individuals and institutions have provided me with invaluable assistance and support. Without their generous help, the book could not have been in its current form.

Jinan University in Guangzhou, Guangdong Province, China, where I have been an adjunct professor at the Institute of Overseas Chinese Studies since 2007, facilitated my field trip to *qiaoxiang*, the ancestral villages of overseas Chinese, in Taishan, Guangdong. Colleagues and graduate students from Jinan University, especially those from the Institute of Overseas Chinese Studies, inspired me with their intellectual energy and ingenuity. My gratitude first goes to Professors Gao Weinong and Chao Longqi of the institute for their hospitality, assistance in my fieldwork, and generosity in sharing sources and research outcomes with me; and I am also thankful to Mo Guangmu, a graduate student of Professor Gao Weinong, for researching data for me. Vice President Ji Zongan at Jinan University also offered hospitality and support during my stay at Jinan University in the summer of 2007.

Mr. Huang Deyi, director of the Overseas Chinese Affairs Office of the town of Duanfen, guided my trip to the *qiaoxiang* of Duanfen and informed me about many families originating from Duanfen. Mr. Wang Minghui, division chief of the Overseas Chinese Affairs Office of the People's Government of Guangdong Province, and Mr. Guan Xinqiang, vice-chairman of the Federation of Returned Overseas Chinese of Taishan City, provided invaluable assistance to my research. My deep gratitude also goes to Mr. Weng Songping and his family, Mrs. Mei Yuqing and her family, and to other local residents for welcoming me into their homes for interviews. I am also very thankful to Professor Mei Weiqiang of Wuyi University in Jiangmen City, Guangdong, who compiled the most recent *Meishi zongqin zupu* and whose scholarship has been invaluable to this book.

I am very thankful to the Overseas Chinese Affairs Office of the State Council of the People's Republic of China, the All-China Federation of Returned Overseas Chinese, the Chinese Institute for Overseas Chinese History Studies, the Overseas Chinese Affairs Office of Guangdong People's Government, the Overseas Exchange Association of Guangdong Province, and the Overseas Chinese Affairs Office of the Fujian People's Government for providing assistance to my research and conference trips in China.

I am indebted to my colleagues and friends in the field of Asian American studies in the United States and Canada, who have encouraged me on this project, commented on parts or the entirety of the manuscript, and offered steadfast support: Ling Z. Arenson, Kendra Boileau, Shehong Chen, Yong Chen, Roger Daniels, Madeline Y. Hsu (for reading chapters and providing suggestions), John Jung, Peter S. Li, Wei Li, Jinqi Ling, Haiming Liu, Lisa Mar, Adam McKeown (for reading chapters and providing suggestions), Soon Keong Ong, George Anthony Peffer, Barbara Posadas (for editing chapters and providing suggestions), Yuan Shu, John Kuo Wei Tchen, Zuoyue Wang, Fenggong Yang, Phillip Q. Yang (for reading manuscript and providing suggestions), Xiaohuang Yin, Henry Yu, Renqiu Yu, Xiaojian Zhao, Da Zheng, Min Zhou, and Li Zong.

I am most thankful to the following individuals in Chicago: Delilah Lee Chan, Ian Roosevelt Chin, Joe Chiu, Grace Chun, Howard Chun, Helen Eng, Eugene Kung, Ruth Kung, Margaret Larson, David K. Lee, Albert Moy, Soo Lon Moy, Thomas O'Connell, John S. Rohsenow, Andrea Stamm, Loong-yan Wong, and Judy Zhu, all volunteers at the Chinese-American Museum of Chicago (CAMOC), for their friendship and hard work preserving the Chinese American heritage in Chicago; Si Chen, branch manager of the Chicago Public Library Chinatown Branch, for assisting my research; and Esther Wong of the Chinese American Service League, Steve Brunton of the Chinese Mutual Aid Association, Leonard M. Louie of the Chinese American Civic Council, and Run-Hao Hu of the Southeast Asian Center for providing information about their organizations. I am especially grateful to Soo Lon Moy and John S. Rohsenow for reading chapters of the manuscript and for offering invaluable suggestions.

The following individuals have generously shared their life histories with me: Grace Chun, Howard Chun, Eugene Kung, Ruth Kung, David K. Lee, Tammy Sun Spencer, Wong Xiaoyu, and Ling Zhang from Chicago; Richard Ho, Don Ko, Annie Leong, Chung Kok Li, and Rachel Wang from St. Louis. I have also benefited from the interviews conducted by the aforementioned members of the CAMOC (the name of each individual interviewer appears in the notes): Celia Moy Cheung, Catherine Wong Chin, Ian Roosevelt Chin, Herman Chiu, Corwin Eng, Susanna Fong, Doc Huang, Yolanda Lee, Jenny Ling, Toung Ling, Cho Tuk Lo, Rich Lo, Benjamin C. Moy, Dato' Seri Stanley Thai, Charles W. Tun, Lorrain Moy Tun, Harry Wu, and Henry Yee. I also want to thank Ruth Kung for sharing her interview of Lorraine Moy Tun and John Jung for introducing me to the CAMOC and for sharing his life history and writings on Chinese Americans. Without their generous participation, this book could not have been completed.

I am grateful to the staff members and officers of the following institutions and organizations: Asian Human Services Chinatown Office, Chaozhou Tongxiang Hui, the Chicago Chinatown Chamber of Commerce, the Chicago Chinese American Historical Society, the Chicago History Museum, the Chicago North Chinese School, the Chicago Public Library Chinatown Branch, the Chinese American Cultural Center, the Chinese-American Museum of Chicago, the Chinese American Service League, the Chinese Christian Union Church, the Chinese Community Center, the Chinese Consolidated Benevolent Association, the Chinese Language School, the Chinese Mutual Aid Association, the Hip Sing Association, the Hong Men Zhigong Tang, the International Overseas Chinese Association Chicago Branch, the Lee Family Association, the Longgang Qinyi Gongsuo, Mercy Medical in Chinatown, Mount Auburn Cemetery, the Moy Family Association, the National Archives Records Administration–Great Lakes Region (Chicago), the Newberry Library, the On Leong Merchants and Laborers

Association, the Chicago chapter of the Organization of Chinese Americans, Pacific Global Bank, Pui Tak Center, Pui Tak Christian School, Rosehill Cemetery, the Special Collection of the Joseph Regenstein Library at the University of Chicago, and St. Therese Chinese Catholic School.

The following Chinese or Asian American businesses have also provided assistance to the project: Anh Linh Restaurant; Argyle Medical Center; C. P. Louie Travel; Chinatown Smoke Shop; Chiu Quon Restaurant and Bakery; Dúc Hûng Video; Fat Lee Grocery; Heng Heng Jewelry; Hon Kee Restaurant; House of Fortune Restaurant; Kim Hing Jewelry; Oriental Gifts and Food; Pacific Realty, Inc.; Speed Kleen Laundromat; Thai Grocery; Three Happiness Restaurant; Tiên Giang Restaurant; and Viêt Hoa Oriental Grocery Store.

Special thanks to Truman State University, my home institution, for providing me with Faculty Summer Research Grants and Sabbatical Grants; to Lori Allen of the Pickler Memorial Library for tirelessly acquiring numerous materials through interlibrary loans for me; to Winston Vanderhoof of Truman State University Publications for creating Map 1 for this book; and to my colleagues in the History Department for giving me endless support, especially to Jason McDonald, a scholar on American ethnicity and immigration, who read the manuscript and provided valuable insights, along with sharing bibliography on ethnic Chicago. I am deeply grateful to the History Department at the University of Missouri–Columbia for sponsoring the sabbatical leave during which I completed this book.

At Stanford University Press, two anonymous readers enthusiastically endorsed my manuscript along with excellent comments and insightful suggestions. Gordon H. Chang has provided steadfast support and encouragement; Stacy Wagner and Jessica A. Walsh have expedited the review process and have guided me through the final stage of the project. Christine Gever's judicious and intelligent copyediting has improved the manuscript immensely. Carolyn Brown and her production team worked with efficiency and professionalism. Together, they have helped transform my manuscript into this beautiful book!

My husband, Sami, has been my creative muse, candid critic, and resilient technical support throughout all my intellectual enterprises. Without his constant counsel, comfort, and companionship, I would not have been able to complete this book.

A Note on Translation and Terminology

Although the Pinyin phonetic system based on Putonghua or Mandarin Chinese has been more widely used in recent academic writings, the earlier Wade-Giles system still persists. In this book, I have used Pinyin whenever the Chinese names of places occur, except those preferred transliterations of certain proper nouns, for example, "Canton" for "Guangzhou" (Pinyin). Regarding the names of Chinese people mentioned in the book, however, the situation is more complicated. While the English-language government records, archival manuscripts, and newspapers recorded the names of Chinese people based on their pronunciation in Cantonese or other local dialects without consistency, the Chinese-language sources provided the names in Chinese characters that are consistent in writing. While such variants make consistency in spelling people's names nearly impossible, I have managed to arrive at some degree of consistency by using the original spellings cited in the English-language sources and Pinyin spellings based on Putonghua from the Chinese-language sources. Nevertheless, inconsistency is inevitable in some cases; for example, the surname "Moy" (according to its Cantonese pronunciation) also appears in its Pinyin form "Mei" in later chapters.

In addition, both the singular form "community" and plural form "communities" have been used in reference to the Chinese settlement in Chicago before and after 1912, respectively. Before 1912, it was primarily a single-sited community, located in the Loop area around South Clark Street. After 1912, when the majority of the Chinatown businesses and residents relocated to the Cermak-Wentworth area, some still remained in the South Clark neighborhood. Since the 1960s, the expansion of South Chinatown, the emergence of suburban communities, and the revival of North Chinatown have resulted in multi-sited Chinese American communities. Moreover, the plural form, "communities," also emphasizes the cultural, economic, linguistic, political, and social diversity among the Chinese in Chicago.

Chinese Chicago

Introduction

Rethinking Chinese Chicago

And each time I roam, Chicago is
Calling me home, Chicago is
One town that won't let you down
It's my kind of town

—Lyrics by Sammy Cahn, music by Jimmy van Heusen

Chicago is a city of hope and promise. Situated in the heartland of America, favored with land, water, rail, and air transportation advantages, and populated by vibrant multiethnic communities, it attracts thousands of people from all across the country who seek to realize their dreams. Barack Obama, a graduate of Columbia University in New York, came to Chicago in the summer of 1985 and worked as a community organizer on the far South Side of the city, thus starting his political journey to the presidency. His historic victory in the 2008 presidential election was a spectacular manifestation of the fulfillment of the American dream through the promise of Chicago.[1]

The vast opportunities presented by Chicago were evident to newcomers even more than a century ago. The city has attracted hundreds of thousands of immigrants from around the world; since the mid-nineteenth century, Canadians, Germans, English, Irish, Scottish, Swedish, Norwegians, Poles, and Italians have poured into the city over time, making it a truly multiethnic community. For the Chinese who first arrived in the 1870s, Chicago offered a growing and attractive economic landscape. Here the Chinese initially established a small but lively community in the downtown Loop area (the downtown business district coinciding with the old cable car service area). Chinese grocery stores, laundries, restaurants, and community associations sustained the residents of early Chinatown. Less than two decades later, the small Chinese community of nearly 2,000 was so successful that it sponsored the "Chinese Village" in the 1893 World's Columbian Exposition, taking the place of the Chinese Qing government, which was boycotting the fair in protest against the Chinese Exclusion Act of 1882. The success of the Chinese Village helped promote China, Chinese culture, and especially the financial abilities of the Chinese merchants who financed the Chinese Village at a key historic moment when American politicians were debating US expansion into the Pacific.

The anti-Chinese sentiments prevalent in the country, embodied in the Chinese exclusion acts since the 1880s, affected relations between the Chinese and the larger society even in Chicago. In the 1910s, downtown property owners raised rents, making it difficult for Chinese businesses to survive and forcing the vast majority of the Chinese to move to the city's South Side in search of cheaper properties. On the South Side, the Chinese soon established a new Chinatown, known as South Chinatown today, which remains a major tourist attraction of the city.

Since the 1970s, the influx of ethnic Chinese from Vietnam, Laos, and Cambodia has revitalized the Argyle Street area on the North Side, which has become known as North Chinatown. Meanwhile, the suburban Chinese communities have also been growing rapidly. Today, more than 100,000 Chinese Americans live in the Chicago area. From the gift shops, grocery stores and supermarkets, restaurants and bakeries, herb stores, medical clinics, insurance agencies, real estate agencies, and accountants in Chinatown, to the Argonne National Laboratory, Fermi Lab, Abbott Laboratories, Motorola, the University of Chicago, Northwestern University, the Illinois Institute of Technology, and many other research institutions, universities, and colleges in the suburbs and nearby, Chinese Chicagoans are making valuable contributions to the larger society.

What attracted the Chinese to Chicago? How did they integrate into this communications and commercial center? How did they survive in this multiracial and multicultural industrial "jungle"? This study attempts to address these questions by exploring the history of the Chinese in Chicago from the three Moy brothers to the present-day Chinese Chicagoans and their transnational links to the homeland.

Legacy of the "Chicago School" and Beyond

Upon joining the Department of Sociology at the University of Chicago in 1914, where he teamed up with other like-minded colleagues such as Ernest Watson Burgess, Homer Hoyt, and Louis Wirth, Robert Ezra Park developed his theory of assimilation, as it pertained to immigrants in the United States, into an approach to urban sociology that became known as the "Chicago School." The sociology professors and their students at the University of Chicago were deeply interested in "the social and economic forces at work in the slums and their effect in influencing the social and personal organization of those who lived there" and were actively involved in studies on settlement houses and ethnic communities.[2] Coinciding with the federally funded Works Progress Administration (WPA) in place in 1935, many joint WPA–Department of Sociology projects were launched, and consequently, numerous scholarly works on Chicago's poor neighborhoods were completed, among them Nels Anderson's *The Hobo*, on homeless men in the city; Louis Wirth's study of Jews, *The Ghetto*; and Clifford Shaw's study of a young delinquent, *The Jack-Roller* (see Chapter 2 for details on these works). Some students recruited to study the "Oriental Problem" investigated the socioeconomic conditions in Chicago's Chinatown.[3] Their theses and dissertations, together with publications of students and scholars in other universities of the region, provide a solid base for studies on Chinese Americans in Chicago as well as in the rest of the country (see Chapter 6 for details on these works).

The existing literature on the Chinese in Chicago addresses the issues of assimilation, social behavior, occupational mobility, landscape, and linguistic diversity but lacks a fuller treatment of the nature and effects of transnational interactions on Chinese Chicagoans.[4] Historical records have indicated significant contacts with the homeland that impacted both the immigrants and the societies at home. This book will try to fill some of the gaps in our knowledge about Chinese Chicagoans. More specifically, it will address the following pertinent questions: How was the transnational migration reflected in native places, such as in land purchased; in houses, schools, and hospitals constructed with remittances from overseas Chinese; in written records of genealogies, gazetteers, and overseas Chinese magazines and in academic writings? How did the Chinese navigate a city marked with sharp racial divisions? How did transnational migration affect the formation of family and community? Situated in a midwestern metropolis and hub of transportation, what role did Chicago Chinese communities play in the regional and national economy?

There are rich and abundant anthropological, archeological, archival, cultural, and intellectual resources in the native places of coastal China that have yet to be widely used by Western scholars. Within the field of Asian American studies, an overwhelming majority of scholarship to date still remains centered on the American coasts, with San Francisco, New York, Los Angeles, and their vicinities as the dominant sites of scholarly work.[5] Although Chicago has been a major national and international center of attention since its birth in 1833 and rapid rise as America's "Second City" in the 1890s, the Chinese Chicagoans have remained relatively understudied. Thus, constructing a Midwest-focused but transnationally comprehensive and comparative study that encompasses race, migration, and community for the nearly century-and-a-half history of Chinese Chicago will be valuable for broadening the understanding of immigration to the Midwest and of the Chinese in the Midwest in particular.

Themes of the Book:
Race, Transnational Migration, and Community

This book focuses on three crucial issues that define the Chinese in Chicago: race, transnational migration, and community. First, it examines how the Chinese have dealt with the complex mix of race and ethnicity in the city. Second, it investigates how transnational migration has penetrated all aspects of the Chinese experience in Chicago. Third, it shows how the Chinese community in Chicago has never been simple and monolithic but always culturally, geographically, linguistically, politically, and socioeconomically complex and diverse.

RACE: SURVIVING THE JUNGLE

In the ethnically complex city of Chicago, the Chinese occupy a delicate position in terms of racial relations. In the early years of the Chinese settlement, the small community was overshadowed by other, more populous ethnic groups including the Germans, Danes, Irish, Poles, Swedes, Jews, and Italians. As a quiet and exotic people, they were initially tolerated by the local residents and welcomed by the Christian missionaries. However, Chicago was not immune to the overall climate of anti-Chinese hostility prevalent in the country as the Chinese exclusion laws were enforced in the late nineteenth and early twentieth centuries. In Chicago, anti-Chinese prejudice and racial tensions propelled local landlords in the 1910s to raise property rents—a form of economic sanction against the Chinese, whose population now reached nearly two thousand. The Chinese opted to relocate to avoid the tension and potential conflicts. In the new Chinatown on the South Side after 1912, they shared neighborhoods first with the Italians and later with blacks who migrated from the American South. There both racial tension and racial harmony characterized relations between the Chinese and their Italian and black neighbors. While there were incidents in which Chinese were called names and were made fun of for their physical appearance by Italians, there were also cases in which strong friendships and bonds formed between Chinese families and their Italian neighbors, and it was also not uncommon for blacks to be hired in Chinese laundries and other businesses.

In Chicago, the Chinese successfully managed to navigate the multiethnic "jungle" by consciously avoiding racial conflicts, by creating and maintaining an insulated ethnic enclave that was largely self-governed, and by cultivating friendships with local authorities.[6] Since the 1960s, the new community leaders have made concerted efforts to bridge Chinatown communities and the larger society. Meanwhile, Chinese professionals are successfully mingling with other ethnic groups at work and in suburban residential communities. The various strategies employed by Chinese Chicagoans in different historical periods indicate their instinct for survival as well as their conscious efforts to adapt and assimilate.

TRANSNATIONAL MIGRATION: A VITAL LINK

Since the 1990s, a growing number of scholars have noted that immigrants have lived their lives across geographical borders and maintained close ties to home. A number of social scientists have begun to use the term "transnational" to describe such cross-national, cross-cultural phenomena. Anthropologists Nina Glick Schiller, Linda Basch, and Cristina Blanc-Szanton (1992) have analyzed and conceptualized transnational migration in more precise language. They define "transnationalism" as "the emergence of a social process in which migrants establish social fields that cross geographic, cultural, and political borders. Immigrants are understood to be transmigrants when they develop and maintain multiple relations—familial, economic, social, organizational, religious, and political—that span borders. . . . The multiplicity of migrants' involvements in both the home and host societies is a central element of transnationalism."[7] Since then, writers from various disciplines have further delineated and evaluated the theorization of transnationalism.[8] As the concept of transnationalism has become a compelling theoretical framework for interpreting manifestations of international migration, a number of historians have also endorsed the idea in their monographs.[9] In their view, transnationalism offers a richer interpretation of Chinese migration by focusing on both native place and host society. At the same time, scholars have also cautioned against the overuse or "abuse" of the term.[10]

This study finds that the Chinese in Chicago have been closely linked with the transnational migration network. Chinese ethnic businesses, from the very beginning, were closely connected to the transnational ethnic economy. In all aspects of business, including capital accumulation, procurement of inventory, business operation, and distribution of merchandise, they have depended on the transnational ethnic network. Although located in the hinterland, the Chinese in Chicago have thus been connected to the homeland and other Chinese communities across the country; and the Chinese ethnic economy in Chicago has also served as a vital socioeconomic link to other Chinese communities in the Midwest, largely thanks to the city's transportation advantages and their transnational connections.

Like Chinese businesses, the lives of Chinese families in Chicago have also been impacted by transnational migration. Money remitted to the homeland by the Chinese in Chicago sustained family members, purchased land, and constructed new houses. Continuing transnational connections with the homeland enabled immigrants to support their trans-Pacific families. To cope with marital separation caused by immigration, a special marital arrangement was invented and practiced within many early families. I conceptualize it as "transnational split marriage—Taishanese 'widow' and American concubine." Under such an arrangement, the wife of an immigrant stayed in the native village to take care of children and in-laws, while a concubine, often chosen by the wife or parents of the immigrant, accompanied the immigrant to the foreign land.

COMMUNITY: DIVERGENCE AND CONVERGENCE

Chicago Chinese communities have been a battleground where interest groups with diverse and sometimes competing and conflicting lineal, geographical, cultural, social, and political orientations have clashed, compromised, and collaborated. The earliest divisions and conflicts emerged among the major clans of the community—the Moys, the Chins, and the Wongs— for economic gain and political influence. The lineal divisions soon evolved into organizational contentions for community power structures: On Leong versus Hip Sing, and later the Chinese Consolidated Benevolent Association (CCBA) versus the newer community service organizations. While all power groups vied for attention from the major political parties in the homeland, whether it be the Emperor Protection Association (Baohuang Hui) or the Nationalist Party (Kuomintang) prior to 1949, the retreat of the Nationalist Party and government to Taiwan and the founding of the People's Republic of China by the Communist Party in 1949 resulted in divided loyalty among the Chinese in Chicago, similar to what transpired in other Chinese communities across the country. The post-1949 political confrontation between Taiwan and mainland China also divided the community into pro-Taiwan, or pro-Nationalist, and pro-China groups. The influx of ethnic Chinese refugees from Vietnam, Cambodia, and Laos following the fall of Saigon in 1975 further complicated the situation, contributing to the expansion of the multiethnic transnational Chinatown on the North Side. The geographical diversity was further enhanced when suburban Chinese Americans formed "cultural communities" beginning in the 1970s, and a working-class Chinese community in Bridgeport expanded South Chinatown in the 1990s. The tripartite division into South Chinatown, North Chinatown, and suburban cultural communities has made the Chinese communities in "Chicagoland" complex and conflicting. Yet in the interest of best serving each group's needs and demands, community organizations have realized the importance of cooperation and collaboration and have strived to bring Chinese Chicagoans together under a common identity as Chinese Americans.

Highlights of the Book

This book covers important historical developments in the Chinese communities of Chicago from the arrival of the three Moy brothers in the 1870s to the present day, highlighting the establishment of transnational communities between the 1870s and 1940s and their transformation in the postwar period. Chapter 1 traces the roots of the transnational community in Chicago from both macroscopic and microscopic perspectives. In a broad sense, the unique position of Guangdong Province, with its ports well developed for international trade and its residents well accustomed to a long tradition of domestic migration and overseas emigration, made it a major source of Chinese emigrants to other parts of the world. The invasion of China by Western industrialized powers and the country's natural calamities in the mid-nineteenth century pushed the local residents to the brink of economic disaster. The lure of gold and other economic opportunities in America attracted hundreds of thousands of Chinese to the new land. The Moys, one of the major clans among the early Chinese immigrants in Chicago, provide a good example of how the patrilineal network assisted and perpetuated transnational migration.

Chapter 2 examines in depth the emergence of the early Chinatown in the multiethnic industrial center of Chicago. It relates how the community gingerly navigated the racial thicket, through a combination of self-government and the maintenance of amicable relationships with local political and law enforcement authorities. It also investigates the early rivalry between the Moys and the Wongs, which cast an adverse shadow of "tong fighting" over an otherwise mostly homogeneous and harmonious community. It then discusses the root causes for the relocation of the early Chinese community from the Loop area to the South Side.

Chapter 3 examines the transnational economic activities of Chinatown. Without English-language and other skills necessary for competition in the larger labor market, the Chinese carved out niche businesses primarily including hand laundries, grocery and general merchandise stores, and restaurants and chop suey shops. Transnational ethnic networks were essential for the sustenance and success of these businesses. Consistent with Chicago's unique position as a transportation hub, the Chinatown businesses served as a center for regional socioeconomic development. Prostitution and gambling were also part of the Chinatown economy. Although considered as vice, they were inevitable in a gender-imbalanced immigrant community, serving as substitutes for an absent family life and as recreation after a long week of toil in a laundry, grocery store, or chop suey shop.

Chapter 4 discusses the marriage patterns and family structures of the community. Three patterns emerged among the Chinese families: (1) the transnational split marriage already mentioned; (2) traditional Chinese marriage; and (3) American-style urban marriages: love unions, interracial marriages, and widow remarriages. The first was a practical arrangement devised by the Chinese to cope with the marital separation due to transnational migration. The second was common among Chinese restaurateurs, grocers, and lottery house keepers, all of whom were merchants exempted from the Chinese exclusion acts and consequently permitted to bring their families with them or send for their wives later. The marriages in the third category were natural products of American life. The chapter also argues that a large gap in age between husband and wife and large family size both characterized the families of the first two types. Life in America also elevated the position of most Chinese women to that of family head, co-provider, and joint decision maker.

Chapter 5 examines the social organizations of the transnational community and their significance in bridging Chinatown, the homeland, and American society. Self-government was a predominant feature of Chinatown prior to the 1960s. On Leong, Hip Sing, the CCBA, and family associations were transplantations of traditional Chinese social organizations. They constituted the early social landscape of the community and endeavored to maintain transnational ties between the immigrant communities on American soil and the native places in the homeland. At the same time, the community also adopted or hybridized American values and established progressive trade and social organizations, Christian churches, Chinese-language schools, and newspapers, connecting Chinatown communities with the larger American society as well as the homeland.

The rich intellectual legacy of the Chinese in Chicago is the focus of Chapter 6. It first provides a collective portrait of Chinese students and intellectuals and then explores the intellectual contributions made by students and scholars in Chicago and nearby regions. It divides the literature on Chinese Chicago into three periods, analyzing the large body of literature produced by the pioneer scholars from the 1920s and 1930s, wartime and postwar scholars from the 1940s to the 1960s, and the more diverse scholars of the city in the years following the 1960s.

Chapter 7 traces and analyzes the emergence and evolution of the newer Chinatown on the North Side, the Chinese cultural communities in the suburbs, and the expansion of South Chinatown, along with the development in Bridgeport that has become part of South Chinatown in recent decades. The tripartite division of Chinese Chicago poses serious challenges. To secure the communities' existence and to promote their further development, various cross-ethnic and cross-cultural community organizations have been formed and are diligently working toward a common goal—celebrating a multiethnic Chicago.

Finally, the Epilogue looks at the "hollow center" phenomenon in the homeland.

Significance of This Study

This book is significant for a number of reasons. Most notably, it is the first comprehensive study of the Chinese in Chicago. While earlier studies have provided valuable information on the subject—see, for example, Tin-Chiu Fan's thesis "Chinese Residents in Chicago" (1926), Paul C. P. Siu's dissertation "The Chinese Laundryman: A Study of Isolation" and its publication in 1987 edited by John Kuo Wei Tchen, and Adam McKeown's *Chinese Migrant Networks and Cultural Change: Peru, Chicago, Hawaii, 1900–1936*—none so far has encompassed the complete history of the Chinese communities of Chicago from the beginning to the present in a single volume. Building on previous work and utilizing primary sources in both English and Chinese—in particular the Immigration and Naturalization Service's Chicago Chinese Case Files (CCCF) at the National Archives Records Administration–Great Lakes Region (Chicago); the Ernest Watson Burgess Papers at the University of Chicago; local newspapers; oral history interviews; sources from the Chicago History Museum and the Chinese-American Museum of Chicago; and Chinese genealogies, gazetteers, and local and regional overseas Chinese magazines—this book reconstructs Chinese Chicago's history over nearly a century and a half. The book's extensive use of Chinese sources in addition to English sources is intended to provide a more transnationalistic, global view of Chinese emigration to America, from not only a Western but also a Chinese perspective. The incorporation of Chinese scholarship on overseas Chinese expands the field of Asian American studies, while making these primary sources available to readers who are unable to access sources in the Chinese language.

This book is also the first comparative study of the Chinese in Chicago. It places the Chinese in the broader contexts of transnational migration and multiethnic Chicago and compares and contrasts the Chinese in Chicago with Chinese immigrants in other areas of the United States. It also compares Chinatown with other poor ethnic neighborhoods in Chicago as presented in Nels Anderson's study of the homeless, Louis Wirth's study of Jews, and Clifford Shaw's work on a young delinquent.

Additionally, this book contributes to the continuing theoretical discourse on transnationalism and migration. Centered on the theme of transnational migration, it examines elements that connect Chicago with coastal China. It also looks closely at the role Chicago has played as a vital link within transnational networks of migration and the translocal migration movement and converses with other significant works on Chinese transnational migration.[11] Finally, this book contributes significantly to ethnic urban studies on the American Midwest. Its data and interpretations provide refreshing and invaluable resources on this region for scholarly research, for public understanding, and for both governmental and private policy making for urban planning and development.

ONE

Searching for Roots of a Transnational Community

樹挪死，人挪活。

A tree would likely die when transplanted; a man
will survive and thrive when migrated.

—Chinese proverb

Migration is an essential survival strategy in human society as well as in the animal kingdom. In an attempt to survive or to better their lives, humans have migrated to every continent, resulting in the colorful racial diversity evident today. Following this natural instinct, the Chinese migrated from north-central China, where they originated, to all of China proper and then emigrated further all around the world. One can trace the roots of Chinese immigrants in America as far back as ancient Chinese history and as close to the present day as the global capitalistic expansions of recent centuries.

Forces of Transnational Migration

GUANGDONG AS A HUB OF OVERSEAS EMIGRATION

The large two-story building, built in 1928, formerly headquarters of the On Leong Merchants and Laborers Association, stands prominently on Wentworth Avenue in the heart of Chicago's Chinatown; it reminds many local Chinese residents of a *yanglou* (Western-style building) or *diaolou* (fortress building or watchtower) in their homeland in Taishan. The striking grandeur and staunch Chinese characteristics of the building also lead curious visitors to marvel over the connections between the Chinese in Chicago and their homeland.

The similarities are hardly coincidental but the natural outcome of emigration. Taishan and the three adjacent counties of Kaiping (Hoiping in Cantonese), Enping (Yanping), and Xinhui (Sunwei) are collectively called Siyi (Sze Yap), or "four counties." Along with Canton and its three adjacent counties, or *Sanyi* (Sam Yap), of Nanhai (Namhoi), Panyu (Panyi), and Shunde (Shuntak), they are internationally known as hubs whence came the overseas Chinese in North America, Australia, and Western Europe, while the neighboring province, Fujian, has been a native place for Chinese emigrants to Southeast Asian countries. The Overseas Chinese Affairs Office of the Nationalist government published statistics in 1945 indicating that among the then 8,546,374 overseas Chinese, 5,992,066 or 70 percent were from Guangdong, mainly from Canton and the Sanyi and Siyi districts.[1]

The Chinese in Guangdong are people with a long tradition of migration. The first group of migrants were more than one hundred thousand Han, or mainstream Chinese, dispatched by the authoritarian government of the Qin dynasty (221–206 BC) to expand the influence of Han culture and to

Old On Leong headquarters on Wentworth Avenue, 2008. Collection of Huping Ling.

develop the region.[2] In migrating, the Han moved from a temperate environment into a debilitating hot, humid subtropical climate and gradually
became accustomed to their habitat in South China. As a coastal province,
Guangdong provided easy access to Southeast and South Asia, where many
Chinese merchants had opened commercial routes by the first century AD.
As early as the third century AD, Canton had positioned itself as an excellent port, attracting Arab merchants from West and South Asia for trade
and becoming a great hub for international trade and overseas emigration.
By the end of the Tang dynasty (618–906 AD), to escape the frequent social
upheavals and civil wars, some Chinese emigrated to Southeast Asian countries, where they were called Tangren (people of the Tang dynasty) by the
locals. This was the first large-scale Chinese emigration from Guangdong.[3]

The Song dynasty (960–1279) saw the rapid development of Chinese
maritime commerce. Residents from Fujian and Guangdong frequently
traveled between the two provinces and trading ports in Southeast Asia.
Merchants stranded by typhoons, illness, or debt became accidental settlers
in these foreign lands. They were later joined by political refugees escaping persecution by the Chinese authorities and others seeking their fortune
overseas. By the thirteenth and fourteenth centuries, Chinese emigration
to Southeast Asia reached its zenith, as a result of Mongol military expeditions and Ming government–sponsored maritime expeditions to the region,
which left behind many Chinese soldiers and civilians in the localities they
contacted.

Quanzhou and Zhangzhou in Fujian together with Canton in Guangdong were well-developed Chinese ports for international trade as early as
the Song dynasty. Canton, however, was selected as the only official port for
international trade by the Qing government (1644–1911) in 1760. Writers
have pointed out a number of reasons why the Qing court chose Canton as
the only open port. First, rampant piracy in the coastal provinces of Fujian
and Guangdong forced the Qing government to close the coastal areas for
self-defense. Second, the Manchu rulers were convinced that the "foreign
devils" would corrupt the Chinese populace and therefore should be contained in the most distant port possible. Third, the Qing rulers believed it
more practical to delegate international trade to the experienced merchants
in Canton (who were therefore called Gonghong, or security merchants)
than for it to be handled by the court.[4] The Canton monopoly in international trade allowed Western influence to penetrate the port city and nearby

regions, making Canton and its adjacent counties premier locations for sending Chinese laborers overseas.

GUANGDONG AS A LINK OF GLOBAL IMPERIALISTIC EXPANSION

Although the emigration overseas, especially to Southeast Asia, continued throughout the centuries, emigration to the Americas did not occur in significant numbers until the end of the Opium Wars (1839–1842), when China was defeated by the cannons and gunboats of the British empire and forced to sign a series of unequal treaties with Britain, France, and the United States. These unequal treaties demanded that the Chinese government pay a $21 million indemnity, abolish the government-chartered Gonghong monopolistic system of trade, open five ports (Canton, Xiamen, Fuzhou, Ningbo, and Shanghai) to trade and to the residence of British consuls and merchants and their families, cede Hong Kong to the British, and fix a tariff at the very low rate of 5 percent. These treaties were imposed by the victors upon the vanquished at gunpoint, without the careful deliberation normally practiced in the course of reaching international agreements in Europe and America. Ironically, though the war was triggered by conflict over the opium trade in China, opium was not even mentioned in the treaties, as the issue of its future status was cautiously avoided by both sides. As a result, opium traffic became essentially unrestrained after the war.

The importation of opium deepened the social and economic crisis. The volume of imports rose from 33,000 chests in 1842 to 46,000 chests in 1848 and to 52,929 chests in 1850. The year 1848 alone witnessed the outflow of more than ten million taels of silver, which exacerbated the already grave economic dislocation and copper-silver exchange rate.[5] The disruptive economic consequences of opium importation were further compounded by the general influx of foreign goods into the open ports. Canton was particularly hard hit because it had the longest history of foreign trade and the most foreign contact; it now lost this advantage to other open ports. Local household industries were swept away and the self-sufficient agrarian economy collapsed. Those who were adversely affected thus became potential emigrants.

In addition to the external invasions, many natural calamities also occurred in China during the 1840s and 1850s. Severe drought occurred in Henan in 1847; flooding of the Yangtze River plagued Hubei, Anhui, Jiangsu, and Zhejiang; and famine struck Guangxi—all in 1849. Flood and famine in Guangdong gave way to the catastrophic Taiping Revolution (1850–1864), which devastated the land, uprooted the peasantry, and dislocated the economy and the polity.

Imperialist invasions and natural disasters, however, can only partly explain the phenomenal emigration to America in the second part of the nineteenth century. The lure of gold upon the discovery of rich deposits in California and other regions in 1848, and the opportunities in the so-called New Continent that resulted, also pulled Chinese emigrants to Gam San, or Gold Mountain, the Chinese nickname for America. In 1849, the news of the discovery of gold in California spread like wildfire to every corner of the world and soon attracted thousands of gold seekers to California. Among them, 325 were from Tangshan, a sobriquet used by overseas Chinese for China proper.[6] In the early 1850s, the number of Chinese increased dramatically—2,716 in 1851 and 20,026 in 1852.[7] By 1882, when the passage of the Chinese Exclusion Act ended Chinese immigration on a large scale, there were about 300,000 Chinese resident in the continental United States.[8]

In view of the popular Chinese expectation that America was a land full of gold, gold played a significant role in the lives of the early Chinese immigrants, with the majority of *gam san haak* (gold mountain guests) working in the mining areas of California. Census statistics indicate that almost 100 percent of the Chinese in the continental United States in 1860 were living in California. Most Chinese miners worked on placer claims, the most labor intensive and least remunerative of the three methods—placer, hydraulic, and quartz—used by miners. They washed the gold-bearing sand in small amounts in a pan or rocker, letting the heavier particles of gold settle to the bottom.

In addition to mining, the construction of the transcontinental railroad absorbed a large number of Chinese laborers, many of whom were former gold miners. After the end of the Civil War, the American government could once again devote its attention to the construction of the railroad. It contracted the eastern part of the railroad to the Union Pacific Railroad Company to be built westward from the Missouri River, and the western part of the railroad to the Central Pacific Railroad Company, nicknamed "the Big Four" as it was formed by four Sacramento merchants—Leland Stanford, Charles Crocker, Mark Hopkins, and C. P. Huntington—to be built eastward from Sacramento. In February 1865, fifty Chinese workers were hired by the Central Pacific Railroad Company as an experiment. As the Chinese workers performed various jobs of blasting, driving horses, handling rock, and wielding picks and shovels and proved to be effective and reliable, the company began to hire more Chinese. During the peak of construction, twelve thousand Chinese, approximately 90 percent of the entire workforce, worked for the Central Pacific Railroad Company.[9]

The Moys, the Taishanese, and Transnational Ties

THE MOYS

One distinctive feature of the Chicago Chinese is the dominance of the Moys, outnumbering any other surnames, especially among the early immigrants. The Moy Family Association has been the largest of the family associations in Chicago since the late nineteenth century. In the over six thousand immigrant files in Chicago for the years between 1898 and 1940, there are at least one thousand files under the surname Moy.[10] Although the Chins and Wongs were also populous clans in the early history of the Chinese in Chicago, for the convenience of discussion I shall use the example of the Moy clan to demonstrate the transnational kinship connections.

According to the Moy family genealogy, its progenitor was a member of the royal family of the Shang dynasty (1766–1122 BC). He was granted a principality in what is now Bo County, Anhui Province, called Mei in Mandarin Chinese (Moy in Cantonese), and therefore was known as Count Moy, whose offspring adopted the name of the principality as their surname. During the Han dynasty (206 BC–220 AD), Bo County administratively belonged to Runan Prefecture (*Nunan jun*), and that is why the Moys were also known as Nunan people.[11]

Though originating in northern China, the Moys eventually migrated south. By the end of the Han dynasty in the second century AD, the court had been weakened by both internal and external disturbances—political rivalries among the powerful aristocratic families and pressures from the nomadic "barbarians" from the north and northwest frontiers. The dynasty was soon usurped by one of the powerful aristocratic clans and then divided into the three states of Han, Shu, and Wu, during what is known as the Three Kingdoms Period (220–265 AD). This was followed by the so-called Period of Division (220–589 AD) and the Northern and Southern Dynasties (420–589 AD), when successive waves of various groups of northern and northwestern nomads invaded northern China and forced the Chinese court to move south. The constant wars among the divided Chinese states and between the nomadic kingdoms and the Chinese courts, together with the subsequent devastation of farmlands, resulted in one of the largest population shifts in Chinese history—hundreds of thousands of people followed the Chinese courts south of the Yangtze River, to an area previously perceived by the northern Chinese as an uncivilized region. For the first time in history, the population in South China exceeded that in the North: during the Han dynasty, the population ratio between the North and the South was 10 to 1; by the time of the northern Song dynasty (960–1127 AD), more than half the Chinese population resided in the South.

The Moys were among the waves of migrants from the North. In 307 AD, after a notorious palace coup that overthrew the Jin court, the Moys began their migration to southern China, following the defeated Jin court.[12] To rule the dislocated populace more effectively, the Chinese court in exile established a *qiaojun*, or migrant prefecture system, among the migrants, setting up prefectures for the migrants in the South in accordance with those in the North where the various groups of migrants had originally resided. Runan Prefecture (presently Anhui Province) was thus established for the Moys, who had originally lived in Bo County, Runan Prefecture. The *qiaojun* system helped maintain social order and stability among the migrants, who therefore willingly cooperated with the government in implementing the practice. Only the prominent aristocratic families, however, migrated in an organized fashion, moving along the patriarchal clan structures collectively, whereas the commoners migrated sporadically and more or less randomly. Thus, the association between a surname and its prefecture name indicates the prominence and prestige of that surname. The Moys, having been transplanted and rerooted in South China, were mindful of their historically prominent northern origins and traced them proudly.[13] Over the nearly two thousand years that followed, the Moys spread widely across China proper. The areas with the highest concentration of Moys include Anhui, Hubei, Henan, Hunan, Sichuan, Jiangxi, Zhejiang, Guangdong, and Jiangsu provinces, with an estimated total population of five million members of the clan.[14]

A branch of the Moy family settled in Duanfen Township, Taishan County, Guangdong. Over time, Duanfen Moys became the largest branch of the Moy family in China.[15] Duanfen Moys also prospered in the region, and Moy remains the predominant surname in the town, comprising 20 percent of the over fifty thousand residents during the period from the 1970s to the 2000s.[16] A survey conducted in 1996 counted 14,500 Moys, or 26 percent of the total population of 55,290 in Duanfen.[17]

What makes the Duanfen Moys stand out among all the branches of the Moy family is their written records, which provide virtually a complete family genealogy, or *zupu*. In 1664, Moy Mingxie, an eleventh-generation member of the Duanfen Moys and a metropolitan scholar during the Qing emperor Kangxi's reign (1662–1722), began compiling the Moys' *zupu* (*Meishi zongqin zupu*) and completed it nine years later. In 1706, Moy Xisi, a twelfth-generation member of the Duanfen Moys, updated the Moys' *zupu*.[18] The Moys' *zupu* thus constitutes an invaluable resource for scholars and genealogists.[19]

The causes of overseas migration from Duanfen in modern times are those that characterize Chinese emigration history in general since the mid-nineteenth century. At the end of the Qing dynasty, economic conditions in rural Taishan rapidly deteriorated. The economic crisis was further compounded by natural calamities. Between 1851 and 1908, reportedly fourteen floods, seven typhoons, five famines, four droughts, four plagues, and four earthquakes occurred. Situated on low-lying land, Duanfen bore the brunt of these various disasters—of droughts, floods, typhoons, and locust plagues. These natural disasters exacerbated the historical feuds between the Guangdong natives and the migrants, or *hakka* ("guest people" from North China from the time of the Song dynasty). Between 1856 and 1867, violent conflicts between the two groups affected Duanfen, resulting in countless deaths. In 1866, the commander-in-general in Guangdong deployed ten thousand troops to suppress the riots. Moy Qizhao, a Duanfen notable, joined the troops in charge of grain procurement. Witnessing the devastation, he wrote a poem to persuade the locals to go overseas to seek a better life, urging: "There are opportunities everywhere / Chinese went overseas for a long while / several hundred thousand in Gold Mountain (San Francisco) / several hundred thousand in India."[20] The numbers he cited might have been exaggerated, but they certainly indicate that many Duanfenese had already chosen to emigrate overseas. Many locals readily took advantage of the situation, becoming brokers in the immoral Chinese coolie trade; a Duanfenese named Moy Yaoguan served as one of the *zhuzai tou*, or "head of the piglets," in the coolie trade.[21]

According to a 1998 survey on the distribution of overseas Chinese originating from Taishan conducted by the Taishan City (Taishan was upgraded
to a city from a county in 1990) Federation of Overseas Chinese, among the
93,285 individuals surveyed from Duanfen Township, their preferred destinations were the United States, Hong Kong, Macao, and Canada in that
order: 65 percent (60,594) went to the United States, 17 percent (15,555) to
Hong Kong, 4 percent (3,492) to Macao, and 3 percent (3,016) to Canada.
The statistics for other towns in Taishan indicate a similar pattern.[22]

No records tell us whether the Moy brothers in Chicago came from
Duanfen, but they were certainly born in Taishan. Oral history interviews and immigration records all report the three Moy brothers' origin as
Taishan, the county in which Duanfen is located, making the probability
that the Moy brothers came from Duanfen rather high, as the majority of
overseas Chinese from Taishan came from Duanfen.[23]

The predominance of the surname Moy among the Chicago Chinese
indicates several things. First, the clustering of a certain surname or a few
surnames is a manifestation of chain immigration. The patrilineal and
patrilocal nature of traditional Chinese villages resulted in the dominance of
a few clans in any given village. As pioneer immigrants sent for their family
members and relatives from the same villages and areas of the homeland to
join them, the number of people from the same place with the same name
in their new location grew accordingly. Second, the clustering of common
surnames testifies to the existence of close and continuing transnational ties,
emotional as well as economic, between immigrants and those in the homeland, ties that enabled the latter to join the former when the time was ripe.

THE TAISHANESE AND TRANSNATIONAL TIES

Taishan is located in the southwest portion of the Pearl River delta. It
belonged to Xinhui County before the Ming dynasty (1368–1644) and
was incorporated into a separate county named Xinning in 1499. In 1914,
it was renamed Taishan County by the Nationalist government to avoid
confusion with other Xinning counties in Hunan, Guangxi, and Sichuan
provinces. With its long and intensive association with Chinese emigration, Taishan has been popularly dubbed the "First County of Overseas
Chinese." In the 1990s, over a million overseas Chinese had roots in
Taishan—more than the population of one million who lived in Taishan

itself—and more than 75 percent of the locals had relatives overseas. According to the Taishan gazetteer, Taishanese had emigrated to Southeast Asia as early as 1774. In the past two centuries, Taishanese have migrated all over the world seeking a better life, spreading to eighty-two nations or more but with a majority in North America.[24]

During this long history of emigration, four major waves of the Taishan exodus occurred. The discovery of gold in California in 1848 prompted the first wave of gold miners, followed by the second wave in 1865 when the construction of the transcontinental railroad began. The repeal of the Chinese exclusion laws in 1943 led to the third wave. The fourth and largest wave came after 1979 with the renormalization of relations between China and the United States and the relaxation of Chinese government policies regarding emigration and overseas Chinese.[25] The majority of the early Chinese in Chicago were from Taishan, including prominent merchants such as Moy Dong Chow, Chin F. Foin, and Hong Sling as well as numerous common laborers.

While living in almost every corner of the world, the overseas Chinese generally maintain close ties with their homeland by sending remittances, visiting home, and investing in homeland enterprises. The Taishanese seem to have demonstrated even stronger attachment to their homeland; their remittances have been recognized by academic studies as one of the most important contributions to China's economic development. According to a study by Wuyi University scholar Zhang Guoxiong (2003), among the over 2 million overseas Chinese from the Wuyi region (the five counties of Xinhui, Taishan, Enping, Kaiping, and Heshan), there are 1.55 million in the Americas, among whom 1.32 million reside in the United States and Canada. Most Chinese in North America are medium- or small-scale entrepreneurs; few have become owners of large companies, unlike their counterparts in Southeast Asia, Hong Kong, and Macao. Yet remittances from North America greatly surpass those from Southeast Asia. In the 1930s, remittances from North America constituted between one-third and one-half of total overseas Chinese remittances. Overseas Taishanese remitted $30 million in 1930, nearly one-third of the $95 million total for overseas Chinese remittances.[26]

Huang Jing, a researcher at the Chinese Institute for Overseas Chinese History Studies, identifies three periods of overseas Chinese remittances since the founding of the People's Republic of China in 1949. During the first period, 1950–1960, overseas Chinese remittances averaged about $100 million annually. These remittances increased rapidly in the second period, 1970–1980, with an annual increase of 16 percent, reaching an all-time high of $696 million in 1979. In the third period, however, from 1980 onward, these remittances decreased annually, with only $180 million in 1985, a decrease of 43 percent from 1984 and 74 percent from 1979. Huang offers several reasons for the decline. First, as the standard of living has risen in the home villages, residents depend less on overseas remittances. Second, since the 1980s more overseas Chinese have been visiting their home villages bringing gifts and cash instead of sending remittances.

Third, the overseas Chinese have also been investing directly in enterprises of the homeland.[27] According to data on overseas Chinese–owned enterprises, by 2007 the overseas Chinese owned approximately 140,000 enterprises in China, 50 percent of the country's total of 280,000 businesses. Qinghua University scholar Long Denggao (2008) estimates that before 1991, 60 to 80 percent of the private enterprises owned by overseas Chinese were concentrated in Guangdong. These data indicate the large magnitude of direct investment in enterprises of the homeland by overseas Chinese.[28]

Consistent with this evidence, Jinan University historians Wang Yuanlin and Deng Minrui (2005) have observed a great change in three aspects of lifestyle and customs in Guangdong *qiaoxiang* (ancestral villages of overseas Chinese): Westernization of attitudes toward what constitute the necessities of life, a new propensity for emigrating abroad, and a view of "civilized" or Westernized behavior as being more fashionable than non-Western behavior.[29] Anthropologist Andrea Louie (2004) has made similar observations concerning the impact of Chinese emigration on villagers remaining in China: "[In Taishan] many with relatives abroad (usually in the United States) place their hopes on eventually going abroad themselves, or on marrying a potential emigrant or U.S citizen."[30]

Conclusion

Most of the early Chinese immigrants in Chicago were Taishanese, a people with a long tradition of migration and emigration. The strong patrilineal tradition in South China has bound the Taishanese immigrants in Chicago, as well as in other places in the United States and around the world, to their home villages with social, economic, and emotional ties. These transnational connections have benefited those on both ends of the migration: the immigrant community receives a constant flow of human resources and emotional support from the homeland, while the native villages receive a continuing flow of remittances and investments from overseas. Owing to the mutually beneficial nature of these connections, transnationalism is a viable and enduring feature of the Chinese communities in Chicago, as it is wherever Chinese immigrants have settled.

Locating Chinatown, 1870s–1910s

They never asked me whether or not I ate rats and snakes. They seemed to
believe that we also had souls to save, and these souls were worth saving. The
Chicagoans found us a peculiar people to be sure, but they liked to mix with us.

—Moy Dong Chow, 1920s

The turn of the nineteenth and twentieth centuries marked the rise of
urban, corporate America and the intertwining of race, ethnicity, and modernity. During these years, the country became racialized as large groups
of immigrants flooded urban industrial areas in the late nineteenth century
and African Americans migrated from the South to the North in the 1910s.
"The problem of the twentieth century is the problem of the color-line,"
W. E. B. DuBois asserted in 1903.[1] Race dominated the geographical and
social landscapes of Chicago, just as in other industrialized cities. In this
time of transition, the Chinese were initially welcomed in Chicago as a quiet
and exotic people. They carved out their businesses—mainly grocery stores,
restaurants, and laundries—along with other ethnic groups in the downtown area. But they were soon discriminated against and were driven out
of their early settlement by the white residents of the city. They relocated
on the city's South Side, one of the city's most impoverished areas, which
they shared with Italians, Irish, blacks, and other ethnic minorities, in what
became the city's new Chinatown.

Chicago: From Swampland to the "Windy City"

Before Europeans settled there, the Chicago region was inhabited by a
number of Algonquian language–speaking Native Americans, including the
Mascouten and the Miami. Through trading and seasonal hunting migra-

tions, they had contacts with their neighbors—the Potawatomi to the east, the Fox to the north, and the Illinois to the southwest. The name "Chicago" reflects these intertribal connections; it is the French version of the Miami-Illinois word *shikaakwa*, meaning "wild leek" or "skunk," after the plants common along the Chicago River.[2]

The location of Chicago naturally attracted many French Canadian explorers and fur traders, such as Louis Jolliet, the first white man to explore the Mississippi River, in 1673. The narrow, swampy stretch of land between the Chicago River flowing into Lake Michigan and the Des Plaines River flowing into the Mississippi River made for an ideal port, which became a transportation hub. In 1683, French Jesuits built the Mission of the Guardian Angel to Christianize the local Wea and Miami tribes and a French fort, Fort Chécagou, commanded by Pierre de Liette. The French abandoned the Chicago portage during the 1720s because of continual raiding by the Fox tribe. During the mid-1700s, the Chicago area was inhabited primarily by the Potawatomi, who took the place of the Miami, Sauk, and Fox who had previously controlled the area.

The land east of the Mississippi River and south of the Great Lakes had been initially fought over by the Indian tribes and the French explorers and then by the Indian tribes and the Americans, in the Northwest Indian War (1785–1795). In 1795, the Indian confederation ceded the area of Chicago to the United States as a military post in the Treaty of Greenville.[3] In 1803, US troops under Captain John Whistler built Fort Dearborn. Though destroyed during the War of 1812, it was rebuilt in 1816 and has remained a Chicago landmark up to the present day.

Chicago was incorporated as a town on August 12, 1833, with a population of 350. The initial boundaries of the new town were Kinzie, Des Plaines, Madison, and State streets, constituting an area of about three-eighths of a square mile. The population of the town grew rapidly, reaching over four thousand in seven years. The state of Illinois granted Chicago a city charter on March 4, 1837. A decade later, two seminal events sealed Chicago's destiny as the transportation hub of the region. First, the Illinois and Michigan Canal opened in 1848, allowing for uninterrupted shipping from the Great Lakes through Chicago to the Mississippi River and thence to the Gulf of Mexico. Second, the Galena and Chicago Union Railroad was completed in the same year, connecting Chicago with lead mines at Galena, Illinois, and providing the first railroad transport out of Chicago.

From the start the city faced what appeared to be almost insurmountable problems, but its residents persevered and solved them. The worst problem was the perennial spring flooding, which made streets so muddy and treacherous that some humorous local residents put signs in places proclaiming, "Fastest Route to China" or "No Bottom Here," to warn people of the hazard. The city authorities handled the problem by building country roads to the west and southwest. The roads crossed the so-called Dismal Nine-Mile Swamp and the Des Plaines River and then ran southwest to Walker's Grove, presently Plainfield, Illinois. The city was also plagued by problems with water and sewage; it was notoriously described as the filthiest city in America. The city tackled the problem by laying a massive network of sewer pipes across the city aboveground.

In 1871, Chicago suffered another blow. The Great Chicago Fire of that year almost burned the entire city to the ground. It was believed the fire began in and around the barn behind the home of Patrick and Catherine O'Leary, who operated a modest local dairy business. The story that one of their cows kicked over a lantern and thus started the conflagration on the night of October 8 was a sensational journalistic invention that became a popular legend. The brutal reality of the severity and cruelty of the fire, however, is engraved forever in the city's cultural memory. The casualties of the fire included 300 people dead, 18,000 buildings destroyed, and 100,000 homeless, one-third of the city's residents. The fire almost consumed the city but could not crush the spirit of its residents. It only affirmed the city's dynamic potential and the residents' boundless ingenuity. As the city's boosters have claimed, the fire accelerated rather than slowed the city's evolution from bustling mercantile center to manufacturing and trading colossus.[4] Although the precise cause of the fire remains unknown, the abundant wood used in the construction of houses, streets, and sidewalks was believed to be a major factor contributing to the rampant spread of the fire. The fire resulted in the passage of strict fire safety codes, including a strong preference for masonry construction. When the soft, swampy ground near the lake proved too unstable for tall masonry buildings, Chicagoans pioneered the use of steel frames and the construction of skyscrapers. Their ingenuity impressed the world and Chicago was looked upon as a model for achieving vertical growth.

With its transportation advantages and architectural advances, Chicago took giant strides in its growth in the last decades of the nineteenth century. In this era of urban expansion, no other city grew so quickly and so much as Chicago. Between 1870 and 1890 it jumped from fifth largest, trailing behind New York, Philadelphia, Brooklyn, and St. Louis, to second largest city in the country. Its abundant grain, livestock, agricultural commodities, coal, iron, and lumber spurred the farm implement and meat-packing industries and advanced manufacturing and shipping. The manufacturers and retailers in Chicago dominated the Midwest and influenced the nation's economy. Canals and railroads positioned the city as a transportation node between the East and the West, linking the hinterland's farms and small towns to the economic centers of the Northeast, especially New York. Historian William Cronon (1991) offers a rich portrait of Chicago as connecting cities and hinterland, port and borderland areas, urban and rural, farms and factories in his marvelous *Nature's Metropolis.*[5]

Chicago's advantageous location and its ability to receive, process, market, and ship goods of all sorts positioned the city as a wholesale-retail giant. Major wholesalers such as John V. Farwell and Company; Field, Leitter, and Company; and Potter Palmer soon replaced eastern suppliers and established networks based on buying and selling. Chicago emerged as an important retailer in the heart of the country. After 1890, foreign observers increasingly regarded Chicago as the prime urban exemplar of the country's economic surge. Ernst von Hesse-Wartegg, a German scholar, wrote in 1891, "I have lived long enough in America and have traveled the two halves of the New World for years. I can say unhesitatingly I consider Chicago the greatest wonder of America, the *Urtypus* of the distinctive American essence, the most American city of this huge land, much more so than New York or Boston or Philadelphia. It is perhaps the most powerful human creation of all time."[6] The city's boosters and politicians assiduously promoted the city. Their lobbying earned the city the pejorative nickname "Windy City" in the New York press, which despite its etymology the city adopted.

The Windy City now became the world's largest railroad hub; the convenience of its railway and waterway transportation stimulated rapid population growth. Waves of newcomers, including natives from rural communities in America and immigrants from Europe, had been pouring into the city since the 1870s. By the turn of the nineteenth century, Chicago had grown almost sixfold, its population swelling from 300,000 in 1870 to nearly 1.7 million in 1900, the fastest growth in human history at the time. The vast majority of the immigrants were German, Irish, British, Canadian, Swedish, Norwegian, and Scottish, later joined by Poles and Italians.[7]

Big or small, all the immigrant groups made lasting contributions to the city's development as an industrial and cosmopolitan center in America and added to the racial, cultural, and religious diversity and complexity of the city. Germans contributed to industry, technology, and high culture, in particular Chicago's world-renowned symphony orchestra.[8] Chicago's Swedes followed similar residential and occupational patterns as the German immigrants; although poor and often just fresh off the boat, they were one of the first nineteenth-century immigrant groups to settle in the less densely populated areas of the city and its suburbs.[9]

Unlike the western and northern Europeans, who were relatively more skilled and arrived with at least some meager savings, Irish immigrants to America were mostly from rural communities, driven to the New World by the "potato famine" that decimated Ireland in the 1840s. Lacking both capital and the skills necessary for survival in the industrial cities, they were forced to start as humble canal diggers and menial laborers. These sons of the Emerald Isle, however, came to dominate the "Irish Trinity" of American urban culture: the priesthood, the police, and politics. Every Catholic bishop in Chicago from 1847 to 1916, with one exception, was Irish. The police force in Chicago was disproportionately Irish by the 1890s. And most Chicago mayors since 1933 have been of Irish Catholic heritage.[10]

Chicago also became the city with the third largest Jewish population in the world, exceeded only by New York and Warsaw. Irving Cutler, a Chicago-based geographer, portrayed the people, neighborhoods, institutions, and events that shaped the present-day Chicago Jewish community. Like other immigrant groups, the Jews were not at all monolithic but diverse. German Jews (Ashkenazim), the earliest group of Jews in Chicago, arrived in the city in the 1830s. Many of them started out as peddlers with packs on their backs. With profits made in this way, they then opened dry goods, clothing, or grocery stores, often along the main commercial streets of early Chicago—Lake and Clark Streets. They generally lived above or behind their stores (a settlement pattern identical to that of the Chinese immigrants). The second wave of Jewish immigrants in Chicago, as well as in the rest of the country, consisted of two million eastern European Jews, predominantly from the Russian Empire, parts of the Austro-Hungarian Empire, and Romania, who migrated to America between 1881 and 1924. Many of them poured into Chicago, constituting 80 percent of the city's Jewish population. Between 1880 and 1910, an estimated 55,000 eastern European immigrants crowded into the Maxwell Street area known as the "Poor Jewish Quarter." While the German Jews by now had largely assimilated into American society, the Maxwell Street community of eastern European Jews resembled a European shtetl, including an open-market bazaar with kosher meat markets, chicken stores, groceries, matzoh bakeries, dry goods stores, tailor and seamstress shops, bath houses, peddlers' stables, sweatshops, and second-hand stores. They dressed as they had in eastern European ghettos: bearded Jewish men wore long black coats, boots, and Russian caps or wide-brimmed hats, and women wore shawls.[11]

The Polish immigrants brought with them to America a deep, resilient attitude toward national identity and "survived through solidarity" in the streets of Chicago. They created "Polonia," a nation within a nation, on the basis of their churches, building and lending associations, parochial schools, and fraternal associations.[12] Northern Italians (mostly from Genoa and Tuscany) founded and dominated Chicago's fast-growing Italian community until the 1880s. The early northern Italians consisted mainly of settled family units, some with large families with as many as thirteen children. Italian men generally worked as skilled or semiskilled laborers or found jobs in service or trade occupations as saloonkeepers, bartenders, hairdressers, or restaurant owners or employees. They usually resided in or near the center of the city, in the Loop area, clustering around Clark Street.[13] After the 1880s they, like their counterparts in New York and other major cities of the country, were joined by immigrants, mostly Catholic farmers, from the impoverished southern part of Italy, the *Mezzogiorno*. These immigrants found employment in Chicago's various industries, railyards, municipal construction projects, and the smaller businesses of shoemaking, fruit and vegetable peddling, barbering, and tailoring.[14]

The Moy Brothers and Early Chinatown

In the mid-1870s, a small number of Chinese also came to the Windy City to join the European immigrants who were already there, in search of a better life. To understand the history of the Chinese in Chicago, we need to place it in the larger context of Chinese immigration to America.

The discovery of gold in California in 1849 led to the first large wave of Chinese immigration to the country. In the following three decades, about three hundred thousand Chinese entered the United States to work primarily as gold miners, as laundry and grocery store operators in urban communities, as farm laborers in agricultural areas, and as fishermen in the fishing villages of California.[15] Although California continued to have the majority of the Chinese population in the United States, its percentage of the total slowly and steadily declined, from 9.2 percent in 1860 to 8.7 percent in 1880 and then to only 3.1 percent in 1900.[16]

The anti-Chinese movement in the United States, exacerbated by the economic depression on the West Coast in the last decades of the nineteenth century, contributed to a redistribution of the Chinese immigrant population. Economic discrimination, in the form of special taxes and levies, targeted the Chinese. For example, in the 1850s, the Foreign Miners Tax was designed to discourage Chinese miners in particular,[17] and an 1870 San Francisco ordinance taxing laundrymen who used horseless delivery wagons likewise deliberately targeted small Chinese operations.[18] Furthermore, anti-Chinese sentiment subjected immigrants and their businesses to violent physical attacks and abuse.[19]

The completion of the transcontinental railroad in 1869 also contributed to the dispersion of Chinese laborers. During the last stage of construction of the Central Pacific Railroad, Chinese constituted 90 percent of the workforce of twelve thousand men. The availability of so many Chinese laborers heightened the competition between them and European Americans. Although most of the railroad workers, once discharged, found jobs in agriculture in California, many others migrated to the South and the East, working on southern plantations or in new, booming towns such as Chicago and St. Louis in the Midwest.[20]

TO THE WINDY CITY

Among the dispersed Chinese laborers, a man named Moy Dong Chow (梅宗周 Mei Zongzhou, a.k.a. Hip Lung) was particularly interested in Chicago. One of the Moy clan from Taishan, Moy Dong Chow was known among his fellow countrymen for his stubbornness, resourcefulness, and shrewdness. The rare photos of Moy show him as a man with a commanding presence and a stern face expressing determination.[21] As his entourage deserted him one by one, remaining in the cities and towns along the way from California to the Windy City, Moy Dong Chow was determined to reach his destination.

In the mid-1870s, Moy Dong Chow arrived in Chicago, and his two brothers, Moy Dong Hoy (梅宗凱 Mei Zongkai, a.k.a. Sam Moy) and Moy Dong Yee (梅宗瑀 Mei Zongyu) followed soon afterward. (As in the case of numerous immigrants from all corners of the world with unfamiliar names, the names of the Moy brothers have been spelled many different ways in many different academic and popular writings. These variations reflect corruption of the Cantonese spelling of the Chinese names. To avoid confusion, I have chosen to use the spellings of the names of the Moys recorded in the Chicago Chinese Case Files.)[22]

Unlike Canton, which is warm, or California, with its temperate climate, Chicago was cold, with a harsh, bone-chilling wind; but the social climate seemed warmer to the pioneer Chinese. A half century later, Moy Dong Chow had become the most senior Chinese resident in the city and something of a local historian. When interviewed by Tin-Chiu Fan, a Chinese Christian graduate student in sociology at the University of Chicago in the 1920s, Moy Dong Chow recalled his earlier encounters with the Chicagoans: "They never asked me whether or not I ate rats and snakes. They seemed to believe that we also had souls to save, and these souls were

Moy Dong Chow in an official outfit as a fourth-rank official, awarded by the Qing government, 1900s. Collection of Ruth Moy, Chinese-American Museum of Chicago.

worth saving. The Chicagoans found us a peculiar people to be sure, but they liked to mix with us."[23]

The accommodating reception in Chicago brought more Chinese to the city. In 1878 Moy Dong Chow sent for his compatriots in San Francisco, and consequently sixty Chinese came to Chicago.[24] By 1880, there were a hundred Chinese in the city. Moy Dong Chow also sent for his family members in the homeland. By 1885, forty members of the extended Moy family from his native village lived in Chicago. By the end of 1890, more than five hundred Chinese lived on South Clark Street between Van Buren and Harrison.[25] The first Chinatown in Chicago was born.

Laundries, grocery stores, and restaurants constituted the businesses of early Chinatown. Two Chinese laundries opened in 1870 in the Loop area. In the mid-1870s, the Kim Kee Company at 293 South Clark Street sold imported Chinese dry goods and cooking ingredients. Below the grocery store in the basement, a restaurant called Quong Lee Yuen shared the building and probably customers with the Kim Kee Company.[26]

EARLY RACIAL CONTACTS

As soon as the Chinese appeared in the city, Christian missionaries began outreach efforts among them. The Reverend R. R. Coon of the First Baptist Church submitted a resolution to his board of directors in 1876. Recognizing the need for "a free social and intellectual intercourse" between the peoples of China and the United States and for "free and fraternal relations" between the two countries, the resolution reminded the board of the "Christian obligation to the Chinese" and called for actions in cooperation with local Chinese "to inaugurate some plan" to bring the Chinese "under the influence of [the] Gospel."[27] As a result, the First Baptist Church launched the Baptist Chinese Mission, located on the second floor of the building at 295 South Clark Street, next door to the Kim Kee Company.

To bring their "Mongolian brethren" within the fold of Christendom, the Baptist church addressed the need to first teach English to the Chinese. As part of Sunday school programs, English classes were offered, where the Chinese were given individual lessons by their American teachers, mostly ladies of the church. The twenty-one Chinese students included a clan leader as well as ordinary Chinese laborers. Yuen Ah Ching, a prominent member of the Yuan clan, another large clan from Taishan, was reportedly one of the

Sunday school students, while the rest were common laborers, including Ah Sam Chong, Fong Sang, Low Lee, R. Gin, and others. Undoubtedly the Chinese were pleased by the attention paid to them. On August 4, 1878, they expressed gratitude to their teachers by inviting them to a Chinese banquet after the lesson and by presenting exotic and expensive presents to their teachers—"an elegant and costly silk and ivory fan" and "a pair of shoes," all imported from China.[28]

This close contact between Chinese males and Caucasian females was similar to cross-racial interactions that took place in other gateway cities such as New York and Boston.[29] These interracial contacts in the context of Christian fellowship in Chicago, however, seem to have been better tolerated by the residents of this city in the last decades of the nineteenth century than in New York and Boston.

THE MOY BROTHERS' DOMINANCE

In the late 1870s, Moy Dong Chow bought a store on Clark and Madison from a fellow Chinese. He named it Hip Lung Yee Kee and Company and sold mostly dry goods. In the 1880s he moved the store to 323 South Clark Street, the heart of early Chinatown. By the late 1880s, the Chinese operated twelve grocery stores, three chop suey houses, and other businesses in the Chinatown district. Charles Kee (Moy Dong Mow), a cousin of the Moy brothers, operated a cigar factory at 327 South Clark Street.[30] On the upper floors of the Chinese grocery store Quong Wing Kee at 311 South Clark Street were a gambling house, several family associations, the headquarters of Hip Sing Tong and On Leong Tong, the office of the Emperor Protection Association, and the First Chinese Baptist Mission.[31]

Of all the Chinese businesses, a laundry was the easiest to operate as it required limited skills and very little capital. All a laundryman needed was a tub, a scrub board, soap, and an iron and ironing board. Chinese laundrymen could canvass a neighborhood, find a low-rent location, and open a business. As a result, Chinese hand laundries developed rapidly. In 1874, there were 18 Chinese laundries, of which 15 were in the Loop and in the area around Madison Street and Roosevelt Road, 2 on the near West Side, and 1 on the near South Side.[32] Nearly a decade later in 1883, the number of Chinese laundries had increased to 198. While more than half of the laundries (107) were still concentrated in the Loop, the rest were scattered across the city. By 1893, the number of Chinese laundries had decreased slightly, to 190, but they were more widely spread around the city than a decade before.[33]

The Chinese population in Chicago also grew rapidly. Within two decades, from the 1870s to the 1890s, it had increased to nearly six hundred according to the US census, although the local estimate was two thousand.[34] Hip Lung became the focal point of Chinatown social life. On weekends or during the Chinese New Year, the Chinese would congregate in the South Clark Street area, to meet kinsmen, get authentic Chinese meals, and relax by playing fan tan (a popular Chinese gambling game of the time) or smoking cigars and opium. Reporters from the local newspapers frequently visited the area to search for "celestial" exotica. Moy Dong Chow, referred to as the "patriarch" and "historian" of Chinatown, would offer his authoritative opinions on the celebration of the Chinese New Year and other China-related topics.[35] On February 17, 1894, one local reporter vividly rendered his firsthand observations of how the people of "the Orient" celebrated their New Year in "the Occident":

> The cosmopolitan character of Chicago may be illustrated in few places to a better advantage than in that "Midway Plaisance" of thoroughfares—South Clark street. Here the representatives of almost every nation under eastern and western skies mingle in the heterogeneous throngs which ceaselessly, day and night, walk the pavements. Nor is there a more picturesque class of humanity than the Chinese when adorned to celebrate the festival of the New Year, which continues for a week, and is packed full of celestial merry-making.
>
> There are nearly 2,000 Chinamen in Chicago, and one who visited Clark Street on several occasions last week would have been prepared to declare that all of them were on hand to honor the occidental traditions, which makes New Year's with them so marked a period of hilarity and fire-cracker joy. They donned their quilted-silk dress coats, with the ample sleeves; they put on their immaculate stockings and their thick soled shoes; they uncoiled yards of Mongolian black hair, and adorned with smiles which would have done honor to Bret Harte's immortal card-player, they assembled in the neighborhood of Hip Lung's store, the center of Chinese society. In the laundries, the cigar stores, the opium "joints," the restaurants, they were found. The Chinese "four hundred" held receptions, at which the guests partook of roast pig, rice, sweetmeats, and drank enough tea to have floated a Chinese junk.[36]

This reporter's writing offers a glimpse of the social life of the Chicago Chinese. Despite the frequent use of terms such as "Celestials," "Mongolians," and "Chinamen," ubiquitous synonyms for "Chinese" in Victorian writing and offensive in the present day, the article contains revealing, detailed information concerning early Chinatown. It confirms that the core population in the South Clark Street district was about "four hundred" and that the total Chinese population in Chicago was "nearly 2,000." The premier businesses of the Chinese were laundries, grocery stores (also dubbed "cigar factories" and "opium joints" by news reporters on account of the recreational activities taking place on their premises), and restaurants. Hip Lung's store was not only the largest grocery store where Chinese bought their weekly provisions but also served as a cultural center for entertainment and recreation, where the Chinese smoked cigars, sipped Chinese rice wine, and gambled in the upper-floor rooms, as well as a de facto Chinese court where Moy Dong Chow exercised his "fatherly" authority in disputes among the Chinese.[37]

The Moy brothers took care not only of the living Chinese residents of Chicago but also of the deceased. An article in the August 10, 1891, *Chicago Tribune* provides a record of a collective memorial ceremony for all the deceased Chinese in Chicago led by Moy Dong Chow at Rosehill Cemetery, the primary burial site for the Chinese at the turn of the century. Established in February 1859 and occupying 350 acres, the Victorian-era cemetery at 5800 North Ravenswood Avenue on the North Side is the largest cemetery in the city. Along with numerous mayors (eighteen as of 2010), famous businessmen, and sports stars, the quiet and hard-working Chinese also found their final resting place there.

> Fourteen carriages containing four Chinamen each rolled into the entrance of Rosehill Cemetery at 2 O'clock yesterday afternoon, and a little later three street car loads of former residents of the Celestial Empire arrived and joined their countrymen. At first the cemetery officials wondered what their visit meant but later on were informed that the Chinamen had come to feed their dead.
>
> Little time was lost getting to the plot of ground belonging to the Chinese and almost instantly Hip Lung, their wealthy leader, was surrounded by his friends and after a few words in his native tongue the entire party was engaged in placing all kinds of edibles upon the grave. Meats, breads, vegetables, and queer dishes, familiar only to these strange

people, were scattered in profusion. While it was all going on a large caldron containing consecrated paper made of an imported punk that had
been prepared by the chief religion officer of China, produced a dense
smoke, as it was arranged to burn slowly.

The strange gesticulations and seemingly funny antics cut by the of-
ficiating people were extremely interesting to the few white people present.
Many thought the pigtails were dedicating their new monument and in
order to learn whether or not this had been done Hip Lung was questioned.
"It is not a dedication of the monument," said he. "It is our custom of feeding the dead. We will not dedicate the monument until next Sunday. We
feed our dead today, tonight we feed some of our living—the laundrymen."

In the evening there was a feast at Hip Lung's store [at] 323 South Clark
Street. The sidewalk was crowded with Chinese from every part of Chicago,
all awaiting the sound of the gong—the tocsin of feast. At 7:30 p.m. the
large dining hall on the second floor of Lung's building was ablaze, and the
laundrymen of Chicago enjoyed a banquet such as was never seen or tasted
here before. It was given because a nephew had been born to Hip Lung.[38]

This description offers a vivid and authentic account of Chinese memorial ceremonies in Chicago at the time, from which one may draw some
useful information. First, the memorial ceremonies closely resembled those
in traditional, especially southern, China.[39] Burning consecrated paper in
a caldron and blessing the graves with various foods are all traditional ways
of ensuring that the deceased has money to spend and enough food to eat
in the next world. Respect and care for one's ancestors and one's deceased
fellow-countrymen was central to the Chinese code of moral conduct according to Confucian values; the Chinese relied on their ancestors and the
deceased for blessings and protections from unforeseen harm or misfortune. According to their beliefs, the precious baby boy born to Moy Dong
Hoy was a blessing from the ancestors and deceased. Thus a memorial
ceremony was held to express the gratitude of the Moy family, especially
the Moy brothers, and it was proper that feeding the dead precede feasting the living as an embodiment of their ancestral and spiritual worship.
These ceremonial rituals indicate that the early Chinese in Chicago were
consciously preserving Chinese traditions in a foreign land. Moreover, the
practical meaning of preserving Chinese memorial customs went beyond
the rituals themselves. These ceremonies were a means of binding members of the community together, providing not only ways for the living to

commemorate the dead but also the shared experience of mourning the deceased. The gathering of Chinese at such memorial ceremonies likely gave them a reassuring feeling of kinship and a sense of solidarity.

INTERCLAN RIVALRY

The authority of the Moy brothers among the Chinese, however, met challenges from rival clans in Chicago—first the Wong clan in the 1890s and later the Chin clan in the 1900s. The bitter strife between the Moys and the Wongs, each having about two hundred members in Chicago in the 1890s, culminated in physical violence in 1893. On the night of March 29, Wong Aloy, a member of the Wong clan and a Chinese student at Evanston, who later became an interpreter in the Office of the Inspector in Charge [of Immigration] in Chicago, was assaulted by Moy Toi Nye and Ung Yok, members of the Moy clan, in front of 307 South Clark Street. Wong Aloy was severely injured and confined to bed at the home of John B. Strassburger, an attorney representing him. State's Attorney Kern, a close friend of the Moys, presented the case. The two assailants were arrested and a $2,000 bond was placed on them by Justice Clemon.[40]

Dissatisfied with the ruling, the Wong clan brought Wong Chin Foo, a renowned journalist and fearless advocate of Chinese civil rights, to Chicago from New York, where he resided. Wong Chin Foo demanded a more vigorous prosecution and punishment of the assailants and the Moy brothers. After his visit to the state's attorney's office, however, he concluded that justice would not be served as long as Kern occupied the office. Wong Chin Foo disclosed that there were close connections between the Moy brothers and Kern to a *Chicago Tribune* reporter in what were allegedly Kern's own words: "I have my information from Sam Moy who is a resident of Chicago and I prefer his testimony to yours. Moreover I want you to understand that if you prosecute Sam Moy or Hip Lung you prosecute me. Those men are my friends and in no case will I prosecute them." Wong Aloy's attorney, John B. Strassburger, confirmed Wong Chin Foo's statement to the reporter. Meanwhile, State's Attorney Kern, who accused Wong Chin Foo of being an "adventurer" and a "trouble-maker," defended his position on the case.[41]

The "bitter factional fight" continued as both sides hurled recriminations at each other. Moy Dong Chow charged that Wong Chin Foo had held a meeting of the Wong family and asked its members to raise $600 to pay for an assassin to kill him, and that Wong Chin Foo had agreed to withdraw the prosecution if the Moy family would pay him $500. Meanwhile, Wong Chin Foo declared both charges to be false and absurd and stated that his personal safety was so threatened that he had had to hire a bodyguard upon his arrival in Chicago.[42] He asserted that Moy Dong Chow had gained his ascendency over the Chinese in Chicago through his position as treasurer and manager of Hip Lung, which had branches in San Francisco and Hong Kong, and charged Hip Lung with using its "financial power" to exert its influence over civil courts.[43]

The rivalry between the Moys and the Wongs was not simply a factional fight or "tong war" between criminal families as it was categorized by the white media and perceived by the general public; more accurately, it manifested "two types of integration," as historian Adam McKeown has correctly observed.[44] Wong Chin Foo was a staunch believer in and visionary advocate for the Americanization of Chinese immigrants, using his sharp tongue and audacity to fight all authorities and opponents; while the Moy brothers deftly navigated their path to the American dream through the operation of transnational family businesses, personal connections with influential and powerful members of the larger society, the employment of effective legal assistance, and participation in and control over the Chinese community in Chicago.

WONG CHIN FOO AS AN ADVOCATE OF ASSIMILATION

Wong Chin Foo was one of the most colorful Chinese intellectuals in America during the late nineteenth century. Born in China in 1851, he came to the United States in 1864 at the age of fourteen, landing in New York.[45] Utterly different from his counterparts in America, he removed his queue (braid) as soon as he arrived in America, wore Western-style suits, and cultivated a cosmopolitan demeanor. He was educated at Yale University in journalism but returned to China after his graduation in the early 1870s. Scion of an aristocratic Chinese family, Wong inherited a strong sense of duty and responsibility for the fate of his homeland and openly expressed his intense anti-Manchu sentiments, a hallmark characteristic of Chinese intellectuals during the Qing dynasty. He called for the overthrow of the Manchu dynasty and the establishment of a republic. His anti-Qing speeches and activities agitated the Qing court, which put him on its most-wanted list with a $1,500 reward for his head, and consequently he fled China in 1872. He went first to Japan, where he continued to be pursued by the Qing government. He barely escaped and sailed back to America with the help of Charles O. Shepard, the US consul in Tokyo, to whom Wong was so grateful that he eventually presented him with a rare chair shipped from China, supposedly used by Confucius, as a gift.[46] Wong soon decided that he had to become an American citizen to exercise his civil rights and to continue advocating his cause. On April 3, 1874, he applied for naturalization to the court in Grand Rapids, Michigan, one of the stops of his lecture tour across the country, and was granted citizenship immediately.[47]

Wong was known as being among the best-educated Chinese and famous as a writer and journalist who contributed frequently to several leading journals in English, as well as traveling around the country to deliver lectures. In his writings and lectures, he was vehement in promoting Chinese civilization, advocating that his compatriots assimilate and defending the Chinese as valuable immigrants and potential American citizens. He engaged in debates with American politicians and commentators on issues pertinent to China and the Chinese. On the negative portrayal of the Chinese as rat-eaters, he declared, "Chinese don't eat rats. I would pay someone $500 if they can prove that the Chinese eat rats." He rejected the notion of Chinese being unassimilable, once telling an audience: "Assimilation? You try it. Anyone here wants to become a Chinese?" In an open debate, he publicly and repeatedly challenged the most prominent anti-Chinese political leader of the era—Irish working-class demagogue Dennis Kearney—to a duel when Kearney was touring the East Coast in 1883. His unconventional attitude and sharp tongue earned him fame as a popular speaker, and his lectures were often packed with large audiences. His debate with William E. Lewis of Chicago on March 23, 1879, for instance, was anticipated as "an interesting one" and was therefore held in the West End Opera-House to accommodate a large audience.

He encouraged the Chinese to invest in business as a means of assimilation. In one of his speeches he praised Hong Sling and other merchants for putting up $90,000 to build a Chinese Village at the 1893 World's Columbian Exposition while the Qing government failed to do so. He started a bilingual newspaper, *Meihua xinbao* (Chinese American), in New York City in 1883 and printed eight thousand copies for a Chinese population of less than a thousand in the city. The venture failed within a year, but his enthusiasm and idealism are vividly demonstrated by this endeavor.[48] Contemporary writers have labeled him a "provocateur," "showman," "master of the sound bite," "muckraker," "rabble-rouser," "Victorian media activist," "civil rights advocate," and the first Chinese to use the term "Chinese American."[49]

A man of influence and eccentricity, Wong Chin Foo was a gallant champion in defending the interests of his fellow Chinese. He fought fearlessly against the New York Police Department and other formidable opponents throughout the country in an attempt to secure justice for his compatriots, including the Moys before they clashed openly with the Wongs. In his visit to Chicago in February 1881, he took two unusual actions on behalf of the Moys, both extremely unthinkable for the Chinese at the time and audacious and shocking to the general public. On February 16, 1881, he called on the mayor of Chicago and tried to convince him to order the Chicago police to leave Hip Lung alone. The store had been raided by the police a few days earlier, as the police believed there was a "gambling-saloon" in the rear part of the store where the "celestials" played "poker" and allegedly smoked opium. Wong explained to the mayor that the back of the store was in fact a type of club, the sums staked in gambling were very small, and the winnings were spent in the grocery for confections—and moreover, the pipes the Chinese used for smoking were for tobacco, not opium. His petition was successful: the mayor instructed Superintendent McCarigle to investigate the matter, and subsequently the Chinese club in the back of Hip Lung appears to have been spared from future police raids.[50]

Encouraged by his victory, on the following day, February 17, Wong Chin Foo took three Moy clansmen, Moy Yee, Moy Sam, and Moy Hong Kee, to the Criminal Court of Northern Illinois in Chicago. He first stopped at the clerk's office to have the names of his companions recorded and the necessary forms filled out and then led the Moys into the courtroom. It was something so unusual that people in the courtroom were shocked and amused when the four Chinese filed in and presented themselves before Judge Moran asking for his attention. Wong Chin Foo explained his mission and passed to the judge a petition to make the Moys US citizens. Then Judge Moran asked the Moys what they thought of American institutions; one of them answered that he liked the country better than he did China and one of the others that he "liked America's peculiarities very much," which sent laughter around the room. Judge Moran told them that he would consider their applications and asked them to come back in a week.[51] It is unclear whether the three Moys were actually granted citizenship. Given the strong suspicion throughout the nation toward Chinese on the eve of passage of the Chinese Exclusion Act of 1882, a denial of their applications for citizenship seems more likely than otherwise. Nonetheless, the incident is illuminating as an example of Wong Chin Foo's unusual courage and charisma. Moreover, at least two Chinese laundrymen in Chicago reportedly had been naturalized by the previous judge, Judge Gary. Wong Chin Foo's mission in the courtroom, therefore, was hardly just a bold and naive endeavor but a reasonable and optimistic quest for the rights of his fellow Chinese.

Wong Chin Foo's encounter with State's Attorney Kern in the 1893 conflict reveals even more of his character. When Kern denied Wong's demand for the retrial of the assailants, Wong declared that his life was "dedicated to the cause of securing them [the Chinese] justice," and if he died in the attempt it would be "an honorable death."[52] Yet despite his extraordinary charisma and courage, Wong Chin Foo was less than practical in his approaches to Americanization, as evidenced by his writings in English, which were largely inaccessible to most immigrants, who were illiterate both in Chinese and in English, and in his recommendations for large investments in business, which were irrelevant to most Chinese immigrants, who had only meager incomes.

The Moy bothers, on the contrary, cleverly and deliberately cultivated broad personal connections with influential figures in the larger society and maintained firm control over the Chinese immigrant community through their wealth and accommodations. Their primary business was the Hip Lung Company, a transnational enterprise consisting of merchant houses in Chicago, San Francisco, and Hong Kong. The company not only dealt in regular merchandise, however, but was also allegedly involved in gambling, drug trafficking, and the smuggling of immigrants.[53] The profits from those businesses may have enabled the Moy brothers to hire the best lawyers to extricate them from legal difficulties, to contribute to local politicians and powerful institutions, and to sponsor charitable activities within the Chinese community.[54] The Moy brothers' circle of friends included State's Attorney Kern, the politician H. H. Stridiron, and a Harrison Station police sergeant, Dan Hogan, among others, all of whom, no matter their status in the social hierarchy, were willing and able to defend the Moys when called upon. While Moy Dong Chow acted as a benevolent fatherly authority among his fellow countrymen, Moy Dong Hoy actively courted friendships beyond the boundaries of Chinatown. Thumbing through the records of the US Immigration and Naturalization Service, one finds that Moy Dong Hoy frequently appeared at the Office of the Inspector in Charge in Chicago during the decades around the turn of the century, giving testimony on behalf of both clansmen and nonclansmen concerning their lawful status as bona fide merchants, as American-born citizens, or as residents qualified for readmission to the United States.[55] The Moy brothers were unanimously regarded by immigration, legal, and law enforcement officers as "prosperous merchants," "peaceful" residents of Chicago, and fun-loving and generous hosts of "merry-making" cultural celebrations.[56]

REFUGEES FROM SAN FRANCISCO

The earthquake and subsequent fire in San Francisco in 1906 altered the demographic makeup of the Chicago Chinese. Devastated by the earthquake, thousands of Chinese whose homes had been ruined fled San Francisco and found refuge in the Chinese settlements of other cities. Chicago received its share of such refugees. Although no relief work was organized in the community, the Chinese reportedly made individual donations to their suffering fellow countrymen in the stricken California city as well as to those taking refuge in Chicago. Arriving by two's and three's, the Chinese refugees made their way to South Clark Street, where they were assisted by the local Chinese until they became independent.[57]

The newcomers were not confined only to Chinatown, however. When the South Clark Street district could not hold any more refugees, they were housed in laundries, restaurants, and every other sort of establishment run by the Chinese throughout the city and suburbs, including Elgin, Aurora, and Joliet. Initially, these Chinese businesses offered shelter and food for the refugees, but they soon offered regular employment as well. Some refugees also found employment as domestic servants and cooks in the homes of American families. The earthquake refugees greatly reinforced the chop suey restaurant businesses in Chicago. The upscale restaurants secured the most experienced cooks by offering them good wages; the more modest restaurants hired the less expensive ones; and the plainest Chinese eateries, where one could get "a full meal for 15 cents," also hired new cooks from San Francisco. The South Side was so filled with Chinese, particularly on 63rd Street from Woodlawn to Chicagolawn, that the local media complained that restaurants "were overrun by Celestials."[58]

Thus Chicago again became a refuge for Chinese from the West Coast.

The ready access to railway and waterway transportation and its comparatively tolerant atmosphere in regard to the Chinese again positioned the city as an important gateway for transnational and transregional migrations. The flow of human resources and socioeconomic connections between the coastal port cities and the hinterland metropolis made Chicago a significant link within the global and transnational Chinese networks.

REACTION TO THE GEARY ACT

Although the Chinese settled in Chicago with relative ease and met with more welcome from the local residents, they nonetheless also endured the nationwide expression of anti-Chinese sentiments embodied in the anti-Chinese exclusion laws and the subsequent hunts and raids for "unlawful" Chinese by immigration authorities and local police.

The renewal of the Chinese Exclusion Act of 1882 on May 5, 1892, known as the Geary Act, prompted another round of anti-Chinese persecution in the country. In Chicago, the situation was made worse by preparations for the World's Fair in 1893. The Office of the Inspector in Charge in Chicago was particularly alarmed by a rumor that scores of Chinese would be smuggled to the fair and would then disappear into the crowds of their fellow countrymen in the city. As in other port cities, the immigration authorities in Chicago photographed the Chinese to further scrutinize them so as to be able to distinguish them from the illegal Chinese smuggled in with staff members of the Chinese displays at the fair.

These actions infuriated the Chinese community. Moy Dong Chow and Moy Dong Hoy led a protest. When a reporter from the *Chicago Tribune* visited the South Clark Street district on August 9, 1892, Moy Dong Chow angrily refused to talk to the reporter—the opposite of his usual easy-going and accommodating manner—and Moy Dong Hoy declined to be included in the group photograph of Chinese outside the Hip Lung store. Chow Tar, whose excellent command of English apparently made him the spokesperson for Chinatown, articulated to a reporter the anger of the Chinese community at the exclusion acts and related measures:

> If that law means that all my countrymen, residents in America are to be measured as criminals and labeled as so many packages of tea it will never be enforced. The ridiculousness of its provisions will kill it. Are we not residents here? Do we not pay taxes as all other property holders? It would

be more nearly justice for them to drive us out. So long as we are accepted as residents we are entitled to some rights. We are not law breakers. There certainly would be a great deal of trouble should an attempt be made, such as you have indicated to place all Chinese residents on a par with professional criminals. For the record of such measurements and pictures would be classed as a "rogues" gallery. Would this Chinese "rogues" gallery be put on exhibition in the World's Fair to show the advancement in civilization that this nation has attained?.No, no, I think that a telegram stating that such measurements and photographs are now being taken of Chinese in the cities which are ports must be a hoax.[59]

Contrary to the public perception of "Mongolians" or "Chinamen" as racially debased, politically naive, and culturally ignorant, Chow Tar was poignant, logical, and piercingly convincing. The Chinese in Chicago protested the Geary Act for singling them out and imposing unjust treatment on them and demanded their rights as law-abiding and tax-paying residents.

Wong Chin Foo, brought back to Chicago on account of the 1893 legal conflict between the Wongs and the Moys, participated in the protest movement. He started a handwritten bilingual, bimonthly newspaper, *Meihua xinbao* (Chinese American), as a revival of his failed newspaper in New York from a decade before. In its inaugural issue of June 24, 1893, Wong Chin Foo declared in English: "[This paper] especially will appeal to the members of the Americanized Chinese of this country who understand the English language and love the institutions and civilization of America, and are willing to cast their life lots with us here instead of with the people of China." He criticized the Geary Act for discriminating against the Chinese and expressed his disappointment with the Chinese Six Companies (fraternal organizations of Chinese immigrants in the United States based on lineage and geographical origin, including the Kong Chow Company, Sam Yup Company, Yeoung Wo Company, Yan Wo Company, Ning Yung Company, and Hop Wo Company), for failing to oppose it successfully.[60]

The Chinese protest in Chicago echoed those in other parts of the country. On September 22, 1892, nearly two hundred English-speaking Chinese from the East Coast rallied at the Cooper Union in the East Village in Lower Manhattan to form the Chinese Equal Rights League to contest the legality of the Geary Act, which had been passed four months previously. Sam Ping Lee, a Philadelphia merchant, was elected president and Wong Chin Foo was elected secretary of the league. The organization published an appeal, declaring, "As residents of the United States we claim a common manhood with all other nationalities, and believe we should have that manhood recognized according to the principles of common humanity and American freedom."[61]

The Geary Act of 1892 resulted in numerous raids and arrests of Chinese throughout the country, including the Chicago area, during subsequent decades. The Civil Case Files of the United States District Court in the Northern District of Illinois show a number of Chicago Chinese arrested in 1911, allegedly for being unlawful residents. Moy Jan, a likely kinsman of the Moy brothers, was arrested in January 1911 on the charge of "contravention of Chinese Exclusion Laws" as "being a Chinese Person unlawfully within the United States." Responding to the arrests, On Leong hired attorneys Thomas E. Milchrist, Frank T. Milchrist, and James P. Greer to provide him with legal representation; Moy Dong Hoy, Wong Aloy, and Lee Ham appeared in court as witnesses on his behalf. Despite their efforts, Moy Jan was ordered to be deported to China by Mark A. Foote, the US commissioner for the Northern District of Illinois.[62] Other Chinese in Chicago— Moy Gwong, Moy Shew, Moy Suey, Mark Song, and Mook Chin, among others—were likewise arrested and convicted on the same charge. Among the indicted Chinese, only Mook Chin appealed the court's ruling and successfully had his conviction reversed.[63]

Similar raids targeting the Chinese in connection with the Chinese exclusion laws of 1882, 1888, 1892, 1902, and 1922 also took place in other major midwestern cities, such as St. Louis. In 1883, the so-called Highbinder Murder Case took place in the St. Louis Chinatown. A black man named Johnson was killed in Hop Alley, the Chinese quarter of the city, and his head was later found in a basket of rice. The local police believed that a conflict between the man and a Chinese gambler connected with the Highbinders, a Chinese secret society allegedly associated with many murders in large Chinese communities, resulted in the murder.[64] Without any witnesses, police arrested six Chinese men from Hop Alley as suspects in the murder. The Chinese men were vigorously prosecuted but the court was unable to convict them owing to the lack of evidence.[65] Not only were the local police quick to suspect the Chinese of being criminals, but the news media even erroneously identified all the Chinese residents of St. Louis as Highbinders: according to the *St. Louis Globe-Democrat*, there were "about three hundred Highbinders in St. Louis" in 1892—a number almost the same as the total Chinese population of St. Louis at the time.[66]

Aroused by the sensational and exaggerated media reports and guided by an anti-Chinese exclusionist mentality, St. Louis law enforcement agencies assumed there to be a large number of illegal laborers and criminals among the Chinese in the city and took serious action, targeting the city's entire Chinese population.[67] The annual reports of the St. Louis Police Department indicate that the years 1895 and 1905–1911 were the peaks of police arrests of Chinese. The heightening of police harassment of Chinese unsurprisingly coincided with the renewals of the Chinese Exclusion Act in 1892, 1902, and 1904. Media reports confirm the arrest data. According to the *St. Louis Globe-Democrat*, on August 25, 1897, St. Louis police rounded up all 314 Chinese in the city as requested by a government agent investigating reports that illegal Chinese immigrants had been smuggled into the city. Thirteen Chinese men were found to be without proper legal documents and were arrested to await deportation.[68] In the first two decades of the twentieth century, St. Louis police repeatedly raided Hop Alley and apprehended scores of Chinese individuals allegedly guilty of smuggling, manufacturing, and selling opium.[69] The nationwide roundup for the purpose of identifying illegal Chinese also included raids in Boston in 1903, when the police and the Immigration Bureau jointly searched the Boston Chinatown for the tong murderers who had allegedly killed a member of a rival tong, and in Cleveland in 1925, when police arrested all of the Chinese in the city following a series of Chinatown murders.[70]

Although the police harassment in St. Louis and other cities might have been worse than that in Chicago, negative media reports and institutionalized legal actions in connection with the Chinese exclusion laws nevertheless effectively demonized Chicago's Chinatown and paved the way for the economic sanctions that came later, collectively imposed by property owners in the Loop area. Here multiple factors of racial prejudice, cultural bias, and economic competition intertwined, culminating in a powerful force that drove the Chinese out of the Loop in 1912.

A Multiethnic Jungle

The Chinese in late nineteenth-century Chicago were probably tolerated more than their counterparts in other cities because they were less conspicuous in this cosmopolitan port, where all nationalities were represented and mixed. In fact, the Chinese were not only well mixed with other ethnic groups, according to historian Adam McKeown, but they also were likely "overshadowed" by the exotic sights and activities in the Loop.[71] The block between Van Buren and Harrison on Clark Street was just inside the south part of the Loop. It was in this multiethnic urban "jungle" that the Chinese built their ethnic enclave. McKeown offers a vivid account of this ethnic milieu:

> Chinese businesses and association halls shared buildings on Clark Street with the Salvation Army, bars, flophouses, pawn shops, barbers, dime museums, and oyster bays run by a variety of ethnic groups. The Sip Sing Tong shared a building with the "Deutsches Gast Haus," an Italian grocery store, and Harrison's lunchroom. Black Mushmouth Johnson's gambling house, famous for clientele of all races and bets as low as a nickel, was right next door to one of the earliest Chinese restaurants, the Bow Wo Fang. The Kenna Saloon, headquarters of Hinky Dink Kenna, John Coughlin's partner as ward boss, was one story below the King Yen Lo, an upscale restaurant with a citywide reputation.[72]

This worldly scene was common to other American metropolises at the turn of the century. But Chicago, as an emerging industrial powerhouse and transportation node in the heart of the country, was particularly impacted by industrialization and immigration, being a preferred destination for European immigrants. In 1871, most foreign-born residents were from Germany (30 percent), Ireland (30 percent), and England (20 percent).[73] Two decades later, in 1909, most were from Germany, Denmark, Ireland, Poland, and Sweden, in descending order.[74]

The prevalence of immigration, with its associated problems of unemployment, homelessness, crowded and unsanitary housing, and crime and delinquency, drew national attention to Chicago. Progressive reformers and scholars zealously attempted to improve the city by performing scientific studies and taking the measures recommended as a result.[75] Scholars of the Chicago School viewed the city as an experimental social laboratory. The arrival of Robert Ezra Park, a charismatic and driven sociologist, in the Sociology Department of the University of Chicago in 1914 prompted a series of sociological studies of the city's poorest neighborhoods and marginal individuals. Published mostly in the 1920s and 1930s, these works paint a vivid and realistic picture of the urban jungle in an industrialized age.[76]

As a transportation, communications, and commercial hub, the city attracted a floating population of 30,000 to 75,000 homeless men, or "hobos," mostly migrant workers drifting in search of jobs, food, and shelter. Nels Anderson, a graduate student in the Sociology Department at the University of Chicago in the early 1920s and previously a hobo himself, recorded the lives of homeless men in Chicago as a participant observer in *The Hobo: The Sociology of the Homeless Man* (1923). The hobos gravitated around Hobohemia, an area less than five minutes' walk from the Loop. Within Hobohemia, West Madison Street was known as the "slave market," where most of the employment agencies sent "man catchers" with whom the hobos searching for jobs bargained. The street was also home to bootleggers, peddlers, beggars, cripples, and old homeless men. Jefferson Park, between Adams and Monroe Streets, supplied the "slave market." Known to the locals as "Bum Park," it was the favorite place for the homeless to sleep in the summer or to pass time reading newspapers and boasting of their adventures to fellow hobos.[77]

While migrant workers and homeless men congregated near the Loop, the German Jews established a ghetto in the south and west sides of the Loop, as recorded by Louis Wirth, another Chicago sociologist, in *The Ghetto* (1928). The center of the Jewish population in 1870 was an area bounded by Van Buren Street on the north, Polk Street on the south, the Chicago River on the west, and Clark Street on the east, in the immediate vicinity of the Loop.[78] Irving Cutler (1996) has described in detail the settlement conditions in the Maxwell Street area for eastern European Jews, who came to the city between the 1880s and 1910s, complementing Wirth's earlier study on the German Jewish community.

Clifford R. Shaw's *The Jack-Roller* (1930) examined the life history of a young delinquent named Stanley in great detail. Basing his account on a short and simple document Stanley wrote prior to his commitment to the House of Correction, Shaw retold the story on a grand scale, including statistics. A twenty-two-year-old male delinquent, Stanley grew up in a broken home in an area with high rates of delinquency. According to Shaw, his career of delinquency began before he'd even started school.[79]

In addition to their work on European immigrants and their neighborhoods, members of the Chicago School of sociology also studied the so-called Oriental problem and subsequently recruited students of Chinese ancestry, including Tin-Chiu Fan, Ching-Chao Wu, Rose Hum Lee, Paul

C. P. Siu, and others.[80] Some of their theses and dissertations focused on Chicago's Chinatown (these works are discussed in detail in Chapter 6).

The city's multiracial makeup and comparatively high level of cross-racial interaction may account for the relatively favorable reception of the Chinese in Chicago. But the city was hardly immune from the racial anxieties and anguish experienced throughout the country in the first decades of the twentieth century, which were manifested in Chicago in its own specific way.

Driven to the South Side

As the Chinese population in Chicago continued to increase, reaching 584 in 1890, the local Chinese grew worried.[81] Their memories of anti-Chinese sentiments on the West Coast, still fresh, haunted them. They dreaded the possible repetition of the crusades that had driven them to the Windy City.

To avoid a humiliating and violent removal by the majority of the population, the Chinese community decided to make its own move. In 1893, the Chinese began voluntarily to disperse themselves throughout the city.[82] As a great number of Chinese businesses were laundries, which catered to a white clientele all over the city, this voluntary dispersal was logical and beneficial to the Chinese.

In the period between 1892 and 1902, while the total Chinese population in the United States declined, the number of Chinese in Chicago more than doubled, from 584 in 1890 to 1,179 in 1900 (see Table 1). Two factors contributed to the population increase. First, feeling more settled in the city, the Chinese had sent for their relatives in China, urging them to come to Chicago. Second, the Columbian Exposition in 1893 had attracted many Chinese from other parts of the country to meet the increased demand for restaurant and laundry services.[83]

The growing presence of Chinese in Chicago had aroused discomfort and suspicion among some of the city's white residents, who were particularly uncomfortable with the interactions between Chinese males and white females taking place at the Chinese missions, where Chinese male laborers, mostly laundrymen, were taught English by white female teachers. The English classes operated by the Presbyterian churches in Chicago initially met with little resistance. But in 1909, in the wake of the murder of Elsie Sigel in New York City, also known as the "Chinatown Trunk Mystery," the suspicion among some white Chicagoans grew into hysteria.

TABLE I Chinese population in Chicago, 1870–2010

Year	Number	Increase
1870	1	0
1880	172	171
1890	584	412
1900	1,179	595
1910	1,778	599
1920	2,353	575
1930	2,757	404
1940	2,018	−739
1950	3,334	1,316
1960	5,082	1,748
1970	9,357	4,275
1980	13,638	4,281
1990	22,295	8,657
2000*	34,370	2,075
2009*	43,227	8,857

SOURCES: For data from 1870 to 1990: US Bureau of the Census, *U.S. Census of Population*, cited in Kiang (1992, 30); data from 2000: US Bureau of the Census, Summary File 2 (SF 2) and Summary File 4 (SF 4), http://www.ameredia.com/ resources/demographics/chinese.html; data from 2009: American Community Survey, http://factfinder.census.gov/.
* Figures do not include Taiwanese.

On the afternoon of June 18, 1909, Sun Leung, the proprietor of a chop suey restaurant in New York, reported to the police that his cousin, Leon Ling, had disappeared. A policeman went to search Ling's room and found a large trunk bound with rope. He opened the trunk and found, not Leon Ling's body, but the body of a young white woman, later identified as nineteen-year-old Elsie Sigel, who had been missing for a week. Further investigation revealed that Sigel, a missionary worker from a prominent family, had been intimate with Leon Ling. The murder of Elsie Sigel immediately occupied the front pages of newspapers throughout the nation, which portrayed Chinese men as dangerous to "innocent" and "virtuous" young white women. This murder led to a surge in the harassment of Chinese across the United States. Despite the combined efforts of police forces across the nation, Leon Ling was never apprehended and the murder remains unsolved to this day.[84]

Agitated by the Elsie Sigel murder in New York, residents in Chicago's Woodlawn neighborhood demanded that the local authorities close the Chinese mission Sunday school at 6446 Drexel Avenue, the residence of Dr. Minerva Kline, a fervent Christian missionary who had worked with the Chinese for nine years. The area's white residents feared that the encounter between Chinese males and Christian females at the mission school would lead to interracial intimacy or even the murder of white women. Timothy Barrett, leader of the protests and a retired policeman who lived across the street from the school, told the authorities, "I noticed that the students came in the back way passing down an alley and through a shed. They were followed by a crowd of girls of various ages, who looked upon them with curiosity. The Chinamen, apparently seemed [to] behave themselves just now, but after the agitation blows over, will they? I noticed some of the boys wore carnations given them by their teachers. That shows the wrong attitude on the part of the instructors." To expel the Chinese mission, Barrett "spent all afternoon trying to get evidence" for prosecuting the case.[85]

On June 28, 1909, nine days after the Elsie Sigel murder, inspectors from the building commissioner's office inspected the building of the Chinese mission and found that the "doors swung in instead [of] out," which was alleged to be a violation of a city ordinance. Then policeman John Kane of the Woodlawn station ordered the class disbanded. Dr. Kline explained that the English lessons were conducted in one large room and that several of the teachers were married and were accompanied by their husbands, who were interested in the mission efforts; she called the protests by Woodlawn residents just "spite work." Many of the teachers remained away from the meeting held by the authorities, but three attended the meeting and were determined to continue their work.[86]

The anti-Chinese agitation occurring in Chicago, as in other major cities of the country at the time of the Chinatown Trunk Mystery, was reaching a climax, ready to be fanned into anti-Chinese riots. Suspicion of and antipathy toward the Chinese in the city on the part of white Chicagoans, however, took a different form—economic sanctions. Property owners in the Loop area drastically raised rents to drive out Chinese businesses and tenants. In the early 1910s, the rent for a medium-size Chinese grocery store in the South Clark Street area, such as Quang Yuan Chong Kee and Company, was $225 a month, while for the same space on West 22nd Street on the South Side, rents ranged from $125 to $190 a month.[87] By 1910, about

MAP 1 Chinese communities in Chicago.

half of the Chinese population had been forced to move out of Clark Street into the South Side.[88]

The move was also prompted by an additional development. In 1911 the federal government announced the construction of a new federal building on Clark Street between Adams and Jackson Streets, right in the heart of the Chinese district, which would require the demolition of many buildings housing Chinese businesses. Alarmed by the pending loss, On Leong took the initiative and obtained a lease through H. O. Stone and Company for approximately fifty commercial spaces near the intersection of Wentworth Avenue and Cermak Road. The businesses associated with On Leong moved from Clark Street to Wentworth and Cermak in February 1912, and the area was immediately proclaimed as the "New Chinatown."[89] (See Map 1.)

The reasons behind the relocation of Chinatown, however, were not only racial prejudice expressed in the form of economic pressure. Writers have speculated that the internal rivalry between the On Leong Tong and the Hip Sing Tong might also have been responsible for the move (see further discussion on this topic in Chapter 5).[90]

The "South Side Story"

The city of Chicago is divided by the Chicago River and its branches into four main sections: downtown, the North Side, the West Side, and the South Side. Downtown, or the Loop, lying approximately between Division Street on the north, Lake Michigan on the east, Roosevelt Road on the south, and Des Plaines Avenue on the west, serves as the city's commercial hub. The city's North Side, extending north of downtown along the lakefront, is the most densely populated residential section of the city. It contains public parkland and beaches stretching for miles along Lake Michigan to the city's northern border. The West Side, extending west of downtown, is made up of neighborhoods such as Austin, Lawndale, Garfield Park, West Town, and Humboldt Park, among others. Some neighborhoods, particularly Garfield Park and Lawndale, have socioeconomic problems including urban decay and crime.

The South Side, extending south of downtown along Lake Michigan, is the largest section of the city, encompassing roughly 60 percent of the city's land area. The section along the lake is marked with public parkland and beaches. The South Side also contains most of the city's industry. Here one can see the industrial might of Chicago: massive industrial plants, grain elevators, lumberyards, and meat-packing houses.

Although the South Side had a reputation for being impoverished and crime ridden, the leaders of On Leong realized it also had a number of advantages. There were a relatively large number of available residential and commercial buildings in the area chosen for the new Chinatown, allowing for population and business growth, as well as both a public school and a private school. Moreover, away from downtown, the encroachment of downtown businesses and the close attention of city officials could be avoided.

In the late 1920s, sociologists at the University of Chicago subdivided the city into seventy-seven distinct community areas. The boundaries of these areas are more clearly defined than those of the over 210 neighborhoods throughout the city, allowing for better year-by-year comparisons. The new Chinatown falls within community area 34, Armour Square (see Map 2).

Armour Square is named after the pork-packing magnet Philip Danforth Armour, who with his brothers founded the slaughterhouse and meatpacking company Armour and Company in this area in 1867, which by 1880 had become Chicago's most important business, helping make the city and its Union Stockyards the center of the American meat-packing industry. The area was occupied by different ethnic groups in succession: Irish, German, and Swedish immigrants had settled there in the last decades of the nineteenth century, and when these groups moved out in the 1900s, Italians and Yugoslavs moved in.[91] In 1912, when the Chinese moved to 22nd Street in the Armour Square area, Italian immigrants were already settled there and were not friendly to their new neighbors. The Chinese were called names and made fun of for their clothing and queues, which they still wore despite the overthrow in 1912 of the Manchu ruler who had forced Chinese males to wear them as a symbol of submission.[92] This friction restricted the new Chinatown to one square block at 22nd Street and Princeton Avenue.

Despite ethnic differences, multiple ethnic communities coexisted side by side in relative harmony. Similar to the ethnic succession in New York City and San Francisco, the new Chicago Chinatown on the South Side coexisted with the established Italian community. While the Chinese took over a large portion of the residential and commercial property, many Italian residents and institutions also remained, for example, Zweifei's Hardware Store at 2508 South Wentworth.[93] Josephine Coco, owner of an Italian

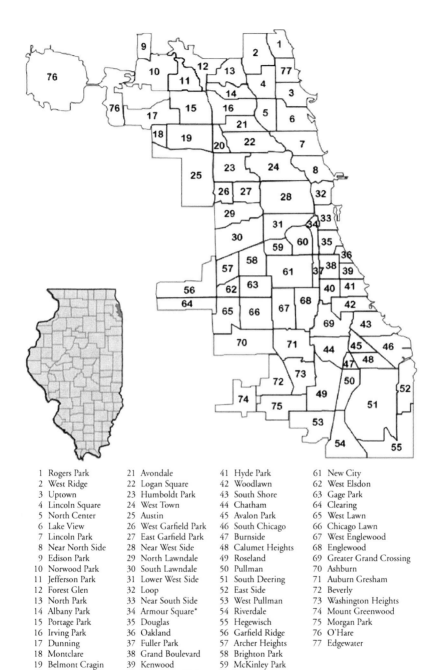

1 Rogers Park	21 Avondale	41 Hyde Park	61 New City
2 West Ridge	22 Logan Square	42 Woodlawn	62 West Elsdon
3 Uptown	23 Humboldt Park	43 South Shore	63 Gage Park
4 Lincoln Square	24 West Town	44 Chatham	64 Clearing
5 North Center	25 Austin	45 Avalon Park	65 West Lawn
6 Lake View	26 West Garfield Park	46 South Chicago	66 Chicago Lawn
7 Lincoln Park	27 East Garfield Park	47 Burnside	67 West Englewood
8 Near North Side	28 Near West Side	48 Calumet Heights	68 Englewood
9 Edison Park	29 North Lawndale	49 Roseland	69 Greater Grand Crossing
10 Norwood Park	30 South Lawndale	50 Pullman	70 Ashburn
11 Jefferson Park	31 Lower West Side	51 South Deering	71 Auburn Gresham
12 Forest Glen	32 Loop	52 East Side	72 Beverly
13 North Park	33 Near South Side	53 West Pullman	73 Washington Heights
14 Albany Park	34 Armour Square*	54 Riverdale	74 Mount Greenwood
15 Portage Park	35 Douglas	55 Hegewisch	75 Morgan Park
16 Irving Park	36 Oakland	56 Garfield Ridge	76 O'Hare
17 Dunning	37 Fuller Park	57 Archer Heights	77 Edgewater
18 Montclare	38 Grand Boulevard	58 Brighton Park	
19 Belmont Cragin	39 Kenwood	59 McKinley Park	
20 Hermosa	40 Washington Park	60 Bridgeport*	

MAP 2   Community areas of Chicago.

SOURCE: Wikipedia, http://en.wikipedia.org/wiki/Community_areas_of_Chicago.

* Uptown (3) hosts North Chinatown, centered around the West Argyle Street Historic District. Armour Square (34) and Bridgeport (60) constitute South Chinatown.

meat and poultry store at 2262 South Wentworth and 23rd Street, and her younger daughter Carmen would pose for a photograph with their Irish customers.[94] Italian American Frank Lizzo and his brothers, Sam, Vincent, and Phil, were born in the 1910s and raised in the Chinatown area; although Frank moved away in 1949, he still returned to Chinatown frequently to visit family and friends.[95]

In the 1920s, another turnover occurred in the Armour Square area. The prosperity of the 1920s created more economic opportunities for the Italian immigrants. Meanwhile, the Great Migration of black laborers from the American South after World War I brought more African Americans to the neighborhood. As a result, many of the Italians moved out and the Chinese gradually bought some of their properties. The Chinatown now expanded east to include State Street, the center of the black community in the 1910s and 1920s. Langston Hughes, the American poet, short-story writer, journalist, and playwright known as a leading member of the Harlem Renaissance in the 1920s but whose career stretched into the 1960s, was thrilled when he arrived in the city in 1918 as a sixteen-year-old teenager. In his autobiography he describes the strong impression made on him by the Armour Square area: "South State Street was in its glory then, a teeming Negro Street with crowded theaters, restaurants, and cabarets. And excitement from noon to noon. Midnight was like day."[96] The *Chicago Whip*, a black newspaper, provided an even more colorful description of the area as a cosmopolitan "Bohemia of the Colored folks" where "lights sparkled, glasses tinkled."[97] However, the Chinese and African Americans generally remained in segregated residential areas and socially separated from each other.

Conclusion

Chicago was more welcoming to the Chinese than cities on the West Coast such as San Francisco. Its racial diversity helped the Chinese "disappear" in the multiethnic "jungle." The initial tolerance of the city fostered steady growth of the Chinese population, leading to the establishment in the Loop area of the first Chinatown, which overlapped with other ethnic neighborhoods and businesses, creating a pattern of ethnic cohabitation. But in the 1910s, the growing Chinese population and the nationwide anti-Chinese crusades aroused anxiety among the white residents of the city. White property owners raised rents, effectively driving the Chinese out of the Loop area, and the displaced community relocated to Chicago's South Side.

This account of the removal and relocation of the Chinese leads to several observations. First, when the larger society perceived itself as being threatened, racial tolerance was immediately replaced by racial suspicion and anger. Second, to avoid direct and possibly violent conflict with the dominant racial group, the Chinese opted for a strategy of retreat—moving to a less desirable neighborhood. This practical and effective means of dealing with the problem of racial conflict reveals both their instinct for survival and their vulnerability in a racialized society.

THREE

Operating Transnational Businesses, 1880s–1930s

This is not a basis to estimate the volume of their business. Indeed they do much more business in these stores than can be estimated by an outsider.

—A Chinese resident in Chicago, 1920s

The new Chinatown on 22nd Street between Clark Street and Princeton Avenue was probably one of the most neglected areas of Chicago in 1912. Here the Chinese built a commercial and residential community sheltering at least one-third of the Chinese population, which numbered more than two thousand in the city during the first decade of the twentieth century. By the 1930s, following two decades of growth and expansion, Chicago's Chinatown was well established as a distinctive and sizeable Chinese American urban community. The development of Chinatown was consistent with the city's overall growth; since 1890 Chicago had become known as America's "Second City," after New York, and was the largest city in the developing West.[1]

Niches

In the Second City, stockyards and factories absorbed the bulk of the city's workforce. In 1919, more than 70 percent of the four hundred thousand wage earners working in Chicago were employed in companies of at least one hundred employees, and nearly a third of them labored in factories employing over a thousand workers. Thus, a typical worker in Chicago in the 1910s and 1920s was an industrial worker, hired by one of the giant employers such as Armour and Swift in the stockyards; Inland, Youngstown, Republic, Wisconsin, and US Steel; the Pullman Company works; International Harvester; Western Electric's Hawthorne Works; and Hart Schaffner

Marx, makers of men's clothing. Ethnic succession followed a similar path-way for both steelworkers and meat packers. The earliest workers in steel plants and meat-packing houses came from Ireland, Germany, and a little later from Bohemia. As the need for skilled workers declined and the sources of immigrant workers changed, Poles, Lithuanians, and Slovaks, along with blacks, filled the ranks of a workforce that had become increasingly semiskilled and unskilled.[2] Only one ethnic group from Asia, however—Filipinos, who worked at the post office and for Pullman—had joined the mainstream labor force by the mid-1920s.[3]

Unlike immigrant workers in other ethnic groups, the Chinese in Chicago did not join the workforce overseen by corporate employers but rather fo-cused on the economic niches of groceries, restaurants, and laundries, ethnic enterprises that were prevalent in other parts of the country with high con-centrations of Chinese population. The racialization of the larger labor mar-ket discouraged the Chinese from seeking jobs there, and so they chose to work for niche businesses, where their lack of English-language skills as well as other skills required for the larger labor market would not be an impedi-ment. Similarly, Japanese and Korean immigrants survived largely as fresh vegetable growers and grocery retailers, respectively. By contrast, Filipinos, as nationals of an American colony who had been exposed to American cul-ture and acquired at least some English-language skills before emigrating to America, worked for employers in the larger society.[4]

Although exhibiting the same occupational patterns as their Chinese counterparts in other parts of the United States, the Chinese businesses in Chicago deserve special attention for a number of reasons. First, the gro-cery businesses in Chicago were well connected with transnational ethnic networks in every aspect of business; they supplied not only the Chinese laundries and chop suey houses in the city but also those in the surround-ing areas, making the Chicago Chinatown a major center for wholesale groceries and other merchandise in the Midwest region. Second, the city's metropolitan atmosphere fostered ambition, a sense of modernity, and a taste for extravagance among the Chinese restaurateurs, who consequently helped create a trend of Chinese fine dining in the country in the late nine-teenth and early twentieth centuries.[5] Third, the Chinese hand laundries in Chicago, which provided a livelihood for thousands of Chinese immi-grants, also served as a fruitful field of study for Paul C. P. Siu's monu-mental work on the Chinese laundryman, which remains unmatched in its depth and scope decades after its eventual publication in 1987. Siu's observations on the "back and forth movement" of the Chinese "sojourners" significantly preceded and strengthened the theory of Chinese transnationalism that emerged in the early 1990s.[6] Chinese laundries in Chicago (as well as those in San Francisco and New York) served as prototypes for those in other midwestern cities and towns. Fourth, the Chinese businessmen in Chicago, from the Moy brothers to Chin F. Foin and Hong Sling, were transnational in their business orientations and operations, constituting prime examples of early Chinese transnational entrepreneurship. Finally, because Chicago was a transportation hub, it was comparatively easy for many Chinese to move between it and other cities of the Midwest, making Chicago a center for the transnational migration of Chinese and their regional socioeconomic development. The sections following provide further elaboration of these points.

WHOLESALE CENTERS AND TRAVELING STORES

Wentworth Avenue and West 22nd Street, the main thoroughfares of Chinatown, hosted most of its businesses and community organizations: 65 on Wentworth Avenue and 60 on West 22nd Street, out of a total of 156 Chinese establishments listed in the local Chinese directories of the 1930s.[7] The majority of the businesses were grocery stores, retailing and wholesaling goods imported from China.[8]

   The larger and more prominent grocery stores (in chronological order) included Hip Lung Yee Kee at 323 South Clark Street, owned by the three Moy brothers; Wing Chong Hai at 281 South Clark Street, owned by Chin F. Foin; Tai Wah and Company at 303 South Clark Street; Quang Yuan Chong Kee and Company at 509 South Clark Street; the Chinese Trading Company at 2214 Archer Avenue; and Sam Lung and Company at 431 South Clark Street, owned by Hong Sling. A close examination of some of the older, established firms in Chicago offers a good picture of the Chinese transnational grocery business in terms of capital investment, partnership, organizational structure, dividends and salaries, daily operation, and business volume.

   Transnational ethnic networking dominated various aspects of the Chinese businesses in Chicago. Ethnic networks were essential for the larger Chinese businesses in raising capital to start a business, procurement of merchandise, and recruitment of employees, both in wholesale and in retail trade. Almost without exception, according to immigrant testimony, Chinese business owners acquired capital by borrowing from kinsmen and friends rather than obtaining loans from banks, the conventional and standard practice in American and other Western societies. A large Chinese grocery store or restaurant might have between ten and twenty partners each investing about $1,000 in the business, with the largest shareholder and organizer of the business normally serving as manager.[9]

Members of the major Chinese clans—the Moys, Chins, and Lims—benefited greatly from kinship networking, as shown by the case of Moy Lung Auk and by those of Hip Lung Yee Kee and Company, Wing Chong Hai, and Quang Yuan Chong Kee and Company. Moy Lung Auk's story illustrates, at the microlevel, how the kinship network was used by resourceful Chinese to initiate and develop businesses. Born in China in 1861, Moy Lung Auk emigrated to the United States in 1881. He came to Chicago in 1902 and soon opened a Chinese restaurant, Wee Ying Lo at 137 North Clark Street, from which he made some money. He then decided to open a second Chinese restaurant, Peking Restaurant at 459 North Clark Street, which required a total investment of $2,500, of which Moy Lung Auk had an $850 share and his three partners put up the rest. The $850 that Moy Lung Auk invested came from $250 in profits from Wee Ying Lo; $550 borrowed from Moy Kee Doy, a kinsman who was also a cook at Wee Ying Lo; and $50 worth of goods he acquired from Tai Wah, a Chinese grocery store.[10]

Hip Lung Yee Kee, or Hip Lung for short, the oldest Chinese company in Chicago, was initially started by an unknown Chinese immigrant before the 1870s. Moy Dong Chow bought it in the late 1870s and named it Hip Lung Yee Kee and Company. The store was moved to 323 South Clark Street in 1880 and then to 2243 Wentworth Avenue in 1912 when Chinatown was relocated to the South Side. The three Moy brothers deftly and strategically divided among themselves the operations of this transnational family business that spanned Chicago, San Francisco, and Hong Kong. Moy Dong Chow, the most charismatic of the brothers and said to be the oldest Chinese in town, handled the task of public relations, negotiating with the mainstream media and the Chinese community on behalf of the Moys. Moy Dong Hoy, steady and calm, oversaw the operation of Hip Lung as its manager from 1885 on. As manager of the company, as well as one who spoke English fluently, Moy Dong Hoy was often summoned by the Office of the Inspector in Charge to testify on behalf of fellow partners in the company. Moy Dong Yee, handsome and shrewd, managed the transnational family business on the other side of the Pacific, traveling between Chicago, San Francisco, and Hong Kong.[11]

In addition to the division of labor and sharing of responsibilities among the Moy brothers themselves, there was also a heavy dependence on clansmen in matters of capital investment and business operation. In 1904, Hip Lung had thirty-five partners, of whom nine actively participated in the store, all of them members of the Moy clan (Moy Dong Chow, Moy Dong Hoy, Moy Dong Yee, Moy Ben, Moy Lee, Moy Toy, Moy Quan, Moy Hen, and Moy Loy). Of the business's total capital of $41,000, over $10,000 was in stock. Its capital investment and partnership fluctuated over time. Two years later, in 1906, the nine active partners of the firm included the three Moy brothers, Moy Ham, Moy Shuk, Moy Choon, Moy Han, Moy Gun, and Moy Lee. The store's worth was $30,000 in goods, not including accounts outstanding and goods on the way. Moy Dong Chow and Moy Dong Hoy served as managers, while Moy Dong Yee served as assistant treasurer, earning $40 a month besides his dividends. When Moy Dong Yee was in China, Moy Toon, a nephew of the Moy brothers, would serve as acting treasurer.[12]

Chinese sources further reveal that, of the major Chinese clans in Chicago, the Moys maintained the most extensive transnational migration network. The Chicago branch of Moy Shi Kung Sow (the Moy Family Association) was founded in 1898, the second branch of Moy Shi Kung Sow in North America (the first was founded in 1894 in New York). Its membership was the largest of all the Chinese family associations in Chicago. A global organization, Moy Shi Kung Sow constitutes a transnational network with connections and influences throughout North America and other parts of the world. The Chicago Moys emerged as leaders of the family association in America as early as the 1920s. It hosted the first national Moy convention in 1927 and several successive national conventions that were held every three years (see Table 3 in Chapter 7).[13] Their broad national and international connections helped the Chicago Moys build their early businesses and reinforced their economic power over time.

The early history of Hip Lung is informative in a number of ways. First, it illustrates the crucial role of the kinship business partnership in securing both venture capital to establish a business and capital for further business growth. Second, while the distribution of capital investment and the makeup of the partnership fluctuated over time, both remained within the kinship network. Third, in order to be competitive, a large firm benefited from being transnational in all or at least most aspects of its business operation.

Transnational ethnic networking was also essential in the recruitment of employees. Immigrants who had settled in Chicago would send for their family members, kinsmen, and fellow villagers, and the latter would work as paid or unpaid helpers in the stores upon arrival in the city. The major Chinese grocery stores in Chicago normally hired kinsmen as employees. While the Moy brothers and their kinsmen operated Hip Lung Yee Kee, in the 1890s the Chin clan established a rival firm, Wing Chong Hai, at 381 (later 319) South Clark Street, that competed with Hip Lung. It imported and sold teas, silks, and general Chinese and Japanese merchandise. Chin F. Foin, a wealthy and flamboyant Chinese merchant, served as its assistant manager from 1895 to 1900 and became the manager in 1900. He hired twenty employees to keep the store running. In 1908 twelve partners, also exclusively Chin kinsmen (Chin F. Foin, Chin Yen Quai, Chin F. Toy, Chin See, Chin Hor, Chin Leng, Chin Wing Yuen, Chin Der, Chin Wing, Chin Fung, Chin Sun Cheong, and Chin Lee), jointly owned the firm and worked as its employees as well. Among the partners, Chin Wing Yuen, a member of the company since 1893, had a share worth $1,000. Chin F. Foin earned a monthly salary of $120 in addition to dividends, while Chin Wing Yuen, who worked in the herb section of the store preparing and packing medicines, earned $60 a month and dividends. The store normally had $25,000 worth of goods at any time and sold $50,000 to $60,000 worth of goods annually in the 1900s.[14] Clearly, as in the case of Hip Lung, Wing Chong Hai also depended heavily on a kinship network for financing and operating the business. The volume of sales of the two firms was also comparable.

Tai Wah and Company was probably the third oldest Chinese grocery store in Chicago. Founded in 1896, it had about $20,000 worth of goods in stock. Eleven partners, mostly Moy clansmen, invested in the company, including Moy Sam (manager), Moy Lum You, Moy Mon, Lee Park, Moy Yee, Moy Hor, Moy Son, Moy Yoke, Moy Yee Wing, Moy Dung, and Moy Sue Hing. The salesmen of the store were paid $35 a month. The store hired experienced employees like Moy Dung, who worked in a Chinese grocery store, Quong Yuen Sing, in New York prior to his employment at Tai Wah.

Tai Wah benefited as well from the transnational ethnic network, through which it recruited better employees. At the same time, the network also provided Chinese immigrants with job mobility. In addition to wholesale and retail sales, Tai Wah, being a large and reputable firm, also oversaw numerous lending transactions and managed savings for many Chinese laborers.[15]

The dual role of the larger Chinese businesses as both merchandise firms and banks grew out of the casual practices of money lending between Chinese kinsmen and friends taking place in the grocery stores. The money lending within kinship networks was highly personal and informal. The Chinese immigrants generally regarded making loans from their savings to kinsmen as either a familial obligation or a form of investment; in neither case was the lending documented formally and properly but rather was handled as an informal and individual transaction between kinsmen. Interpersonal money lending often took place in the Chinese grocery stores, where close kinsmen or distant "cousins" loaned money to each other while also buying groceries or socializing.[16] In such transactions, as "a Chinese custom," no receipt or other document was necessary for Chinese kinsmen; sheer trust in his "cousins" was a sufficient guarantee for a lender.[17] Chinese laundryman Lum Joy, for example, loaned his cousin Lem Quai $600 in 1903 and another cousin Lem Dock $600 in 1904. Both loans were transacted at the Chinese store Quang Yuen; the transactions were recorded in the store's book but Lum Joy did not possess any documentation himself.[18]

As informal money lending took place in grocery stores more and more frequently, reputable Chinese stores operated by prominent merchants began serving as banks or investment brokerages, for both clansmen and nonclansmen, handling numerous monetary transactions that were regarded as part of the store's normal business. Many Chinese laborers deposited their savings in the large firms, which would use the funds in business operations and pay a certain percentage of the business's profit as a return. Moy Kee Doy's story provides a case in point. Moy Kee Doy was born in China in 1871 and came to the United States in 1881. He moved to Chicago in 1902 and worked as a cook for officers at Fort Sheridan for two years. From that job he saved $500, which he put in the care of Moy Lung You, the bookkeeper of Tai Wah. He later asked Moy Lung You to invest his $500 in the Wee Ying Lo restaurant when it opened in 1903. From this investment he received a dividend of $7 for each $100.[19] The 7 percent return was lucrative enough to attract further investors among kinsmen and customers of the business. In addition to managing money for clan members and customers, some stores also handled the sending of remittances to families and relatives in China on behalf of Chinese immigrants.

Transnational ethnic networking was even more indispensable in the procurement of merchandise. Chinese grocery stores largely depended on imports from China, as they carried mostly dry goods, cooking ingredients, herbs, teas, and fabrics produced in China. Madeline Y. Hsu (2000) explains that the need for Chinese groceries overseas generated the businesses called *jinshanzhuang*, or Gold Mountain firms, in Hong Kong to handle the demand on the part of overseas Chinese for Chinese merchandise. *Jinshanzhuang* date as far back as the 1850s, with close links to overseas Chinese businesses that were mostly run by kinsmen or fellow villagers. On behalf of the overseas firms, managers of *jinshanzhuang* took orders for Chinese goods and arranged for their shipment. By 1922, there were 116 *jinshanzhuang* located in Hong Kong doing business with Chinese firms in North America. Owing to increasing demand, by 1930 the number of *jinshanzhuang* had more than doubled, to 290.[20] The typical route for merchandise procured from China—tea, dried foods, cooking ingredients, herbs, fabrics, and porcelain—began in Hong Kong; then the goods were shipped by sea to San Francisco and finally carried by rail to Chicago.

The Chinese grocery stores in Chicago would also dispatch representatives to China to purchase goods directly, as exemplified by the case of Au Tat. Au Tat was born in 1884 in the village of Ng Woo, Kaiping District, Guangdong, in China. He came to the United States in 1911, first landing in San Francisco and then taking the train to Chicago. He joined Quong Hong Chong and Company at 219 West 22nd Street when it was established in 1917. With a total capital of $12,000 and an annual business of $80,000, the store sold Chinese groceries and Chinese medicines. Having a $1,000 interest in the store, Au Tat served as bookkeeper, also undertaking tasks of procurement in Hong Kong from time to time. In 1919, for instance, he went to Hong Kong on a business trip and returned the following year. While in Hong Kong, he did business with the Quong Loon Chung store at No. 1 Bonham Strand, one of the *jinshanzhuang*, from which he ordered merchandise for his company in Chicago.[21]

Reflecting the city's unique economic position as a retail-wholesale giant, the grocery businesses in Chicago served as central suppliers, distributing goods to many hinterland cities and small towns. Apart from the large firms already mentioned, all of which handled wholesale as well as retail transactions, Quang Yuan Chong Kee and Company was typical in wholesaling to smaller grocery stores in the midwestern states. Opened in 1906, it was initially located in Old Chinatown, at 509 South Clark Street, where the store paid $225 a month for rent. In 1912, along with many other Chinese businesses on South Clark Street, it moved to the South Side, to 241 West 22nd Street, with a monthly rent of $190. By 1913 it had twenty-five partners, most of them from the Lim clan, with a total capital of $30,000. Eight of the partners worked in the store: Lim Bon, with a $2,500 share; Lim Chong, $2,500; Lim Foo and Lim Shear Lett, $2,700; Lim Guy, $1,000; Lim Ying, $1,000; Toy Hung Chuck, $1,000; and Lim Yee, $700. Lim Shear Lett, who held the largest share of the firm, served as manager from when the store opened, and Toy Hung Chuck served as bookkeeper. Lim Yee served as a sales clerk, with a monthly salary of $35, selling goods in the store or traveling for the firm in the neighboring states of Michigan, Indiana, and Wisconsin, as well as to smaller towns in Illinois. He often visited Battle Creek and Lansing in Michigan and Indianapolis, Kokomo, Fort Wayne, and Peru in Indiana, where he took orders for goods and collected debts from the local grocers. Being an image-conscious man, Lim Yee purchased his fine suit and hat in Peru, Indiana, when he saw them in a store during one of his business trips.[22]

While Quang Yuan Chong Kee and Company provides an example of how the larger merchandise companies served as wholesale centers to the Chinese grocers in other cities in the Midwest, Annie Leong's family history offers an example of how the smaller grocers in the cities of the Midwest benefited from business connections with Chicago. Annie Leong's father came to St. Louis in 1920 and set up a successful Chinese restaurant. Four years later, he brought his bride to St. Louis from his hometown, Xinhui, Guangdong, in China. Annie and her two older brothers were all born and grew up in Hop Alley, the Chinatown in St. Louis. During the 1920s and 1930s, the Leong family owned a Chinese restaurant downtown and a grocery store in Hop Alley. The family ordered merchandise for their grocery store from wholesalers in Chicago, San Francisco, and New York. The children all spent their time after school working in the family grocery store. Annie Leong recalled her childhood experiences retailing goods: "We got them on credit and we have thirty days to pay. If you don't have a good credit, you have to pay right away. They gave us wholesale price, and we retail them. The whole family helps to do the business. After the operation whatever is left is our profit."[23]

The major Chinese grocery stores in Chicago generally had tight operational structures, with clear job descriptions for each employee. Quong Hong Chong and Company at 219 West 22nd Street, a medium-size store selling Chinese groceries and Chinese drugs, had twelve business partners, each owning a share of $1,000. The six partners actively working in the store divided the work in the following way: Jack Sam Tsai, manager; Au Tat, bookkeeper; Dea Hawk Woon, treasurer; Dea Mer Quong, salesman; Yee Woi Wah, Chinese druggist; and Dea Sung, English correspondent and interpreter.[24]

The operations of the Chinese general merchandise stores in Chicago resembled in most ways those of their counterparts on the West Coast, as documented in scholarly writings.[25] From capital investment to organizational structure to daily business operation, the Chinese businesses were characteristically transnational and clan oriented. Historian Haiming Liu's nuanced account of the family history of Yitang Chang, a Chinese herbalist in Los Angeles during the late nineteenth and early twentieth centuries, makes clear in detail the transnational nature of the business, which required the procurement of hundreds if not thousands of indigenous herbs collected from mountains and valleys in China.[26]

While the large grocery stores in the heart of Chinatown enjoyed steady patronage, many of the smaller Chinese groceries located on the outskirts or outside of Chinatown had to rely on the less stable business of supplying wholesale to Chinese chop suey shops and laundries, as illustrated in the case of Mr. Fung. Mr. Fung was a farmer in China who came to America in the 1890s. His grocery store in Chicago was not located in the center of the Chinatown, and thus his business had to depend on selling wholesale, primarily chop suey supplies of meats and vegetables delivered daily by car to chop suey houses and laundries run by his cousins.[27]

In addition to the regular grocery stores, there were also traveling grocery stores. The traveling stores emerged at the end of World War I and developed rapidly in the 1920s and 1930s, owing to the increase in the number of Chinese laundries and chop suey houses in the city and throughout the country. Paul C. P. Siu counted twenty-five trucks operating daily in the 1930s, making deliveries to Chinese laundries and chop suey houses all over Chicago.[28] They carried laundry supplies, meats, vegetables, cooking ingredients, imported and locally produced food supplies, and household miscellanies. Some of the traveling stores specialized in fresh meats, poultry, vegetables, and Chinese delicatessen foods. Others, dispatched by the larger stores in Chinatown, carried a more complete inventory, including not only foods but also laundry supplies. The laundryman usually did his food shopping on Sunday, the only day he took off from his business. He could carry home dry foods and a certain amount of fresh foods, enough to last a few days. But by the middle of the week he would be out of fresh foods and would have to buy more from the traveling stores. Such demand generated a growing amount of business for traveling stores.

The same was true for the Chinese chop suey houses. They could buy dry ingredients from the Chinese wholesale stores, but perishable foods would have to be purchased daily. Since the chop suey houses used considerable quantities of meat, poultry, fish, and vegetables, daily supplies of fresh foods were essential to their business. As the largest Chinese urban center in the Midwest, Chicago experienced an expansion in the number of Chinese chop suey houses in the 1910s as the trend was spreading across the country; a majority of the 250 Chinese restaurants in Chicago at that time were in fact chop suey houses. One enterprising man perceived the potential demand and started the first traveling grocery store business. When he became successful, many more soon followed, and thus traveling grocery stores or delivery businesses grew into a significant sector of the overall grocery business.

Typically a traveling store keeper would first purchase a truck. He would then buy grocery items from grocery stores and fresh meats and vegetables from local suppliers at wholesale prices and make deliveries to his customers all across town. A key to the success of a traveling store was the owner's kinship networks. If a traveling store keeper had a large circle of "cousins"—members of his lineage or others who came from the vicinity of his ancestral village—and other relatives, he could make a decent living from the business, as did the previously discussed Mr. Fung and as in the following case recorded by Paul C. P. Siu.

> Sieu is once a laundry man. Uncle J. told me that every penny Sieu earned was spent on the "stockings" (prostitute). As he quit the laundry, he bought a car and began to do retail delivery business. By gathering all kinds of groceries, he drives to the doors of Chinese country men in the laundry or in chop suey places. He always finds friends and relatives to be his customers. Later Sieu found the business going along well then he, one step further, opened a dry good store in Chinatown. But the luck is gone! The business was not

so good as he expected. So the short life store was closed in the interval of ten months. Closing up the store, he met a great depression. He didn't have enough money to buy goods for market on the delivering. Sometimes he found his car out of order but he had no money to send it for repair.[29]

Paul C. P. Siu also demonstrated the importance of kinship networks by examining a four-man laundry on Chicago's far North Side. He observed that there were seven traveling grocers stopping in sequence during the week, selling food and laundry supplies. The laundry's account books indicated that the traveling grocers who were relatives of the laundrymen had more and steadier sales, while the grocers who were not kin had only sporadic and random sales.[30]

The traveling store could also be found in other midwestern cities. In St. Louis in the 1920s, Oriental Tea was such a store. Several partners financed and operated the store, selling supplies to Chinese laundries and restaurants. One of the partners was Richard Ho's father, who brought then ten-year-old Richard from Canton, China, to St. Louis in 1928. Richard Ho later worked in the store as a driver of a small panel truck delivering goods ordered by Chinese laundries and restaurants and taking new orders from them for the next round of deliveries.[31]

In the sale of merchandise, the degree to which Chinese businesses had to rely on transnational ethnic networks varied, depending on the type and size of the business. While the larger Chinese mercantile companies engaged in wholesale marketing to Chinese business owners from other cities in the Midwest in addition to retailing to local residents, the small grocers and traveling stores had to rely primarily if not exclusively on retail sales to kinsmen and friends, who felt obligated to patronize these businesses. The transnational migration networks were important to the survival and success of the business in both cases but indispensable in the latter case.

In addition to grocery stores, other specialized stores such as cigar stores and laundry supply stores opened. Wah Kee at South Clark Street, opened in 1890, sold mainly cigars, tobacco, and opium. The company also owned a cigar factory next to the store. In 1904 Moy Doon Yuen and Moy Wah Foon were partners in the company, with $4,000 invested capital, of which $2,000 was in stock, including cigars and other goods.[32] The Joe Pang Laundry Supply Company at 2209 Wentworth Avenue started in 1920. Its owner, Chin Kai Kim, came to Chicago in 1907 and with his own savings and $1,000 borrowed from a kinsman, Chin Sing, was able to start the business.[33]

Apart from their regular business operations, the Chinese grocery stores and other food service businesses also provided temporary or long-term lodging for Chinese laborers, thus serving as boarding facilities or hotels. For instance, Louie Yap, a hired laundryman, lived in the store of Sam Lung and Company at 299 South Clark Street in 1906.[34] Gong Dock Death, a restaurant worker, lived in the Hong Kong Noodle Factory at 152 West 22nd Street in the 1910s and 1920s.[35] Hip Lung, run by the Moy brothers, also served as a hotel.[36]

The Chinese grocery stores constituted a significant part of the Chinatown businesses and provided six hundred people, a quarter of the Chinese population in Chicago in the 1920s, with livelihoods, largely through kinship connections. The multiple functions of the Chinese grocery stores, as wholesalers and retailers, banks, and hotels, diversified and increased the profit margins of the businesses while providing needed services within the transnational migrant community. Moreover, the grocery stores' economic significance went far beyond Chinatown in Chicago, as they supplied merchandise to numerous smaller stores in cities and towns across the Midwest. A local Chinese marveled at the sales volume of the Chinese grocery stores in Chicago, packed tightly along 22nd and South Clark Streets in the 1920s: Although they looked small, "this is not a basis to estimate the volume of their business. Indeed they do much more business in these stores than can be estimated by an outsider."[37]

PIONEERS OF CHINESE FINE DINING

Chinese restaurants were the most important businesses in Chinatown. In 1926, there were about 250 Chinese restaurants, located at "every convenient point along the principal thoroughfares."[38] By 1930, there were at least eleven Chinese restaurants located in South Chinatown. On Wentworth Avenue could be found Mee Hung at 2125, Guey Sam at 2205, Tin Dong at 2206, Eastern Star at 2225, Won Kow at 2235, and Wah Ying Lo at 2254. On West 22nd Street were the San Lee Yuan Company at 158, Pagoda Inn at 202, Little Pomroi at 208, and Great China at 225. In addition, Foo Chow was located at 411 South Clark Street, in Old Chinatown.[39]

In this hub of land, water, and rail transportation, where foreign dignitaries, international celebrities, and wealthy businessmen often made visits or stopped in transit, the Chinese restaurants in Chicago contributed to the national rise of upscale Chinese fine dining, which also flourished in San

Francisco and New York in the 1920s.[40] The upscale Chinese restaurants in Chicago were furnished with abundant capital, lavish interior decor, expensive furniture, large seating capacity, and both Chinese and non-Chinese clients. Their owners were men with vision, a taste for elegance, and a sense of modernity.

Chin F. Foin was arguably the first and best example of a modern Chinese restaurateur in Chicago. Born in Xinning (renamed Taishan in 1914) County, Guangdong, in 1877, Chin came to America in 1892 as a fifteen-year-old teenager, arriving in Chicago in 1895. Young and adaptable, he picked up the English language and American ways of life quickly. He is believed to have spoken German fluently, and he lived a life rivaling that of wealthy and

Chin F. Foin and his wife, 1906. National Archives, Great Lakes Region, Chicago, Illinois.

trendy American businessmen. He rode horseback, owned an automobile when they first became available to consumers, joined an exclusive social club, and had connections with both Chinese diplomats and influential Chicagoans. When Kang Youwei, the eminent Chinese reformer and loyalist, visited Chicago, Chin F. Foin was there to escort him.[41] By 1905, in addition to the Wing Chong Hai grocery store, he also owned the King Yen Lo restaurant at 277–279 South Clark Street, one of the finest Chinese American restaurants in Chicago at the turn of the century. Located in Old Chinatown at the corner of Clark and Van Buren Streets, the restaurant was appointed with sumptuous furniture made in China. The wooden tables were decorated with mother-of-pearl and topped with marble, a popular style at the time. King Yen Lo was patronized by visiting Chinese officials and other prominent Chinese, as well as by upper-class Chicago socialites.[42] As in the case of Wing Chong Hai, his grocery business, Chin F. Foin had a number of partners who also invested in the restaurant, including kinsmen Ham Sam, who invested $1,300, and Hum Sing, who invested $1,200.[43]

Somewhat later, Chin F. Foin invested in King Joy Lo Mandarin Restaurant, probably the most extravagant Chinese American restaurant in Chicago established at the turn of the nineteenth and twentieth centuries. Also located in the Loop area, at 277–279 South Clark Street and the corner of Van Buren Street, it offered all the amenities fashionable in the finest Western restaurants of the time.[44] It featured a live orchestra and a dance floor and provided American customers with Western-style silverware. Its menu guaranteed the diners satisfaction and the restaurant provided special assistance to customers who were unfamiliar with Chinese cuisine: "If you experience difficulty in making selection, the floor walker will cheerfully aid you."[45] A 1930s photograph shows the restaurant lavishly and tastefully decorated with Chinese artwork. The downstairs dining room was spacious and up-to-date, with an elegant and clean appearance. The wide staircase was divided by sumptuous columns. Carved banisters displayed Chinese workmanship, and the walls and ceiling were adorned with carving and paintings with Chinese themes. It is said that the splendid design is unmatched even by Chinese restaurants of the present day.[46]

Another upscale restaurant, Guey Sam, opened in 1901 in the South Clark Street area. It then moved to South Chinatown along with most of the other Chinese businesses in 1912 and was located at 2205 Wentworth Avenue, on the second floor at the corner of Wentworth Avenue and Cermak Road.[47] A postcard of the interior of the restaurant in the 1920s shows its modern-style decor, with Western-style round tables covered by starched tablecloths and napkins. The spacious restaurant was air conditioned and could hold more than a hundred guests at one time. Its distinctive appearance made it one of the major landmarks of the Chicago Chinatown. A photograph of a parade held on October 10, 1928, commemorating the 1911 revolution, shows the grandeur of the exterior of Guey Sam.[48] The restaurant changed hands in 1950 though it kept the same name; its new owner used custom-made chinaware by Shenan Company in New Castle, Pennsylvania, proudly displaying the restaurant's logo.[49] Hoe Sai Gai, at 85 West Randolph Street in the Loop, was decorated in the fashionable Art Deco style of the 1930s, which distinguished it from other Chinese restaurants.[50] The Pagoda Inn at 202 West 22nd Street, on the other hand, was furnished with Chinese decor and a Chinese shrine. It was more popular with and patronized by community organizations; for instance, the progressive Young China Club celebrated its third anniversary at the restaurant in 1936.[51]

Like Chin F. Foin, the Moy brothers invested in and operated Chinese restaurants. Moy Dong Hoy was the primary shareholder and manager of two restaurants, Wee Ying Lo and Song Ying Lo. Opened in 1903 and located at 174 South Clark Street, Wee Ying Lo had $30,000 in capital investment.[52] With their success in Wee Ying Lo, Moy Dong Hoy and his partners opened a branch restaurant in 1903, Song Ying Lo, with $40,000 capital. The two restaurants jointly had twenty-five partners with a total capital of $70,000. The cooks of the restaurants were paid $55 to $60 a month.[53] Although no evidence as to the appearance of the two restaurants exists, the capital investment readily suggests that their decor and furnishings were comparable to rival restaurants, such as King Yen Lo and King Joy Lo run by Chin F. Foin.

Tom Lok was another visionary Chinese restaurateur. Born in Canton, China, in 1868, Tom Lok came to the United States in 1881, landing in San Francisco as a thirteen-year-old. Ten years later he went to New York to learn the restaurant business and then came to Chicago at the turn of the century. He had been interested in a property at 349 South Clark Street, where an Italian restaurant owned by Tom Cincho was in operation. After Cincho's death in 1916, Tom Lok bought the business from his wife and heirs for $15,000 and converted it into a large Chinese chop suey restaurant with a seating capacity of two hundred. Unlike other large Chinese restaurant owners who accumulated capital from kinsmen and fellow villagers, Tom Lok was the sole proprietor of the restaurant. In 1923, the volume of the business was $100,000, of which $3,000 was Tom Lok's net profit. He employed thirteen people: seven cooks in the kitchen and six waiters in the dining room. In addition, two white men were closely associated with the restaurant: Charles F. Hille, an attorney at 109 North Dearborn Street, came to the restaurant once a month; and H. L. Henson, a salesman of wholesale groceries and rice at 251 East Grant Avenue, visited the restaurant once a week to take orders and collect debts. In 1924, eight years after he bought the business, Tom Lok estimated that its worth had more than doubled, to $40,000.[54]

The Chinese restaurants in Chicago at the turn of the century were not only extravagant but also sizeable in seating capacity, indicating the growing demand for Chinese food services in the area. The Golden Pheasant Inn at 72 West Madison Street, opened in 1916, was reportedly the largest Chinese restaurant in Chicago in the 1920s. It had a capitalization of $75,000 from thirty shareholders, each receiving 10 percent dividends, twice as much as the dividends paid by smaller Chinese restaurants. With 175 tables and 75 employees, it would be among the largest restaurants even today. The high volume of diners and large number of employees necessitated that the restaurant have effective management and well-defined responsibilities for employees. Eng Gow, president of the company and general manager, oversaw the operation and dealt with the procurement of supplies from H. L. Henson, the wholesale grocery owner discussed in the previous paragraph. Ng Gar Chung, one of the shareholders, with an investment of $1,250, was first hired in 1917 as a checker, virtually a kitchen manager, whose primary responsibility was to make sure the food on the trays matched the items on the order before the trays were carried out by waiters, in order to avoid mistakes. A year and half later, Ng Gar Chung was promoted to the position of dining room manager, at a monthly salary of $75, possibly because of his fine performance as a checker—which suggests the importance of management in the restaurant's operation and success.[55]

While the Chinese restaurants in Chinatown offered more authentic Chinese food and catered largely to a Chinese clientele, those outside the boundaries of Chinatown apparently served a larger proportion of non-Chinese customers, with a mixed menu of Western dishes, such as sirloin steak and soups, and Americanized Chinese dishes such as chop suey (fried rice with meat and vegetables) and chow mein (fried noodles with meat

and vegetables). A restaurant guide dated around the 1930s lists the restaurants in Chicago in alphabetical order, providing a good idea of the culinary diversity of the cosmopolitan city at the time. The Bamboo Inn at
11 North Clark Street, with a specialty in Cantonese food, for instance,
served "AA" club sirloin steak ($3.00) and fried chicken and bacon ($1.50),
along with beef chop suey or chow mein ($1.60) and chicken chow mein
($2.00). Hoe Sai Gai at 75–85 Randolph Street listed egg rolls ($0.85),
broiled filet mignon ($2.85), Hon Su Gai (chicken fritters and Chinese veg-
etables) ($1.85), and fried half chicken club style ($1.45). Nankin Restaurant
at 230 North Dearborn Street, featuring Cantonese foods, served beef rice
($1.35), chicken subgum chow mein Nankin special ($1.65), and fried ten-
der half chicken "disjoined" ($1.65).[56]

The Chinese restaurants outside Chinatown's boundaries were not necessarily small in size. Canton Café at 9146 Commercial Avenue on the South
Side of Chicago, for instance, had a seating capacity of one hundred people.
Kong Ming and Charlie Get were the joint partners of the restaurant, with
capital of $10,000. Eight employees worked in the restaurant, including
Kong Ming, who served as manager. In 1923, the restaurant did $40,000 to
$50,000 worth of business.[57] Joe Hing Lo at 2020 West Madison Street was
another Chinese restaurant outside of Chinatown. Wong Lung was the sole
owner of the restaurant from 1913 until 1920, when he sold half of the restaurant's interest, $1,000, to Joe Leong. It had nineteen tables and six employ-
ees, including Wong Lung serving as manager and bookkeeper, Joe Leong as
assistant manager, two waiters, and two cooks. Wong Lung paid himself $80
a month plus a 5 percent dividend and the cooks $70 to $80 a month. The
restaurant did $30,000 in business in 1920.[58]

These examples illustrate the rapid growth and economic significance of
Chinese restaurants in Chicago during the last decades of the nineteenth
and first decades of the twentieth century. The annual business volume of
$30,000 for small restaurants and $100,000 or more for large restaurants
would total about $11 million for the 250 Chinese restaurants in town.[59]
With such financial capacity, it is no wonder that the prominent restaurateurs in Chicago could make their establishments the finest and most extravagant of the time.

The Chinese entrepreneurs in Chicago were deft and savvy in promoting
their enterprises through lavish investment. The most illustrative example
is the Chinese participation in the two world's fairs in Chicago in 1893 and

1933–34. The 1893 World's Columbian Exposition was one of America's earliest exposures to Chinese culture and Chinese Americans in a positive light. As the Chinese Qing government boycotted the fair in protest against the Chinese exclusion laws, Chinese participation was sponsored by the Wah Mee Corporation, a private company formed solely for the purpose of participating in the fair. The three managers and main investors of the company were all prominent Chinese businessmen in America. Its president, Dr. Gee Woo Chan, was originally a Chinese government official, who arrived in 1884 to observe the World's Industrial and Cotton Centennial Exposition in New Orleans. Chan overstayed his visa after his official commission had expired and remained in the United States. He first practiced Chinese herbal medicine in San Francisco, then invested his money in real estate and a "higher standard of business enterprises." The second investor, Hong Sling, was a young but wealthy newcomer to town. While living in Omaha, Nebraska, he invested heavily in real estate, particularly in railroads, as a contractor on the West Coast. He moved to Chicago before the 1893 World's Fair, anticipating that it would be a good business opportunity. As a wealthy owner of Sam Lung and Company, he almost certainly played a major role in the Chicago Chinese community up to the 1930s. Although his English was not as proficient as Dr. Chan's, he was well connected and had close associations with several American civic leaders in Chicago. An experienced restaurateur, he was also reportedly responsible for introducing chop suey to the Midwest.[60] The third investor and treasurer of the company was Wong Kee, owner of a grocery store on South Clark Street. Although he was believed to be the richest Chinese in Chicago, Wong Kee was circumspect regarding his fortune.[61] The Wah Mee Corporation created a "Chinese Village" consisting of a Chinese theatre, a joss house, a teahouse, and a shopping bazaar.

The participation of Chinese businessmen in 1893 was motivated partially by patriotic and nationalistic pride and partially by practical business instinct. The exposition proved to be an effective venue for arousing Americans' curiosity; for educating the American public about Chinese architecture, culinary culture, customs, philosophy, religion, and theatrical art; and for promoting the Chinese restaurant business throughout the country, particularly in the Midwest. Historian Mae M. Ngai has made a similar assessment of the commercial effort of the Chinese entrepreneurs involved in the 1893 World's Fair: "The Chinese village was an early prototype for Chinese

American efforts to develop urban Chinatowns as tourist destinations, a trend that began in San Francisco in the 1910s."[62]

The Chinese café in the Chinese Village was believed to be one of the first Chinese restaurants in the Midwest to cater to non-Chinese diners. The owners imported two thousand pairs of ivory chopsticks from China but thoughtfully provided knives and forks as well. Low Luck, "the best cook of Hong Kong," was hired as the head chef of the Chinese restaurant at the fair, but his culinary talent was mainly displayed at the banquets for VIP visitors. At one such banquet, "a feast was spread which demonstrated much perfection in the art of cookery. . . . All sorts of Chinese delicacies were served with American soups and meats, as well as some strong rice wines and brandies and whiskies."[63] The menu seems to have been a well-conceived combination of Chinese food and Western soups and steaks, revealing the Chicago Chinese businessmen's conscious efforts to introduce Chinese cuisine to non-Chinese diners at one of the largest venues available.

The Chinese entrepreneurs' enormous efforts were also noted by the American public. In his *Art and Architecture* (1893), William Walton marveled at the endeavor of the Chinese American entrepreneurs:

> Much was hoped by the Exposition authorities in the way of a worthy exhibit from China, but unfortunate international legislation intervened to prevent that government from taking any official part in the Fair. The Chinese village in the Midway Plaisance is the enterprise of a syndicate of [Chicago-based] Celestial merchants, and the buildings were designed by a Chicago architect. They include a theatre, restaurant, Joss house from which the Joss has departed, and bazaar; some of the tea offered for sale is priced at a hundred dollars per pound, only a few leaves being required to make a pot of the beverage. In the pavilion in the Manufactures Building are exhibited the well-known industrial and artistic productions of the empire, porcelains, ivory carvings, embroideries, textile fabrics, etc.; and in the Transportation Building a number of models of Chinese boats and other modes of conveyance.[64]

In contrast to the Columbian Exposition of 1893, Chinese participation in the 1933–34 World's Fair: A Century of Progress was a concerted and joint effort on the parts of the Chinese government; private Chinese and Chinese American merchants; a Swedish explorer, Dr. Sven Hedin, who provided the replica of the Lama Temple of Jehol (Rehe), also known as the Golden Pavilion; and the Japanese government, promoting its newly acquired Manzhouguo (the Japanese puppet state created after the Japanese invasion of Manchuria in 1931), which was frowned upon by the Chinese in Chicago. The display featured a jade pavilion, Foochow lacquer ware, and in 1934, a "street of Shanghai."

Although not as lavish as that in 1893, the display definitely showed off the local Chinese business community effort. Since the site of the fair was only about a mile from Chinatown, many local merchants financed the concessions there and many Chinatown residents worked at the fair. The "street of Shanghai" in 1934 was financed entirely by the Chinese merchants in Chicago. The highlight of Chinese participation was a parade held on October 1, 1933. Organized by the Chinese Consolidated Benevolent Association (CCBA), commonly known as Zhonghua Huiguan, all of Chinatown participated. The parade consisted of floats, bands, Boy Scouts, and beautiful girls in Chinese costumes. It started from Michigan Avenue, then wound through the fair along the Avenue of the Flags past the Golden Lama Temple and the Chinese Village.[65]

The promotion of Chinese businesses through cultural exoticism may have reinforced the American public's stereotypical notions of the Chinese and Chinese culture, but nonetheless, its effectiveness in attracting non-Chinese patrons is undeniable. The Chinese participation in the two world's fairs demonstrates the vision and acumen of the Chinese business community in Chicago. Its successful participation was possible because the Chinese business community in Chicago consciously employed its transnational human and financial resources.

PAUL SIU'S LAUNDRYMAN AND BEYOND

Like grocery and restaurant businesses, laundering was a niche occupation for Chicago's Chinese. It was meticulously documented by Paul C. P. Siu, in "The Chinese Laundryman: A Study of Social Isolation," a dissertation that took Siu twenty-five years to complete and was finally published in 1987, a year after his death. This empirical study provides invaluable, detailed sources and exhaustively investigates every aspect of the life of a Chinese laundryman; after its publication, it might seem that there is nothing more to be done on the topic. My research on the records of the US Immigration and Naturalization Service (INS), the papers of Ernest W. Burgess that contain some of Siu's essays for classes and his interview notes, and other primary sources, however, indicates otherwise.

While Siu's study of the Chinese laundrymen in Chicago has been recognized as a landmark work, it did not make use of the abundant sources
provided by INS records. The INS records of Chicago Chinese case files
(CCCF) from 1898 to 1940 comprise over six thousand files.[66] Early files often
document alleged violations of laws resulting in the denial of admission to
the country to Chinese laborers. Later files, especially after 1920, refer mainly
to applications for return certificates or for student status. These case files
provide further information to augment Siu's study, especially on capital investment, business volume, and wages and profits. As government records of
affidavits, entry and departing documents such as ship tickets, birth certificates, resident certificates, and testimonies of cross interrogations of Chinese
immigrants or residents and their witnesses, the CCCF documents have
been used extensively by historians and other scholars in recent decades.

The following cases from the INS records provide an official profile of
a laundryman's life in Chicago at the turn of the century. Many laundrymen started businesses with loans from friends or kinsmen, or took over
a laundry business from a friend or kinsman as a debt to be repaid from
profits. Generally, a one-man laundry was worth $550 and could conduct
a monthly business of $200; a two-man laundry would double the value
of the laundry and its business. For instance, Moy Lun borrowed $550 in
1907 from his cousin Moy Gee Nie to invest in a laundry on Cottage Grove
Avenue.[67] Chin Wing and Chin Teng jointly owned a laundry at 3223 Cottage Grove Avenue in 1906. The laundry was worth $1,100 and its weekly
business was about $110; they paid a monthly rent of $32.50 for the laundry.
In 1907, Chin Wing turned over his half of the laundry, $550 in value, to his
friend Chin Show without getting payment; instead, Chin Show owed the
$550 to Chin Wing.[68]

The cases of Mark Do Wea and Chan Wing provide good examples of the
operation of Chinese laundries. Mark Do Wea was born in China in 1860
and operated a laundry at 5631 Wentworth Avenue in the 1900s. His laundry,
worth $500, was equipped with tubs, irons, and a gas ironing machine for
ironing collars, cuffs, and shirts. The weekly business volume was about $50
on average.[69] Similarly, Chan Wing started his laundry on 63rd Street in
1900 with $500 capital. Three years later Charlie Chin joined the laundry,
taking charge of the bookkeeping; when the laundry closed for the night,
Charlie Chin took the money made during the day and looked after it. He
reported the accounts to Chan Wing on a weekly or biweekly basis. In 1905

when planning a visit to China, Chan Wing sold the business to Chin Leung Dum and got $1,380 for it.[70] Within five years, Chan Wing had more than doubled his initial investment of $500 from the laundry business.

While the owners of one- or two-man laundries worked in their laundries as laborers, the larger laundry owners did not work in the laundry, instead hiring workers to do the actual laundering. For instance, Goon Pon Sing bought a laundry at 105 Lake Street, Oak Park, a suburb of Chicago, from Moy Chong in 1904 for $1,400. Goon Pon Sing only came to the laundry every Saturday to pay wages to each of the four laundrymen working for him: Goon Toon, $17; Yik Loon, $13; Fook Seu, $14; and Goon Dai, $14. He also had a bookkeeper, Goon Toon Pak, to keep accounts and to pay all other expenses. He took in about $120 to $140 worth of business each week, from which he drew $30 in profit. He also owned a horse-drawn wagon and paid $3 to $4 a week for the stable where he kept the horse.[71]

Interracial coexistence was also evident in the operation of Chinese laundries. Some Chinese laundry operators hired non-Chinese employees, as illustrated by David Lee's father's laundry. David Lee's father came to San Francisco in 1918 and then to Chicago in 1924, where he operated a Chinese hand laundry to support his large family. He hired a black woman, a white woman, and a Mexican woman to help him with the washing and ironing.[72]

The earning from a laundry was meager, about $50 a month, or 20 percent of the normal business volume in the 1900s. For instance, Kong Choon owned half of a laundry at 4626 Cottage Grove Avenue in the 1900s. His share was $620 and he made $50 to $80 a month.[73] With a frugal lifestyle, however, many laundrymen could save about $1,000 after five years of toiling in the business. For example, Louis Fook came to the United States in 1879. By 1906 he had saved $1,000 from his laundry at 299 South Clark Street, which he had owned for five years.[74] Lum Joy, born in China in 1864, came to the United States in 1881. In 1904 he was a laundryman in Chicago making $55 a month on average. He was able to save more than $1,000 and loaned money from his savings to two of his cousins.[75] Moy Len also saved $1,000 from his laundry at 2036 West North Avenue and deposited it at the Great Lakes Trust Company, arguably the only mainstream Chicago bank that served Chinese immigrants at the time.[76] The more enterprising laundrymen would invest their savings in Chinese restaurants for profit. In 1903, for instance, Hum Sing, a laundryman, invested his $1,200 savings in the King Yen Lo restaurant and received dividends.[77]

Not all laundrymen, however, could realize savings from their meager earnings. Moy Dun owned half of a laundry at 307 East 43rd Street in 1907. From the business, he could only make enough for his living. When his family in China were about to build a house and needed money from him, he had to borrow $500 from a friend to send to his family.[78]

The Chinese laundry business was not only a significant means of support for the Chinese; ownership of a laundry also enabled a Chinese laborer to qualify for a return certificate before departing for China, as the immigration regulations required possession of a minimum of $1,000 worth of property or debts owed to him in order to grant a return certificate.[79] For instance, Goon Pon Sing claimed the ownership of his laundry at 105 Lake Street, Oak Park, worth $1,400, as entitling him to a laborer's return certificate when he was planning a visit to China in 1907.[80] Numerous cases from the INS records indicate that Chinese laundrymen would turn over their businesses to kinsmen or friends, thereby becoming creditors with the right to a return certificate. For instance, Chin Wing applied for a laborer's return certificate in 1907, based on the claim that he was owed more than $1,000, of which $550 had been loaned to Chin Show in the form of the half share of the laundry that Chin Show took over from him, and $500 had been loaned to Chin Mon Pon, who put the sum into a separate laundry.[81]

The Chinese hand laundry was also of vital importance in enabling the Chinese to move around in search of better economic opportunities. The portability of the occupation facilitated the translocal migration of Chinese between Chicago and other cities. St. Louis, the second largest city in midwestern America, was a particularly favored destination for the remigration of many Chinese laundrymen in Chicago; the following stories illustrate that the reverse was also sometimes the case.

The Sam Wah Laundry in St. Louis was almost a replica of the Chinese laundry in Chicago described by Paul C. P. Siu. In 1887, a Chinese man named Sam Wah opened a laundry at 329 Market Street. He seems to have done well in the business, for after 1912 he opened two more laundries, one at 1408 North Jefferson Avenue and the other at 4298B Finney Avenue, and after 1915 he was running four or five laundries simultaneously, including the one at 4381 Laclede Avenue that survived until 1986. In 1922, the aging Sam Wah brought his two nephews, Gee Kee One (also known as Gee Sam Wah) and Gee Hong, from Canton, China, to join him. Gee Kee One and Gee Hong initially arrived in San Francisco, where they learned the laundry business, and then the brothers moved to Chicago to open a laundry. Unaccustomed to the cold weather in Chicago, they moved to St. Louis to join their uncle.[82] At first they worked for their uncle in the laundry at 4381 Laclede Avenue, which they later inherited after Sam Wah passed away. The Gee brothers operated the laundry under the same name using more or less the same techniques until it finally closed in 1986 when both proprietors passed away.[83] A poignant story published in the *St. Louis Post-Dispatch* on November 12, 1978, provides a vivid picture of the laundry:

> The Sam Wah Laundry is on Laclede Avenue, a few hundred feet east of Newstead and a turn north through a door into St. Louis, a half century ago.
>
> Inside—after passing under a rubber tree plant that grows westward along a system of ceiling hooks and jerry-built supports, a plant that soars out of its pot near the wall and achieves the form of a dragon—is the shop of the brothers Gee Sam Wah and Gee Hong, long out of Canton, China. Wah is 88 years old, Gee is 86. With its worn wooden washtubs, its drum dryer powered by a noisy and archaic direct current motor, its naked light bulbs and sagging wooden floors, the Sam Wah Laundry seems ready to stand for a spot in the Smithsonian Institution, or at least the Museum of Westward Expansion, this paint-peeling and dusty memorial to a part of the Chinese role in American history.
>
> . . . The Gee brothers live and work in Spartan quarters. They apparently sleep on mats near an old stove. The walls of the laundry are adorned in places by an odd mixture of pictures and photographs—religious art, mostly Jesus Christ at various ages, a newspaper photo of Chairman Mao and former President Gerald R. Ford shaking hands, 1962 calendars from the Canton Market and the Wing Sing Chong Co., Inc., both of San Francisco, and a glossy photo of a standing room hockey crowd at the Checkerdome. There are numerous snapshots of weddings and assembled families.
>
> Gee Sam Wah still uses an antique hand atomizer when he irons shirts. He has had the atomizer since his days in Canton, which probably means at least 80 years or more. Despite the appearance of disorganization, regular customers do not need a ticket, said Wah. The launderers have a system of numbering the bundles and remembering the faces. They do not forget regular customers, and no one, apparently, has had reason to complain. Not-so-regular customers get a ticket. Everything is lettered in Chinese.
>
> Gee Hong and Gee Wah, by western standards, are certifiable workaholics. Even in their 80s, the two are up ironing and washing early in the morning and are at it still late at night, say longtime customers.

They had a television set, presumably for relaxation, but it has been broken and unused for some time. There is also a sickly-looking radio on the premises.[84]

Like the Gee brothers, Lum Hey also came to St. Louis to help a Chinese "uncle" in his laundry in the 1920s. Lum Hey came to America from China at the age of twenty to join his father, who was running a "Western-style" grocery store in Mississippi. He landed in Seattle, Washington, where he waited for a month while undergoing lengthy interrogations by immigration officers, who cross-checked his answers against those from his father in Mississippi. When released at last, Lum Hey took a train to Chicago and then to Mississippi to help in his father's grocery business. Three years later, Lum Hey and his wife, whom he had brought over from China under the status of a dependent of a merchant, relocated to St. Louis to help a Chinese "uncle" in his laundry. They stayed there for a few months, living in a small room and earning minimal wages. Eventually deciding to go into the laundry business themselves, they bought a downtown laundry for $1,000 from an "old Chinese man."[85]

Lam Lap Goey was a laundryman in St. Louis for some years. In 1901, he moved to Chicago to look for new business while working in a laundry to support himself. Planning to start a laundry, he borrowed $650 from Lam Chee Dai, a laundryman and friend he had known since he arrived in Chicago.[86]

EARNINGS FOR TRANSNATIONAL FAMILIES

The INS records provide us with firsthand information on various aspects of the operation of Chinese businesses in Chicago. Tin-Chiu Fan's (1926) empirical investigation amplifies that information with data on trade distribution and earnings of Chinese laborers. Fan surveyed 161 Chinese male adult students from area schools, 245 Chinese YMCA members, 1,215 Mon Sang Association (a labor union for Chinese waiters in Chicago; see Chapter 5 for more discussion) members, and 3,001 members of the Chinese Association, using the membership cards of the Chinese YMCA, records of the Chinese Association, the weekly publications of the Chinese YMCA, and the monthly publications of the Mon Sang Association, as well as the *Chinese Daily News.* While the survey of the members of the Chinese YMCA shows a slightly smaller percentage (84 percent) engaged in trade (merchants, dealers, and store helpers) and service (laundrymen, restaurant keepers, cooks, and waiters), the surveys of the Chinese students, Mon Song Association members, and Chinese Association members all indicate that more than 90 percent of them were engaged in trade or service.[87] The wage distribution data for Chinese laborers gives monthly earnings of $160 for cooks, $117 for laundrymen, $100 for waiters, and $50 for store helpers in 1926,[88] which is consistent with the data from the INS records.

The Chinese laborers were able not only to sustain themselves on these meager wages but also to keep part of their income as savings. Some of the savings were deposited in banks, lent to kinsmen, or hidden in a trunk in the residence, but a substantial share was sent home to China.[89] In their testimonies, numerous Chinese immigrants stated that they sent money to their families in China. The amount of these remittances to China is difficult to calculate, as they were made in a variety of forms: postal money orders, checks, and drafts. According to Madeline Y. Hsu (2000), from 1903 to 1937 the estimated annual remittances from overseas Taishanese to China increased from 110 million to 517 million Chinese dollars. In the 1920s and early 1930s, remittances from the United States to Taishan constituted one-tenth of all money sent to China from abroad.[90]

These remittances enabled families back in China to purchase land, build houses, make charitable donations, and enjoy a lifestyle less in accord with the Chinese tradition of thrift and frugality. The construction of *diaolou*, or fortresslike buildings, and *yanglou*, or Western-style buildings, was widespread in the villages of Taishan in the 1920s and 1930s when the region was plagued by social instability and turmoil due to local bandits and natural disasters. The frequent bandit attacks and summertime floods caused the overseas Chinese great concern for the safety of their families left behind in the homeland. To ease their worry, they sent money home to construct fortresslike buildings as protection for family members from these menaces. To effectively defend the residents from bandits and floods, such a building was normally six to seven stories tall, often with *meurtrières* on top. Having lived abroad for an extensive period of time, the Chinese immigrants were influenced in varying degrees by Western architecture. They would often design the buildings themselves while living abroad, combining Western architectural styles with Chinese ones, and then send the blueprints back home along with their remittances.[91]

Meijia dayuan (the Moy family compound) was typical of the Western buildings in Tingjiangxu, Taishan. The remittances from the Moys in Chicago and other places abroad in the 1920s and 1930s paid for these buildings.[92] Constructed in 1932, the compound comprised more than one hundred Western-style buildings erected over an 80 *mu* (13 acre) area. The buildings were two or three stories tall, uniform in height, and neatly arranged around a huge rectangular courtyard that served as a local market.[93]

Wengjialou (the Weng family's buildings) in the village of Miaobian, Duanfen Township, Taishan, offers another example. Five family buildings were constructed between 1927 and 1931 by Weng Songping's grandfather, who made his fortune in Hong Kong as an owner of *jinshanzhuang*. Three of the five buildings were named after the heroes in the classical Chinese novel *Romance of the Three Kingdoms*. The architectural design was artistic but practical, combining Eastern and Western styles—traditional Chinese tiled roofs atop Western-style buildings. Unlike the traditional buildings in Guangdong, which featured a broad covered porch in front of the house, *Wengjialou* bears more of a resemblance to buildings in European countries and American cities. The kitchen and storage rooms are in the basement, while the living room and bedrooms are on the first, second and third floors.

Meijia dayuan, or the Moy family compound, in Duanfen County, Taishan, Guangdong, China, 2007. Collection of Huping Ling.

The tall, narrow buildings were easier to protect from flooding or from plundering bandits. These brick/concrete buildings have endured almost eighty years of weathering and are still in good shape.[94] In 2002, they were registered and listed as an official historical site by the Taishan city government.

Meijia dayuan and *Wengjialou* have been featured in a number of television programs and magazine articles in China.[95] They exemplify and concretize the transnational ties between the Chinese overseas and the homeland and demonstrate the profound social and economic consequences of transnational migration. The tall, modern, brick-and-concrete buildings provided protection from natural disasters and depredations due to social instability for members of the extended family back in China. The buildings' modern design and amenities also improved their living conditions, while introducing Western customs and cultural habits to China, such as Western types of toilets, bathrooms, and kitchens, together with a more hygienic way of life.

Remittances from overseas Chinese were also responsible for establishing the numerous elementary and secondary public schools in Taishan beginning in the early twentieth century. By the end of the Qing dynasty, Western influence had penetrated most parts of China, and the zeitgeist was dominated by ideas and experiments that emphasized Western learning, resulting in the establishment of Western schools throughout the country. Taishan, as the premier native place in Guangdong for overseas Chinese, experienced a surge of new elementary and secondary schools funded by donations from overseas Chinese. Between 1907, when the first Western elementary school was founded, and 1919, eighteen local schools were established. The rate accelerated in the 1920s, when forty-two schools were built, probably as a result of the economic prosperity in the United States, which benefited the overseas Chinese. Eighteen new schools were added during the 1930s and seventeen in the 1940s.[96]

Not only did the remittances benefit those who were back home in China but they also provided psychological and emotional satisfaction to those who were overseas. Many of the large, grandiose fortress- and Western-style buildings were the equals of multimillion-dollar mansions of the present day. They conspicuously displayed the wealth possessed by such successful Chinese immigrants. That they were willing to invest substantial amounts of money in real estate back in China suggests the importance of homeland in their minds. For many Chinese immigrants, the ultimate goal and highest

form of success was to return home rich or to be recognized, honored, and/
or envied by fellow villagers for their monetary contributions to the native
place. Such a mentality was instilled and deeply rooted in the minds of most
Chinese immigrants and provided strong motivation for their maintenance
of continuing social, economic, and emotional ties with the homeland.

HONG SLING AS A QUINTESSENTIAL TRANSNATIONAL BUSINESSMAN

The life story of Hong Sling offers a compelling narrative of how a transnational Chinese businessman in Chicago navigated between the shores of
the Pacific Ocean and operated transnational businesses successfully. Born
in China in 1855, Hong Sling came to the United States in 1875 at the age of
twenty, landing in San Francisco. He first worked in Wyoming as a manual
laborer for two or three years, then moved to Utah as a labor contractor and
railroad agent. From these jobs he accumulated enough savings to invest
in businesses in Hong Kong, the United States, Cuba, and Panama, thus
initiating his career as a transnational businessman.[97]

His prosperous business and family life unfolded in Chicago. In 1892
Hong Sling moved to Chicago, attracted by the city's position as a transportation hub and as the site of the coming World's Columbian Exposition. That year, two groups of Chinese merchants competed for the private
Chinese concession at the exposition. Both planned to build a Chinese theatre, to which various shops and other attractions would be added. To the
surprise of many, the newcomer in town, Hong Sling, teamed up with Gee
Wo Chan and Wong Kee to form the Wah Mee Company, won the concession over rival bidders Moy Dong Chow and Moy Dong Hoy, the two
elder Moy brothers and the dominant figures of late nineteenth- and early
twentieth-century Chicago Chinatown.[98]

Hong Sling's bidding success was due in part to his ampler funds. The
three investors in Wah Mee put up $90,000 for the Chinese Village ($1.7 million in 2003 dollars).[99] Moreover, the Moy brothers seem to have had worse
luck with the immigration authorities. With ambitious plans, the Moys
formed the Wah Yung Company in November 1892, intending to build a
second theatre outside the fairgrounds on Cottage Grove Avenue, four blocks
south of the Midway Plaisance. The theatre was to be designed by architect
Francis J. Norton and feature actors from Hong Kong. Unfortunately, the
INS declared the certificates of the 273 putative actors to be forged and denied

them entry at Tacoma, Washington. Although the Moys managed to smuggle 32 of the actors from Tacoma to Chicago, they were unable to appear onstage at the Wah Yung Company's theatre because it was not finished on time.

The victorious Wah Mee Company also sent representatives to import actors from China. In early 1893, 483 putative actors landed in San Francisco and then boarded a Santa Fe Railroad train for fares totaling $32,200. Hong Sling, manager of the Wah Mee Company, was furious at his handlers for bringing so many of them at such an exorbitant cost. He selected only 200 and sent the rest back to San Francisco.[100]

The Chinese Village in the Midway Plaisance—a huge success—was the enterprise of a syndicate funded, sponsored, and operated by Chicago Chinese merchants. Hong Sling's investment and leadership in the enterprise elevated him to a position as one of the most prominent businessmen in the Chicago Chinese community.[101]

Having established himself as a powerful and wealthy merchant in Chicago, Hong Sling began establishing a family. At the end of 1897, he went to China and married Toy Shee, a woman fourteen years his junior who had been born in San Francisco but returned to China at a young age, according to Chinese custom. The newly-weds boarded the steamer *Gaelic* in the spring of 1898, sailing to the United States. They landed in San Francisco and then took the train to Chicago. On October 28, 1898, their eldest son, Harry Hong Sling, was born in the Hong residence, a flat on the third floor at 324 South Clark Street.

The year 1898 was also a prosperous one for the Hongs in business. Cashing in on his newly achieved fame and influence, Hong Sling opened his grocery business, Sam Lung and Company. The store was first located on Wabash Avenue for a couple of years, then moved to 299 (the street number later changed to 431) South Clark Street. Hong Sling invested $1,200 in the store, with nineteen partners each investing $1,000. He served as manager and hired about a dozen employees, mostly Hong clansmen. See Hoo She, the bookkeeper, also served as acting manager whenever Hong Sling was on a transnational business trip. As one of the largest Chinese grocery stores in Chicago, its clientele included not only Chinese immigrants, who stopped by every weekend to purchase groceries and to socialize, but also white patrons, who did business with Hong and befriended the Hong family.[102] The store also often served as an inn for itinerant Chinese immigrants staying in Chicago while in transit or for a short duration.[103]

Apart from Sam Lung and Company, Hong Sling's businesses in Chicago also included Hong Fong Lo, one of the largest Chinese chop suey restaurants in Chicago. Hong served as president of the company. He was also a passenger agent for the Chicago and Northwestern Railroad. By 1913, his business in the United States was worth about $30,000. That sum, however, was dwarfed by his business interests in Hong Kong, where his investments in banking, insurance, and merchandise in five stores were worth about $80,000. His transnational business network also extended to Central America, including interests in Cuba and Panama.[104]

Because of his wealth and frequent overseas travels, Hong Sling was well known to the immigration authorities in Chicago. Immigration inspector Howard D. Ebey regarded him as "a man of wealth and standing."[105] Hong Sling's association with white Chicagoans also helped him obtain approval from the immigration authorities for his return certificates, enabling him to conduct his transnational trips smoothly despite the Chinese exclusion laws and practices. His white friends included local businessmen, physicians, and politicians, who readily served as witnesses for his return certificates by appearing at the Office of the Inspector in Charge [of Immigration] in Chicago. On December 3, 1913, Arthur W. Chapman, a mortgage broker, testified as to the American citizenship of Hong Sling's three children, averring that they had been born in the United States. Chapman had been acquainted with the Hongs for more than twenty-three years, during which time he had made monthly visits to Sam Lung and Company. He praised Hong highly as "one of the leading businessmen among the Chinese in Chicago" and an "unquestionably representative" Chinese "in point of intellect, personality, and general good."[106] H. L. Henson, a wholesale grocery businessman with McNeil and Higgins, who had more than twenty years of business dealings with Sam Lung and Company, also appeared at the Office of the Inspector in Charge [of Immigration] in Chicago on December 12, 1913, to testify on behalf of Hong Sling in the same case.[107]

Hong Sling was thoroughly Americanized in his values, outlook, and lifestyle. Undoubtedly his wealth had helped him achieve a substantial assimilation. On December 26, 1904, his second son, William Hong Sling, was born in the Hong residence. Almost two years later, on November 3, 1906, Hong's youngest child, a daughter named Jennie Hong Sling, was born.[108] Hong Sling hired Dr. Joseph Brennemann to officiate at the births of William and Jennie, while many families in Chinatown could only afford a midwife for

Hong Sling family, ca. 1913. Front row from left: Toy Shee, Jennie Hong Sling, William Hong Sling, Hong Sling, and Harry Hong Sling. The youth in the back row is unknown. National Archives, Great Lakes Region, Chicago, Illinois.

Hong Sling family, ca. 1908. Front row from left: Toy Shee, Jennie Hong Sling, William Hong Sling, and Hong Sling. Back row: Harry Hong Sling. National Archives, Great Lakes Region, Chicago, Illinois.

childbirth.[109] All of his children attended the Jones School, a public elementary school near Old Chinatown on South Clark Street, from kindergarten on.[110] Upon graduation from the Jones School, Harry went to Lane Technical High School on the North Side, in a more affluent part of Chicago than the Clark Street area where the family lived.[111] Many family photographs show Hong Sling's wife and children clad in stylish Western clothing, suggesting Hong's economic prosperity and inclination toward assimilation.

However, as a transnational businessman dealing mostly with Chinese, Hong Sling also preserved Chinese traditions and customs. On Chinese holidays and other important occasions, Hong and his family would don traditional Chinese dress. One of the Hong family photographs, taken by a professional photographer named Gibson whose studio was located on Wabash Avenue over Jevne's grocery store around 1909, shows members of the Hong family adorned in splendid traditional Chinese costumes.[112]

Vice

While the economy of Chicago's Chinatown consisted mainly of grocery, restaurant, and laundry businesses, it also included prostitution and gambling, the urban vice. Rather than viewing the "problems" of prostitution and gambling in Chicago's Chinese communities as "natural" and as "cultural defects" of Chinese people, I consider them as products of immigrant life in America resulting from the institutionalized exclusion of the Chinese and socioeconomic sanctions enforced against them. In the absence of family life, prostitution and gambling readily filled the void left in the spare time of Chinese "bachelors," substituting for family life and offering temporary relief and recreation to Chinese immigrants' otherwise diligent and dull daily existence. And of course, prostitution and gambling have been the classic urban vice since the dawn of urban history, plaguing all racial and cultural groups.

PROSTITUTION

Part of the global movement of laborers, most of the Chinese prostitutes in the late nineteenth century were young women from Hong Kong, Canton, and neighboring areas who were kidnapped, purchased, or stolen by procurers and then smuggled to America.[113] When they arrived in San Francisco, these young Chinese women were transported to Chinatown and housed in temporary quarters known as barracoons, where they were put on display and auctioned. Generally, the more "fortunate" women were sold to well-to-do Chinese as concubines or mistresses. Some merchants considered experienced prostitutes ideal wives because they were attractive, sociable, and adept at entertaining guests. A small number were recruited to high-class establishments. They lived in upstairs apartments in Chinatown and had a more or less long-term regular customer or customers. While they seem to have been well treated, they could be sold at their master's will.[114]

Except for such "fortunate" women, most Chinese women ended up in brothels of various grades, according to their attractiveness. During the typically four-year period of servitude, prostitutes had to work for their owners without wages. They were only allowed to take off a total of one month for their menstrual period during the four years and had to work an extra year if they became pregnant.[115] These lower-grade prostitutes, according to Lucie Cheng Hirata, tended to attract white and Chinese customers, on account of their comparatively low fees of twenty-five to fifty cents. The living conditions of these young women were miserable. Most of them lived in street-level apartments. Their daily activities were restricted to these tiny rooms, usually four by six feet, with a door that held a barred window facing a poorly lit alley.[116]

The early Chinese prostitutes in Chicago followed the same migration pattern as their counterparts in San Francisco. They were purchased by or deceived into marrying a prostitute smuggler in South China, brought to San Francisco as "wife" or "daughter" of the broker, and then transported to Chicago. Prostitution in Chicago's Chinatown was much less established and organized, however, than in San Francisco. The first prostitutes mostly lived with their keepers as couples while being allowed or forced to act as "semi-prostitutes," a term used by Siu. In the 1880s, there were only five or six Chinese families in Chicago; among them, some "wives" were actually prostitutes who practiced the trade. A prostitute's bond with her keeper could be broken if she was redeemed by another man, as in the case of Shiu-Feng. Shiu-Feng was one of the most popular prostitutes in the old Chinatown on South Clark Street. She eventually married a Chinese man named Wong Lum, who paid her "body value," the sum that bought her freedom from her keeper.[117] As the Chinese population increased and the demand for prostitutes grew, a few white prostitutes were also found in Chinese restaurants in the late 1890s.[118]

There were no professional Chinese prostitutes until the 1920s. In 1930, for a sociology class project, Siu conducted interviews with several prostitutes that shed light on the lives of prostitutes in Chicago at that time. There were four Chinese prostitutes and about fifteen non-Chinese prostitutes in China-town in the 1930s. The number may have been higher: Professional prosti-tutes often migrated from one Chinatown to another because when they stayed in one town for awhile, they lost their initial "freshness" and business began to slow down; upon arrival in a new town, they were regarded as new commodities and thus could get more business. Compared to the slave girls who were locked up in the basement cells of brothels in San Francisco, the professional prostitutes in Chicago had more freedom of movement, and their fees were higher as well. They had their own apartments in Chinatown, rented by their owners. They usually picked up their customers in public places such as restaurants or family associations. They charged $5 per service and $15 to $25 for overnight service. The so-called body value of a prostitute varied from as much as $10,000 for a new, young prostitute to $5,000 for an older, less attractive prostitute. Thus it was difficult for a prostitute to accumulate enough money to buy back her freedom. And more often than not, a prostitute would also be entangled in other vices like gambling or drug addiction, which would further reduce her ability to accumulate savings.[119]

The conditions of these prostitutes show that prostitution in Chicago was a rather small and unorganized business whose existence depended on a pool of single Chinese men. There seems to be no evidence of a connec-tion between the prostitutes and any larger community power structures, suggesting that prostitution in Chicago did not become a profitable enough business for the powerful gangs to take an interest in controlling and exploit-ing it. The "underdevelopment" of Chinese prostitution in Chicago may also reflect certain conservative values of the Chinese communities there, which did not provide a favorable environment for the business to flourish.

GAMBLING HOUSES

Compared to prostitution, gambling was a much bigger business in Chica-go's Chinatown. The 1933 Chinese directories listed in the *San Min Morning Paper* show thirteen gambling houses on Wentworth Avenue, nine on West 22nd Street, and three on South Clark Street.[120] That the number of gam-bling houses was twice as large as the number of Chinese restaurants speaks volumes about the severity of the gambling problem plaguing Chinese immigrants in Chicago. Siu's study counted between 80 and 140 fan-tan tables and more than 30 lottery units in operation in somewhere between ten and fifteen gambling houses in the 1920s. As of 1938, eight regular gambling houses had survived the worst of the Great Depression. In 1940, 350 men depended on the gambling business in Chinatown for a living. After the Japanese attack on Pearl Harbor and the United States' entry into World War II, gambling in Chicago's Chinatown reached a new height, as two new gambling houses were in business and people had more money to spend.[121]

Scholars have studied the causes of gambling and its destructive nature. Gambling has been recognized as a universal human instinct;[122] excessive gambling often brings misery and suffering to the gambler and the gambler's family.[123] For the Chinese, gambling was "an old world trait transplanted" to American soil.[124] Throughout Chinese history, the royal families engaged in hunting and the nobility played games such as kicking balls, but outdoor games and sports hardly developed in China among the commoners. Instead, many indoor games providing challenge and excitement became popular. Among them, chess and Go were popular pastimes among the gentry and the scholarly class, while cockfights and cricket fights were games for idle men from well-off and poor families alike. Gambling as a game of thrill and excitement can be traced at least as far back as the Han dynasty, and traditionally it has been denounced as a social vice. Nevertheless, it has persisted as one of the social problems among many affecting all social strata in China.

When emigrating to America, the Chinese readily transplanted this old world pastime to the new land. Chinese scholar Chao Longqi's research has established that the Pearl River delta was a region known for rampant gambling and that the Cantonese emigrants learned to gamble prior to emigration and then gambled as they whiled away the hours on the wearisome journey to America and upon landing in San Francisco.[125]

That gambling became a characteristic peculiar to the early Chinese immigrants in America, however, was more a product of their circumstances than a cultural preference. The socially isolated Chinese bachelors looked to their clansmen for entertainment and relaxation, and gambling was the readiest and easiest way to pass the time. Most Chinese immigrants were laborers, illiterate and unfamiliar with the American banking system, so they would hide their savings where they lived or carry the sum with them. Having cash at their disposal would entice them to gamble, in hopes of winning big and then returning to China with a fortune ready for retirement. Although in reality few Chinese immigrants won a return trip to China by gambling, the glamour and excitement of the gambling world was almost irresistible. Besides, with no family around and no other form of entertainment available, even some Chinese laborers who were morally opposed to gambling would still go to gambling houses as spectators and eventually end up participating in the game themselves, like this Chinese laundryman in Chicago in the 1930s:

> I had no intention of gambling. I was up there looking here and there, trying to amuse myself. Finally I stood beside Kai-chung and he said, "Look at that table there. All of them gambling are clansmen of yours. You had better go over to join them. That will make it a family affair."
>
> I walked over and took a look. It was Shui-lung, Tunk-li, Chang-wai, and Shui-hing. "Hey, why do you have to get together at one table?" I said to them. "It does not look nice at all."
>
> "What of it?" answered Shui-long. "Who knows who we are. Come on, you want to put down your bet?"
>
> I put down one dollar. Ah! Lost. Then I put down two dollars. Ah, lost again. Ah, wah! Del-ka-ma! This was excitement. Then I put down five dollars. It brought no luck either! Next I put only two dollars. I won this time. Next I put down seven dollars. Lost. Then I put on two. No luck.
>
> Within a short time I lost fourteen dollars. Del-ka-ma! I was not going to play it any more. I quit and turned over to bet on fan-tan.
>
> First I put down five dollars. Then I doubled it. I won also. Soon I had fifteen dollars. Then I put it all down. Won again!
>
> So I won forty dollars. By this time Tung-wei saw me. He urged me to keep on. But I was ready to quit.[126]

This laundryman had the will power to stop at the right time. But oftentimes, a regular gambler would not quit, wanting to win more, as described in an interview with another Chicago Chinese laundryman in the 1930s.

> At first I won about sixty dollars. If I had known when to stop, I would be a winner. Del-ka-ma! It was too early to go home. It was only seven o'clock, so I want to eat. After supper, I went back there again.
>
> Then I began to bet again. Finally I lost fifty dollars.
>
> No, I lost what I had in my pocket in addition to twenty-five dollars I got from Sing-chang [a cousin]. It was seventy-five dollars altogether.[127]

Gambling in Chicago was a significant part of the Chinatown economy and a big social problem. Bloody fights over control of the gambling houses took place between the rival Moy and Chin clans in 1907 and tainted the image of the community. Similar tong fighting over the control of gambling houses in California resulted in the deaths of seventeen Chinese in July 1925. The tong war over gambling businesses in the Pittsburgh Chinatown lasted more than two years, from October 1924 to March 1927.[128] Chinese communities in other countries were also troubled by problems due to gambling: Haining Street in Wellington, New Zealand, for example, a hub for Chinese immigrants in that country, was portrayed by the mainstream media and viewed by the general public as a locus of vice, plagued by problems of opium smoking and gambling.[129]

Conclusion

In the past century and a half, especially prior to the 1960s, the survival and success of the Chinese in the United States have chiefly depended on their penetration into niche service industries—laundries, wholesale and retail groceries, and restaurants—that require a minimum of English-language skills and are less attractive to many in the mainstream population. In Chicago these three occupations have without exception remained the pillars of the ethnic Chinese economy.

These niche businesses, however, were not just menial, low-skill trades that were shunned or despised by more privileged Americans, as prescribed by conventional and prevalent notions perceived by the general public. On the contrary, many of the ethnic Chinese businesses, especially the large and complex ones, were deliberately created, sophisticated transnational businesses run by individuals with vision, practicality, and long-term goals. These businesses made effective use of transnational networks to raise the necessary capital to get started, to procure merchandise, and to recruit employees, in their business operations serving the interests of Chinese communities at both ends of the transnational migration network. Chicago's central location and easy access by water, land, and rail enabled the Chinese grocery businesses to become wholesale suppliers to small grocers throughout the Midwest. Its metropolitan atmosphere cultivated pioneers of Chinese fine dining. And the Chinese laundries in Chicago served as prototypes for those in other midwestern cities and towns.

These unique features suggest that the ethnic Chinese communities in Chicago served as a vital link in Chinese transnational and translocal migration and as a center of commerce and trade in the midwestern region of America. The shrewd business sense, practicality, and ingenuity of Chinese entrepreneurs contributed not only to their individual business successes but also to the collective survival, sustenance, and success of the Chinese communities in the Midwest as well as in the homeland.

These niche occupations not only sustained the transnational communities but also spared the Chinese from the harsh and often cruel working conditions in large-scale industrial factories and from harsh racial confrontations and conflicts with whites such as their black and Mexican counterparts were subjected to. Thanks to these occupations, the Chinese did not have to work on the "killing floors" of the slaughterhouses and meat-packing plants, where most black and Mexican migrant workers found employment.[130] This niche economic structure also shielded the Chinese from the violent 1919 race riot in Chicago, resulting from competition for jobs among laborers, expansion of black-occupied territory, and conflict over control of recreational facilities that manifested in racial confrontation and hatred. When it was over, twenty-three blacks and fifteen whites had lost their lives, and well over five hundred Chicagoans of both races had been injured.[131]

FOUR

Living Transnational Lives, 1880s–1930s

當年阿公出遠洋，家里阿婆哭斷腸。

When a man lives overseas, his wife weeps until her death.

—Folk song in Taishan, Guangdong, China

Immigration is often a family enterprise. Without a family, an immigrant remains a sojourner, living a temporary existence; only with a family can an immigrant become more committed to the host society. Through various patterns of marriage and living arrangements, Chinese immigrants in Chicago managed to have a family life or some substitute for it. The immigrant reality also led to changes and adaptations in family life for the Chinese women in Chicago, most of whom now enjoyed a more elevated position in their families.

Portrayals of Marriage and Family

Sociologists pioneered many early studies of Chinese American families and marriages. In her 1947 dissertation, Rose Hum Lee identified thirteen Chinese families residing in Butte, Montana, in 1870, with a large average size, usually seven people.[1] Lee observed that these Chinese women were subject not only to their husbands but also to clan and family associations.[2] Despite such patriarchal control, Lee also noted, they occasionally challenged male predominance by running away from unhappy marriages.[3] Two decades later, in his book, *Chinese Americans* (1974), another sociologist, Stanford Lyman, examined the social life of Chinese immigrants in the United States and spearheaded a discussion on the practice of polygamy among early Chinese immigrants. Lyman interpreted polyandry as a form of marriage among Chinese immigrants resulting from the short-age of women.[4]

Despite such pioneering works, studies of family and marriage of Chi-nese immigrant women have evolved slowly; specialized studies on Chinese families in America did not appear until the 1980s. Evelyn Nakano Glenn (1983) classified immigrant families into three distinct types that emerged in different periods in response to particular political and economic condi-tions—split household (1850–1920), small producer (1920–1960), and dual-wage worker (1960–1980)—and explained them as "strategies for dealing with conditions of life in the United States."[5]

While Glenn's work offered a theoretical analysis of different forms of Chinese immigrant families in the United States, other studies provided additional evidence for the existence of Chinese family life in different re-gions during the period of early Chinese immigration. Sandy Lydon (1985) examined the various Chinese communities in the Monterey Bay region in California. Lydon found that as early as the 1850s, there had been Chi-nese fishing families there. While some Chinese wives went fishing with their husbands, others worked at home processing fish.[6] Family life was also present in agricultural areas. In *This Bittersweet Soil: The Chinese in California Agriculture, 1860–1910* (1986), Sucheng Chan examined family life among Chinese farmers in the Sacramento–San Joaquin delta in 1900, identifying the age difference between married couples as being a notable feature of these families, together with the polyandrous practice among some Chinese miners and laborers in northern rural California in 1900.[7] Sylvia Sun Minnick's *Samfow: The San Joaquin Chinese Legacy* (1988) dis-covered seventeen Chinese marriages recorded between 1857 and 1880 in the San Joaquin County marriage records. Chinese family lives became more apparent after 1900 as forty-three Chinese marriages were recorded between 1900 and 1924.[8] Similarly, Laura Wang (1988) found a family-oriented Chinese community in Vallejo, Solano County, California, be-tween 1910 and 1940.[9] From census and other data, David Beesley (1988) gathered evidence indicating that some of the Chinese laborers in a Sierra Nevada town with regular income had wives or women with them.[10] In addition to California and the mountain region, Chinese families also ap-peared in the Midwest. Sarah R. Mason's (1995) case study of Liang May Seen, an early Chinese immigrant woman living in Minneapolis between the 1890s and 1940s, asserted that Liang May Seen played a vital role economically in her family's survival and prosperity and culturally in their assimilation into American society.[11]

Comprehensive studies on family lives of Chinese immigrant women in America finally began to emerge in the 1990s. Judy Yung's *Unbound Feet: A Social History of Chinese Women in San Francisco* (1995) examines the family lives of late nineteenth- and early twentieth-century Chinese immigrant wives in San Francisco. Yung observes that most immigrant women "presented a submissive image in public but ruled at home" and that their role "as homemakers, wage earners, and culture bearers made them indispensable partners of their husbands."[12]

Along the same lines, my own *Surviving on the Gold Mountain: A History of Chinese American Women and Their Lives* (1998) has been noted by scholars as breaking new ground, the first and "most comprehensive history of Chinese American women to date."[13] It closely examines the lives of Chinese immigrant women as wives of merchants, farmers, and laborers, as prostitutes, and as students and professionals in major gateway cities as well as in rural areas of different regions in nineteenth- and twentieth-century America.[14]

Together, these studies have confirmed the existence of family life among the early Chinese immigrants and greatly contributed to our knowledge of family and marriage of Chinese immigrant women in the United States. However, a number of questions still remain understudied, such as what characterized marriages among Chinese immigrants as well as the implications of these characterizations, the ways in which women's roles in Chinese immigrant families changed, and how such changes occurred.

Marriage Patterns in Chicago

Family life for the pioneers in Chicago Chinatown did not exist until the 1880s. The three Moy brothers and their compatriots first came to the Windy City alone, leaving their families behind in China. The decade of the 1880s saw a steady growth in population, as about thirty Chinese men settled in the city. The Moy brothers and some other Chinese merchants were able to send for their wives from China, since they were exempted from the Chinese Exclusion Act of 1882 that prohibited the entry of Chinese laborers until 1943, when it was finally repealed.

In the mid-1880s Moy Dong Hoy, the second of the three Moy brothers in Chicago, returned to China and brought a young wife back with him a year later.[15] Moy Dong Yee, the youngest of the three Moy brothers, likewise brought his new wife, Luk Shee, from China in 1900.[16] Although there is no record indicating when Moy Dong Chow brought his wife to Chicago from China, it is certain that by the 1910s all three Moy brothers had wives in Chicago, as shown in a family photograph of the three Moy wives taken in the 1910s.[17] A few other Chinese merchants, F. Toy, Y. K. Chan, and M. H. Chan, also lived with their wives in the early decades of the twentieth century.[18]

According to Paul C. P. Siu's fieldwork on Chinese families in Chicago, by the end of the 1880s there were a dozen Chinese groceries and three chop suey houses in the old Chinatown area. To meet the need for chop suey supplies, the bean sprout–producing business emerged in turn. The Chinatown population consequently increased from thirty to about two hundred and the size of an average family also grew to a dozen. Between 1915 and 1925, more than fifty Chinese families resided in the Chinatown area, while many

Moy Tong Wee (Moy Dong Yee) and his wife Luke Shee, ca. 1906. National Archives, Great Lakes Region, Chicago, Illinois.

others lived outside of Chinatown. In the 1930s more than 150 Chinese families lived in Chicago.[19]

Historical records reveal a few distinctive marriage patterns among the early Chinese families in Chicago. I have classified them into the following categories: first, the transnational split marriage—Taishanese "widow" and American concubine; second, traditional marriage; and third, American urban marriages, including love unions, interracial marriage, and widow remarriage. Many of the earlier Chinese women, who came predominantly from rural Taishan, were concubines. The traditional polygamous practice, however, turned into a variant when transplanted to the new land: the husband did not live with multiple wives simultaneously but left his first wife (in most cases) in China to carry out the duties of filial piety and either brought a concubine from China or married a woman in America to carry on family life abroad. While the dominant pattern had been the traditional marriage, in which the Chinese male returned to China, got married, and brought his bride with him when returning to America, the American urban marriage gained popularity, especially among the younger and American-born Chinese, who were more inclined to find mates in their socioeconomic circles in America. Meanwhile, interracial marriages or unions and widow remarriages also emerged in the last category.

TRANSNATIONAL SPLIT MARRIAGE:

TAISHANESE "WIDOW" AND AMERICAN CONCUBINE

Chinese immigrants encountered a series of obstacles to establishing family life in America, including ideological, socioeconomic, and physical restrictions in China and the alienating and often hostile environment in America.[20] Traditional Chinese philosophy supported an ideological system in which women were believed to be inferior and therefore subject to male dominance. Throughout Chinese history, Confucian ideals served as social norms and legal codes to regulate women's behavior and conduct. According to these norms and codes, a woman should possess the "four virtues" of obedience, timidity, reticence, and adaptability. She should subject her entire life to the dominance of men: an unmarried girl should obey her father and elder brother, a married woman her husband, and a widow her son.

This ideology justified and perpetuated women's lower socioeconomic status. Women were excluded from civil service, a main source of income for the ruling class in China. Women were not employed outside the home except for occupations related to reproduction or providing amusement and sexual pleasure for men: matchmakers, midwives, entertainers, prostitutes, and procuresses. Although peasant women largely participated in household handicraft, such as spinning and weaving in North China, and in farm work in South China to help support their families, the income they earned from such activities went to the family—but only the male head of the family could dispose of it.[21]

Physical restriction, such as footbinding, also reinforced the view of women as weaker and inferior creatures. The exact origin of footbinding is obscure, but it has been conjectured that it began with dancers at the Tang imperial court. By the Song dynasty, the custom had spread to upper-class women.[22] During the Qing dynasty, it became a practice throughout China. At quite a young age, between four to seven, a girl's feet were tightly wrapped and gradually bent until the arch was broken and the toes turned under. The "lily foot" produced by this practice crippled a woman to such an extent that she could barely walk without support.

In America, restrictive immigration laws and their enforcement were also responsible for the shortage of women in Chinese immigrant communities. Beginning in 1882, a series of immigration laws (1882, 1888, 1892, 1902, 1907, and 1924) successfully limited the immigration of Chinese women.[23] Even before the passage of the Chinese Exclusion Act of 1882, the Page Act of 1875, which forbade the entry of Chinese, Japanese, and "Mongolian" contract laborers as well as women for the purpose of prostitution, had effectively kept Chinese women out.[24] In the decade before the passage of the Page Act, the state of California had passed several pieces of legislation restricting Chinese women. An Act for the Suppression of Chinese Houses of Ill Fame, passed on March 21, 1866, denounced Chinese prostitution and penalized landlords who allowed their properties to be used for immoral purposes. Additionally, An Act to Prevent the Kidnapping and Importation of Mongolian, Chinese, and Japanese Females for Criminal or Demoralizing Purposes, passed on March 8, 1870, made it illegal "to bring [such females], or land from any ship, boat or vessel, into this state."[25] These exclusion laws effectively prevented most Chinese women from joining their husbands. The records of the INS indicate that the majority of the Chinese women entering the United States between 1882 and 1943 were wives and daughters of Chinese merchants, who were exempted from the exclusion laws owing to class prejudice in American immigrant policy and the US trade with China.[26]

In the face of these obstacles, Chinese immigrants devised a mechanism to negotiate their immigrant reality. I call this mechanism "transnational split marriage: Taishanese 'widows' and American concubines," a marital arrangement in which the husband, as a result of the aforementioned obstacles, left his wife behind in China but brought a concubine with him to America to ease his immigrant life. This pattern is evident among the earlier Chinese immigrants in Chicago.

A popular folk song widespread among the villages of the overseas Chinese starts with the lyric "Dang nian a gong xia nan yang, jia li a po ku duan chang" (When a man lives overseas, his wife weeps until her death), depicting the plight of the wives left behind by their emigrant husbands. The villages with substantial numbers of Chinese overseas were called "widow villages." Such folk songs and sobriquets describe well the split family life a transmigrant and his family had to endure.[27] Numerous literary works also reflect this reality. Louis Chu's (1979) novel *Eat a Bowl of Tea* and the motion picture based on it vividly and light-heartedly portray the life of a split immigrant family. The wife laments that her absent husband periodically sends her modern household gadgets from America while he is the one she wants most.[28] Academics have also studied the issue, with Madeline Y. Hsu's *Dreaming of Gold, Dreaming of Home* (2000) being one of the best accounts.[29]

The plight of the virtual widow of an immigrant Chinese is only part of the trans-Pacific saga. A complete analysis of the transnational split marriage can provide us with a fuller picture of the transnational stories of the Chinese immigrants and their families. It is an arrangement and a practical compromise invented by the immigrants to cope with the marital separation caused by immigration. In many cases, a concubine was arranged for by the parents or the first wife of an immigrant, with the specific purpose of taking care of his physical needs while abroad; at the same time, the first wife remained in the home village to fulfill the duties of filial piety on his behalf. Through such an arrangement, the concubine and the wife jointly fulfilled the biological, socioeconomic, and emotional duties expected of a traditional wife by society. Despite the inferior status of a concubine in the family and society, concubinage was recognized as a viable alternative for girls from impoverished families or in distressed circumstances. Many concubines were illiterate slave-maids from the same or nearby villages, who were sold into servitude at a young age by their impoverished parents. A slave-maid's fate was dictated by her master: she could be married to a male servant or become a concubine of the master at the master and mistress's will. The latter was considered a better alternative in many cases, since as a concubine she was no longer a slave but a member of the master's family, and thus it represented an upward social move. Concubines among the earlier merchant families in Chicago's Chinatown had often been slave-maids prior to their immigration.[30]

M. H.'s family provides a typical example of the transnational split marriage in Chicago. M. H. came to America in 1890, leaving his first wife behind in China. After one of his return trips to China, he brought his concubine, who was from a poor family in a different district and twenty-seven years his junior, back to America with him. While his first wife in China bore him two sons, M. H.'s married life was essentially spent with his concubine in Chicago, who bore him six children of whom only three survived. M. H. later brought his two older sons from China to Chicago, and they helped him in his chop suey house business. For M. H., the transnational split marriage allowed him to take care of his family at both ends of the transnational life.[31]

Concubines were accepted as wives of their husbands by the Chinese immigrant community in Chicago and were socially active. The "young Mrs. M.H." was "a very sociable woman in the community," going to church in Chinatown and participating in "women's affairs." Similarly, Mrs. Fung, also a concubine, was "crazy about ma-jong," often going to a ma-jong party next door or organizing one in her house.[32]

Concubinage was not a monopoly of Chinese culture but a natural product of patriarchal society in traditional China and other patriarchal cultures. The origin of concubinage in China is obscure, but it was certainly related to the patriarchal nature of the society, in which only a male heir could secure that a family's name was passed down, that its fortune was kept intact, and that its social and economic status in the community remained unchallenged. Confucian teachings systematized these patriarchal beliefs and formalized them as cultural institutions that ruled Chinese society and individuals. According to the Confucian ideal, "a man without a son was not a dutiful son." Therefore a man could legitimately have a concubine or concubines if his wife failed to bear him a male heir. The institution of concubinage was further strengthened and developed during the Song dynasty, when urban development and economic prosperity reduced the significance of women's participation in economic activities, and enabled wealthy Chinese gentry-landowners and merchants to enjoy a more leisurely lifestyle.[33] Together with other valuable possessions, concubines signified a man's social status and economic power. Many wealthy Chinese men therefore acquired concubines not only to satisfy their sexual urges but also to display their fortune and power. In one of China's most famous twentieth-century novels, *The Family* (originally published in 1933), Ba Jin (Pa Chin) vividly portrays a typical feudal, patriarchal, wealthy Chinese family, the Gao family, modeled after his own. Grandfather Gao, the patriarchal family head, and his wealthy friends all possess concubines.[34] Although the millennium-long feudal practice of polygamy had been challenged several times in Chinese history—during the Taiping Rebellion (1850–1864) and the May Fourth Movement of 1919—it was not outlawed until 1950, when the new Communist government issued its Marriage Law, which legally prohibited bigamy and concubinage.[35]

Yet, although concubinage had been practiced in China historically, the polygynous practices among Chinese immigrants in the United States were more likely ramifications of immigration than Chinese cultural habits. Not only the well-to-do Chinese merchants had concubines in America; even some Chinese laborers acquired concubines. Before the repeal of the Chinese exclusion laws in 1943, most Chinese immigrant men left their families in China because of financial incapacity, American immigration restrictions, and the dictates of the Chinese patriarchy that women stay in China to take care of children and parents-in-law and to secure remittances from men abroad.[36] A few fortunate men were eventually able to arrange for their families to come to America.[37] Many others managed to return to their native villages in China to see their families periodically.[38] The passage of the Scott Act in 1888, which barred the reentry of Chinese laborers into America even if they left the country only temporarily, however, made the latter practice impossible. Unable to bring their wives to America or go to China to see them, some successful Chinese laborers, such as farmers, employed laborers, service workers, and even gamblers, purchased women from brothels or married those who had successfully escaped servitude, while still legally married to their first wives in China, as indicated in David Beesley's (1988) study on polygynous practices among Chinese immigrants in Nevada.[39]

Furthermore, polygyny as practiced by Chinese immigrant males during the late nineteenth and early twentieth centuries took a different form than its twin in China. Most men had first wives in China and remarried or lived with women under common law marriage in America without divorcing their first wives; they generally did not live with multiple women under the same roof simultaneously, as in China. These marriages were thus more bigamous than polygynous.

Moreover, these bigamous practices among Chinese immigrants in America were more for practical reasons, that is, physical sustenance of the men and survival of the Chinese immigrant communities, than for psychological reasons, that is, the display of one's wealth through possession of concubines, as was the case for many wealthy Chinese in China. An ordinary Chinese migrant needed to meet his basic physical needs (food, shelter, and sex) in order to function normally while working toward his American dream. In the absence of his wife, he had to find an alternative, either another marriage, a common-law cohabitation, or a long-term or short-term relationship with a prostitute.

Among the earlier Chinese families in Chicago, most of the women were concubines, and there often existed a wide age gap between the husband and the concubine. In the case of the three Moy brothers, they all brought their young concubines from China between the 1880s and 1910s. Although no written record exists concerning the age difference of the couples, there is a family photo taken in 1929, about three decades after their marriage, showing Moy Dong Hoy, his wife, and their eight children, ranging from preschoolers to youths in their twenties, in which Moy Dong Hoy appears to be twenty or thirty years senior to his wife.[40] There was also a wide gap in age between Moy Dong Yee and his new wife, shown by photos of the couple from the immigration records.[41] No photo of Moy Chong Chow and his wife is available, but a family picture taken in the 1910s shows the three wives of the three Moy brothers as being of similar age.[42]

Like the Moy brothers, many other Chinese men also brought concubines to Chicago. C. H. Moy brought his concubine from the West Coast in 1920.[43] David Lee's father arrived in San Francisco in 1918 and moved to Chicago in 1924. He had three wives in his hometown, the village of Dongkeng in Taishan; the first wife came to America in 1922, while the second and third remained in China to look after their father-in-law.[44]

Most Chinese immigrants remained lonely married "bachelors" in America. In their case, the role of partner for satisfying their physical needs was filled practically by a substitute for concubinage—prostitution, which has frequently and conveniently been employed as an example of the Chinatown vice. Thus the pattern of transnational split marriage could be said to apply to the majority of the earlier Chinese immigrants.

A wide age gap between husband and wife was also common among Chinese immigrants in other parts of the country. In many Chinese immigrant families, the husband was usually older than his wife. David Beesley's investigation, involving twenty-seven married Chinese couples in a Sierra Nevada town, for example, shows the average age of the women as twenty-two, while the average age of the men was thirty-one.[45] Sucheng Chan's study also notes that among Chinese families in the Sacramento–San Joaquin delta area in the early twentieth century, some farm laborers were twice or even almost three times as old as their wives.[46] The documents from the INS and oral history interviews also suggest the substantial age gap between a married couple to have been a common feature of many Chinese immigrant families.

It is easy to attribute so large an age gap between marital partners to the patriarchal Chinese culture. According to the tradition of Chinese culture, marriage was often a social and economic arrangement between the families of the bride and groom rather than a romantic union between two individuals. A successful and financially secure man was more likely an older man. The sizeable age gap between husband and wife, however, was more prevalent among Chinese immigrants than among those in China, owing primarily to American immigration policies prior to 1943. These policies effectively reinforced the sexual imbalance among Chinese immigrants by restricting the entry of Chinese women. The Page Act of 1875, discussed previously, forbade the entry of Chinese, Japanese, and "Mongolian" contract laborers and prohibited the entry of women for the purpose of prostitution. It also imposed fines and punishment on those convicted of transporting women interstate for the purpose of prostitution. Although the law applied to women of any race and nationality engaged in prostitution, it was executed with Chinese women in mind.[47] The Chinese Exclusion Act of 1882 effectively banned the entry of Chinese laborers and the wives of Chinese laborers who were already in the United States. As a result, from 1906 to 1924, only 150 Chinese women per year on average were legally admitted.[48] The Immigration Act of May 26, 1924, based on the ruling of the Supreme Court in the case of *Chang Chan et al. v. John D. Nagle* on May 25, 1924, excluded Chinese alien wives of American citizens of Chinese ancestry. Consequently, no Chinese women were admitted between 1924 and 1930.[49]

In 1930, an act relaxed this ban by allowing the entry of alien Chinese wives as long as the marriage was legally effective before May 26, 1924. Under this provision, about sixty Chinese women were admitted each year between 1931 and 1941.[50] The records of the INS indicate that the majority of Chinese women entering the United States between 1882 and 1943 were wives and daughters of Chinese merchants.[51] Consequently, American-born daughters of Chinese families were in demand as prospective brides.

The second reason for the age gap was the enforcement of antimiscegenation laws in many states, which prevented Chinese men from marrying women outside their own ethnic group.[52] Antimiscegenation laws in the United States evolved as a reaction of white society to the possibility of racially mixed marriages between whites and blacks resulting from the introduction of black slaves from Africa. In 1661, Maryland passed the first antimiscegenation law to prohibit marriages involving white females and black males. Following Maryland, thirty-eight states in the Union passed similar legislation.[53] In 1850, California lawmakers adopted an antimiscegenation statute to prohibit black-white marriages, which was later included in Section 60 of the new Civil Code in 1872. A drastic evolution of antimiscegenation legislation in California in 1880 also outlawed Chinese-Caucasian marriages along with black-white marriages. In the same year, the California legislature introduced Section 69 of the Civil Code, which restricted the issuance of marriage licenses to unions between a white and a "Negro, Mulatto, or Mongolian."[54] Although the generic term "Mongolian" refers to Chinese, Japanese, Koreans, and other ethnic groups in Asia, the law was designed to target Chinese, echoing the anti-Chinese sentiment at the time on the West Coast. In 1905, to make Sections 60 and 69 consistent and to deal with the fear of the Japanese, the California legislature amended Section 60 to make marriages between whites and Mongolians "illegal and void."[55] These antimiscegenation laws were in force until 1967, when they were finally declared unconstitutional by the United States Supreme Court in the landmark case *Loving v. Virginia.*[56] Prohibited from marrying women of other racial groups, Chinese immigrant males could only look for mates from a very limited supply, mostly American-born Chinese girls who in terms of age could have been their daughters.

Third, the substantial age difference between Chinese husbands and wives was also due to the financial incapacity of most Chinese immigrant men. Many of them worked for almost their entire lifetime to save enough money for marriage. Mrs. C., a second-generation Chinese American woman from Boston in her eighties, recalled her family history in which her parents' marriage provides a good example: "My father spent many years to save money for his marriage. So when he had enough money to support a family, he was already a middle-aged man. He went to Guangdong, China, to marry my mother when she was sixteen."[57]

Transnational split marriages often went hand in hand with a larger family. The three Moy brothers all had large families, with eight or nine children each. Moy Dong Chow had nine children altogether, including three daughters and six sons. His first wife, Ng Shee, bore him four sons in China: Moy Fook Hung, My Fook Choon, Moy Fook Jung, and Moy Fook Ngoon. His second wife, Wong Shee, bore him three daughters and two sons in the United States beginning in 1898: Moy Fung Gu (Lillie), Moy Fung Ying (Marion), Moy Fung Lin (Jumie), Moy Fook Keung (Edward), and Moy Fook Sun (William).[58] Moy Dong Hoy and his wife had three daughters and five sons, and Moy Dong Yee had three daughters and six sons.[59] Siu's study of the Chinese families in Chicago's Chinatown indicates a similar pattern.[60]

TRADITIONAL MARRIAGE

The transnational split marriage pattern, of course, does not encompass all early Chinese immigrant families, and not all the wives of the earlier Chinese immigrants were concubines. Many wives managed to come to America to join their husbands.[61] Thirty-nine of the 137 families in Chicago surveyed by Siu, or 30 percent, fell in the category of traditional marriage, that is, a marriage arranged prior to or after the husband's emigration to America. Eighty percent of the traditionally married couples resided in Chinatown; the majority of these men were restaurateurs, grocers, and lottery house keepers, merchants who were exempted from the Chinese exclusion laws, as illustrated in the following cases.[62]

S. Moy came to Chicago in the 1890s and became a general store owner. During World War I, he made enough money to be able to send for his wife in China and build two houses in Chinatown as rental properties. Unfortunately, he was paralyzed in his midfifties and began to lose money in business as a result of his disability and the economic depression. His wife was "sluggish" and could not take care of him or his business. Both of his houses were therefore authorized to his creditors to collect the room rent.[63]

C. L.'s case offers a counterexample to that of S. Moy in a number of ways. C. L. came to America when he was twenty-three, around the turn of the nineteenth and twentieth centuries. He stayed in Portland, Oregon, for a few years, but lived in Chicago for over thirty years as a general store keeper. His store did well and he made some money. During the 1910s, he went back to China, got married, and brought his bride to Chicago. Twenty years later, they had five children, aged nineteen, eighteen, seventeen, thirteen, and eight. Except for the eighteen-year-old, their children were all males. The oldest son was sent to China for Chinese schooling, while the two youngest worked as newsboys while attending school. During the Depression, C. L.'s business was slow except on Sundays, when his cousins and relatives would come to the store and buy something. He had to supplement his income by selling lottery tickets, earning about $20 a week total. To further supplement family income, his wife worked in a garment factory and later in a bakery.[64]

AMERICAN URBAN MARRIAGE:

LOVE UNION, INTERRACIAL MARRIAGE, AND WIDOW REMARRIAGE

Love Union   Along with the transnational split marriage and the traditional marriage, there were also marriages issuing from romances rather than parental or familial arrangements. The younger, better-educated, and second-generation Chinese often married for love. Such marriages constituted 26 percent of the total number of marriages investigated by Siu. The following are some examples of such marriages.

Mark was a young engineer from Hawaii who found employment in an American company. His wife was also a Hawaiian-born Chinese. The couple had resided in Chicago for six years by the early 1930s. They lived in a little apartment on 26th Street, four blocks from Chinatown. Their apartment was clean and furnished with modern furniture, a rug, a piano, a radio, and musical instruments. Mark played tennis in summer while his wife watched him play. They spoke English and associated mostly with other Chinese from Hawaii.[65]

Dr. D. was a young physician with an office in Chinatown in the 1930s. The son of a Chinese missionary, he went to high school on the West Coast and came to Chicago for his higher education. He graduated from Northwestern University and then Chicago Medical School. His wife was his childhood playmate and a fellow student at Northwestern. They were married immediately after his graduation from medical school. They spoke Cantonese and occasionally English to each other.[66]

Mr. Ying came to America during his teen years and had been in the country for nearly twenty years in the 1930s. His wife was an American-born Chinese from Los Angeles. Ying opened a chop suey house at North Broadway but closed it during the Depression. The couple then became insurance agents and made a sufficiently good living to afford an apartment near Lincoln Park on the North Side.[67]

The case of J. Chung is perhaps the most illuminating of this category:

> Mr. Chung was born in China. At the age 18, he was sent out to Canton by his parents for his high school education. He was there only one year, attending a governmental high school. At the age of 20, he went across [the ocean] to Mexico. When he was in Mexico, he learned Spanish. Later, a Chinese newspaper here in Chicago was established and it was run by a group of his cousins. Mr. Chung was offered a position as a business manager. The newspaper sent him over from Mexico. He finally arrived here and assumed his job. He [worked] in this place for four years and made about from $150 to $200 per month. During that period, Mr. Chung was quite a prostitute and tax-dancing hall patron. He went to dancing hall at least once a week. He had venereal [disease] for once or twice. But, [however] he is a man of will power. Despite of being a [constant] vice patron, he still [could save] a lot of money.
>
> One year before his [return] back to China, he resigned as a business manager of the newspaper company because he had personal conflict with the [editor]. Then, [assisted] by one of his friend[s], he established a pictorial [magazine]. The office was in Downtown. Because of lack of ability and specialization, the [magazine] had a poor circulation. It was stopped from print finally; he [lost] about two thousand dollars probably.
>
> At the same time he imported some Chinese goods from China. At first, those goods were sold only to Chinese people. But since Chung came back from China again, he ordered some goods that can sell to American business houses in whole sale.
>
> Mr. Chung is a new idea person in the immigrant community. In many ways he is different from the other conservatives. He knows many American friends and [constantly makes] contacts with them. Now, since he brought his wife from China, he lives in the Southside instead of . . . in Chinatown. He has lived in the Y.M.C.A. for a while when he [ran] that pictorial [magazine].

Mrs. Chung is a very skinny figure, small, but very sweet. She was educated in Hong Kong, a high school graduate. She speaks a little bit [of]
English. She learned her English when she was in high school at Hong Kong.

They are living in three room apartment. Housing condition is fair; it
furnishes with all modern equipment. They have very seldom gone down
to Chinatown. Mr. Chung do[es] go down there often for only business
purpose.[68]

These cases indicate that love unions were more likely to occur among
American-born or Hawaiian-born second-generation Chinese or the more
Americanized Chinese immigrants who had come to the country at a younger
age. They were mostly better-educated professionals, and they and their marital partners shared similar cultural and educational backgrounds. They lived
outside Chinatown in more affluent neighborhoods and their contacts with
Chinatown were limited to business contacts only.

Interracial Marriage   Despite antimiscegenation laws, interracial marriage
took place among the Chinese in Chicago. The earliest recorded instance
was the union between Quing Kee and his German wife, who was referred as
Mrs. Quing Kee, a hardy and "stout" woman. By 1890, the couple had been
married for some years and lived in the upstairs room over Hip Lung. On
New Year's Day in 1890, Moy Dong Chew and Moy Dong Hoy, the owners
of Hip Lung and leaders of the Chinese community, led other Chinese residents to pay homage to Quing Kee and his wife, according to the Chinese
custom of visiting relatives and friends on New Year's Day. Apparently the
couple were accepted as members of the community. "Complacent" for the
homage, Mrs. Quing Kee reciprocated by offering the greeters Chinese rice-
gin and sending her husband across the street to fill the "growler" with beer;
as she told her husband, "I can't dring dot rice-chin. I lige beer better. Quing go ofer by Lawler's, unt get dree pints."[69]

A significant number of interracial marriages occurred among the Chicago
Chinese. In the 1930s, according to Siu's study, there were at least twenty-seven
such marriages, or 20 percent of the total families investigated. Twenty-six of
the interracial marriages involved Chinese men and white women, mostly
Polish, while one was between a Chinese man and a black woman. The white
women who married Chinese men were generally from one of three social
backgrounds: the Polish dishwasher of a Chinese restaurant, the chop suey
house taker or cashier, or a veteran prostitute. Twelve of the interracial mar-

ried couples lived in Chinatown, while fifteen resided outside.[70] A similar profile of interracial marriage was shared by Chinese in other midwestern cities,
such as St. Louis and Minneapolis–St. Paul.[71]

A few cases of interracial marriage in the 1930s are revealing in regard to
the social acceptance, cultural assimilation, and ethnic identity of the individuals involved. T. Chan met his future wife in a Chinese chop suey house
where she worked as a waitress. Despite the seeming physical incompatibil-
ity—Chan was short and slim and she tall and big—they fell in love. After
the marriage, they lived on the South Side for three years, when T. Chan was
employed in a large company as treasurer. Sometime later he quit his job and
opened a small chop suey shop. Unfortunately, business was so slow that he
could not even pay the rent for the shop; he was evicted from the premises
and lost thousands of dollars on the venture. When the Great Depression
came, the couple had to move to Chinatown to ease the situation. Living in
a small apartment on 25th Street in the Italian community and on the edge
of Chinatown, T. Chan found a job as a waiter at the Pagoda Inn restaurant
in Chinatown. Occasionally, Mrs. Chan would take their son to the restaurant to see her husband and have dinner. Some fellow workers there would
tease the little boy and bribe him with change to make him speak Chinese.[72]

H. Chan, a cook at a Chinese chop suey house, married a Polish woman,
a dishwasher at the same chop suey house. H. Chan was always kind to her
and treated her well, often cooking special dinners for her. The romance
that developed in the kitchen led to marriage. In their first twenty years
of marriage, as the chop suey business was bustling in Chicago, H. Chan
prospered and was able to buy a house on the South Side, and his wife was
able to quit her job and stay home to take care of their three children, two
girls and a boy. The first daughter graduated from a normal school on the
South Side and worked as a bookkeeper in a Chinese restaurant. During her
teen years, she wanted to become a nun and rejected her Chinese heritage,
unwilling to associate with any Chinese. As she matured, however, her entire attitude toward the Chinese changed. She became actively involved in
the Chinese community, attending Chinese social meetings and going to
dancing parties held by the Chinese student association at the University of
Chicago, while her younger sister, a seventeen-year-old high school student,
tagged along. Both girls ended up finding boyfriends among the Chinese
students. When their father was at work managing a Chinese restaurant,
they would have parties with their boyfriends at home.[73]

Mr. Lam was a second-generation Chinese who married a white woman. The couple came to Chicago in the 1930s and set up their tailor shop in Chinatown, although neither of them could speak Chinese. Their clients were young Chinese men who could speak English and were mostly their friends. The Lams, however, were socially isolated from the Chinese community; Mr. Lam was never invited to social meetings in Chinatown and Mrs. Lam had no Chinese women as her friends.[74]

Dr. K. graduated from Northwestern University's medical school first in his class and married a white nurse. Both were in their midthirties in the early 1930s and had a three-year-old daughter. He opened an office in Chinatown, practicing as a physician and surgeon. Although his practice was the most successful among the three doctors in Chinatown at the time, the doctors in Chinatown generally were not doing well, as most Chinese would go to American doctors when they fell ill. Moreover, Dr. K. could not speak Chinese very well, which was a disadvantage for his business.[75]

Frank Moy, the son of Moy Dong Chow and unofficial mayor of Chinatown, also married a white woman twenty years his junior. Frank Moy worked as a laundryman for many years before he was promoted to head of On Leong, a prominent position that made him rich. His family lived in Chinatown for many years but later moved to a comfortable house on the South Side. He would come to Chinatown wearing expensive clothing and big gold chains and driving his big, new, four-thousand-dollar Lincoln that would be parked in front of the On Leong building. The couple's sixteen-year-old daughter, Rita, who liked to dress in boy's attire, could not speak Chinese but understood a little. When coming to Chinatown with her father, she would stop by a gambling house and watch people play ma-jong.[76]

The above stories shed light on the interracial marriages in Chicago. First, shared working experiences made interracial marriages possible, as in the cases of T. Chan and H. Chan, where a common work environment ignited a romance between a man and woman from different cultural and ethnic backgrounds. Second, interracial marriages involving working-class Chinese men seem to have been viewed favorably by the Chinese community, as in the cases of T. Chan and H. Chan, where both couples worked and resided in Chinatown. In contrast, more educated interracial couples, such as the Lams and Dr. K and his wife, who was a nurse, were less connected with the Chinatown community. This difference suggests how class lines crisscrossed and transcended racial lines: Chinatown was then made up predominantly of laborers and small entrepreneurs, and so interracial working-class married couples could easily fit into the community. In all cases, the Chinese men appear to have been devoted husbands and responsible providers for their families.

The interracial marriages in Chicago mirror those across the country. Despite antimiscegenation laws, there were a small number of interracial marriages among Chinese immigrants. Those Chinese men who married non-Chinese women were usually small entrepreneurs or laborers, while the racial and ethnic backgrounds of their wives varied from region to region.[77]

In the South, most Chinese men were laborers from California or Cuba recruited to the South by railroad companies or sugar plantations. They found wives among black women and Irish or French immigrant women. The 1880 census for Louisiana indicates that among the 489 Chinese in the state, 35 were married, widowed, or divorced. Of the married Chinese men, only four had a Chinese wife. The remaining Chinese men married non-Chinese women, among whom four had married mulatto women, twelve black women, and eight white women, including six of Irish or French immigrant background.[78]

In the Midwest, interracial marriages occurred among Chinese small entrepreneurs and laborers, just as in Chicago. In Minneapolis and St. Paul, there were at least six interracially married Chinese men in the early twentieth century. They were laundry and restaurant owners and cooks. The women they married were often Irish or Polish women, who worked as vegetable washers in Twin Cities restaurants.[79]

In New York City, census data and contemporary newspapers reveal a pattern of interracial marriage between Chinese men and Irish women consistent through the last decades of the nineteenth century. *Harper's Weekly* and other magazines and newspapers frequently featured stories of "Chinamen" and "Hibernian" women, in which Irish women praised their Chinese husbands.[80]

Widow Remarriage   Although in the cases studied by Siu only five widows remarried, less than 5 percent of the total number of families in his study, the remarriage of widows provides a contrast to the social taboo in traditional China forbidding a widow to remarry and is therefore more significant than its frequency might suggest.

Several factors made a widow's remarriage not only possible but acceptable to the Chinese community as well. First, the influence of the larger American society helped the Chinese change their values and attitudes toward marriage. Second, the uneven gender ratio made widows ready candidates for marriage. According to a 1931 study by Ifu Chen, a graduate student in the Sociology Department of the University of Chicago, among the 6,000 Chinese (much larger than the census figure of 2,757) then in Chicago, there were only 400 females, or 6.7 percent of the total Chinese population, much lower than the percentage of the total Chinese American population in the country, while the 1930 census shows the total Chinese American population as 74,954, among which 15,152, or 20 percent of the total population, were female.[81] Even using the smaller figure of 2,757 from the census, the percentage of females in Chicago was 15 percent, still considerably lower than the national average. Although the individual situation of a widow was often more complicated than that of a first-time bride, as widows tended to have children from the previous marriage and might be facing financial difficulties that could deter potential suitors, a widow could still get a mate from the much larger pool of males owing to the extremely unbalanced gender ratio. If the widow had money, she would be more in demand. The following cases provide examples of both possibilities.

> Sieu has been in America over fifteen years. He has a wife in the native village in China. He deserted her. He never write[s] to her and support her. Here he is married to Mrs. J Pang, the late chairman of the H. Association. Mr. Pang left to the widow a two stories brick house in the South Side but she [had lost] it because of the failure to meet the payment of the mortgage.
>
> Mr. Pang was immigrated from the Chinese village. She has been here about fifteen years. Her husband died in T.B. and left her in a most regrettable condition. She met Sieu later and he helped her a great deal. Mr. Pang has some cousin[s] in Chicago but [none] of them is willing to take care of the poor widow. She is now married to Sieu and nobody has any opposition toward the new union.
>
> There are four children by her former marriage and a baby son is about one and half year old. . . . The children call Sieu "shok" (younger uncle). In the school they signed their name as follows: Nellie Pang, Arther Pang but Bellie Sieu and Jack Sieu. They are sent also to the Chinese school in Chinatown. During every weekend Sieu usually has the older boy to accompany him to deliver.

They are now living in three rooms apartment in 23rd Place. The housing condition is very poor but the house keeping is much better than any of the Chinese families in Chinatown. . . . To Sieu she expressed her idea as this:

"He is a man I dearly love. I trust he will be able to support me and my children. Oh, he has been so kind to me! When we were in the South side, we had nothing to eat. We were almost starved to death. He was so kind and [brought] us foods everyday and refused to accept a penny. He gave the children this and that each time. You see, [none] of the Pang cousin[s] would do that. My children liked him also. Whenever uncle Sieu came, they cheered with happy laughter.["]

This is Sieu's attitude toward the woman and children: "I don't care how big my responsibility is, I will do my up most to support the kids and her. I need a woman of her kind. I am sick of the street walkers, thru with them! From now on I have my normal marriage life with innocent children and chastity wife. I love the woman and the children. I just can't stand it when I see them in such a sorrowful situation. A widow of four children but [none] of their cousins [could] help her and I [could]."[82]

Unlike Mrs. J. Pang, who had four children and was in serious financial trouble when she became a widow, Mrs. Lin was good-looking and had a lot of money left her by her late husband, although she also had four children from that marriage.

Mrs. Lin's former husband was a tong leader. She was brought over to this country by her former husband. She has been known as the most beautiful house wife among the Chinese immigrants in Chinatown. Her former husband died about eight years ago and he left her four youngsters, two girls and two boys. The first girl has been married to a hybrid boy recently. Mrs. Lin remains to live in Chinatown until she decided to remarry to Lin, her present husband. They are now living in the South side.

Mr. Lin is about five years [older than] the widow. They own a chop suey house in the neighborhood. I was told that the possibility of opening this place was through the widow's promotion. Lin got not a cent but the widow has lot of money that left to her from her former husband. So she gave him the capital to open the restaurant.[83]

These stories of widow remarriage are refreshing in a number of ways. First, the remarriage was beneficial to both parties involved. In the first instance, while the helpless widow found a man who would provide for her and her children, the new husband found a loving, clean, stable, and "normal" family life. In the second instance, the financially better-off widow provided capital to launch a new business, which was possible because of the moral support and manpower provided by her new husband. Both financially and emotionally, the remarriage made a lot of sense. Second, the remarriage of widows offers a stark contrast to the conditions of widows in traditional China, where a widow was expected to remain unmarried to honor her deceased husband and to keep the family wealth within the family. In America, however, rich or poor, a widow was far less restricted by the clan of her deceased husband and freer to follow her own will. Both of the widows just described remarried men of their own choosing and freely and openly displayed their devotion to their new husbands.

Family Lives and Women's Changing Role

WOMEN AS FEMALE HEADS OF FAMILY

Immigration to America changed the role of women in their families. Chinese women became joint heads of their households, a clear promotion from their previous subservient position in China. The traditional and predominant form of the Chinese family was an extended family, in which several generations lived together under the same roof, ruled by the patriarchal familial authority. Once married, a Chinese woman had to serve and please every family member, especially her parents-in-law, in order to conform to the social norms of a filial daughter-in-law, submissive wife, and nurturing mother.[84]

The prevailing family pattern of three or more generations in one household, however, was not transplanted to America, and Chinese immigrant families in America were mostly nuclear ones. Having suffered the pain of leaving familiar surroundings, a month of seasickness, and prolonged detention and interrogation at the American immigration station on Angel Island in San Francisco Bay, Chinese immigrant women, and young wives especially, happily found that they were no longer subject to the authority of their mothers-in-law and that for the first time they were female heads of their families.[85] "It's better to be a woman in America," Helen Hong Wong of San Francisco said. "At least you can work here and rule the family along with your husband. In China it's considered a disgrace for a woman to work and it's the mother-in-law who rules."[86]

In Chicago, most Chinese women lived in nuclear families with husbands and children, running households along with their husbands. For instance, Mrs. J. L. and her husband, owner of a Chinese grocery store in Chinatown, lived in an apartment in Chinatown. She had graduated from a high school in Shanghai and was considered a very educated woman. She stayed at home taking care of their four young children, who were between eight months and six years old in 1930.[87]

Chinese wives in Chicago were also comparatively liberated and exercised more control over their households. Mrs. C. L. came to Chicago in the early 1900s, where her husband kept a Chinese grocery store. Although illiterate, Mrs. C. L. was strong-minded and very much in charge of her family, especially in disciplining the children.[88] Similarly, Lillian Wong was born in China in 1889 and came to Chicago sometime in the 1910s. She was married to Paul Moy, a San Francisco–born Presbyterian minister, eighteen years her senior. She gave birth to eleven children, including ten girls and one boy. While her husband was working in the family laundry, Lillian Wong was the matriarch of her family, who disciplined and provided a loving home for all her children.[89]

The story of Mrs. Chin F. Foin, wife of the famous Chinese business owner in Chicago, however, provides the most compelling example. She was born Yoklund Wong in 1889 into a Chinese immigrant family on Commercial Street in San Francisco. Her father, Duck Wong, came from Xinning (later called Taishan) County, Guangdong, China, and worked in Chinatown as a tailor. As Chinese children were banned from American schools, Yoklund attended the Christian mission school, where she learned some English but had little opportunity to use it either in her Chinese family or in American society, as respectable Chinese women were supposed to remain in the confines of their homes. In 1904, when she was fourteen, her father arranged her marriage to a fellow villager nearly twice her age—Chin F. Foin, who by then had been in Chicago for almost a decade and had established himself as a prominent Chinese businessman there (see Chapter 3). Chin F. Foin married once in China but the marriage ended with the death of his first wife, who left him two children, a daughter of seven and a son of six. The wedding was held on Sacramento Street in San Francisco according to Chinese custom, and then the newly-weds spent their honeymoon at the Grand Pacific

Hotel in Chicago for over a month, in accordance with Western practices. In the following year, 1905, Yoklund bore her husband a daughter named Mee Chin, and in 1907 a boy. The celebration of the boy's one-month birthday and christening was an exciting event in Chinatown. Held on November 6, 1907, at Chin F. Foin's King Yen Lo, the most elaborate Chinese restaurant in town, it was attended by Chicago's prominent professionals, business-men, and politicians, as well as the acting Chinese minister in Washington, Ju Gee Ti, who was given the honor of naming the baby boy. Ju Gee Ti first gave the boy a Chinese name, "Chungow," and then "Theodore Roosevelt," after Chin asked him to choose another one. Chin decided on the name "Theodore Chungow Chin," reflecting his conscious adoption of the host culture. Yoklund and Chin F. Foin led a Westernized life, different from most of the early Chinese immigrants. King Yen Lo was the first Chinese restau-rant in Chicago catering to a white, upper-class clientele. Chin hired an Irish woman, Molly O'Farrell, to act as his business manager while he was socializ-ing with the thriving Chicago business community. As his business grew, the Chins and their two children moved away from Chinatown and into a trendy middle-class white neighborhood on South Calumet Avenue. Yoklund wore modern Western clothing and sent her children to American schools.[90]

While Chin F. Foin was expanding his businesses, Yoklund took excellent care of the domestic front as the female head of the big family. In addition to her own six children, she also looked after her two sisters and two broth-ers from California and her husband's daughter and brothers from China. She also took in some Chinese students as boarders and hosted numerous parties for the Chinese students who worked in the family restaurant.[91]

Yoklund showed great courage and resilience after her husband's sudden and tragic death in 1924, when he fell down an elevator shaft in his restaurant and consequently died of a brain concussion. The family tragedy, compounded by the Great Depression, resulted in the loss of much of Chin F. Foin's fortune in bank foreclosures. To cope with this difficult situation, Yoklund sent two more of her children to China (her eldest son, Theodore, had already been sent to China in 1921 at the age of fourteen to be educated there) and moved to a smaller house at 4913 South Grand Boulevard (presently Martin Luther King Jr. Drive). To support her remaining children in Chicago, she worked as a tailor in a Jewish upholstery shop on the South Side. She put all her children through college and continued to take care of her grandchildren. She lived an independent life until her death in 1986 at the age of ninety-seven.[92]

WOMEN AS CO-PROVIDERS

Chinese immigrant women also found that in America they must become providers for their families. Throughout Chinese history, most Chinese women worked at home weaving in northern China or toiled in the fields in southern China to supplement family income. But Chinese immigrant women's participation in family economic activities or wage-earning work were more essential, in fact indispensable, for the survival of their families in the United States.[93]

In urban communities, as wives of laundrymen, restaurant owners, grocers, cooks, and laborers, the majority of married Chinese women worked side by side with their husbands, in addition to performing their daily household duties. During the late nineteenth and early twentieth centuries, the laundry business was one of the main occupations of the Chinese in the United States. The Chinese laundry shop was not merely a place of work but a place for sleeping and cooking as well.[94] The life of a laundryman's wife was not easier than that of her husband. Her home was in the back of the laundry, where she slept, cooked, and tended her children. The living quarters were humid and dark in all seasons. When she was not busy with her domestic chores, she was expected to help with the laundry work. Her daily life was characterized by long hours, drudgery, and intense loneliness. The only people she saw were customers who brought in their parcels and reclaimed them later. The wives of laundrymen were often worn out from hard work, suffering physical weariness and emotional stress.[95]

Restaurants were likewise one of the main businesses for the Chinese in the United States. In the 1890s, Chinese restaurants sprang up in many parts of the country.[96] Most small Chinese restaurants were run as husband-wife businesses; the husband served as cook and dishwasher in the kitchen, while the wife worked as waitress and cashier in the front. Some Chinese American women even became successful proprietors despite the harsh environment.[97]

The grocery business ranked a distant third among occupations for Chinese immigrants before the 1940s. While the larger firms seem to have pooled their capital and manpower, with each member of the firm having well-defined responsibilities and receiving a regular salary somewhere between $45 and $75, many smaller Chinese stores were run as family businesses, with unpaid family members meeting the demand for requisite labor.[98] The wives of grocers worked alongside their husbands, packing, stocking, and selling goods. For example, Y. L. operated a tin store in Chicago in the 1930s, selling inexpensive merchandise and Chinese dry goods; his wife, though the mother of seven children, worked daily in the store doing whatever was needed.[99]

Mansie (Chung) O'Young provided an inspirational example at the time when few women entered the male-dominated business world. Mansie Chung was born in Oakland, California, in 1901. Her father, who operated an insurance business in Oakland, sent his daughter to the University of California at Berkeley, making her one of the first Asian American women graduates of that university. In 1927, Mansie Chung came to Chicago with her father, who was planning to open a branch office of the Sun Life Assurance Company in the city. Mansie worked closely with Moy Dong Hoy, second of the three Moy brothers. In the following year, she married Henry O'Young, a Chinese businessman selling laundry supplies, at the Fourth Presbyterian Church, and was thereafter known as Mansie O'Young. The couple jointly owned a number of businesses, including a branch office of the Sun Life Assurance Company of Canada in the 1920s and the Hong Kong Noodle Company. While her husband acted as head of the businesses, she managed the payroll. Being American-educated and ambitious, however, Mansie was also a licensed life insurance underwriter and was responsible for numerous life insurance policies purchased by Chinese merchants in Chicago. Mansie O'Young quickly became known for her business abilities, superior to those of her husband, and apparently thrived on the "wheeling and dealing" common to the city's business and political circles.[100]

In this way, Chinese immigrant women played a new role as co-providers for their families, though they were not necessarily making 50 percent of the family income. For most Chinese immigrant women, the focus of their lives was survival through hard work, work—both wage earning and non–wage earning—that was vital for their family's survival in a strange land. As historian Roger Daniels has observed, the fact that many married Chinese women worked "illustrates an important and often unnoticed factor in Asian American economic success: that is, the contribution made by Asian American married women at a time most married women in this country were not in the labor force."[101]

WOMEN AS JOINT DECISION MAKERS

These new roles reinforced Chinese women's position in families and they began to share decision making with their husbands. When working jointly with their spouses, immigrant women generally had more input in family affairs and decision making, as was the case with Irish immigrant women. Historians have found that Irish immigrant men generally experienced a decline in status and power within their families as a result of migration, which pushed women into more authoritative roles than they had experienced in Ireland. The comparatively open range of economic options for many young Irish women made them more influential in their families and communities.[102]

Similarly, when Chinese immigrants came to the New World, they faced a strange and hostile environment, in which they were discriminated against and excluded from the mainstream labor market. Consequently they had to work in trades that white laborers were unwilling to embrace, such as hand laundries, restaurants, and grocery stores, or work as common laborers or farmhands. The necessity of survival required all Chinese family members, wives in particular, to participate in productive activities. The majority of early Chinese immigrant women, as discussed earlier, had to raise their families and help with their husbands' businesses. Moreover, Chinese immigrant families in urban areas often lived in the back of their family businesses. Many small Chinese entrepreneurs had converted the rear part of their stores into family quarters.[103] The overlapping of family life and work life made a wife's involvement in the family business inevitable. At the same time, the expansion of the female sphere enhanced Chinese immigrant women's self-esteem and self-confidence, and they consequently became more comfortable in sharing family decision making with their husbands.

Living Conditions

Most Chinese families in Chicago lived in Chinatown prior to the 1940s, consistent with the distribution of the Chinese population in Chicago. In 1890 almost all Chinese in Chicago lived in the Loop area, particularly around South Clark Street. Of the 567 Chinese recorded by the 1890 census, 142, or 25 percent, lived along South Clark from Van Buren to Harrison Street.[104] In 1934, 1,143 Chinese lived in the Armour Square area on both sides of Cermak Road, constituting 41 percent of the 2,757 Chinese residing in the city around 1930.[105] Within the Chinese population in Chicago, there were more than 150 families, most living in Chinatown.[106]

Piecing together information from immigrant testimonies, Paul C. P. Siu's fieldwork, interviews with Chinatown residents, and the existing scholarship, one can obtain a detailed picture of the living conditions in Chinatown. In the late nineteenth and early twentieth centuries, most families who were relatively well off lived in a flat above a Chinese business. For instance, the wealthy merchant Hong Sling's family lived at 324 South Clark Street, on the fourth floor over Hong Fong Lo restaurant, where Hong Sling owned a large share of the business and served as manager.[107] Another well-to-do merchant, M. H., owner of a chop suey house, had a building in the heart of Chinatown in the 1930s. The first floor was rented to a relative who ran a Chinese drugstore, the second floor to a kinship group as its meeting hall, and M. H.'s family occupied the third floor. The house was decorated with pictures of their ancestors and Chinese furniture.[108] Similarly, T. Tom opened a noodle factory in Chinatown; when he brought his wife from China, they made the upper floor of the factory their home.[109] Generally, an "expensive" apartment in Chinatown would cost $50 per month for rent in 1930.[110]

While the well-to-do merchant families lived in an upper-floor apartment over the business, small store owners made their home in the rear of their stores, where living conditions were poor and crowded. Mr. Y. L. and his wife both came from Sam Yap, Canton, China, and stayed on the West Coast for a while before coming to Chicago. Mr. Y. L. was the only Chinese who established a tin store in Chinatown, selling not only items typical of five-and-dime stores but also Chinese dry goods. The store was located in the heart of Chinatown and business was good enough to support the family in the 1930s. Since the store did not have an upper floor, the family lived in the rear. There were two rooms, "dark and dirty," with only one bed in each room, for the nine-member family that included seven children. A sofa-bed also served as an extra bed at night.[111]

Many Chinese residents also rented basement apartments.[112] Most buildings in Chinatown were old, without steam heat or hot running water.[113] Many chop suey house owners rented apartments near their restaurants, which were often located outside of Chinatown. For instance, T. Wing owned a chop suey house on 63rd Street and rented an apartment for his family at 6000 Champlain Avenue; later he invited his cousin and his wife to live in an adjoining apartment in the same building in the 1910s.[114]

Since living conditions in Chinatown were far from ideal, more Americanized Chinese would rent apartments or purchase homes outside of Chinatown. Chop suey house owner Frank Chan, for example, was married to a young American-born Chinese woman from the West Coast; instead of living in Chinatown, the couple rented a small apartment on South Michigan Avenue.[115] C. Ham married a Polish woman who worked in his chop suey house; they bought their own home outside of Old Chinatown in the South Clark Street area.[116]

Most families in Chinatown were large, with between four and nine children. Although there were some extended families, most were nuclear ones.[117] Many children went to St. Therese Chinese Catholic School, a private school in Chinatown, or the nearby American public schools. Teenagers often worked as newspaper deliverers or helpers in chop suey houses to supplement family income.[118] The older girls in a large family often took care of their younger siblings, as illustrated by Celia's family history. Celia was born in Chicago in 1933. Her family included her father, a laundry keeper, her mother, and eleven children, and they lived on 22nd Place in Chinatown. While her father was busy working in the family laundry and her mother was occupied with the household chores, her elder sister took care of the children.[119]

Overall, about four-fifths of the Chinese lived in rented houses or apartments. To reduce the cost of rental, two or more families often shared a single house or even the same apartment. Many families were also compelled to take in boarders to offset the cost of living.[120] Consequently, congestion and overcrowding became a problem in the Chinese community, although it was not uncommon in other ethnic neighborhoods of the city as well. The Chinese who lived on 22nd Street or in other quarters of the city generally did not enjoy the advantages and opportunities that the city offered. A lack of sewage facilities, absence of paving, and unkempt streets were characteristic of their living environment.[121]

Recreation and Socialization

Gambling has been described both in Paul C. P. Siu's study and in the media as the primary recreational activity of Chinese social life in Chicago. After a week of toiling in laundries, Chinese laborers longed for some relaxation. Many gathered to gamble until they had lost all the money they carried with them.

To Chinese bachelors, Chinatown was not a place of sin and vice but of good food, comfort, enjoyment, and relaxation. Across the city, living behind or in the back of their laundries, Chinese laundrymen would close their shops on Sunday afternoons and hurry to Chinatown for recreation. If the weather was good, many would sit on the benches outside the shops in Chinatown sunning themselves and socializing with one another. After being confined to the dim, damp laundries for a week, they were now temporarily free from the drudgery. They could enjoy the warm breeze, catch up on the news, share some laughter with clansmen, and watch Chinese children play on the street.

The Chinese grocery stores in the Chinatown on South Clark Street before 1912 and in the Chinatown on 22nd Wentworth Avenue after 1912 served as the main venues for recreation and socialization. Among them, the Moy brothers' Hip Lung Yee Kee at 323 South Clark Street, Quang Yuen Company at 321 South Clark Street, and Sing Lung at 309 South Clark Street were the centers of Chinese society in the late nineteenth and early twentieth centuries.[122] On Sundays, the only day the Chinese laundrymen closed their stores, the Chinese residents would congregate in the grocery stores in Chinatown. There they would pick up their weekly food supplies and chitchat with kinsmen and friends to catch up on the latest news about their families and relatives in China. Oftentimes, personal loans between kinsmen and friends would take place during the socialization at these stores.[123]

Many other social activities also took place on Sundays. In the last decades of the nineteenth century, the Chinese in Chicago were very likely to be involved in their clan associations. Like the Chinese on the West Coast, the Chinese in Chicago mostly came from Canton and its adjacent counties, known as Sam Yap (San Yi, "three counties") and Sze Yap (Si Yi, "four counties"). Among the Chinese in Chicago, those who bore the surnames Moy, Lee, Chin, and Yuan from villages in Taishan were predominant, and they set up surname associations for mutual aid and protection. These associations usually rented a flat with a kitchen in an apartment building in Chinatown for clan business meetings and social gatherings. On Sundays, clansmen would bring Chinese ingredients to the associations and use the kitchen facilities there to cook special Chinese dishes that they did not have the time and means to prepare during the busy workweek. Others visited Chinese restaurants to eat authentic Chinese dishes and chat with their clansmen about their families and relatives in China.

Chinatown also served as a substitute for family life in China. Isolated by cultural prejudice, the language barrier, and the drudgery of daily work, Chinese laborers found ethnic solidarity in Chinatown. They came to Chinatown every Sunday, where they were called "uncle" by Chinese children and "cousin" by clansmen, feeling as if they were going home.

Americanization

While preserving Chinese traditions and exploiting the cultural exoticism of Chinatown, the Chinese in Chicago had undergone a profound process of Americanization at the turn of the nineteenth and twentieth centuries. In the first decades of the twentieth century, youth from the better-off Chinese American families were completely in sync with American popular culture. In the 1920s, they wore the Norfolk jackets that were popular for formal occasions and motoring trousers and showed off their newly purchased automobiles. Influenced by the popular American media, which often featured parties on cruise ships, Chinese youth also partied on boats on Lake Michigan. Motion pictures featuring gangsters in the 1920s also fascinated the young Chinese. Toy Chow, for example, a law-abiding vegetable farmer with a lively sense of humor, and a friend posed as gangsters in a photograph, clearly influenced by popular motion pictures of the period.[124]

The children of the Moy brothers were especially Americanized. Fook Chueng, the eldest son of Moy Dong Hoy, appeared every inch the fashionable American boy in his studio-taken photograph in the 1910s, clad in an expensive Western-style jacket and with an eye-catching gold chain indicating a pocketed gold watch. Reputed to be a studious boy, he did well in his public school.[125]

Lillie Moy, the oldest daughter of Moy Dong Chow, was born on February 7, 1898, in Chicago but returned to China with her mother in 1908 when she was ten for an education there, as did many of the American-born Chinese children. She returned to Chicago in 1921 and in the early 1920s married Yusheng Wong, a visiting Chinese student in Chicago. Like her siblings, she received a college degree from the University of Illinois, Chicago. Aspiring to build a career in China, Lillie Moy applied for a return certificate after her graduation from college in 1924, with the intention of working at Nankai University, in Tianjin. Before her departure in early 1925, her photograph was taken with her aging father, Moy Dong Chow, who was eighty years old then but apparently still in good health; he died two years later. Lillie Moy and her husband resettled in China, where her husband attained a high position in government. Lillie Moy was issued a return certificate by the Office of the Inspector in Charge [of Immigration], but she never returned to Chicago, as none of her immediate family members were living in the city.[126]

Lorrain Moy is the daughter of Moy Dong Yee, the youngest of the three Moy brothers. Her recollection of life in early Chinatown sheds light on the experiences of second-generation Chinese Americans of the time. While Lorrain Moy's life might have been relatively privileged, as daughter of a prominent Chinese merchant and community leader, her experiences growing up nevertheless reveal the changing socioeconomic climate for American-born Chinese youth.

> My father's name is Moy Dong Yee and my mother's name is Moy Look Shee. They were both born in Toisan, Kwangtung, China. My father and his two brothers, Moy Dong Hoy and Moy Dong Jui, started Hip Lung Importing and Exporting business located at 2243 S. Wentworth Avenue in 1923. . . .
>
> I was born in Chicago on October 6, 1924. My family consisted of six boys and three girls. We lived at 231 W. Cermak Road from 1924 to 1931. We move to 2243 S. Wentworth Avenue from 1932 to 1949. Both homes had three bedrooms, an old-fashioned bathtub with legs and even hot water.
>
> I attended Haines School in 1930, and graduated from Harrison High School in 1943. I went to the Metropolitan Business School for one year where I developed my shorthand and office skills.
>
> I had quite a few childhood memories growing up in Chinatown. I attended the Chinese Women's Club with my mother at the age of nine or ten. I became the youngest member and I am the sole surviving charter member of the organization. I enjoyed embroidery and crafts from Miss Snape at the Chinese Christian Union Church. I was a drum majorette for the Chinese Boys' Alliance Drum and Bugle Corps.[127]

Like the children of the Chinese elite, most Chinese American girls in Chicago were following the popular American trends as early as the 1920s. Young Chinese American women wore flapper outfits in public—cloth hats and short skirts—like their American peers at the time and went on outings to the beach at Lake Michigan with other young Chinese American men and women. As raccoon-fur coats were fashionable among young people in the 1920s, many Chinese American girls donned fur coats in winter against the chill of Chicago. Influenced by popular teenage horse novels such as *Black Beauty*, Chinese American girls rode horses for recreation.[128] At Chinese weddings, brides and bridesmaids alike wore white dresses, even though the color white was considered unlucky and people dressed in white at funerals in China.[129]

In the 1920s, the Boy Scouts were everywhere in North America and Britain. Chinese Chicagoans, no less progressive than their counterparts in other places, organized their own Boy Scout troops. A group of young boys from Chinatown proudly posed in their uniforms in the 1920s.[130] Girls likewise joined the Girl Scouts to learn American life skills, make new friends, and have fun. The Girl Scout leaders, often Chinese Christian women, helped instill American culture, albeit embedded in Christian beliefs and practices, in the Chinese girls.[131]

Like their white counterparts, Chinese youth also engaged in popular sports of the time. The Chinese YMCA spearheaded the organized sports activities in Chinatown, organizing a basketball team known as the "Cantonese Owls" in the 1920s, for example. The team practiced every Sunday at Harding Square and traveled all across the country, primarily playing other Chinese American teams but occasionally Euro-American teams as well. The team earned distinction in 1926 as champions of the Midwest Conference.[132]

Conclusion

Marriage patterns among the Chinese transnational community in Chicago reveal the practicality and adaptability of the Chinese in coping with the difficult realities of immigration. The transnational split marriage constituted a practical compromise devised to deal with the marital separation resulting from immigration, in which a concubine, arranged for by the parents or first wife of an immigrant with the specific purpose of taking care of his physical needs while abroad, and the first wife, remaining in the home village to perform the obligations of filial piety on behalf of her husband, jointly fulfilled the biological, socioeconomic, and emotional duties expected of a traditional wife by Chinese society. Alternatively, variations on the American urban marriage—love unions, interracial marriage, and widow remarriage—demonstrate the inevitable transformation of the more traditional form of marriage, which as an institution tends to adjust to the prevailing socioeconomic and cultural environment.

In a new environment, Chinese immigrant women experienced changing roles in their lives as female family heads, co-providers, and joint decision makers. The second-generation Chinese American youth were profoundly Americanized, in values as well as in appearance, relishing a lifestyle akin to that of their white counterparts.

FIVE

Bridging the Two Worlds

Community Organizations, 1870s–1945

> "On Leong" means peaceful. If they have problems and don't know
> what to do or if there is a dispute about payment of debt, they go to
> one of the two co-presidents instead of going to a lawyer. The men
> at the meetings hear the story—like a jury. They consult and the co-
> presidents hand down a decision. You know, we Chinese like to keep
> our problems within our community and solve them ourselves.
>
> —Annie Leong, 1962

Self-government was a prominent feature of the early overseas Chinese
communities when they received little protection from either the homeland government or the host country authorities. The Chinese community in Chicago was no exception. The On Leong Association emerged as
an effective self-governing body in Chicago Chinatown at the beginning
of the twentieth century and remained the most powerful community organization. The leadership positions of the community organizations had
been monopolized by the elite members of the community—the Chinese
merchants—a pattern that characterized most of the overseas Chinese communities, as the merchants were more educated than the generally illiterate Chinese laborers. While On Leong maintained its dominance in the
community well into the 1960s, more inclusive community organizations
were also established in the first decades of the twentieth century, providing
services to a broader community base and posing challenges to On Leong.

Transplanting Chinese Social Structure

The earlier community organizations were likely conceived and constructed
according to ideals and practices transplanted from the homeland, as evi-

denced in On Leong, the Chinese Consolidated Benevolent Association (CCBA), and the various family associations. On Leong inherited a tradition of maintaining peace and order from the anti-Manchu secret societies in Qing China, which arose during the time when the Manchu as an ethnic minority ruled a population fifty times its size largely through coercion and consequently aroused great anti-Qing opposition among the Han Chinese. Meanwhile, the CCBA and the family associations were incarnations of the traditional Chinese regional associations and clan associations, which had long traditions and deep roots in South China.

ON LEONG: A SELF-DEFENSE MECHANISM

The national On Leong Association in America was in existence by the 1890s and had branch associations in the eastern and later in the midwestern states.[1] With support and guidance from the national On Leong Association, the Chinese in Chicago established an On Leong Association in 1905.[2] The On Leong Association operated under the leadership of a branch of the Moy family and was initially made up of the extended Moy, Lee, and Chin families.[3]

The term "On Leong" is the Cantonese version of "An Liang," derived from the Chinese aphorism "Chu Bao An Liang," meaning "eliminating despots and bringing peace to people." Generations of Chinese peasant rebels and secret societies had employed this slogan in challenging the established order and promulgating their own political agendas. In a foreign land and surrounded by an unfamiliar culture, merchants, the elite class of Chinese immigrants, felt the need and obligation to establish a social organization to protect their interests and assist newcomers from China. As a vulnerable minority group, Chinese immigrants were unable to "Chu Bao," or eliminate, those who excluded them legally or discriminated against them socially. The best they could do was to maintain peace and social order within their own communities through mutual aid and self-government. Hence, adopting only the term "On Leong," the On Leong Merchants and Laborers Association was formed as a self-reliant, quasi-legal, and social organization of Chinese immigrants.

The On Leong Association was popularly known as the On Leong Tong. The word *tong* in Chinese literally means "hall" and has no implication of crime or secrecy. In China, the term was often used to refer to a school, a church, a district association, or an herbal drugstore.[4] In America, Chinese community organizations using "tong" as part of their names included those providing mutual aid to their members as well as those that were engaged primarily in criminal activities. All of these organizations, however, have been perceived as being secret societies allegedly associated with crime, particularly the tong wars.

Scholars have tried to clarify the confusion on the part of the general public. In 1935 sociologist C. N. Reynolds stated that Chinese organizations or tongs in America had their roots in secret societies in China. He differentiated other Chinese community organizations such as the Six Companies (discussed later) and trade or craft organizations from the fighting tongs. He noted that many tongs in America had modified their criminal activities and developed benevolent-protective functions.[5]

Several decades later, Yung-Deh Richard Chu (1973) systematically explored the origins, structures, functions, and historical development of various Chinese secret societies in America. According to Chu, three types of Chinese social organizations developed in America. The district associations emerged to assist new immigrants by providing free lodging, food, and employment services. Soon the clan associations were also formed, to provide services to those lacking the support of the district associations. Meanwhile, as the district associations grew, different clan associations in the same district began to compete with each other for hegemony. As a result, small clans began to coordinate their efforts secretly in order to avoid the control of bigger clans, and to use violence as a means of forcing larger clans to act reasonably. When the environment in America turned extremely hostile with passage of the Chinese Exclusion Act of 1882, the third type of organization, secret societies, became very active and widespread. Chu concluded that "the tongs have both their vices and positive aspects, especially for the peculiar situation of the Chinese immigrants. They cannot be simply regarded as the Chinese version of Mafia existing merely for pursuing organized crimes."[6]

A more recent study by sociologist Kuo-lin Chen (1995) classifies the Chinese criminal organizations alleged by American law enforcement agencies into the following categories: triads, tongs, gangs, heroin smugglers, and smugglers of illegal immigrants. Based on sworn brotherhood (a typical organizational structure of secret societies in which members are bound by uttering an oath of brotherhood), the tongs in America today include Chih Kung (or Gee Kung, Zhigong), On Leong (Anliang), Hip Sing (Xiesheng),

Tung On (Tongan), Fukien (Fujian) American, Hop Sing (Hesheng), Bing Kung (Binggong), Suey Sing (Cuisheng), and Ying On (Yingduan).[7]

Among the tongs, Chih Kung, On Leong, and Hip Sing are the most influential. Chih Kung, the oldest of all, was formed in 1850 in Hawaii, then extended to British Columbia in the late 1850s, and finally established in San Francisco in 1863.[8] Some members of Chih Kung established On Leong in 1894. Its headquarters were moved to New York a few years later and have remained there ever since.[9]

Although scholars have categorized On Leong as one of the secret societies and characterized such societies as engaging in both beneficial services and criminal activities, On Leong in many ways is more like the Chinese Six Companies. Most Chinese immigrant communities in America were controlled by the Chinese Six Companies up until the civil rights movement in the 1960s. The Chinese Six Companies were fraternal organizations of Chinese immigrants in the United States based on lineage and geographical origins, including the Kong Chow Company (or Gangzhou Huiguan), Sam Yup Company (or Sanyi Huiguan), Yeoung Wo Company (or Yanghe Huiguan), Yan Wo Company (or Renhe Huiguan), Ning Yung Company (or Ningyang Huiguan), and Hop Wo Company (or Hehe Huiguan). They were founded between 1851 and 1862 on the West Coast. In 1882, to react collectively to the harsh treatment of Chinese immigrants by government institutions and the public, these six companies formed a national umbrella organization, the Chinese Consolidated Benevolent Association (CCBA or Zhonghua Huiguan), commonly known to Americans as the Chinese Six Companies.[10]

Unlike the Chinese on the West Coast, Chinese in the Midwest were dominated by the On Leong Merchants and Laborers Association.[11] In 1919, the national On Leong Association underwent two major changes. First, it expanded its membership to include not only merchants but also common laborers. Second, On Leong changed its official name to "On Leong Merchants and Laborers Association." Unlike the CCBA, On Leong was a trade or professional organization; it sought to promote and protect Chinese businesses in the United States regardless of the lineage and geographical origins of its members.

Despite the difference in form of the organizations, On Leong's social functions largely resembled those of the Chinese Six Companies. First of all, On Leong was the unofficial local government of Chinese immigrants in America. It served as the legislative, judicial, and administrative authority within the Chinese community. To avoid competition among Chinese entrepreneurs, On Leong dictated the "one mile one laundry" (later "one mile one restaurant") rule, allowing only one Chinese laundry to operate within a radius of one mile. A similar regulation was established by the Chinese laundry associations in San Francisco and Virginia City in the 1860s. Violators of this regulation were often penalized. Initially they would be issued a warning by On Leong for the offense. Timid offenders would close their shops voluntarily at this point. Those who refused to obey the warning would then be forced to close their business by mysterious tragedies such as the burning of the business premises or the murder of family members.[12] Such measures of law enforcement, though effective, bore a strong resemblance to the cruel and secretive means employed by the secret societies and thus contributed greatly to the stereotypical image of On Leong as a criminal gang. More often, however, On Leong acted as a Chinese court on American soil, using the Chinese legal code or customary laws to convict criminals or wrongdoers in cases presented at its board meetings.[13] The judicial function of On Leong was partly derived from the tradition of Chinese secret societies' taking the law into their own hands, but it was also and more a reaction to their experiences as immigrants in America. When American law enforcement agencies deliberately ignored or delayed prosecuting crimes of murder against Chinese, On Leong decided to handle them within the Chinese community by enforcing Chinese law.[14] The president of On Leong, elected every year by its members, was regarded by the American government and the public as the mayor of Chinatown, particularly for his judicial power. Similarly, the Chinese Six Companies arbitrated disputes among their members and represented Chinese immigrants in dealings with American authorities.[15]

In the second place, On Leong was the most powerful economic force within the Chinese community. The association owned properties that earned considerable income. The presidents of On Leong were generally prominent and successful local entrepreneurs who often donated large sums of money to the association, while the rank and file consisted of small merchants and common laborers. Its economic power was transnational and went well beyond Chicago. Both On Leong and the CCBA in Chicago made arrangements with local American banks to help Chinese immigrants who had difficulty with the English-speaking bank clerks transfer money back to Hong Kong and China.[16]

On Leong's economic control over its members, however, was not absolute. In contrast, the Chinese Six Companies wielded almost complete control over the socioeconomic lives of Chinese immigrants. The Chinese Six Companies mandated that Chinese immigrants register with them upon landing and pay fees and debts before departure for China.[17]

In the third place, On Leong provided useful social services to its members and their families. On Leong assumed that newcomers needed to be guided and helped from the moment they stepped off the train. One of the most valuable services offered by On Leong was translation aid. Since most new Chinese immigrants were unable to speak English, they faced tremendous difficulties and frustrations in their first years in America. On Leong would hire a group of Chinese youths who were able to speak both Chinese and English as interpreters and dispatch them to the train station to meet the new immigrants, bring them to their apartments, help them settle in, and assist them in finding jobs.[18] On Leong helped many new immigrants to get licenses and start laundries in Chicago. It sponsored an after-school Chinese language school in Chicago. On Leong was also a social center for Chinese immigrants, and its headquarters were often used by members at no charge for special events such as weddings, celebrations of newborn babies, funerals, and other social gatherings.[19] The Chinese Six Companies also provided various services to the communities, ranging from offering temporary lodging to newcomers to funding the needy and establishing Chinese language schools.[20]

In the fourth place, On Leong fulfilled the spiritual needs of Chinese immigrants. It regarded performing the burial ceremony for its members as a sacred task.[21] Many Chinese immigrants came to America with the intention to work hard, save as much money as possible, and eventually return to their home village to rejoin their family. Some did return to China with savings after years of "toiling on the gold mountain." Many others, however, met sudden death through violence or became ill and died in America. Their bodies were buried temporarily in local cemeteries awaiting an opportunity to be transported to their homeland. On Leong faithfully performed the duty of sending the bones of deceased members to China.

Like most traditional Chinese organizations, On Leong also held superstitious beliefs and preserved rituals in accordance with them. Members of On Leong depended on Chinese gods for good fortune and protection. The meeting hall of On Leong's headquarters contained an altar with a shrine to

Guan Gong, a Chinese god believed to be a protector of merchants. When On Leong's board members gathered for their monthly business meeting, they would light incense and bow to Guan Gong before conducting the meeting. During the Chinese New Year celebration, the most important ceremony was paying homage to Guan Gong. Members would donate from two to five dollars to cover the cost of this ceremony. The proceeds also served as a source of funds for On Leong, together with the annual membership fee of twenty-five dollars.[22]

Like the Chinese Six Companies, On Leong was a fraternal organization that excluded Chinese immigrant women. Although wives of members were occasionally allowed to attend meetings, women seldom participated in decision making. On Leong provided services to Chinese businessmen and their families, however, that consequently benefited Chinese women. On Leong also opened its meeting facilities to other community organizations, including those for women; for instance, On Leong provided a meeting place for the Women's Association established in the 1930s.[23]

Although On Leong did not exercise complete and deliberate control over its members, as did the CCBA, it was a self-contained community structure that was not intended to reach out and blend into the larger society. This mentality of self-containment was partly a product of the socioeconomic background of the Chinese immigrants and partly of the socioeconomic conditions of American society. Before World War II, most Chinese immigrants came from rural and impoverished areas in China and spoke very limited English at best. The lack of an understanding of American systems due to a lack of education and language ability naturally nourished the mentality of self-containment; the Chinese immigrants clung to each other for comfort and security. At the same time, the Chinese immigrants were legally excluded and persecuted by immigration authorities and law enforcement agencies, economically segregated from the mainstream labor market, and socially isolated from the majority of the population. The hostile climate against Chinese immigrants in America effectively compelled them to develop forms of mutual aid and collective protection for the sake of survival.

Meanwhile, as many writers have suggested, the "mayors of Chinatown," as business leaders, had a vested interest in keeping the community isolated and dependent on its internal socioeconomic structures.[24] An isolated community guaranteed a steady pool of laborers and a profitable market. But the self-contained nature of On Leong in Chicago is due more to cultural and psychological factors. The dominance of the Chinese business class over Chinese immigrants was a pronounced feature of overseas Chinese societies in America and in other parts of the world. This pattern of social control was a departure from the social structure in traditional China, where the elite social class of gentry-scholars dominated every level of the governing machine and merchants were despised as social parasites who would corrupt government and society. Secure in their wealth and power, Chinese gentry-scholars had little incentive to emigrate. The absence of gentry-scholars among Chinese immigrants thus gave Chinese merchants, who were better educated and more sophisticated than common laborers, the opportunity to emerge as leaders of the immigrant communities. The more self-contained a Chinese immigrant community was, the more indispensable the Chinese business leaders were. Undoubtedly these Chinese business leaders enjoyed an elite status and endeavored to maintain the established order in the community.

In performing its legal, economic, social, and spiritual functions, On Leong effectively eased the initial cultural shock and difficulties faced by many newcomers and successfully maintained peace and order in the community. Thus it was instrumental in the successful building of community by the Chinese in Chicago.

THE DOMINANCE OF ON LEONG

Unlike its counterpart in St. Louis, which enjoyed absolute dominance up until the 1970s, the On Leong Tong in Chicago had to compete with its rival tong, Hip Sing, from the very beginning.[25] The Hip Sing Tong was established in the 1870s in San Francisco by a scholar who had lost his business. It soon developed a reputation for aggressive expansion, tight organization, and its readiness to accept Christians.[26] Scholars have observed that, although On Leong and Hip Sing were similar in their goals and forms of organization, a popular distinction between the two can validly be drawn: Hip Sing was viewed as a working man's organization, while On Leong largely represented the Chinese merchant class.[27]

The Hip Sing Tong in Chicago was founded in 1900. The rivalry between Hip Sing and On Leong in Chicago began as a conflict between the Chins and the Moys. As related in Chapter 3, in the late nineteenth century

Chin F. Foin emerged as a prominent Chinese restaurateur, at the same time as the Moy brothers' Hip Lung grocery store was the center of the Chinese community. In addition to the grocery business, the Moys also controlled most of the gambling houses in Chinatown. The possible lineage connection between the New York On Leong founder, Moy Dong Yue, and the three Moy brothers in Chicago made it natural for the Moy brothers to be affiliated with On Leong. Meanwhile, Hip Sing in Portland, Oregon, had put a price on the head of Charlie Kee, an important member of the Moys' circle, in 1899.

By 1907, the conflict between the Chins and the Moys focused on the control of gambling. The conflict reached a climax with the murder of Chin Wai, a Chin clansman, in October 1907. On the evening of October 16, Chin Wai was shot and mortally wounded near the corner of South Clark and Van Buren. Police on duty in the neighborhood heard the gunshots, then chased and arrested Harry Lee, a Chinese laundryman from 43rd Street, as he was going to hide on the Hip Lung Company premises.[28] The murder was followed by an intense legal battle between the Moys and the Chins, each side having arranged for the best legal assistance they could afford. The Chins immediately accused Moy Dong Chow and his brother Moy Dong Hoy of having hired Harry Lee to commit the murder. Chin's lawyers accused Moy Dong Chow of having attempted to "form a Chinese gambling trust with himself at the head, and when he met opposition, instead of resorting to underselling, secret agreements, and rebating, he simply decided to kill off a few of the independents as an object lesson."[29]

The Moys' legal team, led by Robert E. Cantwell, a lawyer with a reputation for salvaging hopeless cases, presented as witnesses John Moseland and H. H. Stridiron, who claimed to have seen the murder and testified that the murderer was someone other than the three accused men. Meanwhile, Frank Moy, the son of Moy Dong Chow, painted Chin Wai as "a known highbinder [who] belonged to the Boston branch of the society."[30] On June 17, 1908, the jury acquitted the Moy brothers and Harry Lee. The Hip Lung trial, as it was known at the time, showcased the invincibility of the Moys, who had shrewdly mastered the winning strategy of the elite in any society when in legal trouble—employment of the best lawyers to defend their case. This strategy saved Moy Dong Chew and his brother from a murder conviction and helped bring about the unquestioned dominance of On Leong in the Chinese community in Chicago after 1912, as was acknowledged by both the Chinese residents and the mainstream press.[31]

The Moys not only always hired the best lawyers but they were also skillful at building a support network and good rapport with the local authorities. The Moys' connections with well-known, powerful men in the area included Edward F. Dunne, a former mayor and future governor of Illinois; Lyman Gage, a Chicago banker, upper-class reformer, and former secretary of the treasury; and the aforementioned H. H. Stridiron, a prominent politician.[32] From the beginning of their taking up residence in Chicago, the Moy brothers were careful and deliberate in courting and maintaining congenial relationships with local authorities. They entertained local police officers on the occasion of important traditional Chinese holidays and cultural celebrations. For instance, on Chinese New Year's Day, January 19, 1890, when the Chinese gathered to celebrate the most important day of the year by feasting and enjoying entertainment, Moy Dong Chow and Moy Dong Hoy invited Sergeant Dan Hogan, a policeman from the Harrison Street station, along with other privileged Chinese, to a performance by a Chinese orchestra. The Moys also instructed a local artist to paint Guan Gong, the historic Chinese war hero turned god who was believed to maintain social order and was worshipped by Chinese merchants overseas, to closely resemble former lieutenant James Bowler of the Desplaines Street station, which immensely pleased Sergeant Hogan.[33]

The two fighting tongs not only competed for resources but also clashed in their political reaction to events in China at the time. Both the Moys and the Chins were interested in the local Emperor Protection Association (a political organization in China founded in 1899 by Kang Youwei and Liang Qichao, which advocated a constitutional monarchy and peaceful reform), regarding it as a useful vehicle for expanding their prestige and influence. The Chicago branch of the association was formed in June 1903 with Moy Dong Chow as its first president; but the Chins were more active in the association's activities and garnered more recognition from prominent reform leaders.[34] On May 23, 1905, Kang Youwei, the famous leader of the 1898 reform movement in China and later a loyalist of the Manchu monarch, passed through Chicago on his tour across the American continent. During his visit, Kang entrusted Chin F. Foin with the operation of a Chinese restaurant, King Joy Lo (瓊彩樓, or Qiongcailou in Mandarin), in Chicago, with the intention that profits from the venture would benefit Chinese students studying in America. Kang Youwei initially provided $7,300, and with other funds raised by members of the Emperor Protection Association and loans from the Commercial Corporation's Huayi Bank in New York, the restaurant opened in May 1906.[35]

The Chins countered in 1909. That year the Chins cooperated with the police in raiding gambling houses on Clark Street.[36] In the 1910s, the Hip Sing Tong was growing rapidly. It opened its new headquarters at 355 Clark Street, opposite the old headquarters. Hip Sing apparently had enjoyed such financial success that it could burn up several thousand dollars' worth of fireworks to celebrate the opening of its new headquarters on the night of June 11, 1911.[37] The expansion of Hip Sing's power made On Leong jealous and uneasy, prompting the latter to move to the South Side. This strategic move consolidated On Leong's dominance in Chinatown.

Nothing better illustrates this dominance than the On Leong Merchants Association Building located on South Wentworth Avenue. The construction of the building was a long and careful process. As early as 1911, On Leong obtained a lease through the H. O. Stone real estate management company for approximately fifty commercial spaces near the intersection of Wentworth Avenue and Cermak Road. Businesses affiliated with the association moved from Clark Street to Wentworth and Cermak in February 1912, and the area was immediately proclaimed the "New Chinatown." On Leong began to plan the construction of its headquarters, which would expand its services to the community as well as enhance the ethnic identity of the new Chinatown.

There were problems, however, in finding a suitable architectural firm. The only large-scale building constructed according to traditional Chinese designs previously in Chicago was the Chinese Joss House located on the Midway of the World's Columbian Exposition in 1893. Unfortunately, along with other structures at the fair, the Chinese Joss House was demolished after the fair was closed in the fall of 1893. In 1919, at the Chicago Architectural Exposition, the architects Purcell and Elmslie had exhibited a drawing of a design accepted for the Institutional Church in Hunan, China, which incorporated traditional Chinese elements. On Leong, however, was not impressed by the design.

In 1920, Jim Moy, one of the directors of On Leong and cousin of Frank Moy, the "mayor of Chinatown," hired the newly founded architectural firm Michaelsen and Rognstad to design a new storefront and interior for his Peacock Inn restaurant in the uptown nightlife district on the North Side of Chicago. Jim Moy's satisfaction with the firm's design for his restaurant eventually led to Michaelsen and Rognstad's receiving the commission to design On Leong's new headquarters in spring 1926.[38]

Although both Christian S. Michaelsen and Sigurd Anton Rognstad were sons of working-class Norwegian immigrants, they had served apprenticeships with prominent architects who specialized in residential design for an upper-class clientele. Upon receiving the commission, Michaelsen and Rognstad studied a number of recent and influential books on historical Chinese architecture, including the two-volume photographic survey *Chinese Architecture* by Ernst Boerschmann, published in Berlin in 1925. Their study gave Michaelsen and Rognstad a better understanding of traditional Chinese style and its underlying philosophy. Their greatest challenge, however, was to construct a building for whose function there was no precedent in the Chinese tradition while preserving the essential elements of Chinese style.

When the final design for the On Leong building was unveiled in July 1926, it was hailed by the Chicago media as an "architectural splash of Chinatown" and "one of the most expensive and elaborate buildings ever erected in America by the Chinese."[39] Above all, the magnificent three-story building was an eloquent expression of the transnational and transcultural features of the Chicago Chinatown. It combined traditional Chinese architectural elements with the practical functionality of the Chinese community in America. The elevation of the building recalled the Chinese Joss House at the Columbian Exposition in its symmetry and the arrangement of its elements, in particular the facade towers, with their close resemblance to the fortress buildings in Taishan. The first floor, the railings of the loggia, the frames of the windows, and the tops of the towers were clad entirely in glazed terra-cotta, custom-made from Rognstad's designs by the American Terra Cotta Company of Crystal Lake, Illinois. The designs were based on Chinese prototypes of animals, figures, foliage, and geometric patterns symbolizing good fortune, longevity, and the Confucian virtues of humanity, righteousness, propriety, wisdom, and fidelity. The colors of the glazed terra-cotta were predominantly red, the traditional color of joy and audacity, and jade green, symbolizing prosperity. The transnational connection between the homeland and Chicago was best displayed in the open loggia on an upper floor and the choice of pier over column, both regional variations favored in Guangdong Province.

Despite its distinctive traditional appearance, the floor plan of the building was designed to suit the community's needs on American soil. The first floor was filled with storefronts to be rented to members of the association. The second floor was designed to hold a Chinese language school, a residential hotel, a lounge, and offices. On the third floor were a kitchen, a dining room, and three large meeting halls that could be converted into one huge meeting hall for the association's large congregation. One of the meeting halls was furnished as a shrine, trimmed in marble and sandalwood inlaid with gold and mother-of-pearl and decorated with tapestries, gilded screens, and antique vases, as well as oil portraits of George Washington and Sun Yat-sen, founding fathers of the United Sates and the Republic of China, respectively.[40] With a headline reading "Chicago Chinese Merchants Plan Gorgeous 'City Hall,'" the *Chicago Daily Tribune* trumpeted the splendor of the new On Leong headquarters.[41]

The quarter million dollars spent in constructing the building, when compared to the monthly wages of Chinese storekeepers, waiters, cooks, and laundrymen—ranging from $50 to $150 in the 1920s—clearly demonstrated the financial power of On Leong and its control over the Chinatown economy.[42] The building's architectural grandeur filled Chinese residents with pride and immediately attracted the attention of visitors. The building was often used as a backdrop for photographic opportunities.[43]

Referred to as the "Chinese City Hall," the On Leong Association building also symbolized the self-governing nature of the Chinese community in America.[44] It hosted all the important community assemblies and ceremonies commemorating national holidays, as well as providing a site for a Chinese school.

The powerful influence of the Moy brothers and their sons on the local community also indicates the dominance of On Leong, as manifested by the funeral of Frank Moy in 1937. Frank Moy was the son of Moy Dong Chow and "mayor of Chinatown" in the first three decades of the twentieth century. Like his father, Frank Moy controlled the community and held every key position within the Chinatown power structure. In addition to serving as president of On Leong, he also served as general director of the Middle-Western Chinese Civilian Relief Association of Chicago, the premier organization among Chinese immigrants for providing aid to the anti-

Japanese war in China. His funeral, attended by thousands, was said to be "the greatest ever seen." Frank Moy died at 6 a.m. on September 17, 1937. The On Leong Association was in charge of his funeral. The service was held at 2 p.m. on September 23, 1937, at the Chinese Presbyterian Church at 23rd and Wentworth Avenue. The church was filled with funeral flowers, together with hundreds of relatives and friends. The Reverend T. Y. Li of the Chinese Christian Church opened the service with a prayer, and Li Shen-Wei, the vice president of On Leong, acknowledged the sympathy of relatives and friends of the deceased. Then immediate relatives of Frank Moy and officers of On Leong escorted the coffin to the hearse. The funeral procession formed with a special police patrol leading the hearse, followed by Frank Moy's white American wife, his daughter, immediate relatives, and friends, both Chinese and American. Dignitaries attending the funeral included the vice-consul, Gung-Hsing Wang, from the Chinese consulate in Chicago and H. Moy, representing the On Leong Association of Washington, D.C.[45]

After Chinatown was relocated to the South Side in 1912, On Leong dominated both the political and social scene in the Chinese community. On Leong and its various activities were widely covered by the media, both English and Chinese, during the first decades of the twentieth century. Hip Sing, however, only appeared occasionally in media reports, mostly in regard to such matters as membership dues.[46]

THE CHINESE CONSOLIDATED BENEVOLENT ASSOCIATION

The Chicago branch of the Chinese Consolidated Benevolent Association (or Zhonghua Huiguan; hereinafter CCBA) was founded in 1906. As already discussed, its functions were legal, economic, cultural, and spiritual, in particular serving as a court of arbitration to handle disputes among Chinese businessmen. It passed and enforced regulations such as allowing only one laundry or restaurant within a radius of five hundred feet and severely punishing violators. When in 1916 a Chinese laundry was found violating the regulations, for instance, the CCBA imposed a fine of $850, which was granted to its rival laundry as compensation. Moy Dong Chew appeared in court as a witness.[47]

The CCBA also sponsored a Chinese language school, the Qing Dynasty Overseas Residents' School. It was opened in March 1909 with twenty-nine

The headquarters of the Chinese Consolidated Benevolent Association on 22nd Place, Chicago, 2008. Collection of Huping Ling.

students. Wu Ting-fang, the imperial Chinese ambassador to the United States, arrived in Chicago to celebrate its opening. The school named Wu its honorary first principal, while Moy Dong Chow served as its president.[48]

THE FAMILY ASSOCIATIONS

There were eight Chinese family associations in Chicago in the 1920s, including Moy Shi Kung Sow (Moy Family Association), Lee Lung Si Tong (Lee Family Association), Du Kin Kung Sow (Association for the Chen, Hu, and Yuan Families), Yu Wu-shi Kung Sow (Yu Family Association), Chi Teh Kung Sow (Association for the Wu, Zhou, Cai, and Ong Families), Chao Lung Kung Sow (Association for the Tom, Hsu, and Hsieh Families), Lim See Ho Tong (Lim Family Association), and Hwang Kiang Shia Tong (Wong Family Association).[49]

In traditional China, family was perceived as the basic unit as well as the society in miniature, and thus ruling a family was equally as important as governing a country. The Chinese believed that harmony within the family brought about prosperity and good fortune, while the breaking of family ties was the greatest misfortune in life. In South China, lineal and patriarchal structure was especially deeply entrenched, controlling virtually every aspect of the lives of family members. When emigrating to foreign countries, the Chinese transplanted their family associations to the host country to alleviate the pain and difficulties of their uprooted lives. Alienated by the anti-Chinese legal restrictions and social and cultural sentiments in America, the Chinese found practical mutual aid and cultural comfort in family associations and naturally gravitated toward them. Like On Leong, the family associations performed a wide range of functions as family record keepers, arbitrators of disputes among members, and facilitators of cultural celebrations. Tin-Chiu Fan's 1926 study provides a vivid and accurate description of the objectives and operations of the family associations.

> The chief objectives of these family societies are to protect the members of each family, to help them in sickness and poverty, to assist them to become familiar with the laws of their adopted country, and yet not to forget their fatherland, language, and family codes: in general, to supervise and lift them as if they were at home. . . .
>
> All these family societies have their regular gatherings at stated intervals. Each one of them has its own Assembly Hall and in each Assembly Hall there is a family Altar. On this altar are placed steps supporting, in the order of their dates, the tablets, photographs or pictures of the ancestors. At a little distance from the altar stands a common square table surrounded with seats; in the middle of the table is a register flanked by books on either side.
>
> On the Assembly Day, before the sun rises, the elder of the society enters the Hall, followed by members of the family or kindred families. They address a short invocation and music, the elder reads the names of the ancestors and lays offerings upon the altar in token of gratitude. This is the first part of the ceremony, solemn but affectionate.
>
> In the second part, the elder, seated before the square table, opens the book in the center. It is the family records, and consists of several volumes, containing in one entries relating to civil life, birth, marriage, and deaths; in the others, the biographies and wills of the dead. Taking the book, the elder reads and exhorts his hearers to follow the examples he has given. Then he reads a chapter from the Confucian classics, and lastly a few articles of the law and the family code.
>
> These lectures finished, as well as the comments and explanation to which they give rise, the object of the meeting changes, and the Hall is

transformed into a Council. The elder again takes the chair and inquires if any one of the family is in debt and if any one has any litigation, or difference of moment, with another family. If anyone has trouble with another family, steps are taken for its peaceful resolution, or if needful, for the appointment of arbitrators. There is nothing revolting or cruel connected with the family gathering, but everything is orderly, kind and simple, calculated to strengthen the family relationship, cement the affection between parents and children, between wife and husband, between brothers and sisters, and upholds habits of filial reverence and obedience.

The elder of the family society is elected annually by a council composed of the head-persons of the family or families affiliated with the society. He holds his office during good behavior, receives such a salary as the council may give him, and may be removed to make way for another whenever the majority of the council is displeased with his conduct. This system of eldership and the influential position the head-persons occupy, is an important safeguard against turmoil and trouble among the Chinese people in the city.[50]

Among the family associations, the Moy Family Association was one of the oldest in Chicago. It was probably founded in 1898 and had the largest membership of all the family associations. A global organization, it embodies a transnational network with connections and influences that transcend Chicago, throughout America and the world.[51] The Moy Family Association was originally located on South Clark Street and moved to its current address on Wentworth Avenue in 1927. The Lee Family Association was the second largest family association in early Chinatown. The founding date of the association is unclear; its first headquarters on Cermak Road were demolished in the early 1960s when a new freeway was constructed, and it moved to its current location on Wentworth Avenue.

The Du Kin Kung Sow, or Association for the Chen, Hu, and Yuan Families, was founded in 1906 and headquartered on South Clark Street. The Chi Teh Kung Sow, or Association for the Wu, Zhou, Cai, and Ong Families, was founded in 1922. The Wong Family Association, founding date unknown, moved to its current building on Wentworth Avenue in 1945.[52]

The Chinese community organizations transplanted from China were generally self-contained and conservative. They nevertheless provided a valuable social structure for the early Chinese community intended to protect the interests of its members, maintain peace and order within the community, and preserve Chinese traditions, which was necessary at a time when the Chinese were a vulnerable and disadvantaged minority group.

Hybridizing and Adapting American Social Structure

In a new land, the Chinese were inevitably influenced by the dominant ways of the host society. They adapted to the environment by creating hybrids combining traditional Chinese organizations with American elements or by forming organizations emulating those in the mainstream society. Hong Men Zhigong Tang offers a good example of the hybridized form of community organization, while the Chinese Association and the Mon Sang Association were closely modeled on American originals. The inclusiveness of the Chinese Association and the Mon Sang Association attracted large followings among the Chinese residents in Chicago, consequently posing challenges to On Leong's dominance. At the same time, the Chinese Nationalist Party (Guomindang or Kuomintang), which led the 1911 revolution that overthrew the Manchu monarchy and became the ruling party thereafter, also drew large support from the Chinese community in Chicago. Chinese churches and schools were integral to the community, providing indispensable social services to community members and promoting Christian values and Americanization. The Chinese-language newspapers also joined the community organizational structure in the 1930s and have since became influential venues for voicing the concerns of the community, promoting commercial activities, and bridging the Chinese community with the homeland as well as with the host society.

ORGANIZATIONS

Hong Men Zhigong Tang   The Hong Men Zhigong Tang (Chinese Freemasons Society) in Chicago was probably established in 1894. Formerly a secret society, the roots of the Hong Men Zhigong Tang can be traced to the 1600s in South China when China was ruled by the Manchu, an ethnic minority originating from the Manchuria area of China. Founded in 1674 in China and aimed at overthrowing the Manchu Qing dynasty (1644–1911), the secret society was credited for supporting Sun Yat-sen's 1911 revolution that finally overthrew the Manchu dynasty. Along with the Chinese immi-grants, the Hong Men Zhigong Tang spread overseas, arriving in the United States in the 1850s. Most Chinese immigrants, coming from South China, were profoundly influenced by anti-Manchu sentiments in China and were therefore readily attracted to the Hong Men Zhigong Tang.

In America, the Hong Men Zhigong Tang was affiliated with Ameri-can Masonic organizations and was thus known as the Chinese Freemasons Association. The Hong Men Zhigong Tang in Chicago was approved by the Masonic lodges of Illinois and used some of the Masonic symbolism. The Hong Men Zhigong Tang in Chicago required its new members to go through an initiation ceremony that involved a series of symbolic ritu-als, performed in front of a shrine, sometimes with temporary "gates" each representing an oath of loyalty that helped bind members together. Some of the ceremonial utensils such as sharp knives, however, may have contributed to the less flattering stereotypes of Hong Men as a secret and violent organi-zation involved in criminal activities.[53]

A document found in the records of deeds at the St. Louis city hall il-lustrates the nature and organizational structure of the Chinese Freemasons Association. The St. Louis Freemasons registered with the city on Octo-ber 21, 1899. The corporation deed stated that "the objects and purposes of this corporation shall be . . . to promote fraternity among and provide for the relief and aid of its members, and the members of Subordinate Lodge of the State of Missouri, their widows, orphans and dependent relatives, to bury the dead, and to engage in such other charitable work as may not be in conflict with its laws."[54] While the document testifies to the organization's philanthropic purposes, it also indicates a mixture of the Chinese secret so-ciety and American social organization. The officers of the organization in-cluded a Grand Master as presiding officer, a Deputy Grand Master as vice presiding officer, a Senior Grand Warden, a Junior Grand Warden, Grand Treasurer, Grand Secretary, and Grand Lecturer.[55] This hybridized combina-tion of elements from secret societies and from democratic organizations re-flects the organization's origin in China and transformation in the American environment, thus providing an impressive example of the cultural adapta-tion of the early Chinese in St. Louis and in Chicago.

The Chinese Association   While trade associations such as On Leong and family associations were exclusive, the Chinese Association was an inclusive organization in North America with branches throughout the United States and Canada. It embraced Chinese from all walks of life regardless of occupation, lineage, region of birth, creed, sex, or political leaning and therefore enjoyed the largest membership of all the Chinese organizations in Chicago, claiming in 1926 to have 3,600 members.[56] Obviously this number was somewhat exaggerated, as the total Chinese population of Chicago was reportedly less than 3,000 in the 1920s. A decade later, according to a report by the organization on its newly elected officers, the number of members present at the election was 541.[57] Nonetheless, it was one of the more influential organizations in the community. Its primary functions included providing social services, arbitrating disputes between Chinese parties, certifying documents and witnessing deeds, maintaining order in the Chinese community, and protecting the rights of Chinese citizens in the city.[58]

It is obvious that many of the functions of the Chinese Association overlapped with those of On Leong and the family associations. But its functions went beyond those of the traditional trade organizations or family associations by reaching out to the higher Chinese governmental authorities such as the Chinese embassy or a consulate for the protection of Chinese citizens. Its organizational structure and management were also more democratic, emulating those of mainstream organizations. Its board of directors, numbering thirty and elected by the members once every three years, oversaw the management of the association, appointing its executive secretary, exercising financial control over and responsibility for the association, and supervising its affairs and activities. Its board members were largely leaders of other Chinese organizations in the city as well. In 1926, the association also created an advisory council composed of the leaders of various family associations, to provide suggestions and advice to the board when necessary. In this way the monopoly over community power by the same elite was also evident in the Chinese Association.

The Mon Sang Association   Like the trade unions of Western societies, the Mon Sang Association demanded a fair day's pay for a fair day's work but with a primary goal of protecting the interests of restaurant workers, including their health and their moral and intellectual welfare.

The organization emerged as a response to the unfair working conditions and pay of restaurant workers in the early twentieth century. Chinese restaurant workers worked seven days a week, fourteen hours a day in the

1910s, thirteen hours a day in 1914, and twelve hours a day in 1918, for an average wage of less than $500 a year. A restaurant worker making an average wage was unable to support a family of average size, which was also the chief reason why most Chinese residents in Chicago could not send or go back to China for their wives. The long workdays and low wages caused stress that challenged their physical and mental health. In the face of such conditions, the progressive Chinese in the city decided to start a Chinese labor union.[59]

On September 1, 1918, thirty-six Chinese restaurant headwaiters in Chicago met in a family association hall and approved a resolution to establish the Mon Sang Association:

> The welfare of the Chinese community demands that the useful labor of every able-bodied man should, as a minimum, be compensated by sufficient income to support in comfort himself, a wife, and at least three minor children, and in addition to provide for sickness, old age, and disability, and should, as a maximum, be allowed to work eight hours a day and six days a week. Under no other condition can a strong, contented and efficient personality be developed.[60]

One can detect little trace here of peasants from a traditional and agrarian society; the resolution, rather, loudly echoes the manifestos of Western labor unions. It is no wonder that in the industrial city where the Labor Day celebration originated the Chinese restaurant workers acquired more class consciousness. It is also significant that in this midwestern metropolis, home to many well-respected public and private universities and colleges, about half the Chinese restaurant workers were university students, who transmitted the reform ideas they learned on campus into the dining rooms and kitchens of the Chinese restaurants where they worked.[61] Chinese restaurants in Chicago not only led the trend in introducing Chinese fine dining but also launched one of the earliest Chinese labor unions in the United States.

This resolution was unanimously approved by the restaurant workers. They enthusiastically embraced the demands for six workdays a week, an increase of the wage rate, and a minimum wage of forty cents an hour for union members. The association immediately inaugurated a welfare program for the restaurant workers by forming music clubs, establishing reading rooms and recreation areas, organizing social gatherings and outings, setting up classes to teach Chinese and English, and creating benefit institutions for relief of the sick, employment services, insurance, and physical examination of employees, all in line with the progressive movements of the time.

As the Mon Sang Association welcomed people from all lineal, regional, and occupational backgrounds, it enjoyed the second largest membership in Chicago, following only the Chinese Association, with more than 1,200 members in 1926 of whom two-thirds were restaurant workers. Its influence was larger than its membership would indicate, however, as many nonmember workers also followed its lead. Meanwhile, like most Chinese community organizations, the Mon Sang Association also kept within the boundaries of the Chinese community. It was not affiliated with the Chicago Federation of Labor nor was it associated with the Waiters Union of American Workers.

The Chinese Nationalist Party   The Chinese Nationalist Party in Chicago was a direct response to Sun Yat-sen's fund-raising movement among Chinese overseas in support of his anti-Manchu revolution in 1911. At the beginning of 1910, Sun Yat-sen visited the major metropolises of the United States, including Chicago. Upon his arrival in Chicago, he was greeted by several hundred Chinese waiters, laundrymen, students, and officials. In his hotel room, Sun received many well-wishers and encouraged them to form a revolutionary party in Chicago. The Chinese Nationalist Party followed Sun's "Three People's Principles," namely People's Nationalism, People's Sovereignty, and People's Livelihood. The first principle called for the overthrow of the Manchu dynasty and the independence of China from the imperialist yoke. The second principle advocated the rights of the people, including the vote, initiative, referendum, and recall. The third principle encouraged agrarian egalitarianism and a nationalized capitalism.

The Chicago Chinese community embraced the party with unusually unified support. In 1911, over one hundred Chinese compatriots in Chicago established a branch of the Chinese Nationalist Party. To celebrate the birth of the new Republic of China, on January 9, 1912, Chinatown set off several hundred thousand rolls of firecrackers donated by various organizations, businesses, and individuals. On Leong, for instance, pledged 200,000 rolls of firecrackers, the King Yen Lo restaurant 20,000 rolls, the King Joy Lo restaurant 10,000 rolls, and community leader Chen Kongfang 10,000 rolls. There were also numerous small donations of fifty cents from the general public.[62]

As with Chinese across America, the transnational nature of immigration made the Chinese in Chicago keenly interested in the political affairs and socioeconomic conditions in China. The Nationalist Party attracted many progressive Chinese Chicagoans, such as Eng Sing, who came to Chicago in 1924 and immediately joined the party and whose membership card, issued by the party's headquarters in San Francisco, was on display at the Chinese-American Museum of Chicago. He paid six dollars for the annual membership dues and another three dollars as a contribution to the party.[63] Like Eng Sing, many Chinese Chicagoans joined the Nationalist Party: by 1926, its membership had reached more than one thousand.[64]

CHURCHES

The pattern of historical development of the Chinese churches in Chicago resembles that of the Chinese churches across the United States.[65] In the early stage, from the 1870s to 1900s, Chinese Christian activities were mostly initiated and sponsored by white Protestant missionary groups. Beginning in the 1900s, the Chinese began establishing independent churches, with assistance from larger Christian organizations in providing funds and organizational structure or in lending church spaces. Chinese Christian organizations, such as the Chinese YMCA, underwent rapid growth in membership and activities during the 1920s and 1930s. Catholic missionaries also preached among the Chinese immigrants as early as the 1920s and enjoyed a growing congregation of Chinatown residents in the 1940s.

The Chinese Christian Union Church   The Chinese Christian Union Church was one of the earliest Chinese churches in Chicago. Three missionary groups—the Presbyterians, Baptists, and Congregationalists—came together to form the Chinese Christian Union Church at 2301 South Wentworth Avenue in 1903. "With a burden and vision to reach the increasing number of Chinese immigrants to the Chicago area that had begun to settle in what is present-day Chinatown," these missionary groups "sensed the suffering and desperation of these folks and felt a desire to meet their physical needs as well as their spiritual needs."[66] The church provided important social and cultural services to the progressive members of the Chinese community, for instance, hosting meetings of the Chinese Women's Club that helped with church-affiliated events in the 1930s and 1940s.

The Chinese Church of Christ   The Chinese Church of Christ was founded in 1915, probably one of the earliest Chinese churches in Chicago. Information on its membership and activities is limited. According to Fan's study, there was very little benevolent work done by the church. Funding for the church came primarily from the Chicago Church Federation, special contributions, weekly pledges, and Sunday collections and was used mainly for the pastor's salary and maintenance of the church building. In 1926 the pastor was able to raise $8,000 from Chinese Christians and $10,000 from the Chicago Church Federation to build a new church at Wentworth and 23rd Street.[67]

The Chinese YMCA   In 1917, Frank Lee, the pastor of the Chinese Church of Christ, with the support of a small group of Chinese Christian young men, founded the Chinese Young Men's Christian Institute. On May 1, 1921, the institute was officially recognized by the metropolitan YMCA as part of the larger association, thus making the Chinese YMCA the first community organization outside the boundaries of the Chinese communities in Chicago. In 1924, however, its affiliation with the metropolitan association was dissolved and its name officially became the Chinese Young Men's Christian Institute. Although the reason for the separation is unclear, the inclination toward and tradition of self-government among the Chinese may have played a part, as is suggested in the congratulatory letter from William F. Hypes, president of the Young Men's Christian Association of Chicago: "I want at this time especially to congratulate the Chinese Department, its officers and members for the fine ways in which they are finding themselves in the matter of ministering to the five thousand Chinese in Chicago through a program of activities which in variety and extent has been well adapted to the needs of your constituency."[68]

The objectives of the Chinese YMCA were completely in line with those of its American counterpart, which included promoting Christian ideals and providing educational training and recreational activities.[69] The institute was most successful in its educational efforts. It established a Chinese school for children. The school held two classes each school day, one in the afternoon and the other in the evening. Each of the two-hour classes taught Chinese literature, history, geography, letter writing, and composition. Fifty-five boys and twenty-eight girls enrolled in the Chinese school in 1926, attending one of the Chinese classes in the afternoon or evening after their public school activities. Two young Chinese teachers, one male and one female and both students of the University of Chicago, were hired to teach the classes.

Committed to Christian values, the institute also closely collaborated with the Chinese Church of Christ. The pastor of the church led the religious programs of the institute, while the secretary of the institute served as an officer and supervised the Sunday school of the church. Religious activities also included personal meetings every Sunday afternoon and midweek prayer meetings in one of the Chinese homes on Wednesday evenings. Although recreational activities were hampered by a lack of equipment and facilities, the institute organized a basketball team, the Cantonese Owls, in cooperation with the Chinese Association; the team practiced at Harding Square and played against American teams. On Sundays, the leaders of the institute took the boys out for games and swimming.

The institute also organized a wide array of cultural activities to promote Christian values as well as Chinese traditions and to enrich the cultural life of the Chinese residents. It held lantern-slide travelogues, moving-picture shows, public entertainments, musical concerts, excursions, picnics, Christmas parties for children, and Chinese-language classes for Americans.[70]

The membership of the Chinese YMCA was smaller than that of the Chinese Association and the Mon Sang Association, with only 245 members in 1926. But it attracted more Chinese professionals and college students, while the Chinese Association and Mon Sang Association were predominantly organizations for Chinese laborers and small business owners. Sixteen percent of the Chinese YMCA members were professionals or college students, while professionals and college students made up only 3 and 2 percent of the membership of the Chinese Association and Mon Sang Association, respectively.[71]

The Chinese YMCA was also the only relief agency in the Chinese community. It was instrumental in providing relief to the needy during the Great Depression, beginning in 1931. More than a thousand people, both American and Chinese, received weekly aid from the Chinese YMCA station.[72] Beginning in 1933, it distributed bread to the poor three times a week, providing an "unusual amount" of bread on Easter Sunday of 1938, in particular. The fund for bread was garnered through voluntary contributions.[73]

St. Therese Church   The Catholic church in Chinatown was formally established in 1947, but missionary work to organize and convert the Chinese began as early as the 1920s, when the School Sisters of Notre Dame and Franciscan friars from St. Peter's Church began teaching Catholicism to Chinese children. In 1940, the Reverend John T. S. Mao, a native of Nanking, China, started instructing classes in Old St. John's Church, and on August 25, 1940, twenty-four Chinese children were baptized in this church. On September 11 of the same year, Reverend Mao rented a store on 2302 South Wentworth and opened St. Therese, the first Chinese Catholic church in Chicago. In 1941, he opened a Catholic grade school in the On Leong Merchants' Association Building, popularly known as the Chinese City Hall, at the corner of 22nd and Wentworth. A few years later, he returned to China, but his work was continued by Rev. Martin Burke, who became pastor on May 14, 1944. Having worked in South China for ten years and being fluent in four Cantonese dialects, Reverend Burke provided effective leadership, and St. Therese Chinese Mission was relocated to the building at 2311 South Wentworth. On October 18, 1947, St. Therese Chinese Mission was formally established by Cardinal Stritch through a special faculty from the Holy See as a national parish for the Chinese community.[74] Together with the Chinese Christian Union Church, the two institutions organized a substantial amount of missionary work in Chinatown in the 1940s.[75]

SCHOOLS

Public Schools   In Chicago, public schools and church-affiliated schools have been credited with increasing literacy among the Chinese and forging a new Chinese American identity. As the population of Chinese students was small, there was no separate Chinese public school established in Chicago as was the case in San Francisco. In 1857, San Francisco opened a segregated school for Chinese children, which two years later was changed to an evening school. In 1871, however, the "Oriental School" was closed by the city. From that time on, Chinese children were denied a public education, until in 1885, following the ruling in favor of the plaintiff in *Tape v. Hurley*, the Chinese were allowed access to public education, albeit still segregated. The new "Oriental School" was opened in 1885, in a rented room above a grocery store in Chinatown.[76] Later on, more Chinese schools were founded, mostly sponsored by Zhonghua Huiguan (CCBA). By 1944, there were ten Chinese schools with a total enrollment of 1,909.[77]

The Jones School was the first public school in Chicago that welcomed Chinese children into its classrooms. In 1894, about thirty Chinese children enrolled as regular students at the school. Located at the corner of Harrison Street and Plymouth Court, it was in close proximity to the old Chinatown on South Clark Street. Consequently, the early Chinese families, from small store owners to prominent transnational businessmen such as Hong Sling, all sent their children to the Jones School. Hong Sling's three children, Harry, William, and Jennie, attended from 1905 to 1913, from 1910 to 1918, and from 1913 to 1921, respectively. Although Thomas C. W. Jamieson, the principal of the school in 1913, provided a certificate to the Office of the Inspector in Charge [of Immigration] in Chicago to substantiate that the three Hong children were enrolled at the Jones School in support of their status as American-born citizens when the Hongs were planning their China trip that year, it was the fluent English spoken with an American accent by the children that convinced Inspector Howard D. Ebey that these children were absolutely "bona fide American-born children."[78] The Chinese children undoubtedly benefited from their education at the Jones School in terms of their Americanization, which enabled them to freely cross national and cultural borders. Most of the leaders of the Chinese community in the early twentieth century connected their successful Americanization to the lessons they received in the little red building on the corner of Harrison and Plymouth Court.[79]

After most Chinese had settled in South Chinatown along 22nd Street, the Chinese children attended the John Charles Haines School at 247 West 23rd Place. Established in 1886, the school was initially named the Harrison School but changed its name to the Harrison Practice School in 1907 and then to the John Charles Haines School in 1913, after the mayor of Chicago from 1859 to 1860, when a new addition was added to the west side of the school building. Although prohibited from living near the school, the Chinese were permitted to enroll at the school. According to Chinese tradition, respectable women were not supposed to appear in public, and so in the first decades of the twentieth century the Chinese children were escorted to school and picked up by their fathers.[80]

Most second-generation Chinese children moved on to high school. They attended Harrison High School or Hyde Park High School and engaged in the same extracurricular activities as their white peers. Samuel Moy, for example, emerged as a star basketball player at Harrison High in 1927.[81]

Owing to financial circumstances, however, few Chinese children went to college. Those who did still faced difficulty in finding jobs after graduation from college because of prejudice and discrimination on the part of the larger society. Many Chinese females went to secretarial school after high school, hoping to have an easier time finding a job. Although a few attended college locally, Chinese females did not attend out-of-state universities and colleges until the end of World War II.[82]

Christian Sunday Schools Earnest American Christians and Christian churches in Chicago also provided English-language education to the adult Chinese. The earliest parochial adult English-language education was provided in 1878 in a third-floor room of Farwell Hall, as part of the Sunday school of a Christian church, and was known as the "Chinese Mission." The Chinese Mission, initiated by David D. Jones, a missionary who had worked for the previous two years among the Chinese in Evanston and was regarded as "an eccentric man with a queer history" by the local media, may have been the founder of the Jones School discussed previously in this section.[83] A vivid description of the interaction between the Chinese students and their "Melican" teachers is illuminating in regard to the media's perception and portrayal of the "Heathen Chinee" by a Victorian writer:

> Ah Ching Yuen, the aristocrat, wore a black satin jacket, a straw hat jauntily tipped on one side of his head, and new felt shoes, which made no sound as he proudly trod across the floor. Lo Bo, being only a hired man on moderate wages, could not be expected to "rag out" very well, but he was neat if not gaudy. Ah Sam Chong, Fong Sang, Low Lee, R. Gin, and the rest of the fourteen Celestials who were present at the banquet (there are twenty-one who actually belong to the Sunday-school) were arrayed in much the same of splendor as Lo Bo.
>
> It is now two months since the Chinese Sunday-school was started in an upper room of Farwell Hall, and already it has attained a place among the prominent religious institutions of the city. An eccentric man with a queer history, David D. Jones, was the founder of it.
>
> It was a great day for the Chinese yesterday. The pupils of the Sunday-school had extended a formal invitation to their teachers to participate in a banquet at the close of the regular exercises.
>
> The regular Sunday-school exercises were gone through as usual. A peculiarity of this Sunday-school is that there is a teacher for every pupil. Most of the teachers are ladies. The teaching is necessarily simple in its scope, as few of the almond-eyed scholars can speak English.
>
> These Chinese are said to be extremely grateful for the attention shown them by the "Melican" ladies, and have manifested their gratitude by making

them several choice presents. One of the ladies was recently presented with an elegant and costly silk and ivory fan imported from China, and another has been notified that there is a pair of shoes coming for her all the way from that far-off shore. Evidently the "Heathen Chinee" of this city is either exceptionally good or else he has been misrepresented on the Pacific slope.[84]

This group of Chinese would have had limited contact with Chicagoans beyond their laundries or grocery stores on South Clark Street, as none of them could speak English. Though isolated, they had a yearning to interact with the society outside of their insulated homes and businesses. Appreciative of what they had learned, they displayed their gratitude nonverbally by offering presents to their teachers. The reporter and likely the teachers were not unaware of the negative conception of the Chinese as ungodly pagans who engaged in criminal activities. But whatever the motives of the American Christian women in teaching English to the Chinese, the Chinese well understood that mastering English was the ticket to their survival and success in America.

In 1894, a group of Christians at West Madison Street established a Chinese mission. Twenty-eight American teachers enthusiastically taught thirty Chinese women lessons in English, the Bible, and home economics. These Chinese women not only studied English but also learned practical methods of raising and educating their children in America. The Chinese mission was viewed as a pilot effort for a later movement to educate the Chinese in the city starting in 1897.

Miss Pickett, daughter of a wealthy property owner, was reportedly one of the pioneers in the movement. In 1897, she visited the first school for Chinese adults organized by the YMCA, which was held in a building in the north part of the Loop. Thus inspired, she convinced her father to allow her to open a second Chinese school in the Central Baptist Church, one of the properties owned by him. Fairly soon, twelve more schools were added to the list of schools teaching English to the Chinese, including the Adams Street Union Church School for the Chinese; Brothern Mission School for the Chinese, located at 3435 West Van Buren Street; Chinese Church of Christ School for the Chinese, at 2131 Archer Avenue; Emanuel Baptist Church School for the Chinese, at 2320 Michigan Avenue; Englewood Baptist Church School for the Chinese, at 62nd Street and Stewart Avenue; Jackson Boulevard Christian Church School for the Chinese, at 2421 Jackson Boulevard and Western Avenue; Metropolitan Church School for the Chinese, at Monroe Street and

California Avenue; North Shore Baptist Church School for the Chinese, at 5300 Broadway; Presbyterian Church School for the Chinese, at 20th Street and Michigan Avenue; Second Baptist Church School for the Chinese, at Lincoln Street and Jackson Boulevard; Second Presbyterian Church School for the Chinese, at Sacramento and Madison Streets; and Woodlawn Baptist Church School for the Chinese, at 62nd Street and University Avenue.

These Christian schools were all Sunday schools, with classes meeting regularly on Sundays. About 360 Chinese adults, predominantly laundry-men and a few restaurant workers, attended these schools on a regular basis. The teaching staffs of the church-affiliated schools were composed chiefly of public school teachers, housewives, businesswomen, and students from the Moody Bible Institute. These English classes were instrumental in promot-ing English literacy among the Chinese immigrants. It was estimated that in the 1920s about 60 percent of the Chinese in Chicago, or 4,500, were literate in Chinese, and of these about 25 percent could read and write plain English very well.[85]

Chinese Language Schools   Various community organizations also sponsored Chinese language schools. In 1905, a local Chinese community leader pro-posed to Wu Ting-fang, the Chinese ambassador to the United States, and other authorities that funds be allocated to establish the Chinese Education Commission in Chicago. The petition was favorably received by the authori-ties and the commission was formed. It was composed of leaders of various community organizations. By 1906, six schools in English and Chinese had been established, affiliated with the Chinese Association. All Chinese chil-dren of school age were expected to attend the Chinese schools, which were run by the Chinese Association or the Chinese YMCA, either in the after-noon (normally from four to six o'clock) or in the evening, after they took off from public school. These schools developed a "Chinese reader" for their students, first teaching basic concepts such as the seasons, domestic animals, musical notation, and numbers in Chinese and then teaching the Confucian classics to advanced students.[86]

The On Leong Merchants and Laborers Association also established a Chinese language school in the 1920s and 1930s. Simply called On Leong School, it hired teachers who had been well educated in China. At the same time, a Chinese (whose name is unknown) set up another Chinese language school, named Pei De (Pui Tek, literarily "educating virtuous students"), in his home near Clark and Van Buren for the Chinese families living in the Old Chinatown area. The operation of this school was later taken over by the Chinese Christian Union Church, which officially began running the school in 1953, with the pastor of the church serving as principal and sometimes as teacher, while most of the teachers were mothers of the students.[87]

On October 1, 1937, the Chinese Church of Christ located on 23rd and Wentworth Avenue opened a new Chinese school. It hired Mr. H. P. Chiao as teacher-principal and Miss H. F. Wang as teacher, both having had many years of teaching experience in San Francisco.[88]

NEWSPAPERS

By 1931, there already existed two 8-page Chinese daily newspapers, *Kung Shong Yat Po* (Workingmen's and Merchants' Daily News) and *San Min Chen Bao*, or the *San Min Morning Paper* (The Three People's Principles Morning Daily News), in Chicago. The press that produced both newspapers was located on West 22nd Street and Archer Avenue. The press was quite impressive in its size and sophistication: eighteen staff members were employed by *Kung Shong Yat Po* alone. Each newspaper cost five cents per copy and had a circulation of seven thousand copies delivered to major cities in North America. The newspapers were printed on old-fashioned flatbed presses, but the type was cast in Shanghai by the largest printing house in Asia.[89]

In 1937, the *Chinese Centralist Daily News*, focusing on news of the Midwest, was established, becoming the third Chinese-language newspaper in Chicago.[90] Although only about two-thirds of the Chinese residents in Chicago were literate, the newspapers were instrumental in connecting the Chinese immigrants with socioeconomic and political affairs in China, reporting the local news, promoting Chinese commercial activities, and bridging the gap between the immigrant community and the larger society.

The three newspapers were largely influenced by and shared the ethical principles and standards of Western journalism—truthfulness, accuracy, objectivity, impartiality, fairness, and public accountability.[91] For instance, C. C. Lee, a reporter with the *San Min Morning Paper*, was dispatched by the newspaper to report on the Chicago laundry unions' activities on April 9, 1937. To give a fair and complete report, Lee attended the meetings held by both the Chicago Westside Laundry Union and the Chicago Northside Laundry Union on the same day. At the meetings, Lee was invited to speak. He stressed that he was not representing any particular Chinese organization but rather was present "as a newspaper reporter" to "secure facts for free discussion and investigation by the Chinese."[92]

These newspapers were relatively small compared to their more prominent and established counterparts in San Francisco, such as the *Chinese World*, founded in 1891 by Kang Youwei and Liang Qichao, two leading reformers in China at the turn of the century, which represented the American Chinatown elite; *Young China* established by Sun Yat-sen, which served as the voice of Tongmenhui and the Nationalist Party (Guomindang); and the *Chinese-Western Daily* (*Chung Sai Yat Po* in Cantonese), started in 1900 by Presbyterian minister Wu Panzhao (Ng Poon Chew), which advocated "reforming and modernizing Chinese cultural practice and adapting to the norms of American mainstream society."[93] All of them were equally influenced by American republicanism, Christianity, and Western middle-class ideologies. They encouraged the local Chinese to absorb American democratic values, and to participate in mainstream society in order to improve their condition. An article in the April 12, 1937, issue of the *San Min Morning Paper*, for instance, urged Chinese laundrymen to attend the American Laundry Union's meeting when the union proposed raising prices for laundering, "We understand that the Westside Laundry Union will have another meeting next Sunday. And we hope that all Chinese laundries in that location will realize that this . . . important matter concerns the future of the laundry business. We hope, that as many Chinese laundries as possible will be represented at that meeting."[94]

Celebrating and Connecting to the Homeland

These community organizations sponsored a wide array of cultural celebrations and activities, which included those promoting Americanization and assimilation. When Japan waged an all-out war against China in 1937, the Chicago Chinese community, like other Chinese communities across the country, enthusiastically rallied to support China's war efforts.

"GLEEFUL CELESTIALS"

A hard-working and industrious people, the Chinese were nonetheless their Western neighbors' equals in their love of amusement. Traditional Chinese holidays were the time for families and the community to gather

together for celebration. The most joyous time of year was the arrival of
the Chinese New Year, celebrated by the Spring Festival. Calculated according to the orbit of the moon, the Chinese New Year, signifying the beginning of spring, usually falls in early February. During the twelfth month of
the lunar calendar, the Chinese would thoroughly clean their houses and
business premises, clearing away the dust along with bad luck and looking
forward to a better year. The tradition of the New Year's celebration was
transplanted faithfully to the New World. The Chinese New Year's celebrations were the optimum occasions for American reporters to hunt for news
on the exoticism of the "Celestials" or "Mongolians." An article entitled
"Gleeful Celestials, Chicago Chinatown Celebrate Their New-Year's Festival" in the *Chicago Tribune* of January 20, 1890, provides a colorful picture
of the New Year's celebration on South Clark Street:

> The Chinese New-Year celebration began last night about dusk. At 3 a.m. It
> had reached the stage of joyous riot, when a Chinaman begins to have fun.
> Clark Street south of Van Buren was crowded with happy Chinamen, and
> more happy Chinamen were bobbling in front of the picture of the Joss in
> the Hip Lung store, Bow Wow Fung's, Sam Moy's, and other pleasant resorts,
> where Chicago Chinamen gather to smoke and have a good time. All the
> shops were lit, red paper signs hung in the windows, friendly parties of China-
> man were tossing off cups of rice gin, while up-stairs, over the Hip Lung
> store, a Chinese orchestra was playing for the pleasure of twenty or thirty
> privileged Chinamen, and a policeman from the Harrison Street station.
> . . . .
>
> When Sam Moy arose yesterday morning his shop was crowded with
> customers and the customers all had their pocketbooks out. They had come
> to settle up their accounts with Sam Moy. On New-Year's every Chinaman
> must pay his "chit"; if he doesn't do it before 4 p.m. he is disgraced. His
> friends do not speak to him on the street. Chinese boys peg bricks at him.
> Chinese women hoot at him from the windows. When he dies he goes to
> a place where he will meet Americans and others. So there was a constant
> stream of Chinamen entering Sam Moy's all day yesterday, and Sam Moy's
> face wore a smile of supreme content. When a customer entered he bowed
> to Sam Moy and said, "Kunghi!" Sam Moy bowed to the customer and re-
> plied, "Kunghi," which means: "I am your everlasting servant. I humbly bow
> myself at your feet. I offer you my sincerest wishes for a happy year. May
> the moon love you, May your head mingle with the stars. May peace and
> prosperity be yours." The customer paid his bill and Sam Moy handed him a

cup of gin and a five-cent cigar. Another customer came in a little while later. The same salutations were exchanged, and he, too, sat down to a cup of gin and a cigar. By nightfall the place was overcrowded. In the little stalls back of the shop half a dozen Chinamen were "hitting the pipe," and in a back room fifteen or twenty were gambling. A fest was set for 6 p.m. This was the menu as at other places: Bird's Nest Soup, Shark's Fin Soup, Fried Flat Fish, Roast Chicken, Roast Pig, Roast Duck, Roast Pigeon, Rice Gin, "Medicine" Wine, Oranges. At 10 p.m. the diners were getting warmed up to the festivities.[95]

Not only Chinese community members were enthusiastic in celebrating Chinese traditions; some progressive Americans also took part in celebrating the Chinese heritage. Miss Olga Huncke was loved and fondly remembered by the children who attended the John C. Haines School in Chinatown in the 1930s. A dedicated kindergarten teacher at the school for many years, she promoted Chinese culture and instilled cultural pride in the children. She made Chinese headwear for her students during Chinese holidays or for special occasions, for instance. Her culture-specific programs made the John C. Haines School special to many children in Chinatown.[96]

In the Century of Progress Exposition in 1933, Chicago Chinese proudly showcased the grandeur of Chinese culture. The Lama Temple, a complete replica of the temple in Rehe, north of Beijing, was the centerpiece of the Chinese displays. A Swedish explorer, Sven Hedin, proposed the idea of having it made in Beijing and shipped to Chicago, and a Swedish American manufacturer named Bendix pledged the cost. Two senior professional builders from Beijing were hired to supervise the construction of the temple. These efforts also gained support from Chinese governmental authorities; Gung-Hsing Wang, vice-consul at the consulate of China in Chicago from 1930 to 1938, who eventually left the Chinese diplomatic service to become an American citizen, real estate developer, and leading member of Chicago Chinatown, was closely involved with the preparation of the temple.[97] The Lama Temple was a media darling in 1933 and 1934 and received extensive coverage.

Since the site of the fair was only about a mile from Chinatown, many Chinatown residents were able to work at the fair, and many others financed concessions there. For instance, in 1934, the entire Shanghai Village was financed by local Chinese merchants. Chinese residents also participated in other ways. One of the high points of the fair was a grand parade organized by the CCBA. The Chicago Chinese community rallied behind the CCBA to put together the first and most spectacular parade for the Chinese community on October 1, 1933. The parade included thirteen floats, five bands, a dragon, lion dances, and pretty Chinese girls in Chinese costume. The Minxin Trading Company, an importer of Chinese food products located in the 2000 block of La Salle Street, sponsored a large float. The parade went up Michigan Avenue and then through the fairgrounds along the Avenue of the Flags to the Lama Temple and the Shanghai Village (also known as a "street of Shangai"). It was hailed as "one of the first times that the full Chinese community of Chicago had asserted itself as the equal of every other ethnic community, parading in front of other Chicagoans and visitors from the entire world."[98]

Such cultural activities in Chicago were very much intertwined with patriotic sentiments. "Double Ten," or October 10, the date commemorating the founding of the Republic of China, was celebrated each year with a flag-raising ceremony and singing of the national anthem of China. On Leong sponsored the celebrations during the first half of the twentieth century.[99] These celebrations of Chinese culture and traditions mirrored those in other American Chinatowns of the time.[100]

CONNECTING CHINA

The Chinese immigrants in Chicago, like their counterparts in other Chinese communities across the country, were closely connected with the homeland socially and politically prior to 1943, when the Chinese exclusion laws that had barred the entry of Chinese since 1882 were finally repealed. Their early participation in politics in China was mainly associated first with Kang You-wei and his Emperor Protection Association and later with Sun Yat-sen's anti-Manchu activities and his Nationalist Party after the 1911 revolution. After Japan's invasion of Manchuria in 1931, Chinese participation in China's affairs reached a zenith.

Kang Youwei's Emperor Protection Association, or Baohuang Hui, was established in 1899 while Kang was in exile following the failure of the Hundred Days Reform Movement a year earlier. Using the organization as a vehicle to advance a program of reform, which had failed to be implemented in the course of the 1898 reform movement, Kang began fund-raising activities overseas to accumulate funds for sending Chinese students to study abroad.[101] The Chinese in Chicago rode the political currents in China by establishing a Chicago branch of the Emperor Protection Association in June 1903, with Moy Dong Chew as its first president. Seeing his rival take a leadership role in the local Emperor Protection Association, Chin F. Foin actively participated in the association's activities, became its next president, and earned the trust of Kang Youwei and his associates.[102]

In 1910, Sun Yat-sen visited Chicago during his tour in America to raise funds for anti-Manchu activities. Sun gathered twelve close followers for a meeting to prepare for the imminent radical uprising to overthrow the Manchu monarchy. Four of them were from the Moy clan: Mei Qiaolin, Mei Guanhao, Mei Naiheng, and Mei Jiu.[103]

In 1931, the Japanese invaded Manchuria. The Nationalist government under Chiang Kai-shek stressed its policy of "unification before resistance," insisting that only after completely eliminating the Communist Party and its influence in China could the Nationalist government organize an effective resistance against the Japanese invasion. Meanwhile, the League of Nations condemned the Japanese aggression without taking any effective action to stop the aggressors. Encouraged by the hesitation and ineffectiveness of the Chinese Nationalist government and the lack of international sanctions, Japan heightened its aggression by waging an all-out war against China beginning on July 7, 1937.

When news of the Japanese invasion reached America, Chinese communities throughout the country rose to organize fund-raisers to assist China's war effort. The Six Companies called an emergency meeting on September 21, 1931, immediately after the Japanese invasion of Manchuria. The meeting gathered together representatives of ninety-one Chinese organizations throughout America and resulted in the founding of the China War Relief Association of America, which eventually comprised forty-seven chapters in the western hemisphere. The most urgent business of the association was to raise money for the war effort in China, one effective means being the "Bowl of Rice Movement," a collective effort on the part of the Chinese in America to raise funds and collect supplies to send to China during the war.[104]

The Chinese in Chicago joined the collective effort at once under the leadership of the CCBA. The major organizations in Chinatown collectively formed the Chinese Civilian Relief Association of Chicago, with Frank Moy as its president. After Frank Moy's death on September 17, 1937, Y. C. Moy succeeded to the presidency.[105] Their collective determination was clearly demonstrated in a resolution passed on the twenty-fifth celebration of the National Day in China on October 10, 1936, which condemned the Japanese invasion of China as "illegal and unjustified" and a "frequent violation of international law, Nine-Power Treaty, Kellogg-Briand Pact and the League of Nations Governance." They pledged their "lives, properties, and everything" they had to strengthen the defense against further Japanese invasion in China. They urged their American friends to institute sanctions against Japan and to support the Chinese war efforts.[106] After the Japanese invasion of China on July 7, 1937, the Chicago Chinese urged the United States and Great Britain to enforce an economic boycott, as 50 percent of Japan's foreign trade was with the United States and Great Britain.[107] Chinese Chicagoans responded to the call from the Chinese Red Cross headquarters in Hankou for cash contributions and medical and other supplies from overseas Chinese in the face of the disastrous conditions in Shanghai following the Japanese invasion of the city in August 1937.[108]

Chinese women formed the Chinese Women's Club to respond to a call from Mme. Chiang Kai-shek to support China's war efforts. They worked in conjunction with the Chinese Civilian Relief Association of Chicago and were very successful in their fund-raising activities. "Through their influence," an article in the September 10, 1937, issue of the *San Min Morning Paper* commented, "even children have turned in their candy money for contribution towards the war fund. Such is the spirit existing in the minds of our women and children. It's not how much we give but it's how we give that counts."[109] Members of the club consisted largely of members of the families of community leaders and activists. Lorrain Moy, the daughter of Moy Dong Yee, youngest of the three Moy brothers, attended the Chinese Women's Club with her mother, Luk Shee, when she was nine years old and remained as one of the charter members of the organization. During World War II, Lorrain became a member of the American Women's Volunteer Service, working on behalf of American service personnel of Asian ancestry.[110]

Mansie O'Young was one of the most active members of the club. She served as the president of the Chinese Women's Club in the 1940s and was directly responsible for the establishment of the Chinatown Unit of the American Women's Volunteer Service, which operated a hospitality center for Chinese American servicemen in Chicago from 1943 to 1945. Located on Cermak Road, the center was used to entertain all servicemen but mostly those stationed at the Chennault Air Force base in Rantoul, Illinois. The center also organized various war relief activities.[111]

Patriotic fervor reached its apogee when Mme. Chiang Kai-shek visited Chicago in late March 1943. In the evening of March 22, Mme. Chiang delivered a speech urging American support to a packed audience in the

Chicago Stadium. Many local Chinese attended the rally with great nationalistic pride.[112]

In addition to war relief efforts, young men from Chicago's Chinatown also enlisted in the army to fight the Axis powers during World War II. Charlie Toy joined the army in 1942 to fight not only the Japanese invaders in China but all the Axis powers in the European theater as well. He was captured by the German army during his tour of duty in France, Belgium, and Germany. His family and friends, who thought he was dead, were overjoyed when he was finally released in 1945 after the war was over. He returned home a hero who had broken the racial barrier and served his country with unwavering loyalty and absolute bravery. Charlie Toy was lucky enough to have returned home while many others fought and died, along with their Euro-American comrades, on the battlefields.[113]

The following story reflects not only the patriotism displayed by Chinese Americans but also the fear among the Chinese of being mistaken as Japanese after the attack on Pearl Harbor by the Japanese navy and the consequent eruption of anti-Japanese sentiment throughout the United States. Charles W. Tun was born in Chicago on October 16, 1927. His father operated a hand laundry on the northwest side of Chicago near Addison and Pulaski; the family lived in a coach house behind the laundry. As Tun recalled, "[When the war broke out,] our greatest concern was the tendency for the Caucasians to group Asians the same. I remember we had to wear buttons indicating we were Chinese." He was drafted in March 1945, inducted at Fort Sheridan, and underwent basic training at Fort Campbell, Kentucky. He was then sent to Fort Meade, Maryland, for military police training, and subsequently assigned to Company B, 503rd Military Police Battalion, stationed in Pisa, Italy, for the duration of his service in the war. After being discharged in 1947, he was assigned to the inactive army reserve for a three-year period and then recalled to serve in the army during the Korean War.[114]

Conclusion

The dominance of the On Leong Merchants and Laborers Association in Chicago was a complex phenomenon. Different from the hierarchical structure in traditional China, in the Chinese immigrant society in America power was wielded by businessmen who possessed superior education and economic means and thus were able to emerge as community leaders. Although publicly known as On Leong Tong, On Leong was in no way an organization connected with "tong wars." The formation and dominance of On Leong was not a result of some cultural peculiarity of the Chinese, who had been charged unfairly with habitually forming secret societies and committing the crimes of gambling, smuggling, tong fighting, and prostitution. On the contrary, the emergence and existence of On Leong, as of other prominent Chinese community organizations, stemmed from the socioeconomic environment of America. As immigrants and a socioeconomically and legally oppressed group, the Chinese received protection from neither the Chinese government nor American authorities. Without the protection necessary for survival in a strange land, the Chinese had to rely on their own resources, and thus On Leong emerged as an organization to meet the social, economic, and legal needs of the Chinese immigrants.

Although its reputation had been tainted by criminal activities committed by some members, On Leong was generally a benevolent-protective trade and community organization, as well as a powerful group of businessmen within the Chinese community. This benevolent-protective function was similar to that of the CCBA and other traditional Chinatown community organizations. At the same time, the power of business leaders over the community suggests the hierarchical nature of the Chinese immigrant society in Chicago and perhaps of Chinese immigrant communities everywhere.

The various functions of On Leong were also comparable to those of the CCBA. During its heyday, On Leong exerted great efforts to protect its members on all fronts. It maintained peace and order in the Chinese community by acting as an unofficial if despotic self-governing body in Chinatown. It represented the Chinese community and negotiated with the American authorities in legal disputes and socioeconomic interactions with the larger society. It provided translation aid, lodging, and business assistance to new immigrants. On Leong also organized various celebrations of traditional Chinese holidays and other significant occasions. The legal, social, economic, cultural, and spiritual functions of On Leong were invaluable and much needed by the Chinese community at a time when the Chinese were segregated from mainstream society and vulnerable to physical attacks and social ridicule on the part of the larger society.

Nonetheless, the protective and hierarchical nature of On Leong also prevented it from reaching out and bridging the gap between the Chinese community and the larger society. The protection provided by On Leong was not only necessary for the social and economic functioning of the community but essential for the commercial success of its business leaders. The self-contained nature of On Leong was shaped both by the alienating socioeconomic environment in the larger society and by the socioeconomic hierarchy within the Chinese community as well.

While On Leong was more of a self-contained and dominant fixture of the early Chinese communities in Chicago, other community organizations that hybridized or adapted American values also arose to bridge the gap between the Chinese communities and the larger society. These hybrid and Americanized community organizations, along with Christian institutions, public and parochial schools, and Chinese-language newspapers, were responsible for the emergence of a new Chinese American identity among the Chinese Chicagoans. At the same time they were also responsible for connecting the overseas Chinese society with the homeland. These transnational connections reached their zenith during the 1930s, when Japan invaded China and waged an all-out war against it.

Connecting the Two Worlds

Chinese Students and Intellectuals, 1920s–2010s

Chicago is an American metropolis known for its many highly regarded institutions of higher learning and for its intellectual prowess in propelling progressive social reform movements. Many preeminent American intellectuals were trained or began their academic careers at the University of Chicago or other area universities.[1] These universities have also attracted large numbers of Chinese students and intellectuals since the late nineteenth century. The Department of Sociology at the University of Chicago, in particular, has recruited a number of brilliant and ambitious Chinese intellectuals from China and from Chinese American communities across the country since the 1920s.[2] Influenced by the Chicago School's progressive spirit and inspired by the millennium-old Chinese tradition that intellectuals should carry with them the burden of educating the masses and worrying about the future of their homeland and their compatriots, Chinese students and intellectuals, either China born or American born, have been catalysts for social reform movements in China and for the assimilation of Chinese in America. They have promoted new ideas for China's socioeconomic development; advocated republicanism, nationalism, and patriotism during times of war and turmoil; and returned to China to serve their country upon graduation or completion of their training abroad. They have also been keenly concerned about the well-being and future of their fellow Chinese in America.

This sense of duty and spirit of social reform are also manifested in their urge to find the best ways for all Chinese to integrate into the host country.

They have enthusiastically advocated for the assimilation of Chinese immigrants into American society, as evidenced in papers, theses, dissertations, articles, and books produced by Chinese intellectuals at Chicago-area universities. Within the rich body of literature on Chinese Chicago, many of these works possess enduring influence, not only for the understanding of Chinese Chicago but also for understanding Chinese and Asian America.

A Collective Portrait

To become familiar with the writings of area Chinese students and intellectuals, we will begin with a collective portrait of Chinese students and intellectuals, tracing their social origins, means of emigration, and educational and professional experiences here.[3] As these features differed at different historical times, I divide the history of Chinese students in America into three periods: (1) pioneer students, 1870s–1930s; (2) wartime and postwar students, 1930s–1960s; and (3) contemporary students, 1960s–2010s, to better demonstrate the distinct characteristics of each historical period.

PIONEER STUDENTS AND INTELLECTUALS, 1870S–1930S

Since the first Chinese male student, Yung Wing, graduated from Yale University in 1854, the flow of Chinese students has never ceased, as Chinese students were one of the nonlaboring classes exempted from the Chinese Exclusion Act of 1882. Between 1872 and 1881, 120 Chinese students studied in the United States supported by Qing government scholarships.[4] In the following two decades, the number of Chinese students entering colleges or universities in the United States totaled 32,[5] and in 1903, there were 50 Chinese students in America.[6] From 1909 onward, however, the number of Chinese students in the United States began to increase more rapidly. There were 239 in 1909, 292 in 1910, and 650 in 1911.[7] This rapid increase was due partly to China's Westernization movement and partly to the Boxer Indemnity Fellowship, which provided scholarships for selected Chinese students to study in the United States.[8]

A few Chinese female students also arrived in the United States as early as 1881. According to a survey conducted by the China Institute in America in 1954, the number of female students continued to increase after the turn of the twentieth century: between 1910 and 1930, their population increased sixfold, in the same proportion as the increase in the Chinese student population as a whole.

While most Chinese male students came to America with Chinese government scholarships, the majority of early Chinese female students arrived in the United States by means of private funding. Christian missionaries were the primary source of support for Chinese female students in America. Once the Opium War had opened China's doors to the Western powers in the 1840s, American missionary workers began preaching in the coastal areas and port cities, where they established schools, hospitals, and other charitable facilities. At a time when public education was not available to women in China, schools run by Christian missions provided opportunities for women to obtain a Western-style education.[9]

The first schools for girls were founded by Christian missionaries in Hong Kong in 1844, in Guangzhou in 1846, and in Shantou in 1860.[10] In 1920, according to a report from the Canton Missionary Conference, there were 236 Chinese girls enrolled in middle schools run by the missions in Guangdong Province.[11] Most of the girls enrolled in the mission schools were from affluent Chinese Christian families. According to a private survey performed in 1933, more than 90 percent of these girls were the daughters of businessmen or professionals, and more than half of them had Protestant Christian parents.[12] Chinese girls who studied in mission schools and daughters of Chinese Christians benefited from their association with the missionaries and were able to enter the United States even during the period when the Chinese exclusion laws were in force (1882–1943).

Although the majority of the Chinese female students of this period were sponsored by Christian missionaries, a few came to America with scholarships from the Chinese government. According to Y. C. Wang, three women were awarded scholarships for study in America in 1907 by Jiangsu Province and one by Zhejiang Province in the same year.[13] Wang's study also indicates that "by 1910 self-supporting female students abroad were competing on equal terms with male students for government scholarships."[14]

After the establishment of the Republic of China in 1912, the new government continued to send students abroad to study. In addition to national scholarships, scholarships for study abroad were also provided by provincial governments and by private organizations.[15] As a result, the number of Chinese students in America increased to 1,446 in 1922, including 135 women.[16]

Most of these female students had obtained a Western education at mission schools in China and had a good command of the English language.[17]

Academic life was a large part of Chinese students' experience in America. While most Chinese male students concentrated in such practical fields as business administration, chemistry, and engineering, most Chinese female students also chose courses that would be useful in their future careers. According to a survey in 1954 by the Chinese Institute in America, the top ten courses of study chosen by Chinese female students were, in descending order, (1) education, (2) sociology and chemistry, (3) home economics, (4) English, (5) general arts, (6) music, (7) history, (8) psychology and nursing, (9) mathematics, and (10) biology, art and archaeology, and medicine.[18] It was expected that they could readily apply the knowledge acquired from these courses upon returning to China.

These pioneer Chinese students also participated in extracurricular activities such as YMCA or YWCA programs, prayer meetings, and club meetings.[19] Above all, most Chinese students were concerned about their home country and conscious of their future roles in China. In an essay written in 1911 for her college magazine, *The Wesleyan*, titled "The Influence of Foreign-Educated Students on China," for instance, Chingling Soong, the second of the Soong sisters, who later married Sun Yat-sen, recommended a Western type of government in China and suggested that the returned Chinese students had already improved the quality of Chinese officialdom.[20]

Chinese students at various American universities had organized local student clubs in the 1900s. On the basis of these clubs a national Chinese students' organization, the Chinese Students' Alliance of the United States of America, was formed in the fall of 1911. The alliance held a conference for Chinese students each summer and published annual, quarterly, and monthly reports containing news of student activities and substantive articles reflecting Chinese students' concerns and ideas.[21]

Chinese students not only associated themselves with political movements in China but also identified themselves with their compatriots in American Chinatowns. Dr. Chi Che Wang, for example, was known for her active participation in civic efforts in Chicago. Born in Suzhou, China, in 1894, Wang was sent by her parents to America for a good education. After receiving a bachelor's degree from Wesley College in 1914, she attended the University of Chicago, where she received a master's degree in chemistry in 1916 and a doctorate in nutrition and chemistry in 1918. She helped to found the Chicago Chinese Women's Club around 1915 and remained active for a decade.[22]

Unlike Chi Che Wang, many of these pioneer Chinese students returned to China after the completion of their education or training and became prominent in their professions. The first four Chinese female students on record who received medical degrees from American colleges became the first women doctors in China upon their return.[23]

A more prominent and concrete example is provided by Dr. Se Moy-Yu, whose story was recorded in the *Chinese Daily Times*, a Chinese-language newspaper in Chicago, on September 5, 1936, when she visited Chicago. Se Moy-Yu was born in Jiangxi, China, and graduated from Michigan University Medical College in 1896, arguably becoming the first female Chinese doctor with Western medical training. She returned to China soon after graduation and "devoted all her life to medicine," establishing hospitals and schools in Shanghai and Zhejiang. Her dedication to medicine earned her great respect and fame in both China and America; her success was especially inspirational to other female doctors. On September 4, during her tour of America, she attended the Chicago Children's Memorial Hospital banquet for all female doctors in Chicagoland.[24]

Other Chinese students in Chicago also returned to China upon graduation and offered their services to the homeland. In the early 1920s, Yusheng Wong, a visiting Chinese student in Chicago, married Lillie Moy, the oldest daughter of Moy Dong Chow, who had just received a college degree from the University of Illinois, Chicago. Aspiring to build careers in China, the couple went to China in 1924 with the intention of working at Nankai University in Tianjin. Yusheng Wong eventually attained "high government positions."[25]

WARTIME AND POSTWAR STUDENTS AND INTELLECTUALS, 1930S–1960S

Nationalistic and patriotic sentiments among the Chinese students and intellectuals reached their height during the 1930s and 1940s, when Japan invaded China, first Manchuria in 1931 and then, beginning in 1937, the rest of China, until 1945, when World War II ended.

Chinese intellectuals in Chicago were also passionate about the welfare of China. They believed that a key to the transition to modernity in China was the establishment and fortification of a nationalized educational system. An editorial commentary with the headline "Essential Factors in the National-ized Education System," published in the March 8 and 9, 1935, issues of the *Chinese Daily Times*, listed eight factors essential for such a system: (1) the organization of a board of education in every town, city, county, and state headed by the executive committee of the education department of the cen-tral government; (2) consultation with national experts; (3) strict execution of the orders of the central office of the department of education; (4) state responsibility in utilizing specialists; (5) local support of the educational boards; (6) city and state financing of the elementary and middle school op-erations; (7) local freedom for educational experiments; and (8) state finan-cial responsibility for any locality that was unable to establish an elementary and middle school.[26] Of course, this nationalized educational system with local freedom and responsibility was inspired principally by the American educational system. Advocating an American model for the modernization of China was a widely held view of the Chinese intellectuals of the time.

In addition to advocating, some Chinese intellectuals worked in China-town as teachers at the local Chinese schools sponsored by community or-ganizations. In 1938, the Chicago CCBA hired two scholars from China as teachers for its Chinese adult school: Mr. C. S. Chang and Miss I. T. Yi. Chang was a graduate of Kunming University in China and had been on the staff of the Canton State Normal School before coming to America. He had been a student at Stanford University and was currently studying at a Chicago-area university. Miss Yi was a graduate of Zhongshan University in China and had been a senior high school teacher at Canton State Normal School for Girls. She came to Chicago as a graduate student at the Univer-sity of Chicago.[27] Both brought their educational experiences in China to Chicago's Chinatown and helped improve the Chinese literacy of its resi-dents, who could then read Chinese-language newspapers to increase their awareness of conditions in China.

The close collaboration between Chinese intellectuals and the Chicago Chinese community is also evident at the conference for the North-American Chinese Student Association (formally the North-American Chinese Student Alliance of the United States of America) held from Au-gust 30 to September 5, 1935. While the Chicago Student Association was working hard to prepare for the conference by renting a meeting hall and finding temporary lodgings for the delegates, local Chinese businesses enthusiastically provided financial assistance to the conference. The CCBA and the Chinese Trade Company sponsored the student delegates' sightseeing trips and one of their dinners.[28]

The trend of Chinese graduates of American universities returning to China was most prominent in the 1930s, owing in part to the less accommodating climate for the Chinese in the American professional job market and in part to Chinese intellectuals' strong feelings of patriotism toward their homeland in its time of trouble. G. P. Moy, for example, the son of Chicago Chinese merchant T. L. Moy, left Chicago for a position in China soon after graduating in 1936 from the Armour Institute's school of electrical engineering with an excellent academic record.[29]

Many Chinese students who were still working on academic degrees in America participated in patriotic activities in America and pledged to return to China as soon as they had completed their education or training. From September 1 to 4, 1937, in response to Japan's full-scale invasion of China on July 7 of that year, the North-American Chinese Students Association held its second conference of delegates at the University of Chicago International House. Over fifty delegates were present, representing Chinese students from university campuses across the United States and Canada.[30] J. Chin, president of the association, announced on the opening day of the conference that it would focus on patriotic activities on the part of Chinese students in North America and divided all issues into two "separate divisions," one dealing with "problems and works in China" and the other with "problems and works abroad." The conference then formed a committee of investigation to assess the accomplishments of the two-year-old association, on the basis of which future plans would be made. The delegates also voted unanimously to send a telegram to the central government of China urging it to conduct a prolonged war of resistance in order to eventually defeat Japan.[31]

On September 4, the closing day of the conference, the student delegates reconfirmed the above decisions and agreed to send an open letter to the CCBA and all other Chinese organizations in the United States. In the letter the students commended the Chinese community organizations' "excellent and unforgettable patriotic activities," encouraged them to continue their "untiring efforts in striving to maintain our national integrity," and offered their own services to China in the near future.[32] The delegates also urged Chinese student organizations throughout North America to participate in the expansion of their patriotic activities. The delegates selected seven schools and regional associations to be responsible for the association's subdepartmental work:

1. Chicago Students Association—publications
2. New York Chinese Students Association—general business
3. California Chinese Students Association—finance
4. Southern United States Chinese Students Association—Chinese merchants
5. Boston Chinese Students Association—exhortation and publicity
6. Michigan Chinese Students Association—research studies
7. Canadian Chinese Students Association—social[33]

The selection of Chicago as the conference site and the organizational structure of the North-American Chinese Students Association clearly reveal the influence and major role played by the Chicago Students Association. Chicago's position as a national center of higher education undoubtedly helped the Chicago Students Association assert a more active role within the North-American Chinese Students Association.

In late September 1937, the student delegates gathered again in Chicago for another conference to discuss the urgent situation in China. C. T. Wong, the Chinese ambassador to the United States, was invited to deliver a speech. Ambassador Wong urged the students, especially those who were majoring in the sciences, to return to China soon to serve their country.[34]

One of the students who responded to the call from the Chinese government and returned to China to serve its anti-Japanese war efforts was Yung-yang Wu. Wu first studied at the University of Indiana and then in 1936 entered the Chicago Aeronautical University, specializing in aeronautical engineering. Actively involved in student organizations and concerned with the affairs of China, he served as president and secretary of the Chicago Chinese Aeronautic Student Association. He graduated on January 27, 1938, with a degree in aeronautical engineering, planning to return to China immediately.[35]

During the World War II years and the aftermath of the Communist takeover of China in 1949, a larger number of educated Chinese came to the United States. According to a 1954 survey by the China Institute in America, the number of Chinese students in America increased from 706 in 1943 to 3,914 in 1948. The ratio of female to male students also increased, from 1 in 6 in the 1930s to 1 in 3 in the 1940s and 1950s.[36] These Chinese students' socioeconomic and cultural connections to the Nationalist government and the elite classes in China differentiated them from their predecessors. Some came to America for further education, with scholarships from the Nationalist Chinese government or from American institutions, or with funds provided by individuals in America.[37] Others were sent by their wealthy families in China to escape Communist rule or to inherit their family estates in the United States. Still others were offspring of former Nationalist diplomats who stayed with their parents when the latter decided to remain in the United States after the Communists took over China. Many of these students completed their educations without interruption and found employment in academic and professional fields in America.

CONTEMPORARY STUDENTS AND INTELLECTUALS, 1960S–2010S

Between the 1960s and 2010s, two large groups of Chinese students came to the United States: one from Taiwan beginning in the 1960s and a second from the People's Republic of China (PRC) after 1979. Most Chinese students of this period were pushed to America by their respective government's drive toward modernization and by a variety of practical reasons for (or impractical illusions about) studying in America. Because the two groups began their emigration at different times, they will be discussed in chronological order.

In the 1960s, under pressure from the civil rights movement, American immigration policy became more liberal and the United States attracted more Chinese immigrants than ever before.[38] The 1965 immigration law reform encouraged the entry of foreign nationals with better education and special training. Students from Taiwan formed the first wave of the large-scale student immigration. According to John T. Ma, from 1950 to 1974 a total of 30,765 students were approved by the Ministry of Education in Taiwan for advanced study in the United States. Although there are no exact data on how many of these Taiwanese students stayed in the United States after completing their education, Ma's study indicates that many of them planned to stay instead of returning home.[39] In the following decades, the number of Chinese students from Taiwan increased rapidly. Between 1979 and 1987, approximately 186,000 students from Taiwan came to America to continue their education, with only 10,000 returning home.[40] The "study abroad craze" in Taiwan was rooted in the success of the postwar Taiwan economy. In the 1960s, Taiwan experienced rapid economic growth accompanied by structural and demographic changes. A dramatic rise in the relative significance of the nonagicultural sector, particularly manufacturing, and industrial development required more highly educated and well-trained personnel.[41]

Many of the students from Taiwan during this period were from families of current or former Nationalist government officials and military personnel who had followed the Nationalist government to Taiwan just before and after the 1949 Communist takeover of the mainland.[42] After moving to Taiwan, however, their family lives were filled with hard work and a scarcity of material goods.[43] Many had to depend on scholarships from the Nationalist government in Taiwan or from American higher educational institutions or private funds to study in American universities and colleges.[44] Many others worked part-time jobs while enrolled as students or worked during summers to earn money for the next school year.[45]

The social origins and means of emigration for Chinese students from Taiwan in the more affluent 1980s and 1990s, however, were different from those in the preceding decades. My own survey of over one hundred female students from Taiwan in 1993 indicates that about 70 percent of the students in this period were the children of Taiwanese businessmen, many of them involved in manufacturing clothing or computers, others selling interior decorating materials or musical instruments, still others working in banks or advertising firms, just to name a few.[46] Most of the students of this period were financially supported either by their parents or their own savings. With more ample funds, they thus had different experiences in America than those of their predecessors. For some, life in America was exciting and full of opportunities; for others, it was a mixture of bitter and sweet experiences. No matter what specific situations they individually faced, however, they all worked hard to achieve their educational and professional goals.

During their first few years in the United States, the chief difficulties for many seem to have been the language problem and cultural unfamiliarity.[47] Financial difficulties also plagued those whose scholarships were insufficient to support their education. Yet despite these difficulties, most Chinese students from Taiwan successfully completed their educations and found employment in the United States; some were employed by educational or research institutions, while others entered the business world as entrepreneurs or brokers. Of the seven students I interviewed who came from

Taiwan during the 1960s and 1970s, for example, three obtained master's degrees in counseling, library science, and special education, respectively, and three received doctoral degrees in economics, food science, and finance. Four of them became professionals working in educational institutions, one as a professor, one a researcher, one a librarian, and one a high school teacher; two others became restaurateurs; and one became a stockbroker.[48]

After the normalization of diplomatic relations between the PRC and the United States in 1979, the so-called study abroad craze in Taiwan spread to the Chinese mainland. Since the establishment of the PRC in 1949, the Communist government, like its predecessors, has relied on foreign countries to train its specialists. As the Soviet Union was the only foreign power friendly to China during its first decades, the Chinese government initially sent its students to Russia, until the 1960s when relations between Moscow and Beijing deteriorated. At that time, Mao Zedong led China into a reclusive existence by advocating and enforcing self-sufficiency and self-reliance. During the decade of the Cultural Revolution (1966–1976), international exchange programs were essentially suspended and almost no one was sent abroad to study, except for 1,629 students who studied primarily foreign languages.[49] Following the Sino-American reconciliation in 1972, the government once again began to view foreign study as a shortcut to the acquisition of world-class scientific and technical knowledge. The decision to initiate scholarly exchanges was made in 1978, even before the normalization of relations between the United States and the PRC in 1979. Since then, cultural exchange has remained a vital link in the relationship between the two countries.

Similar to what had happened in Taiwan two decades before, studying abroad became very popular in the PRC, simply because one was likely to be better off with an American degree. For middle-aged and established scholars, study abroad became a criterion for promotion.[50] For young university or college graduates, an advanced degree from a foreign institution, especially one in the United States (colloquially referred to as *dujin,* "gold plating"), promised a successful career in China.[51]

For many of these people, however, study in America meant not only academic improvement but also material gain in terms of money they could save from their meager scholarships, stipends, or any other type of income. Although small by American standards, these savings were significant to many Chinese in modernizing their daily life. They could equip their families with modern electronic gadgets by converting their hard-currency dollar savings into Chinese currency at a very favorable exchange rate.[52] Others went to study in the United States simply to find an opportunity to stay there permanently.[53]

Motivated by various dreams and expectations, more and more Chinese students and scholars have entered the United States since 1979. According to official Chinese records, between 1979 and 1988, 36,000 Chinese students studied in the United States; 37 percent of them were self-supporting.[54] According to American sources, the number was even larger; Jesse Chain Chou's study indicates that there were 63,000 students and scholars from the PRC during that time period.[55] The INS estimated that there were 73,000 Chinese students in the United States in June 1989.[56] In a statement on December 2, 1989, President George H. W. Bush announced that "as many as 80,000 Chinese have studied and conducted research in the United States since these exchanges began."[57] More recent official Chinese records show that from 1978 to 2008, nearly 1.4 million Chinese students and scholars had studied abroad and that the majority, about two-thirds, had stayed abroad and adjusted their immigrant status.[58]

In contrast to government-sponsored students and scholars (J-1 visa holders), self-supporting students (F-1 visa holders) were financed either by American institutions or by their relatives in the United States.[59] They usually hoped to earn a graduate degree first, then find a job and eventually become permanent residents in America. A survey of over two hundred Chinese students' spouses conducted by the author in 1990 indicates that 90 percent of F-1 students hoped to stay in the United States after the completion of their education. The journey toward this dream, however, has been difficult, even for those who came to the United States with financial support from American relatives. They were usually guaranteed at least one year of financial aid in accordance with immigration regulations, but in fact most of them had to earn their living and tuition from the very beginning. Ms. Z., a student from Shanghai sponsored by her relatives in the United States, recounted her difficulties: "Even though I am sponsored by my relatives here, actually I have to live on my own. I have to make money for my schooling and everything. I work in cafeteria, I work in library, I work in whatever job I could find. Before I came, I never thought life would be this hard."[60]

The sex ratio among Chinese students from the PRC has remained uneven. Since 1979, according to Leo A. Orleans, less than 20 percent of the

J-1 students have been female, while there were no female F-1 students at all until 1983.[61] But this small percentage of female Chinese students in America in fact reflected the sex ratio among students in Chinese higher education. In most Chinese universities or colleges before 2000, the percentage of female students varied from 10 to 45 percent, depending on the field of study. Generally, female students comprised roughly 10 percent of those in the pure sciences and engineering, 30 percent of those in medicine, and 40 to 45 percent of those in the humanities.[62] In other words, female students were underrepresented in all subjects, especially the sciences, within the Chinese higher educational system. This disparity is a complex historical phenomenon. Traditional values together with gender discrimination in both secondary education and university admissions policies worked together to discourage women from pursuing higher education in China. Not surprisingly, this small percentage of female university students in China resulted in an even smaller percentage of female students studying abroad.

Moreover, as a general rule the Chinese government has given first priority to sending students in the pure sciences and engineering abroad. Chinese authorities have always been reluctant to spend the nation's foreign currency reserve on students in the humanities, believing that only those individuals who have special advanced training in the sciences and technology can immediately benefit the country.

The grossly uneven distribution between the sexes among Chinese students began to change in 1985, when the Chinese government revised its policy regarding cultural exchange programs, making it more flexible and less restrictive than before. More students and scholars in the humanities were selected to study in the United States, and consequently more female students crossed the Pacific Ocean, owing to the relatively higher percentage of female students in the humanities. By the end of the 1980s, female Chinese students comprised 30 percent of all Chinese students in the universities and colleges in the United States.[63]

The relaxation of official Chinese policies also contributed to another demographic change. Starting in the early 1980s, many Chinese students began to arrange for their spouses to join them abroad, something never officially permitted before. According to the State Education Commission Provisions on Study Abroad, promulgated in December 1986, "Since the time of studying abroad for the graduate students is relatively longer, applications of their spouses for visiting them abroad should be processed."[64] This same document also stipulated:

> If, during the visiting period, the spouse of the graduate student obtains foreign scholarships or subsidiary funding and applies to study abroad then she/he can report to her/his employing unit for approval during her/his visitation abroad, thus becoming a public- or self-funded student studying abroad through the proper procedures.[65]

Since the inception of this policy, more Chinese women have joined their student husbands and some Chinese men have joined their student wives. According to my survey in 1990, of over two hundred Chinese students' spouses, more than 90 percent of them came to the United States after 1987. Ninety-five percent of the wives of students were college/university graduates, and many came to America planning first, because it was easier, to enter the United States as the dependent of an already-admitted student and then, secondarily, to be admitted to an American institution for a graduate degree herself.[66] These women were potential Chinese female students in the United States, and many have in fact fulfilled their secondary goal of studying in the United States.[67] The presence of Chinese student wives helped balance the uneven sex distribution among Chinese students; in 1990 the ratio of females to males became 3 to 4 in most American colleges and universities.[68]

The socioeconomic background of current Chinese students from the PRC resembles that of their predecessors. About 90 percent of them are children of professionals, including teachers, doctors, and "cadres" (i.e., government officials, the equivalent of civil servants in the United States). The intellectual influence from their families as well as their parents' easier access to power and privileges in China has helped them achieve higher education and obtain government permission for emigration.[69]

Reflecting the academic situation in China, most Chinese students from the PRC are concentrated in the general sciences, engineering, and business and finance, with fewer in the humanities and fine arts.[70] Like their counterparts from Taiwan, many find academic work challenging owing to their lack of proficiency in English.[71] In addition to difficulty with English, computer illiteracy constituted another barrier in academic life for Chinese students prior to the 1990s; most of them had not used computers in China and were therefore intimidated by them. Realizing that the ability to use a computer was indispensable for academic training as well as for virtually any profession, however, they overcame their fears and frustrations and learned to use them.[72]

Also like their predecessors, many Chinese students from the PRC were concerned about the future of China, urging the Chinese government to carry out democratic political and economic reforms and supporting the prodemocracy demonstrations in China in early 1989. The Tiananmen Incident on June 4, 1989, however, disappointed them greatly. Many decided to take advantage of the liberalized US immigration policy toward Chinese students after the Tiananmen Incident, staying in the United States and looking for employment upon or even before the completion of their education.[73] Although we do not have specific statistics on how many Chinese students have entered the professions in the United States, individual cases indicate that many Chinese students have become professionals such as professors, lawyers, researchers, and librarians and that they are making steady progress in their careers.[74] Like their counterparts in earlier decades, Chinese students from the PRC are transforming into members of the Chinese American middle class, whose cultural and socioeconomic importance will grow with time.

While the movement to study abroad in the PRC has continued its momentum, it has abated in Taiwan since the late 1990s. According to my 2001 study, a number of factors have contributed to this decline. First, postgraduate education in Taiwan has developed rapidly since the late 1980s and is now on a par with international standards, largely owing to the large number of returned PhDs from abroad. More university graduates have consequently been attracted to stay in Taiwan for their postgraduate education; moreover, a postgraduate degree from overseas is no longer a requirement for career development and promotion in most institutions of higher education. Second, the rapid development of the information technology (IT) industry in Taiwan provides easily accessible information from around the world to one's home or office without the need to physically go abroad. Third, the younger generation, having grown up during the past two decades in a more affluent and democratic Taiwan, have less desire than their predecessors to go abroad for advanced study. Instead they are more attracted to summer language programs or other short-term training programs or tourism overseas.[75] This changing pattern of the movement in Taiwan to study abroad has obviously changed the composition of Chinese students and intellectuals in the United States. As fewer students come from Taiwan or remain in America after completion of their education or training, students and professionals from the PRC now play an increasingly dominant role among the Chinese students and intellectuals in the United States.

Generally speaking, however, the Chinese students and scholars in the Chicago-area colleges and universities are confined to their campuses, busy with their own academic work, and have only limited contact with the local Chinese communities in Chicagoland. For instance, the members of the Chinese Students and Scholars Association at the University of Chicago, according to its mission statement, strive to "bring social awareness of Chinese culture and traditions, to develop friendship among the Chinese [student] community, and to promote cultural exchange between the Chinese [students] community with other ethnic groups at the University of Chicago."[76] Their activities are in large part aimed at enhancing the educational experience of the Chinese students and scholars on campus. Their connections with the Chinese communities in Chicago are limited to occasional contacts with businesses in Chinatown such as travel agents and restaurants.[77]

Connecting the Two Worlds

THE DUALITY OF "INSIDER" AND "OUTSIDER"

The relationship of Chinese students and intellectuals with Chicago's Chinatown has been ambivalent, characterized by a duality of attachment and detachment, and a status simultaneously of "insider" and "outsider." On the one hand, they are attached to Chinatown for practical reasons. For those who do not have a scholarship to support their studies, Chinatown can provide a livelihood; many Chinese students put themselves through college by working as waiters or waitresses in Chinese restaurants, often illegally. For a few others who study the social sciences, Chinatown can serve as a social laboratory for their research, where they can participate in or observe community activities on which they can perform theoretical analyses and draw conclusions in their academic writings. Those who work or participate in activities in Chinatown during their academic training thereby temporarily become accidental or conditional "insiders."

Even these temporary "insiders," however, detach themselves from Chinatown, both for professional and for practical reasons. As required by their academic training and the nature of academic research, those who conduct fieldwork in Chinatown have to detach themselves from the community in order to gain objective observation and analysis from the perspective of a neutral "outsider." For most of them Chinatown is hardly a destination of their life in America but rather only a transitory or discretional element of their lives. Once finished with their academic training, they move on to somewhere else. Some leave the United States to return to China, while others remain in America and are hired by employers in mainstream society, and so their livelihoods no longer depend on Chinatown. Interaction with Chinatown is no longer a necessity. Those who return to China and only occasionally visit the United States might come back to Chinatown for a brief visit when convenient. Those who remain in America often come to Chinatown on weekends or holidays to shop for Asian ingredients, dine in Chinese restaurants, or participate in cultural activities taking place there; to them, Chinatown is only an auxiliary to their largely Americanized lives.

This dialectic of attachment and detachment determines the identification of Chinese students and intellectuals with Chinatown as a conflicted one. On the one hand, their ethnic consciousness and nationalistic pride lead them to believe that they share a common identity with the Chinatown masses. This shared *Chineseness* pulls them toward Chinatown and makes them sympathetic to its residents. But their social and economic status, on the other hand, separates them from Chinatown, since they do not have to depend on Chinatown for survival or advancement in their career. They are distanced and less affected by conditions in Chinatown; they identify more with educated, middle-class Americans, viewing the immigrant residents and menial laborers in Chinatown as less assimilated working-class Chinese. Thus, their involvement with Chinatown is more motivated by humanitarian or charitable considerations, the detached social obligations of "outsiders," rather than the shared struggle for survival of the "insiders." This contradiction limits the Chinese students and intellectuals in their connection with Chinatown.

Nevertheless, historically some Chinese students and intellectuals, while engaged in activities in Chinatown, whether because of practical considerations or a sense of moral obligation, with their greater proficiency in English and advanced academic training, have helped connect Chinatown residents with the homeland and with mainstream American society. They have acted as catalysts that kindled or rekindled patriotic and nationalistic fervor among Chinatown residents and helped link Chinatown with political affairs in the homeland.

Chinese students and intellectuals have also acted as cultural brokers who help bridge the gaps between Chinese culture and Western culture. As discussed in Chapter 5, Chinese students enrolled at universities and colleges in the Chicago area were responsible for instilling progressive sentiments in the waiters in Chinese restaurants, many of whom were students, and for establishing the Mon Sang Association in 1918, an organization for Chinese restaurant workers similar to a labor union. They demanded a minimum wage sufficient to support a waiter, his wife, and at least three minor children; sickness, old age, and disability benefits; and a maximum eight-hour workday and (only) six workdays a week.[78]

The most recognizable contribution of Chinese students and intellectuals to the Chicago Chinese communities is a rich body of academic literature, which theorized Chinatown in order to promote a greater understanding of Chinese Americans. Through their various disciplines these writings present and interpret Chicago's Chinese American communities to mainstream American readers.

THEORIZING CHINATOWN

Many Chinese intellectuals at area universities and colleges have used Chicago Chinese communities as subjects for their academic research. Over the decades, their studies of Chinese communities naturally have reflected the transformation of the Chinese communities in Chicago over time. To represent this historical evolution, I have grouped the intellectuals who have studied Chinese Chicago into three categories, more or less consistent with the periodization of Chinese students and intellectuals discussed in the previous section. They include the pioneer scholars from the 1920s and 1930s, including Tin-Chiu Fan, Ching-Chao Wu, Ruth Joan Soong, and Bingham Dai; wartime and postwar scholars from the 1940s to the 1960s, typified by Yuan Liang, Rose Hum Lee, and Paul C. P. Siu; and contemporary scholars from the 1960s to 2010, as showcased in the scholarly writings of (in chronological order of their publication dates) Margaret Gibbons Wilson, Peter S. Li, Susan Lee Moy, Harry Ying Cheng Kiang, Minglan Cheung Keener, Linda Qingling Wang, Adam McKeown, Henry Yu, John S. Rohsenow, Yvonne M. Lau, Mae M. Ngai, Shanshan Lan, and Ling Z. Arenson, among others.

Scholars from the first two groups were almost exclusively students from the Sociology Department at the University of Chicago, while scholars from the third group were mostly students or scholars from various universities in the area, reflecting a more diverse profile of scholarship on Chicago in anthropology, education, geography, history, linguistics, and sociology. This wide range of fields reflects the academic expansion of Asian American studies that has evolved from and grown well beyond the Chicago School of sociology in the last half century.

Keen Observers, 1920s to 1930s   Tin-Chiu Fan was a Mandarin speaker who came to Chicago in the 1920s to study in the Department of Sociology at the University of Chicago through his connection with Christian missionary organizations in China. Unable to speak Cantonese (or more specifically Taishanese, the common language of the Chinese immigrants in Chicago), Tin-Chiu Fan compensated for his language handicap with assistance from Alfred S. K. Sze, then a Chinese government minister to the United States, who wrote letters of introduction to various Chinese individuals and Chinese organizations in the city. Surveys and occasional interviews with community leaders who could speak Mandarin constituted the major primary sources of Fan's study.[79]

Fan's master's thesis, "Chinese Residents in Chicago," completed in 1926, is the first known academic study of the Chinese in Chicago. With help from leaders of the local Chinese community civic associations and elders of the Chinese family associations, Fan compiled useful data on occupational distribution, earnings, living conditions, educational status, criminality, and community organizations. His interview of Moy Dong Chow (or T. C. Moy, as given in Fan's thesis) has been cited repeatedly in later studies of the Chinese in Chicago.[80]

Like Tin-Chiu Fan, Ching-Chao Wu was also a Mandarin speaker from northern China who studied at the University of Chicago through the same missionary social network. Like Fan, Wu also had limited contacts with Chicago Chinatown. Alternatively, Wu pulled individual cases from the hundreds of life histories of second-generation Chinese and Japanese Americans on the Pacific Coast gathered during the Survey of Race Relations in the 1920s, a massive survey led by a group of scholars that was intended to investigate economic, religious, educational, civic, biological, and social conditions among the Chinese, Japanese, and other nonwhite residents of the Pacific Coast region of the United States and Canada. In 1928, Wu completed his doctoral dissertation, "Chinatowns: A Study of Symbiosis and Assimilation," focusing on the overall conditions of Chinese immigrants in America. Because of its broader scope, Wu's study is less useful for the understanding of Chinese Chicago than Fan's.[81]

While Fan's thesis was largely a compilation of information with limited analysis or employment of the concepts of the Chicago School of sociology, Wu's dissertation deftly utilized Park's theory of the immigrant as a "marginal man" to understand Chinatowns in America.[82] Wu stated that when a Chinese immigrant experienced such American influences as public schools, Sunday schools, and missionary efforts, "he is, sooner or later, transformed into a marginal man, a new personality which is the subjective aspect of the fusion of cultures." The language Wu used was almost identical to that in Park's discussion on the marginal man: "The conflict of cultures which is inevitable when incompatible ideas and practices are brought together goes on just in the mind of the marginal man. His mind is the real melting pot of cultures."[83]

Little is known about Ruth Joan Soong's family background. Judging from her proficiency in English, research interests and methodology, and sentiments revealed in her 1931 master's thesis in education at the University of Chicago, one may speculate that Soong was a student from China with an advanced Western or Christian educational background or else a second-generation Chinese American woman. An educational sociological work, Soong's thesis combines empirical data, primarily drawn from surveys of 102 students from the On Leong School, with clear and logical analysis. The tables and other data serve as useful supplements to Fan's thesis.[84]

Bingham Dai's 1937 dissertation, "Opium Addiction in Chicago," is a case study of drug addicts in Chicago. Dai had a longtime interest in the opium problem. As a child, he admired his paternal uncle's anti-opium activities, and later he saw the same uncle die as an opium addict. After graduating from college in Shanghai, Dai maintained connections with the Chinese National Anti-Opium Association in Shanghai and the Nationalist government's Opium Suppression Commission in Nanjing in order to educate the masses and help the legislature cope with the opium problem in China. Combining his personal interest and professional training in sociology at the University of Chicago, Dai conducted research from 1933 to 1935 in which he examined over two thousand drug addicts in Chicago.[85]

Dai analyzed the characteristics of opium addicts in terms of race and nationality, nativity, education, occupation, marital status, drug habits and physical well-being, and drug addiction and crime. He found that, among the addicts studied, approximately four-fifths were white, one-fifth black, and the rest of other races, thus discrediting the popular notion that opium addiction was a vicious habit peculiar to a certain race or nationality.[86] Dai's work is arguably the first to study the social behavior of opium addicts in relation to race, class, and national origin. The charts, tables, and maps compiled by Dai from census data also provide useful information on the social conditions of Chicago in the 1930s.

These four scholars (with the possible exception of Soong), like most China-born students studying at the University of Chicago, shared some common traits. They were from major cities in China where American Christian missionary organizations had been active since the late nineteenth century, and their Christian connections assisted their passage to America. Unlike their immigrant counterparts in Chicago, who were chiefly farmers from the Sanyi and Siyi districts of Guangdong with limited or no education who mostly spoke the Taishan dialect of Cantonese, these intellectuals were Mandarin speakers from elite and/or educated families in urban China. These cultural, socioeconomic, geographic, and linguistic differences created a large gap between them and the Chinatown masses. While they felt an affinity with their compatriots in Chinatown in terms of ethnic origin and national pride, they had difficulty identifying themselves with these working-class immigrants.

Most obviously, the language barrier prevented them from having close and personal contacts with Chicago's Chinatown residents. This limitation is reflected in all four scholars' works. Tin-Chiu Fan relied on surveys through the memberships of the civic community organizations of Chinatown and sporadic interviews with a few community leaders; Ching-Chao Wu made use of manuscripts from the Survey of Race Relations; Ruth Joan Soong largely depended on surveys of students from the On Leong School; and Bingham Dai used cases of drug addicts from area governmental and private agencies. None had extensive interviews with the local Chinese. In terms of the participant-observer model of sociological research, they were more observers than participants.

All were keen observers, however, and their nationalistic sensitivity further motivated them to defend their fellow countrymen, despite their linguistic and class differences from the latter. All four scholars made great efforts in their academic writing to repudiate the public anxiety or misunderstanding that the Chinese would take jobs away from white laborers and that Chinese immigrants were detrimental to American society with their "immoral" behavior such as opium smoking, gambling, and prostitution.

In the conclusion of his thesis, Tin-Chiu Fan pointed to the grossly unbalanced ratio of men to women (only 6 percent of the Chinese population in Chicago were females) and the absence of family life as root causes of any so-called immoral behavior on the part of the Chinese, which he said resulted from "crowds of men herded together without the mellowing influence of family life, and subject to terrible temptation." Fan praised interracial marriage as a means of rebalancing the male-female ratio. As the State of Illinois did not forbid interracial marriage between Chinese and whites, there were about eighty such marriages, but these interracial marriages were too few in number to close the gender gap among the Chinese immigrants.[87]

Fan also believed that anti-Chinese propaganda and public misunderstanding were responsible for the social segregation of Chinese from the general public. Despite the Chinese communities' efforts to "acquaint the Chicago Community with what seems to them to be worthy and beautiful in their own group and its literature and its life," he noted, "due to the remaining effect of the propaganda either against or for the Chinese during the anti-Chinese agitation here, the Chinese are over-estimated by the general public in some things and undervalued in others, but misunderstood in most. They are sometimes forced to live in a place surrounded by drab environment; looked upon with contempt and scorn; regarded as undesirable and unworthy. They are not usually equally treated wherever they go."[88]

Last, Fan rebutted the notion that Chinese immigrants would take away jobs from American laborers. "Practically none of the Chinese in the city are now employed in American factories or other industrial establishments. Nor is there a fear of any mischievous influence, morally or socially, through the presence of the 4,500 Chinese in the Chicago community." He further argued, "The presence of Chinese children in the public schools is not resented; they do good work and graduate with credit. The grown-up people, except a very few, have tried their best to live up to the high-sounding principles broadcasted from the American pulpits." Fan concluded his thesis with a strong nationalistic statement: "China is not a nation to be bullied at will. She has the right, and the power, as time will tell to enforce the right, to be treated as a self-respecting and honorable member of the great family of nations."[89]

With similar ethnic sensitivity, Ching-Chao Wu stated in his dissertation, concerning the "immoral" behavior of Chinese, "A man who has been under the influence of two cultures is often described in an unfavorable light. . . . The unfavorable aspect of the marginal man does not need any further elaboration."[90]

With her sharp and accurate intuitions, Ruth Joan Soong provided a profound study of the conditions of Chinese children in Chicago's Chinatown, pinpointing the hybridizing and conflicting nature of Chinatown as a problem inevitably confronting them:

> Chinese children in Chicago, fortunately or unfortunately, have an unusual background—unusual because they are away from their ancient East, living in a "colony" in the modern West. Such a "colony," better known as "Chinatown," exists primarily to promote trade and to regulate life for the Chinese themselves. In one sense, they are not strictly isolated, much to their regret, because the section of Twenty-Second Street and Wentworth Avenue, where they happen to live, brings them near a neighborhood of the worst elements of American culture. On the other hand, they are absolutely isolated, much to their regret, too, because they are segregated from the general American public. . . . Chinatown is neither China nor America, but an offspring of the two. Whether a Chinese child in the town prefers it or not, he is confronted with the fusion or conflict of the two cultures.[91]

Bingham Dai, though indirectly, also rejected the general presumption that associated opium addiction with the Chinese. He concluded in his dissertation: "Opium addiction cannot be considered as a purely physical disease or a vice that is inherent in the individual or race; it is essentially a symptom of a maladjusted personality, a personality whose capacity for meeting cultural demands has been handicapped by inadequate emotional and social development, for which . . . the general cultural chaos and social disorganization that is characteristic of modern society is mainly responsible."[92]

Despite their differences and limitations, these China-born scholars vehemently defended their working-class immigrant compatriots and contributed significantly to the early scholarship on the Chinese in Chicago. Most of the China-born students returned to China upon completion of their education, and some, such as Wu, became influential intellectuals in China.[93]

Participant-Observers, 1940s to 1960s   The Chinese scholars of the next period had closer contacts with the residents of Chinatown, as they were mostly natives of Guangdong; at the same time, American-born Chinese intellectuals had also joined forces to study Chinese communities in America. This marked change enabled the scholarship of the period to be more participant-observatory in nature and to have a more enduring influence, even a half century after its completion.

Rose Hum Lee, a strong-minded yet practical individual, joined the Sociology Department at the University of Chicago in 1942 at the age of 38. Her path to Chicago sociology had been long and winding and she was diverted a few times. As historian Henry Yu observed, Rose Hum Lee "spent the longest time studying Orientals in America and perhaps tried hardest to fulfill the role of cultural translator and marginal man."[94]

Lee was born in Butte, Montana, on August 20, 1904. Her family history was highly representative of the success stories of Chinese immigrants in America. Her father, Hum Wah Long, came to America in the 1870s from Guangdong. Initially landing in California, he worked his way to Montana through manual labor in laundries, in mines, and on ranches and finally settled in Butte, where he became the successful owner of a merchandise store in the Chinatown district, China Alley. As a merchant, he was able to return to China and brought his bride, Lin Fong, back to America with him. The marriage produced seven children, of whom Rose was the second oldest.

Rose Hum Lee's future was significantly influenced by her mother. An illiterate yet extremely determined woman, Lin Fong instilled the values of education and independence in her children, all of whom became honor students at Butte High School and later career professionals. In her dissertation, Lee frequently, though anonymously, used her family, especially her mother, as examples of the successful assimilation of Chinese Americans. After her high school graduation in 1921, Lee worked as a secretary and attended a local college briefly before marrying Ku Young Lee, a Chinese engineering student from the University of Pennsylvania.

The couple moved to China in 1931 and lived in Canton for nearly a decade. This experience of living in China, however, left deep emotional scars. Lee was unable to conceive a child and her in-laws constantly blamed her for her inability to produce an heir for the family, which was considered the primary duty of a Chinese daughter-in-law. Lee later divorced her husband and adopted a daughter from an orphanage where she volunteered. She worked in a variety of administrative positions while in China, including the Guangdong Raw Silk Testing Bureau, the National City Bank of New York, the Sun Life Assurance Company, and the Guangdong Municipal Telephone Exchange. When the Japanese waged all-out war against China in 1937, Lee worked for the Canton Red Cross Women's War Relief Association, the Overseas Relief Unit, and the Guangdong Emergency Committee for the Relief of Refugees, as well as aiding the war effort as a radio operator and translator. In 1939, she returned to America with her daughter, Elaine.

Living in China allowed Lee to reevaluate her Chinese heritage, and she was able to selectively choose the Chinese traits she believed to be valuable and disown those she considered negative, such as unequal gender relations and clannish social structure. Her personal experiences in America and China strongly influenced her intellectual thinking and academic writing.

With encouragement from her mother, Lee returned to college. She financed her education by working at odd jobs and lecturing about Chinese history and culture, as well as about Chinese immigrant experiences in America. She would dress and speak as an American during the lectures and then change into traditional Chinese dress and sell Chinese souvenirs afterwards. Proceeds from these activities enabled Lee to put herself through college.

In her dissertation, "The Growth and Decline of Chinese Communities in the Rocky Mountain Region," which was completed in 1947, Lee used her own family, anonymously, as an example of a success story of Chinese immigrants' assimilation into American society. In fact, the actual identities of all her subjects were erased. This anonymity enabled her to present her work as that of an "outside" observer rather than that of an "insider" who was born and raised in the community.[95]

Compared to Robert Park's theory of the immigrant as a marginal man who lived in conflicting cultures that met and fused, Rose Lee's argument, presented in her dissertation as well as in her later writings, offered a more concrete and definitive solution for the so-called Oriental Problem—the dissolution of Chinatown and complete cultural and racial integration. For Lee, "the completion of the process includes the mixing of cultures and genes so that there are truly no 'dissimilar people.'"[96] As American society becomes ever more multicultural and multiethnic and as the mixed-race American population grows rapidly, Lee's prescription now seems prophetic.

Ironically, despite her sociological training and her career studying Chinese communities in America, Rose Hum Lee's personal interactions

with the Chinatown masses, and especially with the women, were not always pleasant for her, which led to a certain bitterness in her psyche. For
example, she wrote about the reactions of traditional Chinese to the education of women, again citing her own case, in her 1960 book *The Chinese in
the United States of America*, which was published in Hong Kong partly at
her own expense:

> To retaliate for not heeding their wishes, they spread tales of her supposed
> misdeeds in the Midwest, where she attended a famous university. The
> Chinatowners of this prairie city were delighted to have a plum to pick.
> No native-born of this group had ever obtained a doctorate in philosophy,
> though some had received their master's and medical degrees. . . . The local
> Chinese, instead of being sympathetic to professional attainments, dispar-
> aged this girl's achievements. Her personal life was the subject of slander,
> gossip, envy and conspiracy. There were no congratulations when the doc-
> torate was awarded.[97]

In private, Lee's distance from and disappointment with the Chinese
community was more evident, as revealed in a letter to her daughter, Elaine,
in 1958:

> I shall never forget the faces of the women in Chinatown when they heard
> me say I got my Ph.D. The look of envy and greed came forth and instead
> of congratulating me for having arrived after years of struggle and sacrifice
> and malicious gossiping about my "loose ways," they smirked. I guess,
> too, they're mad because I don't socialize with them. . . . Well, I'll never
> do that now.[98]

Yuan Liang's master's thesis, "The Chinese Family in Chicago," completed in 1951, continued Tin-Chiu Fan's earlier work. A native of Guangdong, Yuan Liang had worked in Chicago's Chinatown as a waiter, cashier,
clerk, and salesman for over a year. His ability to speak Cantonese and his
contacts with local Chinese businesses enabled him to interview the Chinese
in the city with ease. In his study, he investigated 80 out of 164 Chinese families, believed to be the total number of Chinese families in the city at the
time. Liang examined the degree of Americanization of the Chinese families
by comparing first-generation (defined as either or both of the couple being
China born) and second-generation (both of the couple American born)
Chinese families across a range of different occupations. He found that in
general the Chinese families in Chicago were considerably Americanized,

that the second-generation families were significantly more Americanized than those of the first generation, and that families with different occupations exhibited different degrees of Americanization, correlating in order with (1) American occupations (positions in American-owned or -run companies), (2) restaurants, (3) other Chinese occupations, and (4) laundries.[99]

Paul C. P. Siu's *The Chinese Laundryman: A Study of Social Isolation*, a dissertation that took him twenty-five years to complete (1932–1957) and was not published in its book form until 1987, a year after his death, is an exhaustive investigation of all the conceivable aspects of the life of a Chinese laundryman.[100] A meticulous empirical study, it provides invaluable, exceptionally detailed and vivid source material on Chinese laundrymen.

Paul Siu's family history itself, as told by John Kuo Wei Tchen in his penetrating introduction to Siu's book, is a compelling story of transnational migration and of the Chinese laundryman. Paul Siu was born in 1906 as Siu Chan Pang (Xiao Chenpeng), the eldest son of a family in a village of three hundred families of the Siu clan in Taishan, Guangdong. Like most of the Taishanese, his father came to the United States through a migration chain of his clansmen and settled as a laundryman in St. Paul, Minnesota. His modest hand laundry supported a family of eight back in China and allowed his eldest son, Chan Pang, to attend an American-run missionary middle school in Canton called the Piu Ying School, where Chan Pang was given his Christian name, Paul. After graduation, Paul taught for a year in China, and then in 1927 he was brought to the United States by his father to further his education. He stayed in his father's laundry for a year, where he first encountered the harsh life of a laundryman.

Paul then moved to Chicago, a bustling and growing industrial metropolis, seeking better opportunities. As a poor immigrant student, he had to work at chop suey houses during the day and attend night school. A few years later, his father came to Chicago and opened a laundry. Paul and his father socialized with their clansmen at the Siu family clan association in Chicago's Chinatown on Sundays. Busy making a living at the laundry and chop suey houses, Paul had insufficient time for his schooling, which went slowly and poorly to the point where he was ready to quit. In the summer of 1932, an old classmate from the Piu Ying School introduced Paul to Ernest Watson Burgess, a distinguished professor of sociology at the University of Chicago specializing in urban studies. Impressed by Siu's intelligence and his connections with the Chinese community, Burgess offered him a scholarship. Thus began the long-term student-mentor relationship between the two men.[101]

The most significant contribution of Siu's dissertation is the notion of "sojourner," a term that came from a fellow student, Clarence Glick, who had used it in his dissertation, "The Chinese Migrant in Hawaii."[102] Siu, however, gave the term a sociological tweak and weight, which helped popularize the so-called sojourner theory. According to his summary of the three characteristics of the sojourner, first was the "temporal disposition" of the sojourner's job. As Siu stated, "The Chinese laundryman does not organize himself to select the laundry work as his life-long career, and his sojourn in America is for one single purpose—to make a fortune or to make enough money to improve his economic well-being at home [in China]." Second, the sojourner exhibits "ethnocentrism and the in-group tendency." Siu asserted that "the sojourner clings to the cultural heritage of his own ethnic group; he is proud of it and thinks of it as the best, and therefore he tries to maintain it by all sorts of means." Third, the sojourner makes "the trip and movement back and forth." Siu observed that the sojourner had the "desire to go home, but when he gets home he finds it hard to stay and wants to go abroad again. This back and forth movement means that the man has gotten into an anomalous position between his homeland and the country of his sojourn."[103]

Siu's conclusions still remain valid today but now can be further understood in the context of transnational migration. The "temporal disposition" of laundry work ensured the Chinese immigrant's sustenance and survival in a foreign land and supported family members back in the homeland. His remittances to China constituted an integral part of the transnational economy. The "in-group tendency" helped form local links to the transnational social network. The "back and forth movement" is the very nature of transnational activities, as defined by authors on transnationalism since the 1990s.[104]

Contemporary Scholars, 1960s to 2010s   The scholars of this period are remarkably diverse in terms of birthplace and cultural, linguistic, and racial backgrounds compared to their counterparts in the earlier periods. They comprise foreign-born Chinese Americans from Hong Kong, Taiwan, and China; native-born Chinese Americans from the Chicago area and other regions of the country or Canada; and white Americans specializing in Chinese studies. Despite this diversity, the scholarship of these contemporary scholars uniformly acknowledges the profound occupational, social, cultural, and residential transformation that has taken place within Chicago's Chinese communities since the 1960s.

Margaret Gibbons Wilson's 1969 master's thesis focuses on the dichotomy between concentration and dispersal of the Chinese communities in Chicago, chiefly using area telephone directories, census tract data, and some professional listings as source material. Wilson asserts that while the early Chinese settlers concentrated in the so-called Old Chinatown on South Clark Street, the propensity toward dispersal began as early as the 1890s and became more powerful than the propensity toward concentration in the postwar years.[105]

Occupational Mobility and Kinship Assistance: A Study of Chinese Immigrants in Chicago (1978) began as Chinese Canadian sociologist Peter S. Li's doctoral dissertation in the Department of Sociology at Northwestern University in 1975.[106] Between 1972 and 1973, Li conducted a survey of 204 adult male Chinese immigrants who had applied for US citizenship between July 1, 1972, and December 31, 1973. Li found polarization in the mobility patterns of the Chinese, with a heavy concentration in the professional and service worker categories. Occupational mobility varied from group to group: professionals were the most stable in terms of retaining their original occupation; service workers were quite stable; the white-collar and blue-collar workers exhibited a moderate degree of mobility; and independent proprietors were the least stable of all.[107]

Susan Lee Moy's master's thesis in education, "The Chinese in Chicago: The First One Hundred Years, 1870–1970," at the University of Wisconsin–Milwaukee in 1978, is an important contribution to the study of Chinese Americans in Chicago. A native resident of Old Chinatown in Chicago, Moy investigated the attitudes of Chicago Chinese Americans in terms of the development and growth of Chinatown and the lifestyles of the Chinese in Chicago. Moy asserts that Chinatown, and especially the community organizations, served the Chinese in Chicago well by providing a vehicle for their national awakening in the early twentieth century but failed to serve the needs of the American-born generations.[108] Moy later contributed a chapter on Chicago's Chinese Americans, based on her master's thesis and further research, to an anthology on the various racial groups of the city, *Ethnic Chicago: A Multicultural Portrait*, edited by Melvin G. Holli and Peter d'A. Jones.[109]

In 1991, Harry Ying Cheng Kiang, a China-born and American-trained geographer (whose master's degree is from Stanford University and doctorate from Columbia University) and an emeritus professor of geography at Northeastern Illinois University in Chicago, published a brief (ten pages) demographical survey on Chicago's Chinatown, based primarily on the US censuses. With a bilingual text, it is geared toward a general readership both inside and outside of Chinatown. The tables and maps Kiang compiled are useful for further research projects.[110]

Three years later, Minglan Cheung Keener, who received her bachelor of science degree from Tongji University in Shanghai, investigated the living conditions of Chicago's South Chinatown in her master's thesis in landscape architecture for the University of Illinois at Urbana–Champaign, using interviews and surveys involving local residents and community leaders. Keener notes that most Chinatown residents were confined in an overcrowded environment because of their social, economic, and linguistic disadvantages and that the quality of their lives largely depended on what Chinatown could provide them: employment opportunities, bilingual services, and Chinese ingredients and foods.[111] Along the same lines, geographer Linda Qingling Wang, in her well-researched 1997 dissertation, suggests that a "highly-structured and well-organized Chinatown" in Chicago provided "physical and cultural identity" to its residents and was "a place with loaded meanings and substances essential" to Chinese suburbanites.[112]

Historian Adam McKeown's *Chinese Migrant Networks and Cultural Change: Peru, Chicago, Hawaii, 1900–1936* (2001), based on his 1997 doctoral dissertation for the Department of History at the University of Chicago, is a comparative study of Chinese migration in the three locales. As to the "disjunctions" and dichotomies in studying migrant experiences from a nation-state perspective, in which the Chinese are either understood as immigrants who settled and helped create a new land or as sojourners who never intended to assimilate into the host society, McKeown favors a "global perspective" that focuses attention on "links" and "connections." His chapter on Chinese Chicago provides intriguing narratives and insightful analysis on the early Chicago Chinese community.[113] Published in the same year, Canadian-born historian Henry Yu's *Thinking Orientals*, based on his dissertation, is a nuanced study on the Chicago School of sociology and its practitioners in Chicago and beyond. Its second section, in particular, provides vivid biographical sketches of some of the earlier Chinese scholars in Chicago—Ching Chao Wu, Rose Hum Lee, and Paul Siu, embellished with insightful analysis of their works.[114]

Chicago-based linguist John S. Rohsenow penned an essay on contemporary Chinese language use in the Chicago metropolitan area. He uses a tripartite division to describe the linguistic differences among the Chinese in three major population concentrations in the greater Chicago metropolitan area: the older "South Chinatown" centered at Wentworth Avenue and Cermak Road, where Taishan and Canton dialects are spoken by most residents; the newer Southeast Asian "North Chinatown" centered along Argyle Street between Broadway and Sheridan in the Uptown area, where Chaozhou and Fuzhou dialects of the Fujian province are spoken, along with Cantonese and Mandarin; and the newer and more dispersed communities of professionals in the surrounding suburbs, where Mandarin is the dominant Chinese language used by residents.[115]

Similarly, Yvonne M. Lau, an American-born Chicago-based sociologist, also notes the divide between the city-dwelling and the suburban Chinese communities. While the residents of urban Chinatowns are "newer immigrants or refugees, lower in socioeconomic status, limited-English speakers, workers in the secondary and service sectors, unemployed or underemployed, young adults or single parents, elderly, and undocumented," Lau states, the educated suburban Chinese Americans "are more homogeneous in socioeconomic status, with sufficient human capital and class resources to afford the lifestyle linked to suburban communities."[116]

In a brief essay published in 2005, historian Mae M. Ngai discusses Hong Sling, the prominent Chinese businessman at the turn of the century discussed previously, and his participation in the Chinese Village at the World's Fair in Chicago in 1893 in the context of transnationalism. Ngai points out the significance of the Chinese Village at the Fair as "an early prototype for Chinese American efforts to develop urban Chinatowns as tourist destinations."[117]

Based on census data and fieldwork in Chicago between 2004 and 2005, Shanshan Lan, a China-born anthropologist who graduated from the University of Illinois at Urbana–Champaign in 2007, documented in her dissertation, with a focus on race and class, the evolution of the Chinese American community in Bridgeport, just southwest of Chicago's South Chinatown. Lan shows Bridgeport to be a part of the "South Chinatown Community" and also argues that by instilling American values into new immigrants, the middle-class Chinese American social service agencies of Chinatown "perpetuate" the existing American racial and class hierarchies by "preparing new immigrants to become an obedient working class of color."[118]

Chicago-based China-born historian Ling Z. Arenson's 2009 essay examines the forces that transformed the Chinese community in Chicago from a relatively homogeneous urban ethnic neighborhood before World War II into fragmented communities since the 1950s. Arenson observes that while the first-generation immigrants struggled to bridge their cultural, class, geographical, and political differences to forge a unified voice, second-generation Chinese Americans are less influenced by homeland politics and are striving to achieve a pan-Asian solidarity.[119]

Conclusion

The history of Chinese students and intellectuals is an integral part of the history of Chinese Chicago. Chinese students and intellectuals from different periods had distinctively different means of emigration, which reflected the conditions in China and the impact of the evolving US immigration policies on Chinese immigrants: when the Chinese exclusion laws prevailed, Chinese students connected with American Christian missions had easier entry; then when American immigration policies turned less restrictive, students sponsored by various governments in China or by private funds began arriving in America in large numbers. The education and professional training of Chinese students and scholars prior to their emigration did not spare them completely from the difficulties and hardships experienced by other Chinese immigrants. Yet despite these hardships, many have enjoyed success in their careers in the United States and have assimilated into the local American communities.

In the course of their education in the United States, however, Chinese students and intellectuals generally had only transitory or conditional contact with the Chinatown communities, owing to the struggle for survival or the academic demands on their time. For some of them, this "outsider" orientation facilitated the observation of the local Chinese communities from a distance and with intellectual assurance and scientific objectivity. Upon completion of their educational training, they moved onward, mostly to work in mainstream companies and institutions, to live in dispersed suburban communities, and to integrate socioeconomically into the larger society. Despite their occupational and residential detachment from the urban Chinese American communities, their academic writings have helped us understand the history of Chinese Chicago as well as the history of Chinese America. The legacy of these Chinese intellectuals in Chicago lies in their bridging the two worlds of China and America.

SEVEN

Diverging and Converging Transnational Communities, 1945–2010s

Compared to the earlier Chinese immigrants, post–World War II newcomers were more diverse in their geographic and socioeconomic origins, contributing to the ever-growing complexity of Chicago's Chinese communities. Ethnic Chinese refugees from Vietnam, Laos, Cambodia, and other immigrants from Southeast Asia following the end of the Vietnam War in 1975 propelled the growth of the new North Chinatown. Students-turned-professionals from Taiwan and the PRC created the suburban Chinese American cultural communities. The tripartite geographical division into South Chinatown, North Chinatown, and the suburban Chinese cultural communities, along with political, occupational, and linguistic differences among the Chinese in Chicago, posed new challenges: how to preserve and promote common cultural values and how to protect and expand the ethnic Chinese economy in a diverse and complex Chinese American transnational community.

New Generation

Although there have been Chinese families in Chicago since the 1880s, the second-generation Chinese American population increased more rapidly in the later 1940s, as more Chinese women entered the country as war brides, fiancées of GIs, displaced persons, refugees, and wives of American citizens.[1] Anti-Chinese sentiment had abated during World War II, when China became a member of the Grand Alliance and public images of the Chinese gradually changed. This trend toward a more favorable attitude in regard to China and Chinese Americans in America continued after the war. Facing pressures from the public and other interest groups, Congress repealed many of the discriminatory exclusion laws that for years had denied Chinese Americans fundamental civil rights and legal protections.[2] On December 17, 1943, Congress passed an act repealing all the Chinese exclusion laws since 1882, permitting Chinese aliens in the United States to apply for naturalization and mandating new preferences for up to 75 percent of the quota allotted to Chinese immigrants.[3]

In spite of the repeal of the Chinese exclusion laws, the Chinese immigrant quota designated by the American government was only 105 per year. This figure was calculated as one-sixth of 1 percent of the number of Chinese in the United States in 1920, as determined by the census of that year.[4] Nevertheless, additional nonquota immigrants were also allowed to immigrate. More Chinese scholars came to teach in the United States, an average of about 137 each year, in comparison with only 10 per year during the previous decade. More important, under the War Bride Act of December 28, 1945, and the G.I. Fiancées Act of June 29, 1946, alien wives and children of veterans and American citizens were also permitted to enter the United States as nonquota immigrants. During the three years in which the War Bride Act was in effect, approximately 6,000 Chinese war brides were admitted.[5] Thus, in 1947, the number of Chinese immigrants entering the United States climbed to 3,191, most of whom came on a nonquota basis.[6]

Many Chinese women also came under other laws. The Displaced Persons Act of 1948 and the Refugee Relief Act of 1953 allowed several thousand Chinese women to immigrate to America. The 1948 act granted "displaced" Chinese students, visitors, and others who already had a temporary status in the United States to adjust their status to that of permanent residents. The 1953 act allotted three thousand visas to refugees from Asia and two thousand visas to Chinese whose passports had been issued by the Chinese Nationalist government, which lost control of mainland China in 1949.[7] On September 22, 1959, Congress passed an act under which more Chinese on the quota waiting list attained nonquota status.[8] Thus, according to the 1960 census, the number of Chinese in the United States had reached 237,292. This included 135,549 males and 101,743 females, of whom 60 percent were American born.[9]

Whereas an average of only 60 Chinese women entered the United States each year during the 1930s, in 1948 alone 3,317 women immigrated. During the period from 1944 to 1953, women comprised 82 percent of Chinese immigrants to America. For the first time, the number of Chinese women and families in the United States noticeably increased. The male-to-female ratio dropped from 2.9:1 in 1940 to 1.8:1 in 1950 and 1.3:1 in 1960 (see Table 2 and the accompanying figure).

TABLE 2   Chinese American population and sex ratio, 1900–2010

Year	Total population	Male	Female	Male-to-female ratio
1900	89,863	85,341	4,522	18.9
1910	71,531	66,858	4,675	14.3
1920	61,639	53,891	7,748	7.0
1930	74,954	59,802	15,152	3.9
1940	77,504	57,389	20,115	2.9
1950	117,629	77,008	40,621	1.9
1960	237,292	135,549	101,743	1.3
1970	431,583	226,733	204,850	1.1
1980	806,040	407,544	398,496	1.0
1990	1,648,696	821,542	827,154	1.0
2000	2,896,016	1,405,107	1,490,909	0.9
2010	3,538,407	1,687,820	1,850,587	0.9

SOURCE: For data from 1900 to 1990, Ling (1998b, 115); data for 2000, US Census Bureau, Summary File 2 (SF 2) and Summary File 4 (SF 4). Data for 2010 is a projection from S0201, "Selected Population Profile in the United States, Population Group: Chinese Alone or in Any Combination," data set, 2007 American Community Survey.

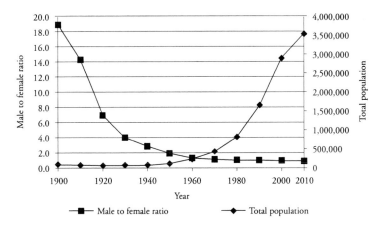

Chinese American population and male-to-female ratio, 1900–2010. Plotted from data in Table 2.

Along with their counterparts across the country, the Chinese in Chicago benefited from these laws, bringing their long-separated families from China, as illustrated by Yolanda Lee's family history. Yolanda's father was born in China in 1903 and came to Chicago in 1924. He later returned to his hometown, Taishan, Guangdong, to get married but had to leave his bride behind. Yolanda was born in Taishan in 1933 and spent her childhood there. During World War II, her father served in the US army in order to bring his family from China. With the G.I. Fiancées Act of June 29, 1946, her father successfully arranged for Yolanda and her mother to come to Chicago in 1947. The family first lived in a trailer camp on the site of present-day Northeastern Illinois University and later in a basement apartment on Alexander Street in Chinatown during Yolanda's high school years. Yolanda attended Von Steuben High School at the age of sixteen and graduated in three years with the rank of number four among the more than two hundred seniors. She was awarded a scholarship to the University of Illinois at Navy Pier. While attending college, Yolanda worked after school and on weekends at her family's restaurant.[10]

As most Chinese in Chicago concentrated in the laundry, restaurant, and grocery businesses, the majority of Chinese youth were children of laundry operators, restaurant owners, or grocers. Many were born in the cramped apartments of tenement buildings in Chinatown or in the back rooms of their family's businesses. Most of them helped with the family business or worked in Chinese restaurants or other establishments after school and during their college years, as reflected in Yolanda's family history as well as in the following stories.

Celia Moy Cheung's growing-up experience was typical of a second-generation Chinese. Her father, Paul Moy, was born in Taishan, Guangdong, in 1871 and later became a Presbyterian minister. He married his wife, Lillian Wong, twenty years his junior, in Taishan through an arranged marriage. At the turn of the century, because of a plague, Paul, Lillian, and their eldest daughter, Mary, left China. They came to America and settled in Chicago. Unable to find employment as a minister, Paul opened a Chinese hand laundry located on the northwest side of Chicago. The family lived in an apartment on 22nd Place in Chinatown, where ten more children were born. In their disciplined but loving home, Celia's mother was the matriarch and her older sister took care of the children while her father was busy making a living for the family in the laundry. Celia was born in Chicago on July 24, 1933, tenth of the eleven children (ten girls and one boy). As a child of the Great Depression, Celia worked as a cashier in a Chinese restaurant, the Junk Restaurant, after school and in a frozen food factory in the summer.[11]

Henry Yee's family history in many ways resembles that of Celia Moy Cheung. Henry Yee was born in 1939 in China and adopted by Shiu Kang Yee at the age of three. Henry immigrated to the United States with his mother in 1951 to join his father, and the family of three settled in Chicago's Chinatown at 225 West 23rd Street in 1953. His father, Shiu Kang Yee, and another relative started the Sun Lite Hand Laundry in Berwyn, Illinois, a western suburb of Chicago. Between 1953 and 1959, his parents had five more children. With his father working long hours at the hand laundry, Henry took on the responsibilities of helping his mother care for his younger siblings.[12]

Harry Wu's life story is similar. Harry Wu's parents, John Eng and Mary Gwan, left Canton, China, in 1929 for a better life in Chicago and opened a family laundry on Cermak Road. Harry was born on November 20, 1933, in Chicago, the third of four siblings. After their mother passed away in 1940 when Harry was only seven years old, his father remarried and expanded the family with two more sons. The family resided on Alexander Street, in the Chinatown district, and the children attended the St. Therese Chinese Catholic School then located in the On Leong building. Harry then attended St. Dominic High School on Chicago and Hudson Streets, graduating in 1954. To help make ends meet, Harry and his siblings worked after school in Chinese restaurants and other establishments in Chinatown. After high school Harry worked for the United States Postal Service and then was drafted into the army in 1956. He served fourteen months, including nine months in Pusan, Korea. Upon leaving the army, Harry rejoined the USPS and retired after thirty-five years of service.[13]

Grace Chun was born in 1938 in Chicago. Her family lived on the North Side, where her parents operated a hand laundry at 953 North Western Avenue. The laundry survived as a family business thanks to all of the children, Grace and her two younger brothers, who worked after school and on weekends, bringing coal for the furnace that heated the irons. The laundry also survived because of its low prices—twenty-two cents for laundering a shirt, for instance.[14]

While a busy routine of schooling and working still marked the lives of many Chinatown youths, it is also evident that the overall socioeconomic conditions for the new generation of Chinese Americans had dramatically improved in post–World War II America, as demonstrated by Corwin Eng's family history.

> My father was born in China and came to the United States in 1925. My mother was born in Chicago. My parents owned and operated the Kai Kai Coffee Shop from 1942 to 1992.
>
> I was born on February 16, 1952, in Chicago. We lived on the second floor of a three-story brick building at 2219 South Wentworth Avenue. The apartment had two bedrooms, hot running water, and gas heat. I attended the Chinese Christian Union Church Nursery School, Haines Elementary School, Midwest Christian Academy, and graduated from Senn High School in 1970. I received a degree in social science from Northern Illinois University in 1974.
>
> My fondest memory in Chinatown was watching the parades of Chinese New Year and Double Ten Celebrations, being a member of the Wah Mei Drum and Bugle Corp. We traveled outside of Chicago and played in New York City and on the steps of the Capitol Building in Washington, D.C.
>
> I was employed as a Public Health Administrator by the Chicago Department of Public Health from 1974 until my retirement in 2004. I worked with Bernice Wong of the Chinese American Service League for twenty-six years to provide services for the Chinese community.[15]

The following family history is a quintessential story reflecting the changing socioeconomic conditions embraced by the new generation. Benjamin C. Moy was born Moy Chin Quong, later known as Ben, in his family home in China in 1921. His grandfather came to the United States in the 1860s to build the western part of the transcontinental railroad and became a crew chief in the 1920s. His father was born in Portland, Oregon, but was sent to China while he was a two- or three-year-old boy, a common practice among the earlier Chinese immigrants in order to save money and provide their children with a Chinese education, and he remained there until his twenties, when he came back to the United States. He then returned to China only twice, once for his marriage in the home village and then to bring his son Ben back to the United States. Ben attended school in China for five and a half years before traveling to the United States with his father on the *President McKinley* in 1934. Inquisitive and intelligent, Ben learned to speak English while staying with a neighbor of his cousin. His intelligence and proficiency in English enabled him to graduate from McClaren

Elementary School in a year and a half. Ben continued his schooling by attending night school at Crane High School for a couple of years while working in a Chinese laundry during the day. He received his high school diploma at the Central YMCA College, which later became part of Roosevelt University. Ben married Susan Lowe in 1949 and the couple had two daughters. Ben had always enjoyed music, so while working and attending school he also started playing the violin. He held a variety of sales jobs before going into business for himself. He started his business operation out of a truck before opening a grocery store in Chinatown, with the grocery store in front and a chicken slaughtering shop in the back. He engaged in a variety of other business ventures and then opened the Bird Restaurant at the Skokie Swift Station on Dempster Avenue in Niles, a northwestern suburb of Chicago. He later moved the restaurant to Melrose Park, a western suburb of Chicago. Ben finally moved to Oak Brook, also a western suburb of Chicago but closer to the city, where he opened a cooking school and taught cooking until his retirement—when he finally had time to play his musical instruments during the day.[16]

These second-generation Chinese Americans were better educated than their parents' generation. Many attained undergraduate degrees and some even postgraduate degrees. Among the college-bound Chinese Americans in the 1930s and 1940s, many majored in engineering and chemistry.[17] The primary reason for the heavy concentration of Chinese in engineering and the sciences was the perception that these fields were more objective and free from social and cultural biases and prejudices and therefore offered more equal opportunities for Chinese. Moreover, the demands on one's spoken English were not as high as in the social sciences.

George Eng's story best illustrates this pattern. George was born into a Chinese immigrant family in 1920 in Chicago. His father, Gow Eng, tried three times before finally obtaining legal entry to the United States in 1910. George's parents owned several Chinese restaurants in Chicago, including the California Inn on California and Madison, the Golden Pheasant on Clark and Madison, and the Golden Pheasant on Lawrence and Broadway. Although he lived in Chinatown for a short time, George attended school on Chicago's West Side, where his family's restaurants were located. After his graduation from John Marshall High School, George went to Virginia Military Institute to study civil engineering. Three years later, George enrolled in the military and then returned to VMI after World War II to complete his degree. He was hired as an engineer by the City of Chicago and served on the commissioner's staff in the Department of Public Works from 1964 to 1970. In the 1970s, he was hired by the city government as deputy commissioner of public works, becoming the first Chinese in Chicago to hold so high a post in the city government.[18]

Howard Chun's life history tells a similar story. Howard was born in New York City in 1936 into a Chinese immigrant family. His father was a cook in a Chinese restaurant and his mother a seamstress. Since his father was often sick, his mother became the primary breadwinner, and the family had to depend on public welfare assistance. A good student, Howard earned his bachelor of science degree in physics with a minor in electrical engineering in 1959. He then joined the army, serving in the Corps of Engineers. While stationed at Fort Leonard Wood, Missouri, Howard met Grace Hong, also a second-generation Chinese, who was majoring in history at Northern Illinois University; they married in 1961. After retiring from the army with the rank of colonel, Howard and his wife came to Chicago in 1977, where he worked as a computer scientist and systems engineer.[19]

Despite their superior educational background, many second-generation Chinese Americans still found it difficult to find employment in the fields in which they were trained, largely because of discrimination in the business and professional worlds.[20] It was not unusual to find college-educated Chinese American waiters and restaurant owners. Discouraged by the limited opportunities in America, some second-generation Chinese Chicagoans went to China after graduation. G. P. Moy, for example, son of local Chinese merchant T. L. Moy, graduated in 1936 with an excellent record from the Armour Institute's school of electrical engineering. Upon graduation, he left Chicago and went to China to look for a position in Shanghai or Canton.[21]

The earliest examples of Chinese professionals are three men hired by the Great Lakes Trust Company (大湖银行), a Chicago bank owned by white Americans together with a few Chinese businessmen. When it opened in 1922, the bank was able to overcome cultural and racial prejudice to start a Chinese department, headed by Howard Ying Fook Moy and staffed by Won Soon Lee and Shule Eng. The Chinese department of the bank provided interpreter services for Chinese customers who were unable to speak English and handled their remittances to China and Hong Kong. Several years later, the bank merged with the Central Trust Bank, which continued the operation of the Chinese department until the three men retired.[22]

Like their white counterparts, Chinese Americans in the professional fields formed organizations to promote their common interests. Owing to discrimination, they formed their own college and professional organizations in the mid-1930s to meet the demands of the college-educated second generation, who were starting to break away from the traditional ethnic occupations of restaurants and laundries. Alpha Lambda was reportedly the first Chinese American professional organization in Chicago, founded sometime in the 1930s.[23] Similarly, in 1950 the Chinese American Citizens Alliance was founded to promote Americanization and assimilation into the American mainstream. In the same year, the Midwest Chinese American Civic Council was also founded, with the same purposes.[24]

Newcomers

Compared to their predecessors, the newcomers after World War II were more diverse in their socioeconomic backgrounds and geographical origins. They came not only from the southern Chinese provinces of Guangdong and Fujian but also from Hong Kong, Taiwan, and Southeast Asian countries, as illustrated by the following cases.

Cho Tuk Lo's family was one of the many that had continually migrated from place to place in order to escape war and political turmoil in China. Cho Tuk Lo was born in Guangdong, China, in 1926, and his family moved to the British colony of Hong Kong when he was eleven. The family lived in a pawnshop owned by Lo's father and uncle, where Lo was introduced to Western musical instruments and learned to play protest songs when the Japanese invaded Hong Kong in 1938. Lo's musical talents made him well known in Hong Kong and China, and he was invited to teach Cantonese opera and folk music in China. Lo came to Chicago in the 1970s, sponsored by his sister, who was an American citizen. While working in a Chinese restaurant, he found time to teach music to many Chinese students for free. On one occasion he played *erhu*, a two-stringed traditional Chinese music instrument, for Mayor Daley.[25]

Catherine Wong Chin was born in Hong Kong on December 23, 1931, into a family of Chinese migrants from Taishan, Guangdong. She had one older brother and two older sisters. During the Japanese invasion and subsequent occupation of Hong Kong, her family, along with all other Hong

Kong residents, suffered greatly. As the Japanese did not permit Chinese children to go to school, Catherine and her mother had to sell their clothing at a flea market to earn money until the war was over. After World War II, Catherine finished high school and college and became a teacher at a boys' school in Hong Kong, where she taught third and sixth grade. In June of 1956 she married David Chin, and the couple moved to Chicago that year. In Chicago, Catherine had various jobs, first as interpreter for the INS and later as an instructor at the Berlitz School of Languages and the Metropolitan Life Insurance Company.[26]

Many of the newcomers had complex transnational backgrounds prior to their immigration to the United States, as evidenced in the stories of Ian Roosevelt Chin, Susana Fong, Dato' Seri Stanley Thai, and Cheryl Tom.

Ian Roosevelt Chin was born in Jamaica, West Indies, in 1943. Ian's great-grandfather left Guangdong, China, in the late 1890s because of poor economic conditions. Although the Chin family sent out scouts throughout the world to find a suitable new home, they could not get into the United States because of the Chinese Exclusion Act of 1882. They finally settled in Jamaica, which permitted families including women to immigrate and whose climate was very similar to that in southern China. Chin Foo Sing, Ian's father, was born in 1900 in China. He came to Jamaica in 1911 with his parents when he was eleven years old. Later he owned a general store in a village called Moneague. The youngest of the family's nine children (five girls and four boys), Ian wanted to come to the United States to further his education, which he did in 1962, as a student at the University of Miami, majoring in architectural engineering. Three years later, Ian transferred to the University of Illinois, thinking there were mountains nearby where he could go skiing. He earned his BA in architecture and an MS in structural engineering. After working for the City of Chicago for a number of years, he joined the prestigious architectural engineering firm Wiss, Janney, and Elstner Associates, Inc., where he is currently vice president and senior principal. He has served on numerous professional committees, such as the Chicago Committee on High Rise Buildings, the Chicago Committee of Standards and Tests, and the American Society for Testing and Materials. He married his wife, Shelia, in 1977 and they raised three children.[27]

Susanna Fong was born on October 7, 1953, and raised in Penang, Malaysia, as the fifth child of Wah Swee Loh (Hong) and Suan Tan, both from

Fujian, China. Susanna's father, Wah Swee Hong, was sold at a young age to the Loh family in Fujian. During the Communist takeover in China in 1949, Wah Swee was fourteen years old. Desperate to leave China and join his four elder birth brothers, who had relocated to Malaysia, Wah Swee traveled alone for four months, without shoes, money, or any other means. By hopping trains and boats, he finally found freedom in Malaysia, although his older brothers and life there were less than welcoming. Nevertheless, he persevered and became a very successful businessman in the Malaysian fashion and fabric industry. Susanna was the first child born in Malaysia after her father brought his entire family there from China. While attending school in Taiwan, Susanna met her husband, Patrick Fong, a Taiwanese. They married in Malaysia in May 1979 and immigrated to the United States in September of that year, beginning Susanna's journey in a new country without her large extended family and friends in Malaysia. With over two decades of perseverance and hard work, Susanna has thrived in Chicago as a successful businesswoman and mother.[28]

Dato' Seri Stanley Thai was born in Malaysia in 1960, as fourteenth of seventeen children in his family. His father had two wives: one he married in China and one in Malaysia. He left China for Malaysia in 1949, with his first wife arriving later. The families of his two wives lived in separate houses side by side, on a farm where they raised poultry and pigs. Stanley worked at the farm in the morning, attending classes in the afternoon. He went to Toronto, Canada, to study business administration at the University of Windsor, where he met his future wife, Cheryl Tom, one of his classmates in the business administration program. Cheryl Tom was born in 1961 in Johor, Malaysia, the second youngest of eight children in her family (five boys and three girls). Her grandfathers were born in Fujian, China, and immigrated to Malaysia as laborers. Her father moved up the social ladder in Malaysia, eventually owning a rubber plantation. Together Stanley Thai and Cheryl Tom founded the Super Max Glove Company, a worldwide business headquartered in Chicago in 1997. In recognition of his business success and contributions, a sultan in Malaysia bestowed upon Stanley Thai the title Dato' Seri, equivalent to knighthood.[29]

Chinese from other American cities also moved to Chicago in the post–World War II era in response to the city's growing business opportunities. James Chiu was a native of Xinhui, Guangdong, China, and immigrated to the United States in 1920 to make his fortune in New York, leaving his young wife and newborn son, Herman, behind in the homeland. It was not until eighteen years later that he met his son and twenty-five years later that he again saw his wife, in Hong Kong. At the age of eighteen, Herman was sent for by his father to attend boarding school in New York. The ship *Empress of Russia* brought Herman from China to New York, where he met his father for the first time. The growing business demand in Chicago attracted James Chiu to Chicago in 1948. That year Yun-Tsung Chao, the proprietor of China Farm, a flourishing Chicago restaurant supplier, invited Chiu to join his business partnership. Together they built China Farm into one of Chicago's largest Chinese restaurant suppliers, with fifteen employees delivering to suburban restaurants that were unable to come into the city for supplies. China Farm was also Chicago's largest bean sprout grower and supplier. Herman, a graduate of MIT, became a chemical engineer. After returning home from his full-time job every day, he assisted in the family business, waiting for late delivery drivers and closing up China Farm.[30]

Unlike the early Chinese immigrants who mostly worked in the traditional Chinese businesses of laundries, grocery stores, and restaurants, the newcomers now branched out to embrace other economic opportunities, largely in professional fields, and resided in the suburban areas. In 1950, the Chinese resided in sixty-five of the seventy-six community areas. Although the South Chinatown area still held the highest concentration of Chinese, numbering 1,250, almost twice as many, 2,084, lived outside of Chinatown, mostly on the North Side.[31] In 1961, a large majority, 84 percent, of the suburban dwellers were professionals.[32]

The "Santa Fe Project" and South Chinatown Expansion

The construction of the Dan Ryan and Stevenson Expressways in the 1950s had cut through South Chinatown and reduced its size by half. In 1962 Chinatown was bounded by Archer, 25th, Stewart, and LaSalle Streets. In 1969 the apartment buildings and houses located along the east side of Wentworth Avenue from 18th Street to Cermak Road and from 21st Place to Wentworth Avenue were demolished. These losses caused a severe housing shortage in the Chinatown area, and waves of new immigrants further compounded the problem. The acute situation in Chinatown caught the media's attention; as an article in the *Chicago Sun-Times* on June 17, 1962, noted, "The need for action to preserve the character of the community became evident early in 1959."[33]

The leaders of the Chinese community did take action. Gung-Hsing Wang was a central figure in the community's response to the issue. Wang had been a prominent presence in the area since the 1930s when he served as vice-consul of the Chinese Consulate in Chicago and frequently appeared at important community events. He then served as consul general in the Chinese Consulate in New Orleans from 1938 to 1949. When the Communists took over China in 1949, he stayed in the United States and lectured at Tulane University in New Orleans for several years. In 1952 he came to Chicago, the city to which he was socially and emotionally very attached, and became a private developer. In 1959, along with two other businessmen, Wang formed Neighborhood Redevelopment Assistance, Inc. (later changed to Chinatown Redevelopment Assistance, Inc.), a nonprofit organization, serving as its managing director. The organization had three primary objectives: to rehabilitate and restore the neighborhoods within or near the Chinatown area, to construct and sell residential properties to meet the housing needs of Chinatown on a nonprofit basis, and to own and operate residential properties on a cooperative basis.[34]

During the next two decades, with government funding and private donations, Chinatown Redevelopment Assistance, Inc., acquired land and constructed a total of 66 new townhouses at different locations in the vicinity of Chinatown and the nine-story Chinatown Elderly Apartments, comprising 139 units. In addition, the agency donated a strip of land located on 24th Place to the city to be developed as a public park, later named Dr. Sun Yat-sen Park. By 1980, the agency had 8 townhouses designated as public housing at 312–326 West 24th Street, the Wah-Yuen townhouses with 8 living units, 12 condominium apartments at the northwest corner of 24th Place and Wentworth Avenue, 12 townhouses at the southwest corner of 24th Place and Wentworth Avenue, 8 townhouses at the northwest corner of 25th Place and Wentworth, the Appleville condominium with 132 units at Canal and 24th Place, and Chinatown Courts, a five-building development with 22 units at 26th Street and Shields Avenue. These developments helped solve the housing problem in Chinatown, stabilize the community, and expand Chinatown's boundaries. By that time, Chinatown had expanded south to 25th Place and west to Canal Street.[35]

While Chinatown Redevelopment Assistance, Inc., was significant in pushing the boundaries of South Chinatown further south and west, the "Santa Fe Project" was monumental in terms of expanding Chinatown's territory further north. In 1984 the Chinese American Development Corporation was formed, with an ambitious plan to acquire the thirty-two-acre property located just north of Chinatown then owned by the Santa Fe Railroad. If the housing developments undertaken by Chinatown Redevelopment Assistance, Inc., were chiefly meant to solve the housing shortage, the "Santa Fe Project" was a more complex and full-fledged venture, with development of both residential and commercial properties. It aimed not only to attract suburban Chinese American families but also to accommodate the influx of immigrants from Hong Kong, an expected annual arrival of one hundred to two hundred families once the British colonial government handed Hong Kong back to the PRC government in 1997. The architectural design of the project combined modern urban residences with traditional Chinese artistic values, building with an Eastern appearance and Western amenities. It would not only provide residential properties for Asian Americans but also create more commercial opportunities for area business owners. Phase I and Phase II of the project each planned for 52 two-story commercial units, along with 180 townhouses, a hotel, a riverfront marina, a museum, and botanic gardens. Phase III and Phase IV envisioned an Asian Trade Center.[36]

In 1993, land in the old Santa Fe railroad yards along the Chicago River north of Cermak Road and Archer Avenue was developed into a new Chinatown Square featuring a two-level retail commercial center with a multitude of colorful shops and restaurants. In the center of the square stands the Pan Asian Cultural Center, surrounded by twelve bronze Chinese zodiac figures. In front of the square stands a dramatic forty- by eight-foot mural, made of one hundred thousand hand-painted tiles from China, depicting the history of Chinese immigrants to Chicago. At the four ends of the square are four imposing bronze gates illustrating the four greatest Chinese inventions: gun powder, the compass, paper, and printing.[37] In 1999 the twelve-acre Ping Tom Park along the Chicago River just north of Chinatown Square was completed, and in 2004 the new building of the Chinese American Service League (CASL) at 2145 South Tan Court was finished, further expanding the northwest boundaries of South Chinatown. The CASL, the Chicago Chinatown Chamber of Commerce at 2169-B South China Place, and the Pan-Asian Cultural Center in Chinatown Square jointly combine community service, ethnic business promotion, and the preservation of the Asian cultural heritage in the Chinatown Square area, the new focal point of South Chinatown. Throughout the year, Chinatown residents, city-dwellers, and out-of-town visitors now enjoy cultural celebrations and cultural performances in the plaza of Chinatown Square and recreational activities in Ping Tom Park.

Within the ten-block commercial and residential area of South Chinatown, nearly eight thousand Chinese now make their homes. According to the Chinatown Business Listing provided by the Chicago Chinatown Chamber of Commerce in 2004, there are a diverse range of businesses, including 56 restaurants; 55 retail and wholesale groceries; 37 gift, book, and video stores; 36 health service providers; 25 florists and beauty shops; 22 attorneys; 18 travel agencies and hotels; 17 Chinese herb stores and drugstores; 15 construction and remodeling companies; 14 accountants; 7 real estate companies; and 7 noodle companies. In addition, South Chinatown is also home to 45 associations including churches as well as nonprofit and civic groups.[38] These numerous commercial and cultural services make South

South Chinatown, Chicago, 2008. Collection of Huping Ling.

Chinatown a magnet for new immigrants and one of the primary tourist attractions in Chicago.

While these new residential and commercial developments in South Chinatown improved the living conditions of those residents who could afford them, the overall residential living conditions were still less than ideal, a common problem shared by other major Chinese urban communities.[39] South Chinatown was one of the highest-density neighborhoods in Chicago. Constructed in the 1940s, most of its residential buildings were substandard and deteriorating. Twenty to 32 percent of the residents in South Chinatown were living in overcrowded units, with more than one person per room.[40]

Many working-class new immigrants found themselves confined in such substandard apartments in Chinatown. Xiaoyu Wong and her husband came to Chicago in 2003 as immigrants sponsored by her husband's brother. Prior to immigration, Wong had worked as an accountant in a large food retailing company in Jiangmen, Guangdong; Wong's husband had been a manager in a video camera company that had gone bankrupt, leading to the couple's emigration. Upon their arrival in Chicago, Wong's husband found a job as a cook in a Chinatown restaurant, working more than ten hours daily from Monday to Saturday and bringing home a monthly income of $1,000. Two years later, their son came to join them and enrolled at Chicago City College downtown, meanwhile working both as a food deliverer for a Chinese restaurant in Chinatown and as a cashier in a supermarket. To supplement the family income, Wong found a job as a housekeeper at the Hyatt Hotel downtown, starting at $7.25 per hour. With this meager income, they were only able to rent a two-bedroom basement apartment in Chinatown at $700 per month.[41]

While South Chinatown was undergoing a steady expansion, Bridgeport, the adjacent area just southwest of it, has quietly but rapidly been growing into a major Chinese American population center, exceeding South Chinatown itself. According to the 2000 census, the Chinese population in Bridgeport was 8,273, while in the Armour Square area, where the original South Chinatown is located, the Chinese population was only 7,148.[42] This rapid population growth in Bridgeport has prompted community leaders and academics to redefine South Chinatown as the "Chinatown vicinity" or "Chinatown communities" and to suggest redrawing the geographical boundaries of the South Chinatown community to include Bridgeport as an integral part.[43]

Historically a white working-class neighborhood, Bridgeport embraced dif-

ferent waves of European immigrants: Irish, Germans, Lithuanians, Czecho-
slovakians, Poles, Ukrainians, and Italians. Among these ethnic groups, the
Irish remained politically active and dominated the political scene in Chicago
for over a century; five of Chicago's mayors emerged from Bridgeport, including the famous Richard J. Daley and his son, Richard M. Daley. Bridgeport
was a focal point of a devastating anti–African American race riot in 1919 during which many assaults and casualties occurred; the Chicago Commission on
Race Relations identified the Stock Yards district, an area within Bridgeport,
as having the highest number of injuries in the riot. The chronic racial confrontations between white and black citizens in the following decades have
kept the surrounding black neighborhoods from expanding into Bridgeport.[44]

Bridgeport began experiencing a multiracial transformation in the 1980s,
however, when an influx of immigrants from Asia and Latin America led to
an exodus of some of the white population along its eastern and northern
borders. By 2000, Asian Americans accounted for 26 percent, Latinos 30 percent, whites 41 percent, and blacks 1 percent of the population of Bridgeport.[45] The rapid increase of the Chinese population in Bridgeport started
in the 1980s and 1990s, when a number of Chinese American developers
began constructing townhouses in Bridgeport that were marketed toward
Chinese Americans and Chinese immigrants, who purchased properties
there because of its proximity to the core of South Chinatown. Gradually,
block by block, the Chinese have taken over much of the neighborhood.[46]

While the presence of Chinese homeowners revitalized the area real estate market and increased property prices, tensions between Chinese Americans and the more established white residents also rose. Racial harassment
of Asian Americans occurred. On November 3, 1999, two Asian American
male teens were physically assaulted by three white male teens; the white
youths shouted racial slurs and beat the Asian teens.[47] In the following year,
a Chinese restaurant on South Halsted Street in Bridgeport was set on fire,
causing the frightened owner to move his business to the suburbs.[48]

Bridgeport's history of white racial violence against blacks has no doubt
also affected its Chinese residents, and violence against Chinese has often
paralleled that against blacks. In 1998, an eighteen-year-old Chinese American was beaten by several white youths in Bridgeport. The assailants reportedly yelled, "I'll beat you like a fucking nigger. I hate nigger and Chinaman,"
while beating the victim.[49] In 2002, a Chinese high school student was walk-
ing on the border between Bridgeport and Chinatown when a car drove by

and three white teens inside yelled at him, "Hey, are you a nigger?" They then jumped out of the car and punched the Chinese youth in the eyes.[50]

This "overlap" of Chinese American and African American experiences, Shanshan Lan asserts, testifies to the "persistence of the Black/White binary and the die-hard nature of anti-Black racism in Bridgeport."[51] Lan further observes that new Chinese immigrants are more likely to remain invisible to mainstream American racial politics, as their racial experiences are often overshadowed by the public understanding that blacks are the "default targets" for racism in the United States.[52]

Multiethnic North Chinatown

Since 1975, when South Vietnam fell to the Communists, over two million refugees have fled Vietnam, Laos, and Cambodia, forming waves of refugees escaping the turmoil. The Indochinese refugee exodus was shaped by complex political and socioeconomic factors. The first wave of Vietnamese refugees were primarily from an elite class, who fled the Communist takeover of Vietnam; they included army officers and their families, government bureaucrats, teachers, doctors, engineers, lawyers, students, businessmen, and Catholic priests and nuns. The later flows were from more modest backgrounds, many of them ethnic "overseas Chinese," including farmers and fishermen fleeing the continuing regional military conflicts and deteriorating economic conditions.[53] The Vietnamese elites and professionals were soon joined and outnumbered by the masses of later refugees who were temporarily relocated to American bases in Guam and the Philippines under the emergency conditions after the fall of Saigon before being transferred to the United States. As the Communist government consolidated its rule over South Vietnam, it discriminated heavily against the ethnic "overseas Chinese" community, particularly in the Cholon district of Saigon (now Ho Chi Minh City), because of their involvement in business and their historical overseas connections with China.

In North America, Chicago became one of the major loci of settlement for Indochinese refugees. When the Vietnamese refugees first set foot in Chicago in the mid-1970s, Chinatown, the traditional point of entry for new immigrants, had already been overwhelmed by an influx of newcomers since 1965, mostly from Hong Kong, and was unable to provide adequate housing, social services, and employment opportunities, thus forcing these new Southeast Asian refugees to find alternative areas for settlement. They quickly found refuge in an emerging new Chinatown located on Argyle Street between Sheridan Road and Broadway, on Chicago's North Side.

This burgeoning new ethnic Chinese neighborhood traced its roots to the relocation of the headquarters of the Hip Sing Merchants' Association from the remnants of the older Chinatown just south of the downtown Loop area. In 1974 the federal government had acquired the Hip Sing property on Clark Street by eminent domain in order to construct a jail and a parking garage. With assistance from the Nationalist government in Taiwan, Hip Sing purchased several buildings along Argyle Street on the city's North Side and made ambitious plans for an elaborate mall complete with fountains and pagodas.[54] Although this new Chinatown in Argyle was less successful than the leaders of Hip Sing had envisioned, it did form the nexus of a new Chinese American community and thus attracted the ethnic Chinese and other refugees from Southeast Asia to settle there and revitalize the neighborhood. Hip Sing and the newly founded Chinese Mutual Service Agency welcomed these newcomers and encouraged further development of the area. The resident Chinese Americans and Southeast Asian refugees together transformed Argyle Street into a productive Asian business district, now referred to as North Chinatown. The elevated train stop at Argyle Street was specially designed with a Chinese-style red-and-green roof, becoming a conspicuous symbol of this new North Chinatown and competing with the Chinese memorial arch over Wentworth Avenue at Cermak Road in South Chinatown.

North Chinatown, however, was much smaller than and distinctively different from its rival on the South Side. While the businesses in the older South Chinatown were exclusively Chinese, serving local Chinese residents, non-Chinese Chicagoans, and tourists, the North Chinatown businesses catered primarily to ethnic Chinese from Vietnam and other immigrants from Southeast Asia. The North Chinatown major thoroughfares of Argyle Street and Broadway are lined with restaurants, grocery stores and minisupermarkets, gift stores, and jewelers, as well as real estate offices, banks, accountants, and medical doctors, mostly catering to ethnic Chinese and others from Indochina. Many grocery stores sell meats, vegetables, and cooking ingredients to the Chinese and Southeast Asian immigrant families living in the neighborhood, and most of the restaurants combine Chinese and Vietnamese cuisines.

According to my MapQuest search in 2009, among the more than twenty most popular Vietnamese restaurants in the metropolitan Chicago area, half are located in the Argyle area, including the Vietnamese Thai Binh Restaurant at 1113 West Argyle, Pho Viet at 4941 North Broadway, Viet My at 1119 West Argyle, Dong Ky Chinese & Vietnamese at 4877 North Broadway, Dong Thanh at 4925 North Broadway, the Pho Xe Tank Restaurant at 4953 North Broadway, the Hoang Café at 1010 West Argyle, the Anh-Linh Restaurant at 1032 West Argyle, and the Hai Yen Restaurant at 1055 West Argyle. While most are modest in decor and service, a few restaurants have adopted a more modern design and interior decor, appealing to a broader-based clientele. For example, Hai Yen Restaurant, one of the Vietnamese restaurants with a fresh and sleek look, was ranked as the Best New Restaurant by *Chicago Magazine* in May 2001 and featured in the *Chicago Tribune* in November 2001.[55]

As many ethnic Chinese from Southeast Asia opened businesses on or near Argyle Street, they also purchased homes in the area. Residents of North Chinatown are more likely to be ethnic Chinese from Vietnam,

Vietnamese Chinese grocery store and restaurant on Argyle Street, North Chinatown, Chicago, 2008. Collection of Huping Ling.

Cambodia, Laos, and other South Asian countries, as exemplified by Duc
Huang, Jenny Ling, and Toung Ling. Duc Huang was born in China in
1934. His father had owned a tea import business in Vietnam, and after
World War II his family moved to Vietnam from China. Duc Huang had
five years of formal schooling in China and finished middle school in Vietnam. After South Vietnam fell in 1975, Duc Huang and his family fled
in two small boats: he took some of his children in one boat and his wife
took the rest of their children in another. They all arrived at an island off
the coast of Malaysia, where they lived in refugee camps, waiting for clear-
ance and sponsorship in the United States. The Huang family finally arrived in Los Angeles, California, in 1977 and then moved to Chicago in
1978. While in Vietnam, Duc Huang had owned a factory manufacturing
agricultural motors and engines; in Chicago he started a garment factory,
among his other various businesses. Duc Huang's business success enabled
him to emerge as a community leader; he founded the Chinese Mutual Aid
Society in North Chinatown and remained very active in ethnic Chinese
organizations, for which he received numerous awards from state and local
governments.[56]

Jenny Ling is an ethnic Chinese born in Cambodia in 1963 and has three
younger brothers. She started her schooling at the age of six or seven. Unfortunately, her father passed away when she was eight, and she had to live
with an uncle. After the Khmer Rouge took over the Cambodian government when she was thirteen, her family obtained passports to Laos and
from there moved to a refugee camp in Thailand, where she attended school
and learned English. Jenny Ling and her family finally came to the United
States in the late 1970s. In 1988 she moved to Chicago and attended Truman
College near North Chinatown. She has worked as a hairstylist in North
Chinatown since 1990.[57]

Toung Ling, another ethnic Chinese, was born in Cambodia in 1962. He
escaped from Cambodia in 1982 and stayed in a refugee camp in Thailand
with three friends for about a year; then a cousin in Texas sponsored him to
the United States, where he found his first job in a donut shop. He moved
to Chicago in 1990, where he married Jenny Ling, whom he had known in
Cambodia.[58]

Historically, the Uptown area where North Chinatown is now located
has hosted successive waves of migrants, including impoverished whites
from the American South and later, after World War II, relocated Japanese

Americans from the West Coast. The new influx of Southeast Asian refugees from Vietnam, Laos, and Cambodia redefined the area, making it an active multiethnic commercial and residential urban community.[59]

The Suburban "Cultural Communities"

While new immigrants have revitalized or expanded the inner-city Chinatowns, they have also accelerated the suburbanization of the Chinese population around the city of Chicago, mostly in surrounding Cook County and its suburbs. In 1980, there were 721 Chinese residents recorded in the village of Skokie, north of Chicago. Nine other cities, towns, and villages in Cook County each had 100 or more Chinese residents. By 1990, twenty-one cities, towns, and villages in Cook County had a sizeable Chinese population. The western suburb of Naperville in nearby DuPage County had over 1,000 Chinese residents.[60] Together there were 20,700 Chinese living in the suburbs, nearly half of the Chinese population reported by the 1990 census.[61] According to the 2000 census, the Chinese American population in Illinois increased by 54 percent, rising from 28,597 in 1980 and 49,936 in 1990 to 76,725 in 2000. The largest number of Chinese Americans, or 48,058, resided in Cook County, representing 0.9 percent of the county's population.[62] This trend continued in 2010.[63]

Occupationally, most of the Chinese American suburbanites are American-educated professionals from Taiwan and mainland China employed by the area's high-tech industries and research institutions, such as the Argonne National Laboratory, Fermi Lab, Abbott Laboratories, Motorola, the University of Chicago, Northwestern University, the Illinois Institute of Technology, and many other such research institutions, universities, and colleges located in the western, northwestern, and northern suburbs surrounding Chicago.

Their stable income, human capital, and class resources afford them the lifestyle associated with suburban communities. Gravitating toward new housing developments, better school systems, and newly emerging ethnic supermarkets and services in the suburbs, Chinese American suburbanites readily blend into the dominant American suburban culture. They are satisfied with their suburban living conditions and rarely depend on the traditional Chinatown for employment, services, or entertainment except for occasional visits on special occasions.

As the Chinese American suburban population climbed, ethnic shops and supermarkets soon sprang up in and around these population centers to serve the needs of this fast-growing population. The most illuminating example is the DiHo Supermarket complex in the suburb of Westmont, which attracts a large number of Chinese American residents from the nearby areas.

Owing to their occupational and residential patterns, these suburban Chinese Americans form distinctly different communities from their counterparts in South and North Chinatowns in the city. While they are dispersed in their mainstream workplaces and dwell in predominantly white suburban neighborhoods, they congregate during weekends and holidays at Chinese language schools, churches, or Chinese social gatherings. In my earlier study on the Chinese community in St. Louis, *Chinese St. Louis: From Enclave to Cultural Community*, I defined such fluid and flexible community structure as a "cultural community."[64]

In my view, a cultural community is not defined by physical geographical boundaries but rather is defined by the common cultural practices and beliefs of its members. The cultural community is constituted by the language schools, religious institutions, Chinese community organizations, Chinese cultural agencies, Chinese political coalitions or ad hoc committees, and the wide range of cultural celebrations and activities facilitated by these agencies and groups. The St. Louis Chinese community since the 1960s is a typical cultural community. Its members dwell throughout the city and suburban municipalities, and there are no substantial business and residential concentrations or clusters constituting a "Chinatown" or a "suburban Chinatown." Rather, the Chinese of St. Louis have formed their community through various cultural activities organized by such community organizations and cultural institutions as language schools, churches, and other cultural agencies. They have preserved their Chinese cultural heritage and achieved ethnic solidarity without a recognizable physical community. Such a community is therefore better understood as a cultural community.[65]

A cultural community can also be identified by its economy and demography. Economically, the overwhelming majority population of a cultural community is professionally integrated into the larger society; therefore, the specific ethnic economy of the community does not significantly affect the well-being of its members and the community as a whole. Demographically, a cultural community contains a substantial percentage of professionals as well as self-employed entrepreneurs whose economic well-being is more dependent on the larger economy than on an ethnic economy. The professionals are mostly employed by employers in the larger society, and the self-employed also depend on the general population for their economic success. Working-class members, in terms of population, constitute only a minor portion of the suburban Chinese American community.[66]

The suburban Chinese American communities in Chicagoland are strikingly akin to their counterparts in St. Louis. The members of these communities work largely in American companies and reside in dispersed suburban neighborhoods. They visit the inner-city Chinatowns only occasionally for dining or ethnic food shopping needs, although the latter needs can adequately be met as well by the large suburban Asian supermarkets such as the DiHo in suburban Westmont. Chicago-based historian Ling Z. Arenson, in her study on the post-1945 Chinese American communities in Chicago, observes the detachment of the Chinese American suburbanites from the urban Chinatowns and notes that most suburban Chinese Americans "rarely participate in the social structure of the two Chinatowns."[67]

While maintaining their distance from the inner-city Chinatowns, the Chinese American suburbanites congregate in cultural and social activities among themselves regularly and frequently. The Chinese language and heritage schools serve as fundamental community structures among the Chinese American suburban population. Although most are bicultural and bilingual, often with advanced educational degrees from both their homeland and the host country and able to speak English fluently at work and Mandarin or Taiwanese at home, they are eager to have their children preserve their Chinese linguistic and cultural heritage. This strong desire for linguistic and cultural preservation motivates them to form weekend Chinese language schools, usually on Saturdays. In 1971, Chinese American professionals from Taiwan founded the Cooperative Chinese Language School in the western suburbs. While the earlier Chinese American suburbanites from Taiwan formed Chinese language schools teaching the classical, or old-style, Chinese characters, schools founded by the newer residents from mainland China, such as the Xilin Association of Chinese Schools, founded in 1989, which operates seven affiliated schools throughout Chicago's suburbs, teach the new standard "simplified" Chinese characters used in the PRC since 1954.[68] The 1998–99 Chicago Chinese Yellow Pages lists thirty-five Chinese language schools, among which eight are in South Chinatown, one in North Chinatown, and twenty-one in the Chicagoland suburbs, not counting the seven Xilin schools.[69]

Tripartite Divides

The development of separate Chinese communities comprising greater South Chinatown including Bridgeport, North Chinatown on Argyle, and the cultural communities in the northern and western suburbs may be termed a "tripartite division" (see Map 1).[70] Indeed, the contemporary Chinese in Chicagoland are not only divided geographically but more profoundly by their diverse orientations in regard to homeland and host country politics, educational level, professional training, language, and origin of birth.

While the traditional divisions in Chinatown, which have been discussed in previous chapters, were by and large along patrilineal and patrilocal lines, in recent decades the Chinese communities in Chicagoland, like their counterparts across the country, have been affected by politics in both the homeland and the United States. Traditional Chinatown organizations such as the CCBA, On Leong, Hip Sing, and the family associations had long been fervent supporters of President Sun Yat-sen and his Nationalist Party and remained pro-Nationalist after its defeat by the Communists and retreat to the island of Taiwan in 1949. In the 1950s, with the "Red Scare" of McCarthyism, many Chinese in Chicago disavowed any connection with the Communist Party in China.[71] This staunch anti-Communist stance was reinforced by new immigrants from Taiwan, Hong Kong, and the non-Communist Southeast Asian counties. In 1972, however, the Nixon administration's reconciliation with the PRC, followed by the establishment of formal diplomatic relations between the two countries in 1979, led to new political divisions among the Chinese communities across geographical boundaries.

Chinese from Taiwan, Hong Kong, and the Southeast Asian countries were mostly pro-Taiwan, while many Chinese from the PRC supported the Communist government in China. As already noted, most residents in the suburban Chinese cultural communities were American-educated professionals from Taiwan and the PRC. While members of the two groups mingle and collaborate at work and may even form individual friendships, as groups they form their separate Chinese language schools and community organizations. In addition to the major division between those who are pro-Taiwan and those who are pro-PRC, there are further subdivisions. For instance, among immigrants from Taiwan, tensions between those who are pro–Nationalist Party (mostly those who followed Chiang Kai-shek's forces to Taiwan in 1949) and those who support the native Taiwanese Democratic Progressive Party are almost as high as tensions between those who support Taiwan and those who support the PRC, especially during election years in Taiwan. Ling Z. Arenson's work well documents these complex divisions between and among mainland Chinese and Taiwanese in the United States.[72]

Linguistically, John Rohsenow has scrupulously analyzed the differences in language use in Chicago's three Chinese-speaking communities, which correlate with historical and contemporary sociopolitical forces. Historically, the majority of the immigrants in Chicago's South Chinatown comprised rural and urban working-class Cantonese speakers from southern China, Hong Kong, and Southeast Asia. They were generally less educated than the later and suburban-bound immigrants from Taiwan and mainland China. In 1980, the median number of years of schooling completed among those aged twenty-five years or older in South Chinatown was 10.4 years, while their counterparts in Cook County had 12.46 years of schooling. As a result, 92 percent of the South Chinatown residents spoke Chinese (mostly Cantonese) only. In 1990, more than 60 percent of the Chinese in the South Chinatown area did not speak English very well.[73] After the 1970s, moreover, because of increased immigration from Hong Kong and other parts of South China and Southeast Asia, the Chinatown "lingua franca" shifted from the rural Taishan dialect of Cantonese to the more standard Guangzhou City Cantonese.[74]

In North Chinatown, the majority of the ethnic Chinese refugees from Indochina were originally from coastal Fujian, the Chinese province that had historically dispatched its residents to Southeast Asia (popularly known among Chinese as Nanyang), who brought their Fujianese dialect with them but also learned Cantonese and Mandarin to conduct business.[75] Immigrants from Taiwan and mainland China were mostly students-turned-professionals who all spoke Mandarin, although with different accents depending on their province of origin. They came to Chicago for postgraduate education in area universities and colleges. Upon completing degrees, mostly in engineering, computer science, or accounting, from the University of Chicago, Northwestern University, the University of Illinois at Chicago, the Illinois Institute of Technology, or other area universities, they joined the high-tech companies in the suburbs. On campus they had formed their own separate student organizations, and such social separation tended to continue after their graduation.[76]

These linguistic differences are correlated with the class distinctions among the Chinese. While the well-educated professionals are employed in mainstream US high-tech companies or in the health industry, receiving stable incomes and living in new developments including million-dollar luxury homes, the residents of South and North Chinatown are concentrated in low-skill jobs, mainly in the ethnic businesses of grocery stores, restaurants, noodle factories, or the like, earning minimum wage and residing in substandard housing. This socioeconomic polarization results in a social distancing between the two groups.[77]

Converging as Chinese Chicagoans

While Chicagoland Chinese Americans are divided by their differences in politics, socioeconomic status, language, and origin of birth, they also realize that their well-being and hopes for a better future depend on ethnic solidarity. In recent decades, they have made concerted efforts to rise above their intergroup differences and have focused more on issues affecting the Chinese communities that are of common concern, such as housing shortages, employment training, English language proficiency, elderly assistance, youth development, preservation of their ethnic heritage, and protection of civil rights. To better meet these needs, they have formed cross-cultural, political, and social organizations to provide social services and worked side by side with other Asian ethnic groups and Euro-American citizens as well.

In comparison to the previous power structure of the old Chinatown-based community organizations such as the CCBA, On Leong, Hip Sing, and various family associations, these new community organizations share a number of distinguishing features. The prominent new community organizations are more akin to service organizations or agencies in the larger society. While decision making rests with boards of governors, consisting largely of successful professionals and business leaders from various subcommunity organizations or business corporations, social services are executed by professionals and paid staff members. They garner revenues primarily from government funding and donations from private and corporate sources. Their social services also reach out to a broader range of constituencies. Among these social service organizations, the Chinese American Service League and the Chinese Mutual Aid Association provide exemplary cases in point.

CHINESE AMERICAN SERVICE LEAGUE

In 1978 a group of Chinese Americans gathered for a potluck dinner where they discussed the needs of the Chinese community for English language assistance, refugee settlement assistance, and help with applications for social security and decided to form the Chinese American Service League (CASL). The initial community reaction was mixed, as the concepts and values of social service agencies were culturally unfamiliar to the majority of Chinese residents, and traditionally Chinese have shunned assistance from outside their own groups to resolve personal problems. By 1980, however, CASL had become a permanent member of Chicago's United Way and thus attracted groups from outside of Chinatown to join its efforts. The enlarged CASL added more programs: a core service program and an employment and training service. By 1983, CASL had grown into an agency with seventeen staff members, and its seven-hundred-square-foot office at 219 West Cermak Road had become too small. By May 1985, after an unprecedented capital campaign that brought visibility, recognition, and support from diverse constituencies of the CASL community, CASL began operating in a newly renovated ten-thousand-square-foot facility, formerly a truck warehouse, at 310 West 24th Place.

In this new home, CASL was able to provide more services. Soon a multilingual and multicultural day-care center was established. A chef training and baking program was also added to the list of services. CASL formed a neighborhood-development and community-organizing program to respond to issues that affected the Chinese community citywide. Later, after-school programming, youth outreach programming, and academic tutoring and youth mentoring came into operation. What had initially seemed an enormous building quickly became crowded, and CASL launched its second fund-raising campaign and added a nine-thousand-square-foot facility—the Children and Youth Center—on nearby Canal Street. By 1995 a small one-story building at 306 West 24th Place was added to house the expanding Elderly Service Department. Between 1996 and 2004, with the arrival of more immigrants, additional new programs were created to meet the ever-growing needs. An innovative Adult Day Care Service program was added, necessitating the acquisition of new facilities at 300 and 302 West 24th Place. CASL also began to operate a fleet of vehicles to transport clients and to expand the youth and family programs. In 1998, CASL opened a ninety-one-unit residential facility for elderly Chinese. This rapid expansion again required CASL to look for a new facility so that it could combine its disparate sites into a single unit. In the fall of 2002, CASL broke ground for its new community service center at 2141 South Tan Court. By 2004 the new building was completed and occupied, ushering in a new era in CASL's history.

Correspondingly, the financial capacity of the agency had grown exponentially during these decades. In 1985, CASL operated with a budget of less than $300,000. A decade later, in fiscal year 1995, its budget was over $2.5 million. In 2010, its budget soared to $10.3 million, and it employed over three hundred multilingual and multicultural professionals and supporting staff members. Its programs in child education and development, employment services, and counseling and social services now reach more than seventeen thousand clients annually, most of whom live in surrounding South Chinatown, Armour Square, and Bridgeport. Additional clients from across Chicago, neighboring suburban communities, and adjacent midwestern states also make use of CASL's services.[78]

As a nonprofit agency, CASL acquires its support primarily from government funding and from middle-class Chinese Americans. About 70 percent of its budget comes from government funding, while the remaining 30 percent must be raised by the agency itself from private foundations, corporate contributions, and individual donations.[79]

THE CHINESE MUTUAL AID ASSOCIATION

The Chinese Mutual Aid Association (CMAA) also began as a volunteer group serving ethnic Chinese immigrants from Southeast Asia in the late 1970s. In 1981, it was formally incorporated as a nonprofit social service agency with government funding, located at 1016 West Argyle Street, in the heart of the city's North Chinatown. With a mission to serve the needs, promote the interests, and enhance the well-being of Chinese and other immigrants and refugees in Chicago and to foster their participation in American society, CMAA has also garnered funding from federal, state, and local

governments, foundations, and corporations, as well as from private individuals. With generous financial support, CMAA has evolved into a vibrant
and multifaceted social service agency. In 2010, the agency had $3.5 million
expenses and employed close to forty full-time multilingual administrators,
professionals, and staff members working in the agency's various depart-
ments: education and workforce development, computer and information
technology, citizenship and immigration, social services, youth, and the
multicultural youth project.[80]

Many of CMAA's programs serve the basic needs of new immigrants
for English language education, job training, and citizenship assistance.
Its literacy programs, which are designed to help new immigrants improve
communication, gain better employment, understand American culture,
and prepare for US citizenship, include English as a second language (ESL)
classes, one-on-one tutoring, and Families Learning Together. By fiscal year
2001, these programs served nearly five hundred clients.

Although it continued to focus on the most urgent survival needs of immigrant and refugee Chinese, the agency has broadened its initial vision by
expanding the scope of its services and the diversity of its clients. Recognizing the higher rate of depression among and growing health care needs of
the aging parents of suburban middle-class Chinese Americans, CMAA also
established an office in suburban Westmont near the DiHo Supermarket
complex to provide medical workshops, transportation to and from medical
facilities, and English and citizenship classes.[81] CMAA's Multicultural Youth
Project (MCYP) cooperates with five other North Side agencies, including
the Bosnian Herzegovinian American Community Center, the Cambodian
Association of Illinois, Centro Romero, the Ethiopian Community Association of Chicago, and the Vietnamese Association of Illinois. The presence
and cooperation of so many cultural groups in the Uptown area around
North Chinatown created an opportunity to build a strong and diverse
community organization. The MCYP project brought together young people from different backgrounds for fun, friendship, dialogue, skill building,
team building, service, and community activism. Interaction among young
people from the six partner agencies occurs during events and activities such
as sports leagues, outings, camp retreats, workshops, training, community
celebrations, and cultural exchanges. In 2002, MCYP directly served 295
young people, whose ages ranged from ten to eighteen. In 2009, its diverse
programs served over 13,000 people in the Chicago metropolitan area.[82]

CMAA has excelled in promoting interethnic harmony and collaboration with other Chinese community organizations and other ethnic agencies. It has developed a close partnership with its sister agency, CASL, as
well as with such traditional community organizations as the CCBA and
with other Southeast Asian immigrant community organizations such as
the Vietnamese Association of Illinois and the Lao American Community
Services, to provide social services in twenty different dialects and languages
to a wide diversity of immigrant families in Chicago's North Side.[83] CMAA's
multicultural programs provide excellent examples of ethnic harmony in
crowded urban ethnic communities.

CASL and CMAA are social service organizations that help transform
new immigrants into American citizens and promote ethnic harmony and
cohesion while maintaining ethnic heritage. Other prominent community organizations likewise work in collaboration to promote the Chinese
American economy and culture. The Chicago Chinatown Chamber of
Commerce (CCCC) focuses on the business development of South Chinatown. Formed in 1983 with a mission to improve and expand business opportunities and to educate others on the history, culture, and customs of the
Chinese American community, the CCCC aims to increase revenue streams
for local businesses by making Chinatown a major destination for visitors
to the Midwest, the state of Illinois, and the city of Chicago. Its board of
directors comprises business leaders from banks, real estate and insurance
companies, travel agencies, law firms, food factories, and restaurants.

The CCCC's services are focused on promoting and marketing Chinatown, community beautification, and business and development assistance
to its members and community businesses. Working in conjunction with
city hall and with other organizations, the CCCC holds educational workshops, classes on sanitation, and a Chinatown Luncheon Series. It promotes
partnerships with the local police district and with other Asian American
organizations. It has created landscaped entrances along the nearby express-
way ramps and maintains beautification throughout Chinatown. It also provides a free Summer Shuttle Service and concierge programs at local hotels
to attract tourists. Its colorful tourist brochure highlights Chinatown's businesses and attractions, with eye-catching photos depicting the community's
cultural activities. To preserve cultural heritage and promote tourism, it
sponsors popular annual cultural events such as the Chinese Lunar New
Year's Parade in January or February, Asian American Heritage Month in

May, the Chinatown Summer Fair and Dragon Boat Race in summer, the
LaSalle Bank's Chinatown Marathon in October, and the Miss Friendship
Ambassadors of Chinatown Pageant in November.[84] This combination of
ethnic-flavored tourism and business development follows recent trends in
the larger Chinese ethnic communities on the East and West Coasts.

In addition to promoting tourism and business to outsiders, the activities
organized by the CCCC also reinforce a common ethnic identity among the
diverse groups of Chinese Americans in the metropolitan area. For instance,
the top finalists of the 2010 Miss Friendship Ambassador contest included
young Chinese American women of varying ethnic backgrounds. Jessica
Lin, who placed first, and Christine Trinh, who was first runner-up, are
descendants of Taiwanese Chinese and Vietnamese Chinese, respectively.[85]

The Chinese-American Museum of Chicago (CAMOC) is another
unique community organization that strives to promote the cultural and
historical heritage of Chinese Americans in Chicago. The CAMOC is gov-
erned by the board of directors of the Chinatown Museum Foundation,
founded in February 2002 by a group of area businessmen, professionals,
and individuals interested in the research, education, and promotion of the
Chinese American heritage in the midwestern United States; in 2009 there
were twenty-three board members. Since its inception and incorporation as a
tax-free cultural institution, the members of the foundation, many of whom
are retirees, have assiduously collected rare historical photographs and arti-
facts, interviewed residents of the Chinese American communities, and organized two exhibits each year since 2005, when the museum at 238 West
23rd Street, in the heart of South Chinatown, was opened to the public. The
CAMOC was inspired by the Ling Long Museum in Chicago, reportedly
the first museum in America operated by Chinese immigrants.[86] While the
CAMOC had been operating successfully, unfortunately a fire occurred on
September 19, 2008, destroying many of the museum's permanent collections. Twenty-three historic dioramas, antique embroidered wall hangings,
and a Peking Opera costume were lost in the blaze. Devastated by the fire
and the loss of these valuable collections, the surrounding community rallied
to assist the members of the Chinatown Museum Foundation in restoring
and rebuilding the museum, which reopened on September 25, 2010.[87]

In addition to such community-focused organizational efforts, many
community volunteers also work across ethnic and cultural lines. To give
but two examples, Howard Chun, the retired military officer and engineer

discussed previously, has volunteered since 1990 for the Chicago branch of the Korean American Community Service, where he offers private tutoring in computer skills to elderly Korean immigrants. His wife, Grace Chun, has been a longtime supporter of Boundless Readers, the Rochelle Lee Fund to Make Reading a Part of Children's Lives, a literacy group that provides books to classrooms and libraries throughout the Chicago area.[88]

Transnational Connections Renewed

The formal reconciliation between the United States and mainland China in 1972 and the consequent influx of Chinese immigrants from the PRC have prompted a renewal of transnational connections between Chinese American communities and their native places. Taishan, the most common place of origin for American overseas Chinese, witnessed a rapid increase in remittances and contributions from the United States. As in the early days of the Chinese in Chicago, the Moy (Mei) family, together with other Chinese in Chicago and other Moys throughout the world, resumed playing an active role in renewing transnational connections with their villages of origin near Canton (Guangzhou).[89]

In 1975, Mei Youzhuo and other clan leaders of the Moy family proposed establishing an international Moy family association, a proposal that was warmly received by the Moy family associations throughout the world. On September 20, 1975, representatives of the Moy family associations around the globe gathered in Taipei, Taiwan, for the First International Moy Family Reunion Convention and announced the establishment of the International Moy Family Association. The association emphasizes its nature as a nonpolitical and nonprofit same-surname family organization and states its mission as "promoting harmony among members of the Moys, encouraging connections between the native place and the host countries, and uniting all members of the Moys."[90] Since then, the International Moy Family Reunion Convention has been held every three years. On November 13, 2006, the association celebrated its thirtieth anniversary in Jiangmen, Guangdong, China, with more than five hundred attendees. After the conclusion of this convention, attendees paid homage to their ancestral tombs in Duanfen Township, Taishan, and then visited the Moy family associations in Guangzhou (Canton) and in Shunde County.[91]

TABLE 3   The Moy family reunion conventions, 1927–2006

Convention no.	Time	Place	President(s)
1	1927	Chicago	景祥 秀迺
2	1932		宗堯 迺鑒
3			
4			
5			
6			
7			周迺 友煦
8	1947	Chicago	友煦 穆迺
9	1958	Boston	奕強 穆迺
10	1960	Washington, D.C.	友鏡 國康
11			銳康 友謀
12	1972	New York	友謀 毓均
13*	1975**	Taipei	忠和
14	1978		忠和
15	1981		伯儀
16	1984	Miami	伯儀
17	1987	New York	伯儀 勁群
18	1990	New York	勁群 賢添
19	1993	Boston	國莊 錫銳
20	1996	Chicago	悅文 國明
21	1999	Qingshuiwan	犖揚 楹仲
22	2003		
23	2006	Jiangmen, Fujian	

SOURCE: Shijie Meishi Zongqin Zonghui (1991, 113); *Xin Ning Magazine* 新寧雜誌, no. 4 (2006): 32.

* Changes in board of directors.

** Since 1975, when the International Moy Family Association was founded in Taipei, the convention had been international, with attendees representing the Moy family associations from all over the world.

Reenergized by the International Moy Family Association and with donations from its members, in 1976 the Moy family revived its same-surname magazine, *Runan zhihua* 汝南之花 (Nei Nam's flower, or the Moy family magazine), which was initially founded in 1931 and has arguably become the leading same-surname magazine of overseas Chinese native places.[92] A semiannual magazine, it publishes articles and reports on the successes and achievements of the Moys overseas; the social, economic, and political developments in their native place; and recognitions of donations and is distributed internationally to members of the association. Given the dominance of the Taishanese among Chinese immigrants in the United States (prior to the 1960s, at least, more than 50 percent of the Chinese immigrants in the United States originated from the Taishan area of Guangdong province[93]), *Runan zhihua* is typical of overseas Chinese magazines, known as *qiaokan* in China, which first appeared in the 1890s when China was in the midst of the turmoil of the first Sino-Japanese War and the historic Qing dynasty's Hundred Days' Reform and then experienced a revival after the 1970s when China reopened its doors to the world resulting in waves of Chinese emigrants overseas.

The significance of these *qiaokan*, according to academics such as Madeline Y. Hsu, lies in their being "material expressions of belonging" that provide "a sense of community among Chinese overseas."[94] Indeed, *Runan zhihua*, like other overseas Chinese magazines, has itself created a community that transcends geographical borders and connects transnational migrants and their native place. In this magazine, loyalty to their clan and native place on the part of Moys all over the world is abundantly displayed in their donations, investments in enterprises in their native place, and visits to home villages. Such loyalty is honored and recognized by the community in the pages of the magazine, which also highlights the overseas Moys' socioeconomic achievements in their host countries as well as their contributions to their native place. A report on Chicagoans Mei Renguang and his wife, Wu Yuxian, in a 1993 issue of *Runan zhihua* provides an example:

> Mei Renguang and his wife Wu Yuxian were natives of Renheli Village, Shandi District, Duanfen. The entire family emigrated to America, and settled in Chicago in the 1950s. Since then Mr. Mei and his wife have visited their native place more than ten times. They are honorary board members of Shandi Middle School and Chikan Elementary School; to each of the schools they have donated funds for constructing classrooms, greatly contributing to the educational cause of their native place.

Mei Renguang and his wife Wu Yuxian also pay great attention to their children's education. Their daughter Mei Aihua graduated from the University of Minnesota and is currently working as an assistant fashion designer at a large and well-known company. Their son Mei Jianhua, age twenty-seven, graduated from the University of Minnesota and Columbia University, and was then hired by the US Department of State. In 1992, he was appointed vice-consul of the American Embassy in South Korea. It is anticipated that he will be appointed vice-consul of the American Embassy in China. This would be the highest position held by a Chinese American in the US Department of State.

This year, Mr. Mei Renguang and three other brothers of our Moy clan in Chicago visited their hometown and invested in the newly opened Hong-mei Seafood Restaurant in Jiangmen City.[95]

This report praises Mei Renguang and Wu Yuxian as exemplary emigrants of their native place. The couple have maintained close ties with their native place through numerous visits to their hometown, generous donations to the educational projects there, and investment in local enterprises. Their contributions to their native place are thus publicly and prominently recognized. At the same time, the report also commends the couple's success in raising two high-achieving children. Such recognitions provide immense pride and emotional satisfaction to the greater Moy clan, a psychological return for their loyalty and contributions to their native place, and encourage members of the family to sustain such connections and contributions and to encourage others to do likewise.

The magazine also reports on socioeconomic and political developments in Duanfen, mostly on construction projects such as schools, hospitals, roads and bridges, and government buildings. For instance, on September 23, 1994, a ribbon-cutting ceremony celebrated the completion of three major projects: the academic building of Duanfen Middle School, the administrative building of the Duanfen town government, and the Duanfen Nursing Home for the Elderly.[96] Donations from overseas Chinese greatly promote public education in Duanfen. Duanfen Middle School and the numerous elementary schools in the area have contributed to its growing rate of college-bound students. These donations also promoted a "volleyball craze," as volleyball became a popular sport in Duanfen. In the 1980s, Taishan City (Taishan was upgraded from a county to a city in the 1980s) became known as the "home of volleyball," and most members of the city's volleyball team came from Duanfen, where volleyball teams exist in almost every village.[97]

At the end of each issue, the magazine lists the names of donors and the amount of their donations. Although local members also donate money, the overwhelming majority of the donors are overseas Chinese in the United States, Canada, Hong Kong, Taiwan, and Macau. While some donors contribute hundreds or thousands of US dollars, the majority of the donors contribute ten or twenty dollars, showing that the magazine enjoys popular support among ordinary overseas Chinese.

Conclusion

Chinese Chicagoans have found an answer to the challenge posed by the ever-growing diversity of ethnic communities. They have made concerted efforts to form more inclusive and broader community service organizations that attempt to embrace a cross-regional, cross-cultural, and cross-ethnic clientele. To increase their capacity to serve this broader clientele, they have largely relied on funds from government, private agencies, and individual donors and have hired professional staff to operate these ambitious and complex service programs. Melding together a large ethnic community with geographical, cultural, and occupational differences is a difficult task, however, requiring understanding and cooperation on the part of all these concerned groups, a goal that Chinese Chicagoans are still striving to achieve. At the same time, their successes in the United States have allowed them to join with other overseas Chinese to celebrate and support their connections with their native places in China.

Epilogue

The "Hollow Center Phenomenon"
and the Future of Transnational Migration

In the summer of 2007, I was invited by the Institute of Overseas Chinese Studies at Jinan University, Guangzhou (Canton), to give a series of lectures on Chinese American studies in conjunction with my field research in Taishan, Guangdong Province. The beautiful tropical city by the Pearl River was soaked in humid summer heat. The friendliness and eagerness to learn demonstrated by the faculty and students at the institute more than compensated for the heat, however, and made my stay at Jinan University memorable. What excited me most was my upcoming field research in Taishan City and especially in Duanfen Township, where the Duanfen Moys reside and where many Chinese Chicagoans originated. Accompanied by Dr. Chao Longqi, the director of the institute at that time, and Dr. Gao Weinong, a well-known historian of overseas Chinese and a prolific writer, I went to Duanfen and Taishan in the hot July summer. The fieldtrip was extremely fruitful. In addition to many interviews with local residents, a large number of photographs, and a variety of statistics on overseas Chinese from the Bureau of Overseas Chinese Affairs in Taishan City, I obtained a copy of the recent compilation of the *Meishi zongqin zupu* (梅氏親族譜, the Moy family genealogy) prepared by the International Moy Family Association.

Weng Songping, owner of *Wengjialou* (the Weng family's buildings) in the village of Miaobian, Duanfen Township, Taishan City (discussed in Chapter 3), received us. The family history of the Wengs is an exemplar of transnational migration. Weng Songping's grandfather migrated to Hong Kong in the 1910s and made money in the 1920s in the trans-Pacific merchandise business. With his new wealth, he built five sumptuous buildings for his family, known as *Wengjialou*, which were the envy of the villagers. In the wake of the Communist takeover in 1949, the family were forced to move out of the buildings, which were occupied by other families during the Cultural Revolution. Fortunately, the Weng family had kept the title to the property and so were able to win a strenuous nine-year-long lawsuit, after China reopened its doors to the Western world in the late 1970s. Weng Songping was the eldest son of the family. He had two younger brothers, one running a Chinese restaurant in Chicago and the other residing in New Zealand, while Weng Songping had to stay in the home village to look after the family property and to take care of his mother, who was by then in her seventies. Weng Songping's daughter, Weng Xuee, emigrated to America in 2004, joining her uncle in Chicago and working in his restaurant; she also found a boyfriend, who worked in Chinatown. The family buildings now were all empty and looked neglected, except for the one that Weng Songping and his mother occupied.[1]

On the same day we visited with Mei Yuqin (Moy Yuqin), a neat woman in her forties, who was relaxing inside the spacious living room of a well-kept *yanglou* (foreign building) in *Meijia dayuan*, the Moy family compound, in Tingjiangxu, Duanfen Township, Taishan. The building was owned by her husband's distant relative, Moy Zongxian, whom they call "Great-grandfather." Moy Zongxian left Duanfen in the 1950s and settled in Chicago, where he worked in the Chinese restaurant business until he retired. He had brought his children and grandchildren to America beginning in the 1980s, and they are now residing in Chicago, Boston, and New York City. Since all of his relatives had emigrated to America, Moy Zongxian invited Mei Yuqin to occupy the house. He would send money from time to time to Mei Yuqin, as compensation for her work and to provide funds for fixing and keeping up the house. Since Mei Yuqin's own house was nearby, the job was not too difficult for her. Her husband took care of the family field, while her children worked in factories in Guangdong and Shenzhen.[2]

While Weng Songping was willing to stay in the home village and great-grandfather Moy Zongxian was lucky enough to find a relative to occupy the house and keep it in good shape, many owners of the *yanglou* or *diaolou* had abandoned their properties when the last family member emigrated to America. The large-scale emigration from Taishan in recent decades has caused a massive abandonment of properties, which have turned into ghost towns. Chinese scholars have referred to the situation as *kongxinhua*, or the "hollow center phenomenon." In 2007, the total population of Duanfen, for instance, the township where the Moys and many other Chinese Chicagoans originated, was 600,000, whereas there were about 1.2 million relatives overseas, mostly residing in the United States and Canada.[3] The term "hollow center phenomenon" is borrowed from a widespread phenomenon in villages throughout China in recent decades in which new houses and businesses are clustering and crowding along the edges of villages and major roads and highways, while the centers of the villages are left with old and abandoned houses and deserted lands. Geographers, sociologists, and scholars from other disciplines in the social sciences have written a great deal about the phenomenon,[4] but little has been written about the hollow center phenomenon in *qiaoxiang*.

At the same time, Chinese migrant workers from villages in hinterland provinces, mostly Guangxi, Sichuan, and Hunan, gradually moved in and settled in these hollow villages. They rented houses or fixed up abandoned properties. Those who had made enough money built their own new-style *yanglou* alongside the abandoned old *yanglou*. The increasing number of domestic migrants from hinterland China has thus resulted in the so-called *qiaoxiang neidihua* (hinterlandization of the overseas Chinese villages).

The hollow center phenomenon and the hinterlandization of the overseas Chinese village began in the 1980s, when the Chinese government loosened its policies and regulations on issuing permits and passports to relatives of the overseas Chinese. The new process was greatly simplified and took less time than before. The procedure for a relative of an overseas Chinese to acquire a passport generally requires obtaining a letter of invitation and proofs of financial support from the overseas Chinese who would act as sponsor and filing an application form with the Bureau of Overseas Chinese Affairs in a city, which would forward the application to the Bureau of Public Security in the city, and the latter would issue a passport.[5] Few applicants had been denied a passport by the Chinese bureaucracy; the major obstacle for emigration to the United States rested with the American Embassy, which could accept an application or turn it down, depending on the visa-granting officials' judgment as to whether an applicant might become a burden upon American society. Seventy-five percent of the applicants were relatives of Chinese in America—a spouse, a child, or a sibling—who would join their family members or relatives in the United States and would most likely end up working in restaurants, grocery stores, garment shops, or performing other manual service jobs. According to official statistics from the Taishan City Bureau of Overseas Chinese Affairs, there were more than 8,000 passport applicants annually, out of a population of 1.3 million in the city. A majority of the applicants were Moys.[6]

Since the opening up of China from the late 1970s until 2007, the overseas Chinese from Taishan had contributed US$233 million to the homeland, with annual contributions of around $7.1 million. These contributions had enabled the constructions of roads, schools, and hospitals in the city totaling 13,218 projects.[7]

At the same time, the new policy and the relatively easy process contributed to the loss of local population, which could result in a decrease of remittances and contributions from overseas. At the theoretical level, it could also mean the decline and eventual cessation of transnational migration. Thus, the hollow center phenomenon raises a serious issue for local Chinese governments concerning overseas Chinese affairs, as well as for scholars in overseas Chinese studies.[8]

In the short run, the decreased population in home villages will have a significant impact on transnational migration. When those who were able and ambitious enough to leave home have all left for overseas, the number of potential immigrants will be smaller. When the hollowed overseas Chinese villages have been gradually repopulated by domestic migrants, however, who will in turn become new sources of emigration overseas, there will be new "Moys" coming to America and other developed countries, thus repeating the epic presented in the Moy family genealogy.

Further, the ongoing back and forth movement between China and America should be understood in the larger context of "Chinmerica," a term christened by the Harvard historian Niall Ferguson in 2007, according to which the relationship between China and America will be the most important factor in understanding world economy, and China and America will be viewed as a single economy. Chinmerica accounts for a quarter of the world's population, a third of its gross domestic product, and over half of global economic growth between 2003 and 2009.[9] The mutual engagement between and mutual benefits enjoyed by the two countries will perpetuate the transnational human movement.

Reference Matter

Notes

Abbreviations

ARCHIVAL SOURCES

CAMOC   Chinese-American Museum of Chicago
CCCF   Chicago Chinese Case Files, 1898–1940
EWB   Ernest Watson Burgess Papers
OH   Olga Huncke Papers

NEWSPAPERS

CCDN   *Chinese Centralist Daily News* (English translation), 1937–1938
CD   *China Daily*
CDN   *Chicago Daily News*, 1922–
CDT   *Chicago Daily Tribune*, 1872–1963
CHDT   *Chinese Daily Times* (English translation), 1935–1936
CJ   *Chicago Journal*, 1906–
CRH   *Chicago Record-Herald*, 1908–
CST   *Chicago Sun-Times*, 1973–
CSTR   *Chicago Sunday Tribune*
CT   *Chicago Tribune*, 1878–
G-D   *St. Louis Globe-Democrat*, 1875–1986
NYT   *New York Times*, 1880s–
SFC   *San Francisco Chronicle*, 1943–
SMMP   *San Min Morning Paper* or *San Min Chen Bao* [Three People's Principles Morning Daily News] (English translation), 1931–1938
S-PD   *St. Louis Post-Dispatch*

Introduction

Lyrics reproduced with the permission of the Van Heusen Music Corporation. The song had been performed perhaps most memorably by Frank Sinatra.

1. The terms "Chicago" and "Chicagoland," which appears later in the book, refer to the metropolitan Chicago statistical area as defined by the US Census Bureau, generally including the city of Chicago and its suburbs.

2. Burgess and Bogue (1964, 5).

3. Historian Henry Yu's brilliantly written *Thinking Orientals* offers a comprehensive depiction of the Chicago sociologists and their research. Similarly, in his introduction to Paul C. P. Siu's *The Chinese Laundryman*, historian John Kuo Wei Tchen provides penetrating discussions of the Chicago School and works by students of Robert Park and Ernest Burgess.

4. See, for example, works by sociologists Tin-Chiu Fan (1926), Yuan Liang (1951), Margaret Gibbons Wilson (1969), and Paul C. P. Siu (1987); by educator Ruth Joan Soong (1931); by historians Susan Lee Moy (1978), Adam McKeown (2001), and Henry Yu (2001); by geographers Henry Ying Cheng Kiang (1992) and Linda Qingling Wang (1997); by anthropologist Shanshan Lan (2007); and by linguist John S. Rohsenow (2004).

5. See Ling (2004a, 8–10).

6. The term "jungle" is borrowed from journalist and writer Upton Sinclair's novel *The Jungle* (1906), which depicts the plight of the immigrant working class in Chicago's meat-packing industry during the early twentieth century.

7. Glick Schiller, Basch, and Blanc-Szanton (1992, ix).

8. See, for example, Ong (1999); and Portes, Guarnizo, and Landolt (1999, 224).

9. For historical works with a transnationalist approach, see, for example, Yu (1983, 1992); Chen (2000); Hsu (2000); McKeown (2001); and Liu (2005).

10. See, for example, Yang (2006).

11. In particular, Chen (2000); Hsu (2000); McKeown (2001); and Liu (2005).

Chapter One

1. *Guangdong qiaohui* (1945), cited in Liu Quan (2002, 2–3).

2. Gao et al. (2005, 3).

3. Ibid., 8.

4. Fairbank (1973); and Hsu (1990).

5. The tael was a unit of Chinese silver currency used in imperial China that was based on weight, equivalent to 1.3 ounces. In the late eighteenth and early nineteenth centuries, a tael was approximately equal to a Spanish dollar.

6. Takaki (1989, 79).

7. Ibid.

8. Sandmeyer (1973, 16).

9. Takaki (1989, 85).

10. The author's tally for the list of cases comes from CCCF.

11. Shijie Meishi Zongqin Zonghui (1991, 8–11).

12. Ibid., 10.

13. Shijie Meishi Zongqin Zonghui (1991).

14. Ibid., 48.

15. Shijie Meishi Zongqin Zonghui (1991).

16. *Dufen zhenzhi* (2003, 37–38).

17. Shijie Meishi Zongqin Zonghui (1991, 90).

18. Ibid., 81.

19. I had been aware of the Moys' *zupu* but did not have an opportunity to access it until the summer of 2007, when I did my field research in Taishan and obtained a copy.

20. Shijie Meishi Zongqin Zonghui (1991, 90–91), author's translation.

21. Shijie Meishi Zongqin Zonghui (1991, 90). The Chinese coolies were called *zhuzai* (piglets) because they were stuffed into the crowded lower compartments of ships like livestock during their arduous passage overseas from Hong Kong to the Americas; such traffic has been called the "piglet trade," or "coolie trade."

22. Author's tally and computation from *Taishan shi qiaolian pucha* (Taishan Shi Qiaolian 1998).

23. Lorraine Moy Tun (daughter of the second Moy brother, Moy Dong [Tong] Yee), interview by Ruth Kung, September 1, 2007; testimony of Moy Tong Yee, March 30, 1906, CCCF Case 463.

24. *Taishanxian huaqiaozhi* (1992, 5–6).

25. Ibid., 6.

26. Zhang (2003).

27. Huang (2003).

28. Long et al. (2008).

29. Wang and Deng (2005).

30. Louie (2004, 158).

Chapter Two

1. W. E. B. DuBois (1903, 23).

2. McCafferty (2003); Swenson (1991).

3. Dowd (1992).

4. Smith (1995, 101).

5. Cronon (1991).

6. Hesse-Wartegg (1891, 160–161).

7. Merchants' Chicago Census Report, 1871, http://www.chicagoancestors.org/downloads/1871census.pdf.

8. Melvin G. Holli, "German American Ethnic and Cultural Identity from 1890 Onward," in Holli and Jones (1995, 93–109).

9. Anita R. Olson, "A Community Created: Chicago Swedes, 1880–1950," in Holli and Jones (1995, 110–121).

10. Michael F. Funchion, "Irish Chicago: Church, Homeland, Politics, and Class—The Shaping of an Ethnic Group, 1870–1900," in Holli and Jones (1995, 57–92).

11. Cutler (1996, 7, 40–61).

12. Edward R. Kantowicz, "Polish Chicago: Survival through Solidarity," in Holli and Jones (1995, 173–198).

13. Nelli (1970, 22–23).

14. Dominic Candeloro, "Chicago's Italians: A Survey of the Ethnic Factor, 1850–1990," in Holli and Jones (1995, 229–259).

15. Chan (1986); Chinn (1989); Chiu (1967); Lydon (1985); Minnick (1988); and Saxton (1971).

16. Daniels (1988, 70).

17. Chan (1991a, 46).

18. Ibid.

19. Ibid., 48; Sandmeyer (1973, 48, 97–98).

20. Cohen (1984, 82–83).

21. Held by the Chinese-American Museum of Chicago.

22. Tin-Chiu Fan's 1926 thesis refers to T. C. Moy as the first Chinese. When Paul C. P. Siu entered the graduate program in the Sociology Department of the University of Chicago in 1932, he would have known Fan's work, but Siu used different spellings. His study on the Chicago Chinatown in the 1930s records the names of the Moy brothers as Moy Chong-Chow, Moy Chong-Hoi, and Moy Chong-Yee. Given that Siu, the son of a Chinese laundryman, was an "insider" and that his father visited the Siu Family Association and other clan associations in Chicago frequently, Siu's account is probably more reliable. Susan Lee Moy, in her master's thesis (1978) and later writings, refers to "Moy Dong Jue and his brothers." Adam McKeown (2001) quotes Fan's interview with T. C. Moy but uses the name Moy Dong Chew. The Chinese-American Museum of Chicago (CAMOC), which opened in 2005, gives the Moy brother's names as Moy Dong Chow, Moy Dong Hoy, and Moy Dong Yee, which is consistent with most instances in the Chicago Chinese Case Files; see, for example, the testimony of Lillie Moy (daughter of Moy Dong Chow), August 8, 1924, CCCF, file 2005/1628. Similarly, the Civil Case Files of the US District Court in the Northern District of Illinois recorded the name Moy Dong Hoy.

23. Fan ([1926] 1974, 13–14).

24. Ibid., 14.

25. Ibid.

26. Photography displayed at CAMOC.

27. *CT*, October 21, 1876.

28. "Chinese Sunday-School," *CT*, August 5, 1878.

29. Tchen (1990, 1999); Lui (2007); and Wong (1996).

30. "The Celestial New Year Begins Saturday, at Midnight," *CT*, February 6, 1891.

31. Moy (1978, 380); CAMOC.

32. Wilson (1969, 5).

33. Siu (1987, 28–30).

34. "Where Orient and Occident Meet," *Graphic*, February 17, 1894.

35. Ibid.

36. Ibid.

37. See another news report, quoted in Chapter 5, "Gleeful Celestials, Chicago Chinatown Celebrate Their New-Year's Festival," *CT*, January 20, 1890; "Chinese Colony Indignant at the Plan for Detecting Chinamen," *CT*, August 10, 1892.

38. "Feast Dead Chinamen," *CT*, August 10, 1891; see also "Celebration of Chinese New Year's," *CT*, January 30, 1892, 7:4.

39. Chung (2002).

40. "Wong Chin Foo Thinks Kern Opposed to His Family," *CT*, April 16, 1893.

41. Ibid.

42. "Burning Joss Sticks in Court, Wong Chin Foo Mulcted in $1,000 for Libeling Chin Fou Tip," *NYT*, March 4, 1885.

43. "Wong Chin Foo Thinks Kern Opposed to His Family," *CT*, April 16, 1893.

44. McKeown (2001, 200).

45. Wong Chin Foo Naturalization Paper, April 3, 1874, RG 89-28, Kent Country Naturalization Records of the 17th Circuit Court 1860–1929, Archives of Michigan (hereinafter "Wong Chin Foo Naturalization Paper").

46. Shepard (1921).

47. "Wong Chin Foo Naturalization Paper."

48. "Wong Chin Foo," *CT*, March 23, 1879; Moyers (2003).

49. Moyers (2003); Andrew Hsiao, "100 Years of Hell-Raising: The Hidden History of Asian American Activism in New York City," *Village Voice*, June 23, 1998 (http://www.villagevoice.com/1998-06-23/news/100-years-of-hell-raising/); Qingsong Zhang (1998); Ngai (2005).

50. "Chinese Club," *CT*, February 17, 1881.

51. "Naturalizing Chinamen," *CT*, February 18, 1881.

52. "Wong Chin Foo Thinks Kern Opposed to His Family," *CT*, April 16, 1893.

53. "Chinese Club," *CT*, February 17, 1881.

54. "Feast Dead Chinamen," *CT*, August 10, 1891; "Chinese Colony Indignant at the Plan for Detecting Chinamen," *CT*, August 10, 1892.

55. See, for example, *United States v. Moy Jan*, Case 10576, March 30, 1911, USDC/NDI-Chicago, Civil Records, 1871–1985, Civil Case Files, 1871–1911, RG 21, National Archive Records Administration–Great Lakes Region (Chicago).

56. Testimony of Lillie Moy, CCCF, file 2005/1628; *CT*, April 16, 1893; and *CT*, January 20, 1890.

57. "Chinese Refugee Flock to Chicago," *CJ*, May 23, 1906.

58. Ibid.

59. "Chinese Colony Indignant at the Plan for Detecting Chinamen," *CT*, August 10, 1892.

60. *Meihua xinbao* [Chinese American], June 24, 1893.

61. Chinese Equal Rights League, 1892, *An Appeal of the Chinese Equal Rights League to the People of the United States for Equality of Manhood* (New York: Chinese Equal Rights League), p. 2.

62. *United States v. Moy Jan*, Case 10576, Civil Case Files, 1871–1911, RG 21, National Archive Records Administration–Great Lakes Region (Chicago).

63. Cases 10577, 10641, 10642, 10654, and 10666, Civil Case Files, 1871–1911, RG 21, National Archive Records Administration–Great Lakes Region (Chicago).

64. "Highbinder" was the name given by American police and the press to members of certain oath-bound Chinese secret societies in American cities. It was believed that these secret societies had their origin in the Great Hung League, or *Hung-men*, a political organization aimed at overthrowing the Manchu Qing dynasty in China. The terms "Highbinder" and "tong" were often used interchangeably.

65. Hyde and Conard (1899, 1024).

66. "75 Years Ago—Thursday, June 9, 1892," *G-D*, June 9, 1967.

67. The Chinese Exclusion Act of 1882 banned laborers for ten years. It was renewed in 1892 and 1902 and extended indefinitely in 1904.

68. "75 Years Ago—Wednesday, August 25, 1897," *G-D*, August 25, 1972.

69. Chinese Exclusion Cases Habeas Corpus Petitions, 1857–1965, US District Court for the Eastern District of Missouri, St. Louis, Records of the District Courts of the United States, RG 21, National Archives–Central Plains Region, Kansas City, Missouri.

70. K. Scott Wong (1996); Tam (1988).

71. McKeown (2001, 193).

72. Ibid., 194.

73. Merchants Chicago Census Report, 1871, http://www.chicagoancestors.org/downloads/1871census.pdf.

74. Chicago Association of Commerce and Industry (1909).

75. Lewis (1997).

76. Anderson (1923); Wirth (1928); Shaw (1930); Young (1932); Whyte (1943).

77. Anderson (1923, 3–6).

78. Wirth (1928, 169).

79. Shaw (1930, 10–11).

80. The Sociology Department at the University of Chicago also recruited students of Japanese ancestry in the 1930s and 1940s, including Yukiko Kimura, who was born in Japan but migrated to Honolulu later where she became a social worker; and Frank Miyamoto and Tamotsu Shibutani, both of whom grew up outside Little Tokyo in California.

81. US Bureau of the Census, *U.S. Census of Population, 1890*, http://www.census.gov/prod/www/abs/decennial/1890.html.

82. Fan ([1926] 1974, 14).

83. Ibid., 15.

84. Lui (2007).

85. "Police Close Up Chinese Mission," *CDT*, June 28, 1909, p. 3.

86. Ibid.

87. Testimony of Lim Yee, December 5, 1913, CCCF, file 2005/183; testimony of Au Tat, June 5, 1924, CCCF, file 2005/1608.

88. Fan ([1926] 1974, 15).

89. Wittman (1988, 3).

90. Moy (1978, 43); McKeown (2001, 212).

91. Nelli (1970, 43).

92. Moy (1978, 44).

93. Photos displayed at CAMOC.

94. Italian American Collections, Department of Special Collections, University Library, University of Illinois at Chicago.

95. CAMOC.

96. Hughes (1945, 33).

97. *Whip*, August 15, 1919.

Chapter Three

1. Joiner (2007, 21).

2. Cohen (1990, 13, 28).

3. Posadas (1990).

4. For Japanese in agriculture on the West Coast, see Roger Daniels (1988, 157–159); and Modell (1977). For Koreans in the retail grocery business, see Min (1984, 1996).

5. For works related to the development of the Chinese food service industry in the United States, see, for example, Yu (1987); Hsu (2008); and Liu and Lin (2009).

6. See Chapter 6 on Siu's research and dissertation.

7. Author's tally and computation from the directories in various issues of the *San Min Morning Paper* (*SSMP*) for 1933, EWB, box 138, folder 9.

8. Ibid.

9. Testimony of Hong Sling, December 2, 1913, CCCF, file 2005/182-E; testimony of Moy Dong Hoy, April 11, 1906, CCCF, file 463.

10. Testimony of Moy Kee Doy, July 17, 1905, CCCF, file 365.

11. McKeown (2001, 202–203).

12. Testimony of Moy Dong Hoy, April 11, 1906, CCCF, file 463.

13. Shijie Meishi Zongqin Zonghui (1991, 111–113).

14. Testimony of Chin Wing, October 25, 1907, CCCF, file 616; testimony of Chin F. Foin, January 16, 1906, CCCF, file 440; testimony of Chin F. Foin, June 25, 1908, CCCF, file 660.

15. Testimonies of Moy Dung and Moy Sam, September 18, 1907, CCCF, file 596.

16. Numerous case files indicate that personal loans to kinsmen or friends took place in major grocery stores in Chicago such as Wing Chong Hai at 281 South Clark Street and Sing Lung at 309 South Clark Street. See, for example, testimony of Chin Wing, October 25, 1907, CCCF, file 616; testimony of Moy Gee Nie, November 4, 1907, CCCF, file 617.

17. Numerous case files indicate this; see, for example, testimony of Lum Joy, September 7, 1904, CCCF, file 360; testimony of Moy Kee Doy, July 17, 1905, CCCF, file 365; and testimony of Chan Wing, August 23, 1905, CCCF, file 369.

18. Testimony of Lum Toy, September 7, 1904, CCCF, file 360.

19. Testimony of Moy Kee Doy, July 17, 1905, CCCF, file 365.

20. Hsu (2000, 41).

21. Testimony of Au Tat, June 5, 1924, CCCF, file 2005/1608.

22. Testimonies of Lim Yee and Lim Shear Lett, December 5, 1913, CCCF, file 2005/183.

23. Annie Leong, interview by author, December 17, 1998, St. Louis.

24. Testimony of Jack Sam Tsai, June 5, 1924, CCCF, file 2005/1608.

25. Ling (1998b, 65–67).

26. Liu (2005, 47–49).

27. Paul C. P. Siu, "Chinese Family in Chicago," Case no. 2, "Fung's family," EWB, box 137, folder 8.

28. Siu (1987, 101).

29. Paul C. P. Siu, "Chinese Family in Chicago," Case no. 32, "Sieu family," EWB, box 137, folder 8.

30. Siu (1987, 103–104).

31. Richard Ho, letter to author, August 3, 2002.

32. Testimony of Moy Doon Yuen, July 27, 1904, CCCF, file 425.

33. Testimony of Chin Kai Kim, September 28, 1920, CCCF, file 2005/767.

34. Testimony of Louie Yap, June 26, 1906, CCCF, file 375.

35. Testimony of Gong Dock Death, November 2, 1926, CCCF, file 2005/1613.

36. "Celebration of Chinese New Year's," *CT*, January 30, 1892, 7:4.

37. Fan ([1926] 1974, 39).

38. Ibid., 38.

39. *SSMP*, various issues for 1933, EWB, box 138, folder 9.

40. Hsu (2008).

41. Testimony of Chin F. Foin, January 16, 1906, CCCF, file 440; Paul C. P. Siu, "A Case of Assimilation," EWB, box 136, folder 7.

42. Testimony of Ham Sam, September 18, 1905, CCCF, file 374; Ho and Moy (2005, 43).

43. Testimony of Ham Sam, September 18, 1905, CCCF, file 374.

44. Testimonies of Hum Sing and Hum Sam, September 16, 1905, CCCF, file 374.

45. Ho and Moy (2005, 42).

46. Ibid., 43.

47. *SSMP*, various issues for 1933, EWB, box 138, folder 9.

48. Christoff (1998, 45).

49. Ho and Moy (2005, 46).

50. Ibid., 44.

51. CAMOC.

52. Testimony of Ah Song, August 16, 1906, CCCF, file 405.

53. Testimony of Moy Sam, August 16, 1906, CCCF, file 405.

54. Testimonies of Tom Lok, Charles F. Hille, and H. L. Henson, July 1, 1924, CCCF, file 2005/1614.

55. Testimony of Eng Gow, October 8, 1920, CCCF, file 2005/763.

56. CAMOC.

57. Testimony of Kong Ming, July 15, 1924, CCCF, file 2005/1615.

58. Testimony of Wong Lung, October 27, 1920, CCCF, file 2005/739.

59. Author's tally and tabulation.

60. CAMOC exhibit.

61. *Chinese American* (Chicago) 1, no. 1, 1893; Christoff (2001); and Soo Lon Moy, Chinatown Museum Foundation, http://camoc.homestead.com/More_1893 .html#anchor_218.

62. Ngai (2005, 63).

63. *CDT*, February 18, 1893, p. 10; May 20, 1893, p. 3; "Chinese-Americans at the 1893 Chicago World Fair," CAMOC, http://camoc.homestead.com/ More_1893.html#anchor_218.

64. Walton (1893). See also http://columbus.gl.iit.edu/artarch/arch.html.

65. "1933 World's Fair Objects & Scenes," CAMOC, http://camoc.homestead
.com/More_1933.html.

66. Author's tally.

67. Testimony of Moy Gee Nie, November 4, 1907, CCCF, file 617.

68. Testimonies of Chin Wing and Chin Show, October 25, 1907, CCCF, file
616.

69. Testimony of Mark Do Wea, August 9, 1905, CCCF, file 367.

70. Testimony of Chan Wing, August 23, 1905, CCCF, file 369.

71. Testimony of Goon Pon Sing, October 17, 1907, CCCF, file 598.

72. David K. Lee, interview by author, April 19, 2008, Chicago.

73. Testimony of Kong Choon, November 7, 1913, CCCF, file 2005/171.

74. Testimony of Louis Fook, June 26, 1906, CCCF, file 375.

75. Testimony of Lum Joy, September 7, 1904, CCCF, file 360.

76. Testimony of Moy Len, July 16, 1920, CCCF, file 2005/719.

77. Testimony of Hum Sing, September 18, 1905, CCCF, file 374.

78. Testimony of Moy Gee Nie, November 4, 1907, CCCF, file 617.

79. Although the 1888 Scott Act nullified twenty thousand reentry certificates, the applications during the 1900s in the INS's CCCF were recorded as for
laborer's return certificates.

80. Testimony of Goon Pon Sing, October 17, 1907, CCCF, file 598.

81. Testimonies of Chin Wing and Chin Show, October 25, 1907, CCCF, file
616.

82. Papers Relating to the Campaign to Save Sam Wah Laundry, Correspondence, 1978–1986, 9 folders, Eliot F. Porter Jr., Papers, Missouri Historical Society,
St. Louis.

83. *Gould's St. Louis Directory*, 1872–1952, St. Louis, MO: Gould Directory
Co.; *Polk's St. Louis City Directory*, 1955–1980, St. Louis, MO: R. L. Polk & Co.

84. John M. McGuire, "Chinese Laundry Being Pressed," *S-PD*, November 12,
1978, p. 3G.

85. Organization of Chinese Americans (1993, 2).

86. Testimony of Lam Lap Goey, November 7, 1905, CCCF, file 383.

87. Fan ([1926] 1974, 33–37).

88. Ibid., 41.

89. Testimony of Moy Gee Nie, November 4, 1907, CCCF, file 617; testimony
of Kong Choon, November 7, 1913, CCCF, file 2005/171.

90. Hsu (2000, 40–41).

91. *Xin Ning Magazine* 新寧雜誌, no. 4 (2006): 14–15.

92. Ibid.

93. Author's field research, July 2007.

94. Ibid.

95. See, for example, "Exploration and Discovery," CCTV, channel 10, July 6, 2007; and *Xin Ning Magazine* 新寧雜誌, no. 4 (2004): 14–15.

96. *Taishanxian huaqiaozhi* (1992, 120–127).

97. Testimony of Hong Sling, August 27, 1924, CCCF, file 2005/1638; testimony of Hong Sling, December 2, 1913, CCCF, file 2005/182-E.

98. "Wrath over Chinese Trouble," *CT*, April 19, 1893.

99. Ngai (2005).

100. "Chinese-Americans at the 1893 Chicago World Fair," CAMOC, http://camoc.homestead.com/More_1893.html#anchor_218.

101. Testimony of H. L. Henson, December 12, 1913, CCCF, file 2005/182-E; testimony of Arthur W. Chapman, December 13, 1913, CCCF, file 2005/182-E; report of Howard D. Ebey, December 17, 1913, CCCF, file 2005/182-A-B-C-D-E.

102. Testimony of Harry Hong Sling, December 1, 1913, CCCF, file 2005/182-C; testimony of Hong Sling, December 2, 1913, CCCF, file 2005/182-E.

103. Testimony of Hong Sling, August 31, 1911, CCCF, file 282.

104. Testimony of Hong Sling, December 2, 1913, CCCF, file 2005/182-E; testimony of Hong Sling, August 27, 1924, CCCF, file 2005/1638.

105. Report of Howard D. Ebey, December 17, 1913, CCCF, file 2005/182-A-B-C-D-E.

106. Testimony of Arthur W. Chapman, December 3, 1913, CCCF, file 2005/182-E.

107. Testimony of H. L. Henson, December 12, 1913, CCCF, file 2005/182-E.

108. Testimony of Toy Shee, December 1, 1913, CCCF, file 2005/182-D; testimony of Hong Sling, December 2, 1913, CCCF, file 2005/182-E.

109. Testimony of Dr. Joseph Brennemann, December 12, 1913, CCCF, file 2005/182-E.

110. Report of Howard D. Ebey, December 17, 1913, CCCF, file 2005/182-A-B-C-D-E.

111. Testimony of Harry Hong Sling, December 1, 1913, CCCF, file 2005/182-C.

112. Testimony of Hong Sling, December 2, 1913, CCCF, file 2005/182-E.

113. Hirata (1979, 6); Goldman (1981, 96).

114. Ling (1998b, 54).

115. See MacLeod (1948, 180–181).

116. Hirata (1982).

117. Paul C. P. Siu, "Prostitution in Chinatown," EWB, box 137, folder 8.

118. Ibid.

119. Ibid.

120. *SMMP*, various issues for 1933, EWB, box 138, folder 9.

121. Siu (1987, 227–228).
122. Thomas (1901).
123. E. W. Burgess, report to Governor Hornor, June 24, 1935, EWB.
124. Siu (1987, 228).
125. Chao (2010).
126. Siu (1987, 234–235).
127. Ibid., 235.
128. Chao (2010, 48).
129. Shum (2003).
130. See Halpern (1997); Grossman (1989); and Cohen (1990).
131. See Tuttle (1970).

Chapter Four

1. Lee (1947, 234–239).
2. Ibid., 241–253.
3. Ibid., 253–254.
4. Lyman (1974, 94).
5. Glenn (1983, 42).
6. Lydon (1885, 156–161).
7. Chan (1986, 390).
8. Minnick (1988, 246).
9. Wang (1988, 153–168).
10. Beesley (1988, 168–179).
11. Mason (1995).
12. Yung (1995, 77–79).
13. Review by Evelyn Nakano Glenn; see Ling (1998b, book jacket).
14. Ling (1998b).
15. Siu, "Chinese Family in Chicago," EWB, box 137, folder 8; CAMOC.
16. Testimony of Moy Dong Hoy, April 11, 1906, CCCF, file 463; Ho and Moy (2005, 50).
17. Ho and Moy (2005, 84).
18. Siu, "Chinese Family in Chicago."
19. Ibid.
20. Ling (1998b, 18–20, 25–39).
21. Huang (1985, 192; 1990, 13).
22. Fairbank (1973, 142); Xu (1997).
23. Tang (1980, 48–56).
24. Peffer (1999).
25. Sucheng Chan, "The Exclusion of Chinese Women," in Chan (1991, 128–129).

26. Entry 132, Chinese General Correspondence, 1898–1908; Entry 134, Customs Case File No. 3358d Related to Chinese Immigration, 1877–1891; Entry 135, Chinese Smuggling File, 1914–1921; Entry 136, Chinese Division File, 1924–1925; Entry 137, Applications for Duplicate Certificates of Residence, 1893–1920. RG 85, National Archives, Washington, D.C.

27. For more discussion on folk songs in overseas Chinese villages reflecting the socioeconomic conditions of the "Taishanese widows," see, for example, Zhang (2008).

28. Chu (1979).

29. Hsu (2000).

30. Siu, "Chinese Family in Chicago."

31. Ibid.

32. Ibid.

33. Fairbank (1973, 142).

34. See Ba Jin (1972*)*.

35. Zhonghua Renmin Gongheguo Hunyin Fa (1987).

36. For examples of the financial incapacity of Chinese immigrant men, see Case 19571/18-5, RG 85, National Archives, Pacific Sierra Region, San Bruno, CA; "Survey of Race Relations," document 251, Hoover Institution on War, Revolution and Peace archives; and Ling (1998b, 25–26). For examples of Chinese patriarchal control, see Cases 19571/18-5 and 14284/4-4, RG 85, National Archives, Pacific Sierra Region, San Bruno, CA; Ling (1998b, 26–27); and Chan (1991a, 104).

37. Case 3358d, Entry 134, Customs Case File No. 3358 Related to Chinese Immigration, 1877–1891; Case 1355, Entry 132, Chinese General Correspondence, 1898–1908, RG 85, National Archives, Washington, D.C.

38. Case 19571/18-5, RG 85, National Archives, Pacific Sierra Region, San Bruno, CA; and Lin Yutang (1948, 196–197).

39. Beesley (1988, 174).

40. Siu, "Chinese Family in Chicago"; CAMOC.

41. Testimony of Moy Dong Hoy, April 11, 1906, CCCF, file 463.

42. Ho and Moy (2005, 84).

43. Siu, "Chinese Family in Chicago."

44. David K. Lee, interview by author, April 19, 2008, Chicago.

45. Beesley (1998, 174).

46. Chan (1986, 395).

47. For further discussion on the impact of the Page Act on Chinese immigrant women, see Peffer (1986).

48. Daniels (1988, 96).

49. Ibid.

50. Ibid., 96–97.

51. Entry 132, Chinese General Correspondence, 1898–1908; Entry 134, Customs Case File No. 3358 Related to Chinese Immigration, 1877–1891; Entry 135, Chinese Smuggling File, 1914–1921; Entry 136, Chinese Division File, 1924–1925; and Entry 137, Applications for Duplicate Certificates of Residence, 1893–1920, RG 85, National Archives, Washington, D.C.

52. For works on antimiscegenation laws, see Pascoe (2009); Chan (1999a, 59–60) together with her "Exclusion of Chinese Women" in Chan (1999b); Osumi (1982); Sickels (1972, 64); and Sung (1990, 2).

53. *NYT*, March 13, 1966, 4:12; Harper and Skolnick (1962, 96–105). On antimiscegenation laws, see Pascoe (2009).

54. *California Statutes*, 1880, Code Amendments, ch. 41, sec. 1, p. 3.

55. *California Statutes*, 1905, ch. 481, sec. 2, p. 554.

56. *Loving v. Virginia*, 388 U.S. 1 (1967).

57. Mrs. C., interview by author, June 10, 1992, Berkeley, CA.

58. Testimonies of Lillie Moy and Moy Dong Chow, August 8, 1924, CCCF, file 2005/1628.

59. Lorraine Moy Tun, interview by Ruth Kung, September 1, 2007, Chicago (hereinafter "Lorraine Moy Tun interview").

60. Siu, "Chinese Family in Chicago."

61. See, for example, Ling (1998b).

62. Siu, "Chinese Family in Chicago."

63. Ibid.

64. Ibid.

65. Ibid.

66. Ibid.

67. Ibid.

68. Ibid.

69. "Gleeful Celestials, Chicago Chinatown Celebrate Their New-Year's Festival," *CT*, January 20, 1890.

70. Siu, "Chinese Family in Chicago."

71. Ling (2004a, 26–27, 65); Mason (1982, 163).

72. Siu, "Chinese Family in Chicago."

73. Ibid.

74. Ibid.

75. Ibid.

76. Ibid.; OH, box 4, 1911–1943.

77. Cohen (1984, 147); Loewen (1971, 75); Mason (1982); and Tchen (1990).

78. Tenth Census, 1880, New Orleans, Louisiana, population schedules, cited in Cohen (1984, 147).

79. Mason (1982, 163).

80. Tchen (1990, 176–177).

81. Ling (1998b, 115).

82. Siu, "Chinese Family in Chicago."

83. Ibid.

84. For works on traditional family and marriage in China, see, for example, Lang (1946); Yang (1959); Hsu (1970); and Levy (1971).

85. For more discussion on Chinese immigrant women's experiences on Angel Island, see Ling (1998b, 30–39).

86. Yung (1986, 44).

87. Case no. 6, "J. L. Family," in Siu, "Chinese Family in Chicago."

88. Case no. 5, "C. L.'s Family," in Siu, "Chinese Family in Chicago."

89. Celia Moy Cheung, interviewed by Grace Chun, Thomas O'Connell, and Andrea Stamm, 2007, Chicago.

90. Testimonies of Chin F. Foin, January 3 and 16, 1906, CCCF, file 440; testimony of Chin F. Foin, June 25, 1908, CCCF, file 660; *CDT*, November 2, 1907; and Christoff (1998, 46).

91. Christoff (1998, 47).

92. Ibid.

93. Huang (1985, 192; 1990, 13).

94. Siu (1987, 58).

95. Sung (1967, 197–198).

96. Liu (1981, 297).

97. Chung (1989).

98. Cases 16135/5-11, 19938/4-11, 12017/36900, and 33610/7-1, RG 85, National Archives, Pacific Sierra Region, San Bruno, CA.

99. Case no. 7, "Y. L. Family," in Siu, "Chinese Family in Chicago."

100. Christoff (1988, 49).

101. Daniels (1988, 78).

102. Diner (1983, 46).

103. Siu, "Chinese Family in Chicago."

104. Author's tally from CCCF; Fan ([1926] 1974, 30).

105. Kiang (1992, 6).

106. Siu, "Chinese Family in Chicago."

107. Testimony of Toy Shee, December 1, 1914, CCCF, file 2005/182-D.

108. Case no. 1, "M. H.'s Family," in Siu, "Chinese Family in Chicago."

109. Siu, "Chinese Family in Chicago."

110. Case no. 28, "W. L. M. Family," in Siu, "Chinese Family in Chicago."

111. Case no. 7, "Y. L. Family," in Siu, "Chinese Family in Chicago."

112. Rich Lo, interview by members of CAMOC, 2007, Chicago.

113. Case no. 6, "J. L. Family," in Siu, "Chinese Family in Chicago."

114. Siu, "Chinese Family in Chicago."

115. Ibid.

116. Ibid.

117. Ibid.

118. Case no. 1, "M. H.'s Family," and Case no. 5, "C. L.'s Family," in Siu, "Chinese Family in Chicago."

119. Celia Moy Cheung, interviewed by Grace Chun, Thomas O'Connell, and Andrea Stamm, 2007, Chicago.

120. Fan ([1926] 1974, 47).

121. Ibid., 54.

122. Testimony of Lum Toy, September 7, 1904, CCCF, file 360; testimony of Moy Gee Nie, November 4, 1907, CCCF, file 617.

123. Ibid.

124. Ho and Moy (2005, 116–117).

125. Ibid., 108.

126. Her name in the CCCF file is recorded as "Lillie" but spelled "Lillian" in Ho and Moy (2005, 85). Testimony of Lillie Moy, August 8, 1924, CCCF, file 2005/1628.

127. Lorrain Moy Tun interview.

128. Ho and Moy (2005, 118–120).

129. Ibid., 98–99.

130. Ibid., 115.

131. Ibid., 101.

132. Fan ([1926] 1974, 85–86); Ho and Moy (2005, 115).

Chapter Five

1. Gang and Grant, 157; *G-D*, April 1, 1949; Chen (1995, 42–43). Presently, On Leong has more than twenty branches in eastern and midwestern states.

2. Fan ([1926] 1974, 16). The Chicago On Leong Merchants and Laborers Association, however, claims that it was founded in 1893.

3. Wittman (1988).

4. Chu (1973).

5. Reynolds (1935).

6. Chu (1973, 23–24).

7. Chen (1995, 35–37).

8. Chu (1973, 27); for the development of Chih Kung in North America, see Chung (2002).

9. Chen (1995, 42–43).

10. Hoy (1942); Lai (1987); Ling (1998b, 47–50).

11. The reasons why the CCBA did not spread in the Midwest may be associated with its unsuccessful challenge of immigration authorities in the 1890s.

12. Chung Kok Li (owner, Lee's Family Buffet; co-president, On Leong), interview by author, October 12, 1998, St. Louis (hereinafter "Li interview"); Don Ko (proprietor, Chinese laundry, restaurants, and trading company; co-president, On Leong), interview by author, October 19, 1998, St. Louis (hereinafter "Ko interview); telephone interviews, January 11 and February 22, 1999.

13. Wittman (1988); "Chinese in St. Louis," *G-D*, November 19, 1956; "Chinese Cook Up Tasty Convention," *G-D*, April 19, 1962.

14. Li interview.

15. Lai (1987); Chinese General Correspondence, 1898–1908, RG 85, National Archives, Washington, D.C.

16. Ho and Moy (2005, 62).

17. Lai (1987, 19–20).

18. Li interview.

19. Wittman (1988).

20. Lai (1987); Ling (1998b, 96).

21. "Feast Dead Chinamen," *CT*, August 10, 1891.

22. Ko interview.

23. Ho and Moy (2005, 59).

24. Lee (1960); and Loo (1991).

25. See Ling (2004a, 85–107).

26. McKeown (2001, 187).

27. Ibid.

28. *CT*, October 17, 1907, p. 3

29. *CT*, June 7, 1908, p. 4

30. *CT*, October 17, 1907, p. 3.

31. "Chicago's Chinatown: A Melting Pot of the Old and the New," *CSTR*, September 20, 1931, pt. 1, p. 6 (hereinafter "Chicago's Chinatown").

32. "Chin Clan in Terror in Chinatown's War," *CRH*, June 15, 1908; McKeown (2001, 208).

33. "Gleeful Celestials, Chicago Chinatown Celebrate Their New-Year's Festival," *CT*, January 20, 1890 (hereinafter "Gleeful Celestials").

34. *CRH*, June 15, 1908, p. 11.

35. Larson (1998; 2004).

36. CCCF file 2008/5.

37. "Chinatown Rivals Celebrate," *CRH*, June 12, 1911, p. 1.

38. Wittman (1988).

39. *CDT*, July 4, 1926, pt. 3.

40. Ibid.; Wittman (1988).

41. *CDT*, July 4, 1926, pt. 3.

42. Ibid.; Fan ([1926] 1974, 41).

43. Ho and Moy (2005, 60).

44. *CDT*, July 4, 1926, pt. 3.

45. "Mr. Frank Moy's Funeral," *CCDN*, September 24, 1937.

46. *CHDT*, October 5, 1936.

47. Ho and Moy (2005, 61).

48. Ibid.

49. Fan ([1926] 1974, 76).

50. Ibid., 77–78.

51. Shijie Meishi Zongqin Zonghui (1991).

52. Ho and Moy (2005, 68–76).

53. Ibid., 65.

54. "Chinese Grand Lodge of Free Masons of the State of Missouri," *Corporation Book* 18, p. 499 (11-3-1899), Recorder of Deeds.

55. Ibid.

56. Fan ([1926] 1974, 35).

57. *CCDN*, September 28, 1937.

58. Fan ([1926] 1974, 78–79).

59. Ibid., 79–80.

60. Ibid., 80.

61. "Chicago's Chinatown."

62. Ho and Moy (2005, 64).

63. Ibid.

64. Fan ([1926] 1974, 81–82).

65. See Yang (1999).

66. Chinese Christian Union Church, http://www.ccuc.net/ccuc/.

67. Fan ([1926] 1974, 82–83).

68. Ibid., 85.

69. Ibid., 86.

70. Ibid., 85–86.

71. Ibid., 34–37.

72. "The Chinese Y.M.C.A. Relief Activities," *CHDT*, March 25, 1935.

73. "Distribution of Food by Chinese Y.M.C.A. on Easter Sunday," *SMMP*, April 13, 1938.

74. St. Therese Chinese Catholic Mission, http://www.sttThereseChinatown.org/history_part3.html.

75. Ho and Moy (2005, 77–78).

76. Lai (2000).

77. Chen (2000, 228–232).

78. Report of Howard D. Ebey, December 17, 1913, CCCF, file 2005/182.

79. Fan ([1926] 1974, 56).

80. Moy (1978, 100–101).

81. Ibid., 101.

82. Ibid., 101–102.

83. "A Sunday School for Their Benefit," *CT*, June 17, 1878, 8:2.

84. "Chinese Sunday-School," *CT*, August 5, 1878, 8:3.

85. Fan ([1926] 1974, 56–59).

86. Ibid., 58–61.

87. Moy (1978, 99–100).

88. "Opening of a Chinese School by the Chinese Church," *CCDN*, September 29, 1937.

89. "Chicago's Chinatown."

90. *CCDN*, September 12, 1937.

91. See the "Canons of Journalism" adopted by the American Society of Newspaper Editors (ASNE) in 1922, http://asne.org/kiosk/archive/principl.htm.

92. *SMMP*, April 12, 1937.

93. See, for example, two excellent works on the Chinese-language newspapers and their role in cultivating a new Chinese American identity among Chinese immigrants in the first decades of the twentieth century: Chen (2002, 6); and Chen (2000, 173–174). See also Ling (1998b, 217–218).

94. *SMMP*, April 12, 1937.

95. "Gleeful Celestials."

96. OH.

97. Rachel Wang (daughter-in-law of Gung-Hsing Wang), interview by author, September 26, 2007, St. Louis.

98. CAMOC exhibition, "1933 World's Fair Objects & Scenes," http://camoc .homestead.com/More_1933.html.

99. "Independence Commemoration Program by the On-Leong Chinese School," *CHDT*, October 13, 1935.

100. See, for example, Yeh (2008).

101. Hsiao (1975, 388–389); and Larson (1998; 2004).

102. *CRH*, June 15, 1908, p. 11.

103. Shijie Meishi Zongqin Zonghui (1991, 18).

104. Ling (1998b, 107).

105. "Commemoration of 'September 18th,'" *SMMP*, September 21, 1937.

106. "Chinese Community Pledges Strong Support in Move to Oust Japan—Resolution Asks for American Cooperation," *CHDT*, October 8, 1936.

107. *SMMP*, October 11, 1937.

108. *CCDN*, February 5, 1938.

109. *SMMP*, September 10, 1937.

110. Lorrain Moy Tun, interview by Ruth Kung, September 1, 2007, Chicago.

111. Christoff (1998); CAMOC exhibitions on Chinese in Chicago.

112. *CDT*, March 22, 1943.

113. Charlie Toy, interviewed by Albert Moy and Helen Eng, 2007, Chicago; Ho and Moy (2005, 125).

114. Charles W. Tun, interviewed by Albert Moy and Helen Eng, 2007, Chicago.

Chapter Six

1. For example, John Dewey, the preeminent pragmatist philosopher, was on the faculty at the University of Chicago between 1894 and 1904 before his career at Columbia University (1904–1952).

2. See, for example, Henry Yu (2001, 28–29, 37n.17).

3. "Means of emigration" here refers to the physical and financial support that facilitated the emigration of Chinese students.

4. Yung (1909).

5. China Institute in America (1954, 26).

6. Y. C. Wang (1966, 158).

7. Ibid.

8. When the anti-imperialist Boxer Uprising occurred in China in 1900, the Western powers invaded China and forced the Qing government to sign an unequal treaty and pay an indemnity of 450 million taels to the victors. In May of 1908, however, the United States Congress passed legislation to return part of the indemnity to China to quiet China's growing anti-imperialist sentiment. The legislation stipulated that the refund should only be used to improve education. Beginning in 1909, when the United States began to pay the refund, the Qing government used the refund to send students to America under what was called the Boxer Indemnity Fellowship.

9. For studies on the educational efforts by Protestant missionaries on behalf of Chinese women, see Anderson (1943).

10. Anderson (1943, 83, 88, 94).

11. Canton Missionary Conference, "Program of Advance," 27, cited in Anderson (1943, 198).

12. Anderson (1943, 202).

13. Y. C. Wang (1966, 73).

14. Ibid.

15. Ibid., 99–120.

16. China Institute in America (1954, 27).

17. Li (1922).

18. Chinese Institute in America (1954, 34–35); see also Li (1922).

19. Li (1922, 674).

20. Chang (1986, 25–26).

21. China Institute in America (1954, 23).

22. Chi Che Wang Playlot Park–Chicago, http://www.mylakeview.com/maps_parks.html#chi.

23. Y. C. Wang (1966, 49).

24. "Dr. Se Moy-Yu Visited Chicago," *CHDT*, September 5, 1936.

25. Testimony of Lillie Moy, August 8, 1924, CCCF, file 2005/1628.

26. "Essential Factors in the Nationalized Education System," *CHDT*, March 8–9, 1935.

27. "A Bulletin from the Chicago Consolidated Benevolent Association," *CCDN*, January 27, 1938.

28. "All America Chinese Student Association," *CHDT*, August 14, 1935.

29. "Mr. G.P. Moy Leaves for China after Graduation," *CHDT*, September 22, 1936.

30. "North-American Chinese Student Delegate Conference," *SMMP*, September 4, 1937.

31. Ibid.

32. "North-American Chinese Student Delegate Conference—Continued," *SMMP*, September 8, 1937.

33. Ibid.

34. "Ambassador C. T. Wong's Speech to the Chinese Student Delegate Conference," *SMMP*, September 25–27, 1937.

35. "Mr. Wu Yung-Yang Graduated from Aeronautic Engineering," *SMMP*, January 29, 1938.

36. China Institute in America (1954, 18).

37. Y. C. Wang (1966, 130–133, 136–137).

38. Chan (1991a, 145); see also Tsai (1986, 151–152).

39. John T. Ma, "Chinese Americans in the Professions," in Wu (1980), esp. pp. 67 and 85.

40. See Chou (1989, 1, 87); interviews 13 and 15 by author. Interviews with Chinese students by the author in this chapter are cited numerically.

41. Gold (1986). Some other scholars have also associated the study-abroad wave in Taiwan since the 1960s with the island's political instability; see Tseng (1995).

42. Interviews 10, 11, 12, 13, 14, 15, and 41 by author.

43. Long (2009). Long interviewed 191 individuals who migrated to Taiwan following the Nationalist government in 1949.

44. Interviews 11, 12, 14, and 15 by author.

45. Interview 13 by author; see also Yen.

46. Survey conducted by the author of over one hundred students from Taiwan; also interviews 42, 43, 44, 45, 46, 48, 51, 52, 53, and 55 by author.

47. Interviews 10, 11, 12, 13, 14, 15, and 20 by author.

48. Interviews 10, 11, 12, 13, 14, 15, 20, and 35 by author.

49. Shiqi Huang, "Contemporary Educational Relations with the Industrial World: A Chinese View," in Hayhoe and Bastid (1987, 226–227).

50. Since the 1980s, it has become a common practice for many universities and colleges in China to promote faculty members who have studied in a foreign institution, in accordance with the open-door policy of the Chinese government. Among the twenty-seven visiting scholars from the PRC interviewed by the author between 1985 and 1987, most indicated that the major motivation for their coming to America was to be promoted when they returned to China after the completion of their training or research projects in America. Interviews 75–101 by author.

51. Of the thirty-two interviewees who came to America from the PRC since the 1980s as students, a majority of them originally intended to return to China after the completion of their education in America and hoped their training in the United States would facilitate their future careers in China. Interviews 2, 17, 18, 19, 22, 23, 24, 25, 26, 27, 28, 29, 30, 34, 59, 62, 63, 64, 65, 66, 67, 68, 69, 70, 71, 72, 73, 74, and 102 by author.

52. Ibid.; interviews 75–101 by author.

53. Interviews 58, 60, and 61 by author.

54. *CD*, February 15, 1988.

55. See Chou (1989, 61).

56. "Chinese Students Win Waiver," *Congressional Quarterly Weekly Report* 47, November 25, 1989, p. 3245.

57. "Bush Veto of Chinese Immigration Relief," *Congressional Quarterly Weekly Report* 47, December 2, 1989, p. 3331.

58. "Chinese Students Studying Abroad Exceed 1.39 Million," *People's Daily Online*, March 26, 2009, http://english.people.com.cn/90001/90776/90882/6622888.html.

59. The so-called J-1 visa requires its holder to return home for at least two years before seeking an adjustment in immigration status (usually permanent residency in the United States, commonly known as a "green card"), whereas the F-1 visa has no such restriction. The J-1 visa was designed to alleviate the "brain drain" suffered by other nations when their students acquired an education in the United States and then refused to go home. Normally, the government-sponsored Chinese students or scholars are issued J-1 visas. American immigration restrictions as well as the support they have received from the Chinese government thus obligate them legally and ethically to serve their country upon completion

of their education or training in the United States. The Administrative Measures for PRC Nationals issued by President George H. W. Bush after the Tiananmen Incident of June 4, 1989, however, lifted virtually all restrictions on J-1 visa holders by allowing all Chinese nationals who were present in the United States on December 1, 1989, to stay and to be employed.

60. Interview 2 by author.

61. Orleans (1988).

62. This percentage comes from the author's analysis of interviews and surveys of female students from the PRC.

63. According to the author's survey.

64. State Education Commission of the People's Republic of China, 1986, "State Education Commission Provisions on Study Abroad," sec. 5, p. 9.

65. Ibid.

66. In a survey of Chinese students' wives at Miami University of Ohio conducted by the author in 1990, 96 percent expressed their desire to earn a graduate degree at an American university; see also interviews 18, 19, 22, 23, 24, 25, 26, 27, 28, and 29 by author.

67. Interviews 18, 19, 22, 23, 26, and 29 by author.

68. According to surveys conducted by the author in 1990.

69. Interviews 17, 18, 19, 22, 23, 24, 25, 26, 27, 28, 29, 58, 59, 60, 61, 62, 63, 64, 65, 67, 68, 69, 70, 71, 72, 73, 74, and 102 by author.

70. Interviews 17, 18, 19, 22, 23, 24, 25, 26, 27, 29, 30, and 34 by author.

71. Interview 19 by author.

72. Interviews 17, 18, 19, and 22 by author.

73. Responding to pressure from Congress and the general public, President George H. W. Bush issued Administrative Measures for PRC Nationals on November 30, 1989, to protect Chinese students involved in the Tiananmen Incident. The order contains such measures as the waiver of the two-year foreign residence requirement for any Chinese national who was present in the United States on December 1, 1989, and of the employment requirement for all Chinese nationals who were in the United States on June 5, 1989 (according to a cable sent to all INS field offices on December 4, 1989).

74. Interviews 17, 18 19, 22, and 30 by author.

75. Ling (2001).

76. Chinese Students and Scholars Association, University of Chicago, https://studentactivities.uchicago.edu/php/public/detail.php?org=78.

77. Ibid.

78. Fan ([1926] 1974, 80).

79. Ibid., vii.

80. See, for example, McKeown (2001, 198).

81. Wu (1928).
82. Ibid., 327–328.
83. Ibid.
84. Soong (1931).
85. Dai (1937).
86. Ibid., 187.
87. Fan ([1926] 1974, 88).
88. Ibid., 89.
89. Ibid., 90.
90. Wu (1928, 329–330).
91. Soong (1931, 106–107).
92. Dai (1937, 191).
93. Yu (2001, 116).
94. Ibid., 125.
95. Sources for the preceding section include Lee (1947); Yu (2001, 125–133); and *Encyclopedia of World Biography*, s.v. "Rose Hum Lee," http://www.encyclopedia .com/doc/1G2-3404707842.html.
96. Lee (1956).
97. Lee (1960, 387).
98. Letter from Rose Hum Lee to Elaine Lee, January 8, 1958, quoted in Yu (2001, 133).
99. Liang (1951, 108–109).
100. Siu (1987).
101. Siu (1987, xxv–xxvi).
102. Glick (1938).
103. Siu (1987, 296–297).
104. See, for example, Glick Schiller, Basch, and Blanc-Szanton (1992, ix).
105. Wilson (1969, 29, 39, 60, 101).
106. Li (1978).
107. Ibid., 123.
108. Moy (1978, 175–176).
109. Moy (1995).
110. Kiang (1992).
111. Keener (1994).
112. Wang (1997, 350–353).
113. McKeown (2001, 1–6).
114. Yu (2001, 114–116, 125–140).
115. Rohsenow (2004).
116. Lau (2004).
117. Ngai (2005).

118. Lan (2007, iv).
119. Ling Z. Arenson (2009, 65–86).

Chapter Seven

1. Ling (1998b, 2, 113–114).
2. Riggs (1950, 43–183).
3. Tung (1974, 79–80).
4. Ibid., 32.
5. Immigration and Naturalization Services, 1945–1949, *Annual Reports.*
6. Ibid., 1948.
7. Ibid., 1945–1954.
8. Tung (1974, 39).
9. US Bureau of the Census, 1960, *U.S. Census of Population.*
10. Yolanda Lee, interviewed by Grace Chun and Soo Lon Moy, 2007, Chicago.
11. Celia Moy Cheung, interview by Grace Chun, Thomas O'Connell, and Andrea Stamm, 2007, Chicago.
12. Henry Yee, information provided to CAMOC in 2007 by Lily Ng, a relative of Henry Yee.
13. Harry Wu, interview by Delilah Lee Chan, 2007, Chicago.
14. Grace Chun, interview by author, April 19, 2008, Chicago.
15. Corwin Eng, interview by Ruth Kung, 2007, Chicago.
16. Benjamin C. Moy, interview by Grace Chun, 2007, Chicago.
17. Moy (1978, 131).
18. Ibid., 167–168.
19. Howard Chun, interview by author, April 19, 2008, Chicago.
20. Moy (1978, 101).
21. "Mr. G. P. Moy Leaves for China after Graduation," *CHDT*, Sept. 22, 1936.
22. Moy (1978, 97).
23. Ibid., 101.
24. Ibid., 132.
25. Cho Tuk Lo, interview by Grace Chun and Soo Lon Moy, 2007, Chicago.
26. Catherine Wong Chin, interview by Sheila Chin, 2007, Chicago.
27. Iran Roosevelt Chin, interview by Andrea Stamm, 2007, Chicago.
28. Susanna Fong, interview by Delilah Lee Chan, 2007, Chicago.
29. Dato' Seri Stanley Thai, interview by Grace Chun and Soo Lon Moy, 2007, Chicago.
30. Herman Chiu, interview by Delilah Lee Chan, 2007, Chicago.
31. Chicago Fact Book Consortium (1984); Wilson (1969, 101).
32. Keener (1994, 20).
33. Ibid., 25.

34. Rachel Wang, interview by author, September 26, 2007; Keener (1994, 26).

35. Keener (1994, 26).

36. Ibid., 28.

37. See the Chinatown brochure created by the Chicago Chinatown Chamber of Commerce.

38. Cited in Lau (2004).

39. For living conditions in major Chinatowns in San Francisco and New York, see, for example, Loo (1991, 3); and Kwong (1979, 1987).

40. Keener (1994, 1); and Kiang (1992, 9).

41. Xiaoyu Wong, interview by author, April 19, 2008, Chicago.

42. Northeastern Illinois Planning Commission, "Variables from 'Table DP-1, Profile of General Demographic Characteristics: 2000' presented in database format, Summary of General Demographic Characteristics for the City of Chicago and Its 77 Community Areas (hereinafter "General Demographic Characteristics").

43. See K. Kennedy, "Chinatown Returns to Center Stage," *CT*, February 20, 2003, p. 16; Kiang (1992, 6); Rohsenow (2004); and Lan (2007).

44. Lan (2007, 83); Hirsch (1983, 13).

45. "General Demographic Characteristics."

46. Lan (2007), 92.

47. Chicago Commission on Human Relations, *1999 Hate Crime Report*, p. 13, cited in Lan (2007, 92).

48. *CT*, July 18, 2004.

49. Chicago Police Department, July 15, 2004, cited in Lan (2007, 94).

50. Ibid.

51. Lan (2007, 94).

52. Ibid., 210.

53. Rumbaut (1989).

54. *CDN*, February 14, 1974; Don DeBat, "Chinatown: Quiet Island," *CDN*, July 5, 1974; *CT*, December 5, 1976.

55. Hai Yen Restaurant, http://haiyenrestaurant.com/home.html.

56. Duc Huang, interview by Grace Chun and Soo Lon Moy, 2007, Chicago.

57. Jenny Ling, interview by Grace Chun and Soo Lon Moy, 2007, Chicago.

58. Toung Ling, interview by Grace Chun and Soo Lon Moy, 2007, Chicago.

59. Arenson (2009).

60. Ibid., 76.

61. US Bureau of the Census, 1990, *U.S. Census of Population.*

62. US Bureau of the Census, 2000, *U.S. Census of Population.*

63. Ana-Maria Udrica, "Asian Population Booms in Illinois and Chicago, Census Data Show," March 9, 2011, *Medill Reports—Chicago*, Northwestern Uni-

versity. A publication of the Medill School, http://news.medill.northwestern.edu/chicago/news.aspx?id=182462.

64. Ling (2004a).

65. Ibid., 12.

66. Ibid., 13.

67. Arenson (2009, 77).

68. Ibid., 82.

69. Rohsenow (2004, 339).

70. I use the term from Rohsenow's essay on the linguistic diversity among the Chinese in Chicago (Rohsenow 2004, 321).

71. "Homeland Run by Reds, a Saddened Chinatown Marks Its '4th of July,'" *CDN*, October 11, 1950.

72. Arenson (2009, 81).

73. Rohsenow (2004, 325).

74. Ibid., 332.

75. Ibid., 333.

76. Ibid.

77. Lau (2004).

78. Chinese American Service League, 1990–1997, 2007, *Annual Reports*, Chicago History Museum; Chinese American Service League, *History*, http://www.caslservice.org.

79. Lan (2007, 153).

80. Chinese Mutual Aid Association, "Statement of Activities for the Fiscal Year Ended June 30, 2010," p. 3, http://www.chinesemutualaid.org/sites/default/usruploads/FY2010_audit_report.pdf; Chinese Mutual Aid Association, http://www.chinesemutualaid.org/.

81. Arenson (2009, 80).

82. Chinese Mutual Aid Association, http://www.chinesemutualaid.org/.

83. Arenson (2009, 79).

84. Chicago Chinatown Chamber of Commerce (CCCC), http://www.chicagoChinatown.org/cccorg/about.jsp.

85. CCCC website: http://www.chicagoChinatown.org/cccorg/home.jsp.

86. Founded in 1933 on Wentworth Avenue in response to the Century of Progress Exposition, it displayed twenty-four dioramas portraying stories from China's history and various statues designed by a San Francisco–based Chinese artist and made in Foshan, Guangdong, along with a painting of the Buddhist goddess Guangyin. The interior of the Ling Long Museum later became a Chinese restaurant and the museum was closed in the 1970s. CAMOC, http://www.ccamuseum.org/About_Us.html; Soo Lon Moy's presentation at a roundtable session on the Chinese-American Museum of Chicago, Association for Asian American Studies

annual meeting, April 18, 2008, Chicago; Ho and Moy (2005, 53); and CAMOC exhibitions: see http://www.ccamuseum.org/Object_Photos.html.

87. Vikki Ortiz, "Fire Cleanup Begins at Chinese-American Museum of Chicago," *CT*, September 22, 2008.

88. Howard Chun and Grace Chun, interviews by author, April 19, 2008, Chicago.

89. As noted previously, "Mei" is the standard spelling and pronunciation of the common Cantonese surname "Moy."

90. *Xin Ning Magazine* 新寧雜誌, no. 4 (2006): 32.

91. Ibid.

92. Duanfen Office for Overseas Chinese Affairs, "A Brief Introduction of *Duanfen qiaokan runan zhihua*," Duanfen, Taishan: Duanfen Office for Overseas Chinese Affairs, January 19, 2006.

93. Mei (1979).

94. M. Hsu (2000, 124).

95. *Runan zhihua* 汝南之化 [Nei Nam's flower, or the Moy family magazine], no. 34 (December 1993): 27 (author's translation).

96. Ibid., no. 36 (December 1994): 3–12 (author's translation).

97. Ibid., 3.

Epilogue

1. Weng Songping, interview by author, July 7, 2007, Duanfen Township, Taishan, China.

2. Mei Yuqin, interview by author, July 7, 2007, Moy family compound, Duanfen Township, Taishan, China.

3. Taishan Shi Qiaolian (1998).

4. See, for example, the following articles by geographers Qin Zhenxia, Yang Mingjin, and Song Song, "Kongxincun wenti jiqi jiejue duice" [Hollow-center villages and policies on resolving the problem], *Nongcun jingji* [Countryside economics] 3 (2009): 96–99; sociologist Zhou Zhuping, "Zhongguo nongcun renkou kongxinhua jiqi tiaozhan" [China's hollow-center phenomenon in the countryside and its challenge], *Renkou yanjiu* [Population research] 32, no. 12 (March 2008): 45–52; geographers Wang Chengxin, Yao Shimou, and Chen Caihong, "Zhongguo nongcun juluo kongxin wenti shizheng yanjiu" [Empirical study on "village-hollowing" in China], *Dili kexue* [Scientia Geographica Sinica] 25, no. 3 (June 2005): 257–262; and sociologist Zhang Chunjuan, "Nongcun kongxinhua wenti jiqi duice yanju" [A study of the countryside hollow-center phenomenon and its solutions], *Zhexue shijie* [Philosophy studies] 4 (2004): 83–86.

5. See "Rules and Regulations on Application for a Passport," a brochure available from the Taishan City Bureau of Overseas Chinese Affairs.

6. Guan Xinqiang, interview by author, July 10, 2007, Taishan, Guangdong, China.

7. Statistics from Taishan City Bureau of Overseas Chinese Affairs.

8. See note 4.

9. Niall Ferguson, "What 'Chimerica' Hath Wrought," *American Interest Online*, January–February 2009, http://www.the-american-interest.com/article .cfm?piece=533.

Bibliography

Archival Collections

Asian American Small Business Association Records, 1999–2000. Chicago History Museum.

Burgess, Ernest Watson. Papers. Special Collections Research Center, Regenstein Library, University of Chicago.

"Chicago, Central Baptist Chinese Mission." Reports, 1894–1896. Chicago History Museum.

Chicago Association of Commerce and Industry. 1909. *A Guide to the City of Chicago*. Chicago: Chicago Association of Commerce and Industry.

Chicago Chinese Case Files (CCCF), 1898–1940. Records of the Immigration and Naturalization Service, Record Group (RG) 85. National Archives Records Administration–Great Lakes Region, Chicago.

Chicago Chinese Directory. 1951. New York: Chinese Directory Service Bureau.

Chicago Commission on Race Relations. 1922. *The Negro in Chicago*. Chicago: University of Chicago Press.

Chicago Department of Human Services. 1979. *At Your Service: A Guide to Chicago's Northeast Neighborhoods*. Chicago: Department of Human Services.

Chicago Fact Book Consortium, ed. 1984. *Local Community Fact Book: Chicago Metropolitan Area, Based on the 1970 and 1980 Censuses*. Chicago: Chicago Review Press.

———, ed. 1995. *Local Community Fact Book: Chicago Metropolitan Area 1990*. Chicago: University of Illinois at Chicago.

————, ed. 2005. *Working the Boundaries: Race, Space and "Illegality" in Mexican Chicago.* Durham, NC: Duke University Press.

Chicagoland Atlas. 1988. Chicago: Creative Sales.

Chicago Plan Commission. 1942. *Forty-Four Cities in the City of Chicago.* Chicago: Chicago Plan Commission.

Chicago Public Library, comp. 1942. *Chicago Foreign Language Press Survey Chinese, 1928–1938.* Chicago: Chicago Public Library.

Chicago's Chinatown Chamber of Commerce. 1985. *Chicago Chinese Commercial Guide Book.* Chicago: Chicago's Chinatown Chamber of Commerce.

China Institute in America. 1954. *A Survey of Chinese Students in American Universities and Colleges in the Past One Hundred Years.* New York: China Institute in America.

Chinese-American Museum of Chicago (CAMOC).

Chinese American Service League (CASL). 1982–1985. *Newsletter.* Chicago: Chicago History Museum.

————. 2005. *Annual Report.* http://www.caslservice.org/pdf/AnnualReport2005 .pdf.

————. 2006. *Annual Report.* http://www.caslservice.org/pdf/AnnualReport2006 .pdf.

Chinese Consolidated Benevolent Association of Chicago, comp. 2000. *A Century of Chicago Chinatown.* Chicago: CCBAC.

Chinese Mutual Aid Association. 1994. *Annual Report.* Chicago: Chicago History Museum.

Chicago Race Commission. 1922. "The Negro in Chicago." Chicago History Museum.

City of Chicago, Department of Development and Planning. 1976a. *Historic City, the Settlement of Chicago.* Chicago: Department of Development and Planning.

————. 1976b. *The People of Chicago: Who We Are and Who We Have Been: Census Data on Foreign-Born, Foreign Stock, and Race, 1837–1970. Mother Tongue Addendum, 1910–1970.* Chicago: Department of Development and Planning.

City of Chicago, Department of Public Works, Bureau of Maps and Plats. 1973. *Chicago Atlas.* Chicago: Department of Public Works, Bureau of Maps and Plats.

City of Chicago Directory (Chicago Criss Cross Directories). 1983. Chicago: Partridge and Anderson.

Dickens, Albert E. 1942. "Southwest Side: Armour Square, Fuller Park, McKinley Park, Bridgeport, and New City." In *Forty-Four Cities in the City of Chicago,* ed. Chicago Plan Commission, 56–58. Chicago History Museum.

Directory of Chinese Professionals & Students of Chicago Area. 1964. Chicago History Museum.

Fang, Min-Lin Emily, and Li-Mei Ku, eds. 1991. *Chinese American Resources Directory in the Greater Chicago Area, 1991.* Chinese-American Librarians Association, Midwest Chapter.

Huncke, Olga. Papers, 1911–1976. Chicago History Museum.

Linton, Cynthia, ed. 1996. *The Ethnic Handbook: A Guide to the Cultures and Traditions of Chicago's Diverse Communities.* Chicago: Illinois Ethnic Coalition.

———, ed. 2000. *The Ultimate 2000: Directory of Ethnic Organizations, Ethnic Media and Scholars for the Chicago Metropolitan Area.* Chicago: Illinois Ethnic Coalition.

Newspaper Clippings on Chinese, 1939–1991. Chicago History Museum.

USDC/NDI–Chicago Civil Records, 1871–1985. Civil Case Files. RG 21. National Archives Records Administration–Great Lakes Region, Chicago.

Wang, G. H. 1966. "Some Basic Facts about Chicago's Chinatown." In *Chinese American Progress*, Chinese American Civic Council, 7. Chicago: Chinese American Civic Council.

Chinese-Language Sources

Chao Longqi 潮龙起. 2010. "Weixian de yuyue: Zaoqi meiguo huaqiao dubo wenti yanjiu (1850–1943 nian)" 危险的愉悦:早期美国华侨赌博问题研究 (1850–1943) [Dangerous pleasure: Gambling in early overseas Chinese society in America (1850–1943)]. *Huanqiao huaren lishi yanjiu* 華僑華人歷史研究 [Overseas Chinese history studies], no. 2 (June): 41–53.

Chen Kuo-lin 陳國林. 1995. *Hua ren bang pai* 華人幫派 [The Chinatown gangs]. Taipei: Juliu Publishing House.

Chen Pen-ch'ang 陳本昌. 1971. *Mei-kuo hua ch'iao ts'an kuan kung yeh* 美國華僑餐館工業 [Chinese American restaurants]. Taipei: Taiwan Far East Books.

Chen Yiping 陳奕平. 2006. *Renkou bianqian yu dangdai meiguo shehui* 人口變遷與當代美國社會 [Demographic changes and contemporary American society]. Beijing: Shijie zhishi chubanshe 世界知識出版社 [World Knowledge Publishers].

Dufen zhenzhi 端芬鎮志 [Duanfen Township history]. 2003. Duanfen Town Government.

Gao Weinong et al. 高偉濃等著. 2003. *Guiji yimin huanjing xia de zhongguo xinyimin* 國際移民環境下的中國新移民 [New Chinese immigrants in the context of international migration]. Beijing: Zhongguo huaqiao chubanshe 中國華僑出版社 [Chinese Overseas Publishing Company].

———. 高偉濃等著. 2005. *Yueji huaqiao huaren yu yuedi duiwai guanxishi* 粵籍華僑華人與粵地對外關係史 [A history of the relationship between the overseas

Chinese from Guangdong and foreign countries]. Beijing: Zhongguo huaqiao chubanshe 中國華僑出版社 [Chinese Overseas Publishing Company].

Guangdongsheng dituce 廣東省地圖冊 [Guangdong Province atlas]. 2007. Guangdong: Guangdong Map Publishing Company.

Guo Yucong 郭玉聰. 2006. "Zhongguo xinyimin de xingcheng yuanyin jiqi tedian zuoyong" 中國新移民的形成原因及其特點，作用 [The origins, characteristics, and impacts of the new Chinese immigrants]. In Xia Chenghua, ed. 夏誠華主編, *Xinshiji yimin de bianqian* 新世紀移民的變遷 [The changing Chinese immigrants in the new century]. Xinzhu, Taiwan 台灣 新竹市: Xuanzang daxue haiwai huaren yanjiu zhongxin 玄奘大學海外華人研究中心 [Overseas Chinese Studies Center, Xuanzang University].

Hao Shiyuan, ed. 郝時遠主編. 2002. *Haiwai huaren yanjiu lunji* 海外華人研究論集 [Selected papers on overseas Chinese]. Beijing: Zhongguo shehui kexue chubanshe 中國社會科學出版社 [Chinese Social Science Academy Publishing Company].

He Fengjiao, ed. 何鳳嬌編. 1997. *Dongnanya huaqiao ziliao huibian* 東南亞華僑資料匯編 [A collection of sources on Southeast Asian overseas Chinese]. Taipei: Academia Historica.

Huang Jing 黃靜. 2003. "Chaoshan yu zhongguo chuantong qiaoxiang: Yige guanyu yimin jingyan de leixingxue fenxi" 潮汕與中國傳統僑鄉：一個關於移民經驗的類型學分析 [Chaoshan region and other traditional qiaoxiang in China: A typological analysis of migration experience]. *Huanqiao huaren lishi yanjiu* 華僑華人歷史研究 [Overseas Chinese history studies], no. 1 (March): 24–36.

Lee Ying-hui 李盈慧. 1997. *Huaqiao zhengce yu haiwai minzu zhuyi* (1912–1949) 華僑政策與海外民族主義 [The origin of overseas Chinese nationalism (1912–1949)]. Taipei: Academia Historica.

Li Anshan 李安山. 2000. *Feizhou huaqiao huarenshi* 非洲華僑華人史 [A history of overseas Chinese in Africa]. Beijing: Zhongguo huaqiao chubanshe 中國華僑出版社 [Chinese Overseas Publishing Company].

Li Minghuan 李明歡. 1995. *Dangdai haiwai huaren shetuan yanjiu* 當代海外華人社團研究[Contemporary overseas Chinese community organizations]. Xiamen: Xiamen daxue chubanshe 廈門大學出版社 [Xiamen University Press].

Li Qirong 李其榮, Tan Tianxing 譚天星, and Lin Xiaodong 林曉东主编, eds. 2009. *Haiwai gaocenci rencai yu renli ziyuan jianshe* 海外高层次人才与人力资源建设 [A study of overseas talent and China's development]. Beijing: Zhongguo huaqiao chubanshe 中國華僑出版社 [Chinese Overseas Publishing Company].

Liang Yingming 梁英明, Liang Zhiming 梁志明, Zhou Nanjing 周南京, and Zhao Jing 趙敬. 1994. *Jin xiandai dongnanya* (1511–1992) 近現代東南亞 (1511–1992) [Modern and contemporary Southeast Asia (1511–1992)]. Beijing: Beijing daxue chubanshe 北京大學出版社 [Beijing University Press].

Liu Bo-ji 劉伯驥. 1981. *Meiguo huaqiao shi* 美國華僑史 [History of the overseas Chinese in the United States]. Taipei: Li Ming Publishing Co.

Liu Quan 劉權. 2002. *Guangdong huaqiao huarenshi* 廣東華僑華人史 [A history of overseas Chinese from Guangdong]. Guangdong: Guangdong renmin chubanshe 廣東人民出版社 [Guangdong People's Publisher].

Long Denggao 龍登高. 2007. *Kuayu shichang de zhangai: Haiwai huashang zai guojia zhidu yu wenhua zhijian* 跨越市場的障礙: 海外華商在國家, 制度, 與文化之間 [Beyond market obstacles: Overseas Chinese merchants among nation-states, systems, and cultures]. Beijing: Kexue chubanshe 科學出版社 [Science Publishing Company].

Long Denggao 龍登高, Zhao Liang 趙亮, and Ding Jian 丁騫. 2008. "Haiwai huashang touzi zhongguo dalu—jieduanxing tezheng yu fazhan qushi" 海外華商投資中國大陸:階段性特征與發展趨勢 [Investment of overseas Chinese in mainland China: Features and trends]. *Huanqiao huaren lishi yanjiu* 華僑華人歷史研究 [Overseas Chinese history studies], no. 2 (June): 10–17.

Long Yingtai 龙应台. 2009. *Dajiang dahai: Yijiu sijiu* 大江大海，一九四九 [Great rivers and oceans, 1949]. Taipei: Tianxia Magazine Publishing Company.

Qin Zhenxia 秦振霞, Yang Mingjin 杨明金, and Song Song 宋松. 2009. "Kongxincun wenti jiqi jiejue duice" 空心村问题及其解决对策 [Hollow-center villages and policies on resolving the problem]. *Nongcun jingji* 农村经济 [Countryside economics] 3:96–99.

Runan zhihua 汝南之花 [Nei Nam's flower, or the Moy family magazine], 1976–2009. Duanfen Town, Taishan: Runan Zhihua Qiaokan Publisher.

Shijie Meishi Zongqin Zonghui 世界梅氏宗親總會 [International Moy Family Association]. 1991. *Meishi zongqin zupu* 梅氏宗親族譜 [Moy family genealogy]. Taipei: Shijie Meishi Zongqin Zonghui 世界梅氏宗親總會 [International Moy Family Association].

Taishan Shi Qiaolian 台山市僑聯 [Taishan City Federation of Overseas Chinese]. 1998. *Taishan shi qiaolian pucha: Huaqiao huaren fenbu shijie gedi qinkuang tongbiao* 台山市僑聯普查:華僑華人分布世界各地情況統表 [Taishan City Federation of Overseas Chinese survey: Table of the distribution of overseas Chinese]. Taishan: Taishan Shi Qiaolian 台山市僑聯 [Taishan City Federation of Overseas Chinese].

Taishanxian huaqiaozhi 台山县华侨志 [Taishan County gazetteer on overseas Chinese from Taishan]. 1992. Taishan: Taishan County Gazetteer Compilation Committee.

Wang Chengxin 王成新, Yao Shimou 姚士谋, and Chen Caihong 陈彩虹. 2005. "Zhongguo nongcun juluo kongxin wenti shizheng yanjiu" 中国农村聚落空心化问题实证研究 [Empirical study on village hollowing in China]. *Dili kexue* 地理科学 [Scientia Geographica Sinica] 25, no. 3 (June): 257–262.

Wang Xiuhui 王秀惠. 2006. *Zhongzu qishi yu xingbie: Erzhan qian meiguo dalu nanxing uaren zhi jingli* 種族歧視與性別:二戰前美國大陸男性華人之經歷 [Racial discrimination and gender: The experiences of Chinese males on the American mainland prior to World War II]. Taibei: Yunchen wenhua shiye gufen youxian gongsi 允晨文化實業股份有限公司 [Yunchen Culture Ltd.].

Wang Yuanlin 王元林 and Deng Minrui 鄧敏銳. 2005. "Jindai Guangdong qiaoxiang shenghuo fangshi yu shehui fengsu de bianhua: Yi chaoshan he wuyi weili" 近代廣東僑鄉生活方式與社會風俗的變化--以潮汕和五邑為例 [Change of lifestyle and customs in qiaoxiang in modern times--with special reference to Chaoshan and Wuyi]. *Huanqiao huaren lishi yanjiu* 華僑華人歷史研究 [Overseas Chinese history studies], no. 4 (December): 56–62.

Wu Tai, ed. 吳泰主編. 1994. *Jinjiang huaqiaozhi* 晉江華僑志 [Jinjiang County gazetteer on overseas Chinese from Jinjiang]. Shanghai: Shanghai renmin chubanshe 上海人民出版社 [Shanghai People's Publisher].

Xiamen huaqiaozhi bianweihui 廈門華僑志編委會. 1991. *Xiamen huaqiaozhi* 廈門華僑志 [Xiamen gazetteer on overseas Chinese from Xiamen]. Xiamen: Lujiang chubanshe 鷺江出版社 [Lujiang Publishers].

Xin Ning Magazine 新寧雜誌 [Xin Ning Magazine]. 2006. Guangdong sheng taishan shi xin ning zazhi she 廣東省台山市新寧雜志社 [Xin Ning Magazine, Taishan City, Guangdong Province].

Xu Xishan 徐錫山. 1997. "Sancun Jin Lian" 三寸金蓮 [Bound feet]. 世界日報 [World Journal] (March 8–10).

Zeng Shaocong 曾少聰. 1998. *Dongyang hanglu yimin: Mingqing haiyang yimin Taiwan yu feilubin de bijiao yanjiu* 東洋航路移民:明清海洋移民台灣與菲律賓的比較研究 [Migration eastward by way of the ocean: A comparative study of migration to Taiwan and the Philippines during the Ming and Qing dynasties]. Jiangxi: Jiangxi gaoxiao chubanshe 江西高校出版社 [Press of the Universities of Jiangxi].

Zhang Chunjuan 张春娟. 2004. "Nongcun kongxinhua wenti jiqi duice yanju" 农村 "空心化" 问题及对策研究 [A study of the hollow center phenomenon in the countryside and its remedies]. *Zhexue shijie* 哲学视界 [Philosophy studies] 4:83–86.

Zhang Guoxiong 張國雄. 2003. "Cong yuemin qiaoxiang kaochan erzhanqian haiwai huaqiao huaren de qunti tezheng—yi wuyi qiaoxiang weili" 從粵閩僑鄉考察二戰前海外華僑華人的群體特征—以五邑僑鄉為例 [A study of the collective character of overseas Chinese in Guangdong–Fujian qiaoxiang before World War II—with special reference to Wuyi qiaoxiang]. *Huanqiao huaren lishi yanjiu* 華僑華人歷史研究 [Overseas Chinese history studies], no. 2 (June): 26–34.

Zhang Yunhua 张运华. 2008. "Cong wenhua shijiao guanzhao wuyi qiaoxiang shehui yu funu--jianyu chaoshan qiaoxiang bijiao" 从文化视角观照五邑侨乡社

会与妇女--兼与潮汕侨乡比较 [A study of women and society in Wuji overseas Chinese villages: In comparison with Chaozhou, Shantou, overseas Chinese villages]. *Wuyi daxue xuebao* 五邑大学学报 (社会科学版) [Wuyi University social science journal] 10, no. 1 (February): 1–6.

Zhao Heman 趙和曼. 2004. *Shaoshu minzu huaqiao huaren yanjiu* 少數民族華僑華人研究 [A study of the Chinese ethnic minorities as overseas Chinese]. Beijing: Zhongguo huaqiao chubanshe 中國華僑出版社 [Chinese Overseas Publishing Company].

Zhonghua Renmin Gongheguo Hunyin Fa 中華人民共和國婚姻法 [Marriage law of the PRC]. 1987. In *Zhongguo falu nianjian 1987* 中國法律年鑒 1987 [Law Yearbook of China 1987], Zhongguo falu nianjian bianjibu [Editorial Department of the Law Yearbook of China], 168–169. Beijing: Falu chubanshe.

Zhou Nanjing 周南京. 2001. *Fengyun bianhuan kan shijie* 風雲變幻看世界 [Observing the world through changes]. Hong Kong: Nan Dao Publishers.

Zhou Zhuping 周祝平. 2008. "Zhongguo nongcun renkou kongxinhua jiqi tiaozhan" 中国农村人口空心化及其挑战 [China's hollow center phenomenon in the countryside and its challenges]. *Renkou yanjiu* 人口研究 [Population research] 32, no. 12 (March): 45–52.

Zhu Hongyuan 朱浤源. 1993. "Qingmo yilai haiwai huaren de minzu zhuyi" 清末以來海外華人的民族主義 [The nationalism of overseas Chinese since the latter part of the Qing dynasty]. *Si yu yan* 思與言 [Thinking and speaking] 3, no. 3 (September): 1–66.

Zhuang Guotu 庄國土. 1989. *Zhongguo fengjian zhengfu de huaqiao zhengce* 中國封建政府的華僑政策 [The Chinese feudal governments' policies on overseas Chinese]. Xiamen: Xiamen daxue chubanshe 廈門大學出版社 [Xiamen University Press].

English-Language Sources

Abbott, Andrew. 1999. *Department and Discipline: Chicago Sociology at One Hundred.* Chicago: University of Chicago Press.

Abelmann, Nancy, and John Lee. 1995. *Blue Dreams: Korean Americans and the Los Angeles Riots.* Cambridge, MA: Harvard University Press.

Allswang, John M. 1971. *A House for All Peoples: Ethnic Politics in Chicago, 1890–1936.* Lexington: University Press of Kentucky.

Anderson, Benedict. 1991. *Imagined Communities: Reflections on the Origin and Spread of Nationalism.* London: Verso.

Anderson, Kay J. 1991. *Vancouver's Chinatown: Racial Discourse in Canada, 1875–1980.* Montreal and Kingston: McGill-Queen's University Press.

Anderson, Mary Raleigh. 1943. *A Cycle in the Celestial Kingdom.* Mobile, AL: Heiter-Starke Printing Company.

Anderson, Nels. 1923. *The Hobo: The Sociology of the Homeless Man.* Chicago: University of Chicago Press.

Anderson, Philip J., and Dag Blanck, eds. 1992. *Swedish-American Life in Chicago: Cultural and Urban Aspects of an Immigrant People, 1850–1930.* Urbana: University of Illinois Press.

Arenson, Ling Z. 2009. "Beyond a Common Ethnicity and Culture: Chicagoland's Chinese American Communities since 1945." In *Asian America: Forming New Communities, Expanding Boundaries,* ed. Huping Ling, 65–86. New Brunswick, NJ: Rutgers University Press.

Arredondo, Gabriela F. 2004. "Navigating Ethno-Racial Currents: Mexicans in Chicago, 1919–1939." *Journal of Urban History* 30, no. 4 (March): 339–427.

Asian American Institute. 1994. *Asian American Political Empowerment in Illinois.* Chicago: Asian American Institute.

Ba, Jin. 1972. *Family.* Garden City, NY: Doubleday.

Barrett, James R. 1987. *Work and Community in the Jungle: Chicago's Packinghouse Workers, 1894–1922.* Urbana: University of Illinois Press.

Barth, Gunther. 1980. *City People: The Rise of Modern City Culture in Nineteenth Century America.* New York: Oxford University Press.

Basch, Linda, Nina Glick Schiller, and Cristina Blanc-Szanton, eds. 1994. *Nations Unbound: Transnational Projects, Postcolonial Predicaments and Deterritorialized Nation-States.* Langhorne, PA: Gordon and Breach.

Beesley, David. 1988. "From Chinese to Chinese American: Chinese Women and Families in a Sierra Nevada Town." *California History* 67 (September): 168–179.

Biles, Roger. 1995. *Richard J. Daley: Politics, Race, and the Governing of Chicago.* DeKalb: Northern Illinois University Press.

Blusse, Leonard. 2008. *Visible Cities: Canton, Nagasaki and Batavia and the Coming of the Americans.* Cambridge, MA: Harvard University Press.

Bodnar, John. 1985. *The Transplanted: A History of Immigrants in Urban America.* Bloomington: Indiana University Press.

Boehm, Lisa Krissoff. 2004. *Popular Culture and the Enduring Myth of Chicago, 1871–1968.* Routledge.

Bonacich, Edna. 1972. "A Theory of Ethnic Antagonism: The Split Labor Market Theory." *American Sociological Review* 37: 547–559.

Bowly, Devereux, Jr. 1978. *The Poorhouse: Subsidized Housing in Chicago, 1895–1976.* Carbondale: Southern Illinois University Press.

Brooks, Charlotte. 2000. "In the Twilight Zone between Black and White: Japanese American Resettlement and Community in Chicago, 1942–1945." *Journal of American History* (March): 1655–1687.

Bulmer, Martin. 1984. *The Chicago School of Sociology: Institutionalization, Diversity, and the Rise of Sociological Research*. Chicago: University of Chicago Press.

Burgess, Ernest Watson, and Donald Joseph Bogue, eds. 1964. *Contributions to Urban Sociology*. Chicago: University of Chicago Press.

Butler, Anne M. 1987. *Daughters of Joy, Sisters of Misery: Prostitutes in the American West, 1865–90*. Urbana: University of Illinois Press.

Calhoun, Craig, ed. 2007. *Sociology in America: A History*. Chicago: University of Chicago Press.

Chan, Jason. 1995. "Evaluating the Programs of Five Chinese Churches in Chicago in Relation to Their Context." Master's thesis, Wheaton College.

Chan, Sucheng. 1986. *This Bittersweet Soil: The Chinese in California Agriculture, 1860–1910*. Berkeley: University of California Press.

———. 1991a. *Asian Americans: An Interpretive History*. Boston: Twayne Publishers.

———, ed. 1991b. *Entry Denied: Exclusion and the Chinese in America, 1882–1943*. Philadelphia: Temple University Press.

———, ed. 2006. *Chinese American Transnationalism: The Flow of People, Resources, and Ideas between China and America during the Exclusion Era*. Philadelphia: Temple University Press.

Chan, Sucheng, and Madeline Y. Hsu, eds. 2008. *Chinese Americans and the Politics of Race and Culture*. Philadelphia: Temple University Press.

Chang, Jung. 1986. *Mme Sun Yat-Sen*. New York: Viking Penguin.

Chen, Hsiang-Shui. 1992. *Chinatown No More: Taiwan Immigrants in Contemporary New York*. Ithaca, NY: Cornell University Press.

Chen, Jack. 1982. *The Chinese of America*. San Francisco: Harper & Row.

Chen, Julia I. Hsuan. 1974. *The Chinese Community in New York*. San Francisco: R & E Research Associates.

Chen, Shehong. 2002. *Being Chinese, Becoming Chinese American*. Urbana: University of Illinois Press.

Chen, Wen-Hsien. 1940. "Chinese under Both Exclusion and Immigration Laws." PhD diss., University of Chicago.

Chen, Yong. 2000. *Chinese San Francisco, 1850–1943: A Trans-Pacific Community*. Stanford, CA: Stanford University Press.

Chinn, Thomas W. 1989. *Bridging the Pacific: San Francisco Chinatown and Its People*. San Francisco: Chinese Historical Society of America.

Chiu, Ping. 1967. *Chinese Labor in California: An Economic Study*. Madison: University of Wisconsin Press.

Chou, Jesse Chain. 1989. "A Survey of Chinese Students in the United States, 1979–1987." EdD diss., Columbia University Teachers College.

Christoff, Peggy Spitzer. 1998. "Women of Chinatown." *Chicago History* (Spring): 44–55.

———. 2001. *Tracking the Yellow Peril: The INS and Chinese Immigrants in the Midwest.* Rockland, ME: Picton Press.

Chu, Louis. 1979. *Eat a Bowl of Tea.* Seattle: University of Washington Press.

Chu, Yung-Deh Richard. 1973. "Chinese Secret Societies in America: A Historical Survey." *Asian Profile* 1, no. 1: 21–38.

Chung, Angie Y. 2007. *Legacies of Struggle: Conflict and Cooperation in Korean American Politics.* Palo Alto, CA: Stanford University Press.

Chung, Sue Fawn. 1989. "Gue Gim Wah, Pioneering Chinese American Woman of Nevada." In *History and Humanities,* ed. Francis X. Hartigan, 45–79. Reno: University of Nevada Press.

———. 2002. "Between Two Worlds: The Zhigongtang and Chinese American Funerary Rituals." In *The Chinese in America: A History from Gold Mountain to the New Millennium,* ed. Susie Lan Cassel, 217–238. Walnut Creek, CA: AltaMira Press.

Cohen, Lizabeth. 1990. *Making a New Deal: Industrial Workers in Chicago, 1919–1939.* Cambridge: Cambridge University Press.

Cohen, Lucy M. 1984. *Chinese in the Post–Civil War South, a People without a History.* Baton Rouge: Louisiana State University Press.

Conzen, Kathleen Neils. 1976. *Immigrant Milwaukee, 1836–1860: Accommodation and Community in a Frontier City.* Cambridge, MA: Harvard University Press.

Cressey, Paul Frederick. 1938. "Population Succession in Chicago: 1898–1930." *American Journal of Sociology* 44 (July): 59–69.

Cronon, William. 1991. *Nature's Metropolis: Chicago and the Great West.* New York: W. W. Norton.

Cutler, Irving. 1996. *The Jews of Chicago: From Shtetl to Suburb.* Urbana: University of Illinois Press.

Dai, Bingham. 1937. "Opium Addiction in Chicago." PhD diss., University of Chicago.

Daniels, Roger. 1988. *Asian America: Chinese and Japanese in the United States since 1850.* Seattle: University of Washington Press.

Diner, Hasia R. 1983. *Erin's Daughters in America: Irish Immigrant Women in the Nineteenth Century.* Baltimore: Johns Hopkins University Press.

Djang, Helen. 1940. "The Adjustment in American Culture of the Chinese Children in Chinatown, Chicago, and Its Educational Implications." PhD diss., Northwestern University.

Do, Hien Duc. 1999. *The Vietnamese Americans.* Westport, CT: Greenwood Press.

Dowd, Gregory Evans. 1992. *A Spirited Resistance: The North American Indian Struggle for Unity, 1745–1815.* Baltimore and London: Johns Hopkins University Press.

Dreiser, Theodore. 1997. *Sister Carrie: Unexpurgated Edition*. New York: Doubleday.

DuBois, W. E. B. (1903) 1961. *The Souls of Black Folk*. New York: Fawcett.

Duis, Perry R. 1983. *The Saloon: Public Drinking in Chicago and Boston, 1880–1920*. Urbana: University of Illinois Press.

Duncan, Timms. 1971. *The Urban Mosaic: Towards a Theory of Minority Residential Differentiation*. London: Cambridge University Press.

Erdamans, Mary Patrice. 1998. *Opposite Poles: Immigrants and Ethnics in Polish Chicago, 1976–1990*. University Park: Penn State University Press.

España-Maram, Linda. 2006. *Creating Masculinity in Los Angeles's Little Manila: Working Class Filipinos and Popular Culture, 1920s–1950s*. New York: Columbia University Press.

Espiritu, Yen Le. 1992. *Asian American Panethnicity: Bridging Institutions and Identities*. Philadelphia: Temple University Press.

Fairbank, John King. 1973. *East Asian, Tradition and Transformation*. Boston: Houghton Mifflin.

Fan, Tin-Chiu. (1926) 1974. "Chinese Residents in Chicago." Master's thesis, University of Chicago; reprint, Saratoga, CA: R & E Research Associates.

Fong, Timothy P. 1994. *The First Suburban Chinatown: The Remaking of Monterey Park, California*. Philadelphia: Temple University Press.

Ford, Richard G. 1950. "Population Succession in Chicago." *American Journal of Sociology* 56:156–160.

Freeman, James M. 1991. *Hearts of Sorrow: Vietnamese-American Lives*. Stanford, CA: Stanford University Press.

Fu, Xuan. 1991. "Chinese Moon Pavilion at Montrose Harbor Chicago, Illinois." M.Arch, Ball State University.

Fung, Silas H. 1970. *A History of the Chinese Christian Union Church of Chicago*. Chicago: Chinese Christian Union Church.

Glenn, Evelyn Nakano. 1983. "Split Household, Small Producer and Dual Wage Earner: An Analysis of Chinese-American Family Strategies." *Journal of Marriage and the Family* 45, no. 1: 35–46.

———. 1986. *Issei, Nisei, War Bride: Three Generations of Japanese American Women in Domestic Service*. Philadelphia: Temple University Press.

Glick, Clarence Elmer. 1938. "The Chinese Migrants in Hawaii." PhD diss., University of Chicago.

———. 1980. *Sojourners and Settlers: Chinese Migrants in Hawaii*. Honolulu: University Press of Hawaii.

Glick Schiller, Nina, Linda Basch, and Cristina Blanc-Szanton, eds. 1992. *Towards a Transnational Perspective on Migration: Race, Ethnicity, and Nationalism Reconsidered*. New York: New York Academy of Science.

Gold, Thomas B. 1986. *State and Society in the Taiwan Miracle*. Armonk, NY: M. E. Sharpe.

Goldman, Marion S. 1981. *Gold Diggers and Silver Miners: Prostitution and Social Life on the Comstock Lode*. Ann Arbor: University of Michigan Press.

Gong, Eng Ying, and Bruce Grant. 1930. *Tong War*. New York: Nicholas L. Brown.

Gordon, Milton. 1964. *Assimilation in American Life*. New York: Oxford University Press.

Griswood, Robert L. 1988. "Anglo Women and Domestic Ideology in the American West in the Nineteenth and Early Twentieth Centuries." In *Western Women: Their Land, Their Lives*, ed. Lillian Schlissel, Vicki L. Ruiz, and Janice Monk, 15–33. Albuquerque: University of New Mexico Press.

Grossman, James R. 1989. *Land of Hope: Chicago, Black Southerners, and the Great Migration*. Chicago: University of Chicago Press.

———. 1991. "The White Man's Union: The Great Migration and the Resonance of Race and Class in Chicago, 1916–1922." In *The Great Migration in Historical Perspective: New Dimensions of Race, Class and Gender*, ed. Joe William Trotter Jr., 83–105. Bloomington: Indiana University Press.

Gu, Chien-Juh. 2006. *Mental Health among Taiwanese Americans: Gender, Immigration, and Transnational Struggles*. New York: LFB Scholarly Publishing LLC.

Guglielmo, Thomas A. 2003. *White on Arrival: Italians, Race, Color, and Power in Chicago, 1890–1945*. Oxford: Oxford University Press.

Gyory, Andrew. 1998. *Closing the Gate: Race, Politics, and the Chinese Exclusion Act*. Chapel Hill: University of North Carolina Press.

Halpern, Rick. 1997. *Down on the Killing Floor: Black and White Workers in Chicago's Packinghouse, 1904–54*. Urbana: University of Illinois Press.

Handlin, Oscar. 1954. *Adventure in Freedom: Three Hundred Years of Jewish Life in America*. New York: McGraw-Hill.

Harden, Jacalyn D. 2003. *Double Cross: Japanese Americans in Black and White Chicago*. Minneapolis: University of Minnesota Press.

Harper, Fowler V., and Jerome H. Skolnick. 1962. *Problems of the Family*. New York: Bobbs-Merrill.

Hauser, Philip Morris, and E. M. Kitagawa. 1953. *Local Community Fact Book for Chicago*. Chicago: University of Chicago Press.

Hayhoe, Ruth, and Marianne Bastid, eds. 1987. *China's Education and the Industrialized World*. Armonk, NY: M. E. Sharpe.

Hesse-Wartegg, Ernst von. 1891. *Tausend und ein Tag im Occident*. Vol. 1. Leipzig: Carl Reissner.

Hirata, Lucie Cheng. 1979. "Free, Indentured, Enslaved: Chinese Prostitutes in 19th Century America." *Signs* 5:3–29.

———. 1982. "Chinese Immigrant Women in Nineteenth-Century California."

In *Asian and Pacific American Experiences: Women's Perspectives*, ed. Nobuya Tuschida et al., 38–55. Minneapolis: Asian/Pacific American Learning Resource Center and General College, University of Minnesota.

Hirsch, Arnold R. 1983. *Making the Second Ghetto: Race and Housing in Chicago, 1940–1960.* Cambridge: Cambridge University Press.

———. 2003. "Second Thoughts on the Second Ghetto." *Journal of Urban History* 29, no. 3 (March): 298–309.

Hirsch, Eric L. 1990. *Urban Revolt: Ethnic Politics in the Nineteenth-Century Chicago Labor Movement.* Berkeley: University of California Press.

Ho, Chuimei, and Soo Lon Moy, eds. 2005. *Chinese in Chicago, 1870–1945.* Charleston, SC: Arcadia Publishing.

Hogan, W. 1984. "Armour Square." In *Local Community Fact Book: Chicago Metropolitan Area, Based on the 1970 and 1980 Censuses*, ed. Chicago Fact Book Consortium. Chicago: Chicago Review Press.

Holli, Melvin G., and Peter d'A. Jones, eds. 1995. *Ethnic Chicago: A Multicultural Portrait.* Grand Rapids, MI: William B. Eerdmans.

Hoy, William. 1942. *The Chinese Six Companies.* San Francisco: California Chinese Historical Society.

Hoyt, Homer. 1933. "One Hundred Years of Land Value in Chicago." PhD diss., University of Chicago.

Hsiao, Kung-chuan. 1975. *A Modern China and a New World: K'ang Yu-wei, Reformer and Utopian, 1858–1927.* Seattle and London: University of Washington Press.

Hsieh, Theodore T. Y. 1968. "The Chinese and the Chinese Church in Chicago: A Socio-Cultural Study of Their Missionary Implications." Master's thesis, Trinity Evangelical Divinity School.

Hsu, Francis L. K. 1970. *Americans and Chinese.* Garden City, NY: Doubleday Natural History Press.

Hsu, Immanuel C. Y. 1990. *The Rise of Modern China.* New York: Oxford University Press.

Hsu, Madeline Y. 2000. *Dreaming of Gold, Dreaming of Home: Transnationalism and Migration between the United States and South China, 1882–1943.* Stanford, CA: Stanford University Press.

———. 2008. "From Chop Suey to Mandarin Cuisine: Fine Dining and the Refashioning of Chinese Ethnicity during the Cold War Era." In *Chinese Americans and the Politics of Race and Culture*, ed. Sucheng Chan and Madeline Y. Hsu, 173–193. Philadelphia: Temple University Press.

Huang, Philip C. C. 1985. *The Peasant Economy and Social Change in North China.* Stanford, CA: Stanford University Press.

————. 1990. *The Peasant Family and Rural Development in the Yangzi Delta, 1350–1988.* Stanford, CA: Stanford University Press.

Hughes, Langston. 1945. *Big Sea: An Autobiography.* New York: Hill & Wang.

Hurley, Andrew, ed. 1997. *Common Fields: An Environmental History of St. Louis.* St. Louis: Missouri Historical Society Press.

Hyde, William, and Howard L. Conard. 1899. *Encyclopedia of the History of St. Louis, a Compendium of History and Biography for Ready Reference.* 3 vols. St. Louis, MO: Southern History Company.

Ip, Manying. 2005. *Aliens at My Table: Asians as New Zealanders See Them.* Auckland: Penguin Books.

Jackson, John L., Jr. 2001. *Harlemworld: Doing Race and Class in Contemporary Black America.* Chicago: University of Chicago Press.

Jacobson, Matthew Frye. 1998. *Whiteness of a Different Color: European Immigrants and the Alchemy of Race.* Cambridge, MA: Harvard University Press.

Jeffrey, Julie Roy. 1979. *Frontier Women: The Trans-Mississippi West, 1840–1880.* New York: Hill & Wang.

Jewish Federation of Metropolitan Chicago. 1978. *Welcome to Chicago: Indo-Chinese Resettlement and Career Development Services Program.* Chicago: Jewish Federation of Metropolitan Chicago.

Joiner, Thekla Ellen. 2007. *Sin in the City: Chicago and Revivalism, 1880–1920.* Columbia: University of Missouri Press.

Judson, Clara Ingram. 1949. *The Green Ginger Jar: A Chinatown Mystery.* Cambridge, MA: Tribune Press.

Kantowicz, Edward. 1975. *Polish-American Politics in Chicago, 1888–1940.* Chicago: University of Chicago Press.

Keener, Minglan Cheung. 1994. "Chicago's Chinatown—A Case Study of an Ethnic Neighborhood." Master's thesis, University of Illinois at Urbana–Champaign.

Keil, Hartmut. 1983. "The German Immigrant Working Class of Chicago, 1875–90: Workers, Labor Leaders, and the Labor Movement." In *American Labor and Immigration History, 1877–1920s: Recent European Research*, ed. Dirk Hoerder, 156–176. Urbana: University of Illinois Press.

Kiang, Harry Ying Cheng. 1992. *Chicago's Chinatown.* Lincolnwood, IL: Institute of China Studies.

Kitagawa, Evelyn M., and Karl Taeuber, eds. 1963. *Local Community Fact Book: Chicago Metropolitan Area, 1960.* Chicago: University of Chicago Press.

Kivisto, Peter. 1990. "The Transplanted Then and Now: The Reorientation of Immigration Studies from the Chicago School to the New Social History." *Ethnic and Racial Studies* 13, no. 4: 455–481.

Kleppner, Paul. 1985. *Chicago Divided: The Making of a Black Mayor.* DeKalb: Northern Illinois University Press.

Ko, Yu. 2003. "Functional Health Literacy among Chinese Population in Chicago: A Preliminary Study." MS thesis, University of Illinois at Chicago.

Kurtz, Lester R. 1984. *Evaluating Chicago Sociology: A Guide to the Literature with an Annotated Bibliography.* Chicago: University of Chicago Press.

Kwoh, Belulah Ong. 1947. "American-Born Chinese College Graduates." Master's thesis, University of Chicago.

Kwong, Peter. 1979. *Chinatown, New York: Labor and Politics, 1930–1950.* New York: Monthly Review Press.

———. 1987. *The New Chinatown.* New York: Hill & Wang.

———. 1997. *Forbidden Workers: Illegal Chinese Immigrants and American Labor.* New York: New Press.

———. 2005. *Chinese America: The Untold Story of America's Oldest New Community.* New York: New Press.

Laguerre, Michel S. 2000. *The Global Ethnopolis: Chinatown, Japantown, and Manilatown in American Society.* New York: St. Martin's.

Lai, David Chuenyan. 1988. *Chinatowns: Towns within Cities in Canada.* Vancouver: University of British Columbia Press.

Lai, Him Mark. 1987. "Historical Development of the Chinese Consolidated Benevolent Association/Huiguan System." In *Chinese America: History and Perspectives 1987,* ed. Chinese Historical Society of America, 13–51. San Francisco: Chinese Historical Society of America.

———. 1990. "The Chinese Press in the United States and Canada since World War II: A Diversity of Voices." *Chinese America: History and Perspectives, 1990,* ed. Chinese Historical Society of America, 107–156. San Francisco: Chinese Historical Society of America.

———. 2000. "Transmitting the Chinese Heritage: Chinese Schools in the United States Mainland and Hawaii." In *Intercultural Relations, Cultural Transformation, and Identity—The Ethnic Chinese: Selected Papers Presented at the 1998 ISSCO Conference,* ed. Teresita Ang See, 124–158. Manila: Kaisa Para Sa Kaunlaran.

Lam, George Chung Yan. 1977. *The Mission and Ministry of the Church among the Chinese Community in Chicago.* Chicago: n.p.

Lan, Shanshan. 2007. "Learning Race and Class: Chinese Americans in Multicultural Bridgeport." PhD diss., University of Illinois at Urbana–Champaign.

Lang, Olga. 1946. *Chinese Family and Society.* New Haven, CT: Yale University Press.

Larson, Jane Leung. 1998. "The Chinese Empire Reform Association's Movement to Send Students Abroad: Evidence from the Papers of Tan Zhangxiao (Tom Leung)." Paper presented at the International Symposium on the Centennial of the 1898 Reform Movement, Beijing University, China, August 20–23.

Larson, Louise Leung, Shirley Hune, and Jane Leung Larson. 2001. *Sweet Bamboo: A Memoir of a Chinese American Family.* Berkeley: University of California Press.

Lau, Yvonne M. 2004. "Chicago's Chinese American Communities in Transition." Paper submitted to the 99th Annual Meeting of the American Sociological Association, Section on Asia and Asian America, August 9, 2004. http://www.all academic.com/meta/p_mla_apa_research_citation/1/1/0/5/9/p110590_index.html.

———. 2006. "Chicago's Chinese Americans: From Chinatown and Beyond." In *The New Chicago: A Social and Cultural Analysis*, ed. John Koval et al., 168–181. Philadelphia: Temple University Press.

Lee, Jae-Hyup. 1998. *Dynamics of Ethnic Identity: Three Asian American Communities in Philadelphia.* New York: Garland.

Lee, Jennifer. 2002. *Civility in the City: Blacks, Jews and Koreans in Urban America.* Cambridge, MA: Harvard University Press.

Lee, Rose Hum. (1947) 1978. "The Growth and Decline of Chinese Communities in the Rocky Mountain Region." New York: Arno Press.

———. 1949. "The Decline of Chinatowns in the United States." *American Journal of Sociology* 54 (March): 422–432.

———. 1956. "The Marginal Man: Re-evaluation and Indices of Measurement." *Journal of Human Relations* 5 (Spring): 27–28.

———. 1960. *The Chinese in the United States of America.* Hong Kong: Hong Kong University.

Lee, Stacey. 1996. *Unraveling the "Model Minority" Stereotype: Listening to Asian American Youth.* New York: Columbia University Press.

Leonard, Karen Isaksen. 1992. *Making Ethnic Choices: California's Punjabi Mexican Americans.* Philadelphia: Temple University Press.

Levy, Marion J., Jr. 1971. *The Family Revolution in Modern China.* New York: Octagon Books.

Lewis, Arnold. 1997. *An Early Encounter with Tomorrow: Europeans, Chicago's Loop, and the World's Columbian Exposition.* Urbana: University of Illinois Press.

Li, Peter S. 1978. *Occupational Mobility and Kinship Assistance: A Study of Chinese Immigrants in Chicago.* San Francisco: R & E Research Associates.

Li, Rosalind Mei-chung. 1922. "The Chinese Revolution and the Chinese Women." *Chinese Students' Monthly* 8 (June): 673–675.

Li, Wei. 2009. *Ethnoburb: The New Ethnic Community in Urban America.* Honolulu: University of Hawaii Press.

Li, Xiaolan. 1998. "A Study of Marketing Techniques of Chinese Restaurants in Chicago." Master's thesis, University of Wisconsin–Stout.

Liang, Yuan. 1951. "The Chinese Family in Chicago." Master's thesis, University of Chicago.

Liao, P. Y. 1951. "A Case Study of a Chinese Immigrant Community [Arkansas]." Master's thesis, University of Chicago.

Lien, Pei-te. 2001. *The Making of Asian America through Political Participation.* Philadelphia: Temple University Press.

Light, Ivan. 1980. "Ethnic Enterprise in America: Chinese, Japanese and Koreans in Small Business." In *Self-Help in Urban America*, ed. Scott Cummings, 33–57. New York: Kennikat Press.

Lin, Jan. 1998. *Reconstructing Chinatown: Ethnic Enclave, Global Change.* Minneapolis: University of Minnesota Press.

———. 2008. "Los Angeles Chinatown: Tourism, Gentrification, and the Rise of an Ethnic Growth Machine." *Amerasia Journal* 34, no. 3: 110–126.

Lin, Yutang. 1948. *Chinatown Family.* New York: John Day.

Lindberg, Richard. 1997. *Passport's Guide to Ethnic Chicago: A Complete Guide to the Many Faces and Cultures of Chicago.* 2nd ed. Lincolnwood, IL: Passport Books.

Ling, Huping. 1993. "Surviving on the Gold Mountain: A Review of Sources about Chinese American Women." *The History Teacher* 26, no. 4 (August): 459–470.

———. 1994. "Chinese Merchant Wives in the United States, 1840–1945." In *Origins and Destinations: 41 Essays on Chinese America*, ed. Chinese Historical Society of Southern California, 79–92. Los Angeles: Chinese Historical Society of Southern California and UCLA Asian American Studies Center.

———. 1997. "A History of Chinese Female Students in the United States, 1880s–1990s." *Journal of American Ethnic History* 16, no. 3 (Spring): 81–109.

———. 1998a. "Chinese American Professional and Business Women in a Midwest Small Town." In *Ethnic Chinese at the Turn of the Century*, ed. Guotu Zhuang, 398–421. Fujian: Fujian People's Publishing House.

———. 1998b. *Surviving on the Gold Mountain: Chinese American Women and Their Lives.* Albany: State University of New York Press.

———. 2000a. "Chinese Female Students and the Sino-US Relations." In *New Studies on Chinese Overseas and China*, ed. Cen Huang, Zhuang Guotu, and Tanaka Kyoko, 103–137. Leiden, Netherlands: IIAS.

———. 2000b. "Family and Marriage of Late-Nineteenth and Early-Twentieth-Century Chinese Immigrant Women." *Journal of American Ethnic History* 19, no. 2 (Winter): 43–63.

———. 2001. "The Changing Patterns of Taiwanese Students in America and the Modernization in Taiwan." In *Modernity and Cultural Identity in Taiwan*, ed. Hanchao Lu, 179–207. River Edge, NJ: Global Publishing.

———. 2002. "Hop Alley: Myth and Reality of the St. Louis Chinatown, 1860s–1930s." *Journal of Urban History* 28, no. 2 (January): 184–219.

———. 2003. "The Rise and Fall of the Study in America Movement in Taiwan." *Overseas Chinese History Studies*, no. 4: 21–28.

———. 2004a. *Chinese St. Louis: From Enclave to Cultural Community.* Philadelphia: Temple University Press.

———. 2004b. "Governing 'Hop Alley': On Leong Chinese Merchants and Laborers Association, 1906–1966." *Journal of American Ethnic History* 23, no. 2 (Winter): 50–84.

———. 2004c. "Growing Up in 'Hop Alley': The Chinese American Youth in St. Louis during the Early Twentieth Century." In *Asian American Children,* ed. Benson Tong, 65–81. Westport, CT: Greenwood Press.

———. 2005. "Reconceptualizing Chinese American Community in St. Louis: From Chinatown to Cultural Community." *Journal of American Ethnic History* 24, no. 2 (Winter): 65–101.

———. 2007a. *Chinese in St. Louis: 1857–2007.* Charleston, SC: Arcadia Publishing.

———. 2007b. "New Perspectives on Chinese American Studies—Cultural Community Theory." *Overseas Chinese History Studies,* no. 1: 25–31.

———. 2007c. *Voices of the Heart: Asian American Women on Immigration, Work, and Family.* Kirksville, MO: Truman State University Press.

———, ed. 2008. *Emerging Voices: Experiences of Underrepresented Asian Americans.* New Brunswick, NJ: Rutgers University Press.

———, ed. 2009. *Asian America: Forming New Communities, Expanding Boundaries.* New Brunswick, NJ: Rutgers University Press.

Ling, Huping, and Allan W. Austin, eds. 2010. *Asian American History and Cultures: An Encyclopedia.* 2 vols. New York: M. E. Sharpe.

Lipsitz, George. 2006. *The Possessive Investment in Whiteness: How White People Profit from Identity Politics.* Philadelphia: Temple University Press.

Liu, Haiming. 2005. *Transnational History of a Chinese Family: Immigrant Letters, Family Business, and Reverse Migration.* New Brunswick, NJ: Rutgers University Press.

Liu, Haiming, and Lianlian Lin. 2009. "Food, Culinary Identity, and Transnational Culture: Chinese Restaurant Business in Southern California." *Journal of Asian American Studies* 12, no. 2 (June): 135–162.

Loewen, James W. 1971. *The Mississippi Chinese: Between Black and White.* Cambridge, MA: Harvard University Press.

Loo, Chalsa M. 1991. *Chinatown: Most Time, Hard Time.* New York: Praeger.

Louie, Andrea. 2004. *Chineseness across Borders: Renegotiating Identities in China and the United States.* Durham, NC: Duke University Press.

Louie, Vivian S. 2004. *Compelled to Excel: Immigration, Education, and Opportunity among Chinese Americans.* Stanford, CA: Stanford University Press.

Lowe, Lisa. 1991. "Heterogeneity, Hybridity, Multiplicity: Marking Asian American Differences." *Diaspora* 1:24–44.

———. 1996. *Immigrant Acts: On Asian American Cultural Politics.* Durham, NC: Duke University Press.

Lui, Mary Ting Yi. 2007. *The Chinatown Trunk Mystery: Murder, Miscegenation, and Other Dangerous Encounters in Turn-of-the-Century New York City.* Princeton, NJ: Princeton University Press.

Lydon, Sandy. 1985. *Chinese Gold: The Chinese in the Monterey Bay Region.* Capitola, CA: Capitola Book Company.

Lyman, Stanford M. 1968. "Marriage and the Family among Chinese Immigrants to America, 1850–1960." *Phylon* 24:321–330.

———. 1974. *Chinese Americans.* New York: Random House.

MacLeod, Alexander. 1948. *Pigtails and Gold Dust.* Caldwell, ID: Caxton Printers.

Manalansan, Martin F., IV. 2000. *Cultural Compass: Ethnographic Explorations of Asian America.* Philadelphia: Temple University Press.

Mann, Josiah Sungyan. 1985. *A Marriage Preparation Manual for the Chinese Christian Union Church of Chicago.* Chicago: Trinity Evangelical Divinity School.

Mason, Sarah R. 1982. "Family Structure and Acculturation in the Chinese Community in Minnesota." In *Asian and Pacific American Experiences: Women's Perspectives,* ed. Nobuya Tsuchida, 160–171. Minneapolis: Asian/Pacific American Learning Resource Center and General College, University of Minnesota.

———. 1995. "Liang May Seen and the Early Chinese Community in Minneapolis." *Minnesota History* (Spring): 223–233.

McCafferty, Michael. 2003. "A Fresh Look at the Place Name Chicago." *Journal of the Illinois State Historical Society* 95, no. 2 (Summer): 116–129.

McKeown, Adam. 2001. *Chinese Migrant Networks and Cultural Change: Peru, Chicago, Hawaii, 1900–1936.* Chicago: University of Chicago Press.

Mei, June. 1979. "Economic Origins of Emigration: Guangdong to California, 1850–1882." *Modern China* 5, no. 4 (October): 463–501.

Merriner, James L. 2004. *Grafters and Goo Goos: Corruption and Reform in Chicago, 1833–2003.* Carbondale: Southern Illinois University Press.

Min, Gap Pyong. 1984. "A Structural Analysis of Korean Business in the United States." *Ethnic Groups* 6:1–25.

———. 1996. *Caught in the Middle: Korean Communities in New York and Los Angeles.* Berkeley: University of California Press.

Minnick, Sylvia Sun. 1988. *Samfow: The San Joaquin Chinese Legacy.* Fresno, CA: Panorama West Publishing.

Modell, John. 1977. *The Economics and Politics of Racial Accommodation: The Japanese in Los Angeles, 1900–1942.* Urbana: University of Illinois Press.

Mormino, Gary Ross. 1986. *Immigrants on the Hill, Italian-Americans in St. Louis, 1882–1982.* Urbana and Chicago: University of Illinois Press.

Moy, Susan Lee. 1978. "The Chinese in Chicago: The First One Hundred Years, 1870–1970." Master's thesis, University of Wisconsin–Milwaukee.

———. 1995. "The Chinese in Chicago: The First One Hundred Years." In *Ethnic Chicago: A Multicultural Portrait*, 4th ed., ed. Melvin G. Holli and Peter d'A. Jones, 378–408. Grand Rapids, MI: William B. Eerdmans.

Moyers, Bill D., Thomas Lennon, Joe Angier, Mi Ling Tsui, and Steve Cheng. 2003. *Becoming American: The Chinese Experience.* Program 2, "Between Two Worlds." New York: Public Affairs Television.

Nee, Victor G., and Brett de Bary. 1972. *Longtime Californ': A Documentary Study of an American Chinatown.* New York: Pantheon.

Nelli, Humbert S. 1970. *Italians in Chicago, 1880–1930: A Study in Ethnic Mobility.* New York: Oxford University Press.

Ng, Franklin. 1992. *The Taiwanese Americans.* Westport, CT: Greenwood Press.

Ngai, Mae M. 2004. *Impossible Subjects: Illegal Aliens and the Making of Modern America.* Princeton, NJ: Princeton University Press.

———. 2005. "Transnationalism and the Transformation of the 'Other.'" *American Quarterly* 57, no. 1 (March): 59–65.

Okihiro, Gary Y. 2001. *Common Ground: Reimagining American History.* Princeton, NJ: Princeton University Press.

———. 2009. *Island World: A History of Hawai'i and the United States.* Berkeley: University of California Press.

Olson, Audrey L. 1980. *St. Louis Germans, 1850–1920: The Nature of an Immigrant Community and Its Relation to the Assimilation Process.* New York: Arno Press.

Omi, Michael, and Howard Winant. 1986. *Racial Formation in the United States from the 1960s to the 1990s.* New York: Routledge.

Ong, Aihwa. 1999. *Flexible Citizenship: The Cultural Logics of Transnationality.* Durham, NC: Duke University Press.

———. 2003. *Buddha Is Hiding: Refugees, Citizenship, the New America.* Berkeley: University of California Press.

Ong, Hwei-Lan. 1940. "Study of Chinese Clients Known to Chicago Relief Administration." Master's thesis, University of Chicago.

Ong, Paul. 1984. "Chinatown Unemployment and the Ethnic Labor Market." *Amerasia Journal* 11, no. 1: 35–54.

Ono, Kent A., and John M. Sloop. 2002. *Shifting Borders: Rhetoric, Immigration, and California's Proposition 187.* Philadelphia: Temple University Press.

Organization of Chinese Americans, St. Louis Chapter. 1993. *Ironing Out the Fabric of Our Past: An Oral History of Five Chinese Americans in St. Louis, The Early 1900's.* St. Louis, MO: Organization of Chinese Americans, St. Louis Chapter.

Orleans, Leo A. 1988. *Chinese Students in America: Policies, Issues, and Numbers.* Washington, DC: National Academy Press.

Osumi, Megumi Dick. 1982. "Asians and California's Anti-miscegenation Laws." In *Asian and Pacific American Experiences: Women's Perspectives*, ed. Nobuya Tuschida et al., 1–37. Minneapolis: Asian/Pacific American Learning Resource Center and General College, University of Minnesota.

Pacyga, Dominic A. 1991. *Polish Immigrants and Industrial Chicago: Workers on the South Side, 1880–1922.* Columbus: Ohio State University Press.

Palmer, Vivian. 1932. "Documents of the Near South Side Communities, Chicago." Prepared for the Chicago Historical Society and Local Community Research Committee, University of Chicago.

Park, Kyeyoung. 1997. *The Korean American Dream: Immigrants and Small Business in New York City.* Ithaca, NY: Cornell University Press.

Park, Kyeyoung, and Jessica Kim. 2008. "The Contested Nexus of Los Angeles Koreatown." *Amerasia Journal* 34, no. 3: 127–150.

Park, Kyu Young. 2003. *Korean Americans in Chicago.* Charleston, SC: Arcadia Publishing.

Park, Lisa Sun-Hee. 2005. *Consuming Citizenship: Children of Asian Immigrant Entrepreneurs.* Palo Alto, CA: Stanford University Press.

Park, Robert Ezra. 1923. "A Race Relationship Survey." *Journal of Applied Sociology* 8:195–205.

———. 1928. "Human Migration and the Marginal Man." *American Journal of Sociology* 33, no. 6 (May): 881–893.

Park, Robert Ezra, and Ernest W. Burgess. (1921) 1969. *Introduction to the Science of Sociology.* Chicago: University of Chicago Press.

———, eds. 1964. *Contributions to Urban Sociology.* Chicago: University of Chicago Press.

Park, Robert Ezra, Ernest W. Burgess, and Roderick D. McKenzie. 1925. *The City.* Chicago: University of Chicago Press.

Parot, Joseph J. 1981. *Polish Catholics in Chicago, 1850–1920.* DeKalb: Northern Illinois University Press.

Pascoe, Peggy. 2009. *What Comes Naturally: Miscegenation Law and the Making of Race in America.* New York: Oxford University Press.

Pattillo, Mary. 1999. *Black Picket Fences: Privilege and Peril among the Black Middle Class.* Chicago: University of Chicago Press.

Peffer, George Anthony. 1986. "Forbidden Families: Emigration Experiences of Chinese Women under the Page Law, 1875–1882." *Journal of American Ethnic History* 6:28–64.

———. 1999. *If They Don't Bring Their Women Here: Chinese Female Immigration before Exclusion.* Urbana: University of Illinois Press.

Perez, Gina. 2004. *The New Northwest Side Story: Migration, Displacement, and Puerto Rican Families.* Berkeley: University of California Press.

Persons, Stow. 1987. *Ethnic Studies at Chicago, 1905–45.* Urbana: University of Illinois Press.

Philpott, Thomas L. 1978. *The Slum and the Ghetto: Neighborhood Deterioration and Middle-Class Reform, Chicago, 1880–1930.* New York: Oxford University Press.

Pickle, Linda Schelbitzki. 1996. *Contented among Strangers: Rural German-Speaking Women and Their Families in the Nineteenth-Century Midwest.* Urbana: University of Illinois Press.

Pollock, Mica. 2003. *Colormute: Race Talk Dilemmas in an American School.* Princeton, NJ: Princeton University Press.

Popkin, Susan J., Victoria E. Gwiasda, Lynn M. Olson, Dennis P. Rosenbaum, and Larry Buron. 2000. *The Hidden War: Crime and the Tragedy of Public Housing in Chicago.* New Brunswick, NJ: Rutgers University Press.

Porter, Raymond Willis. 1931. "A Study of the Musical Talent of Chinese Attending Public Schools in Chicago." PhD diss., University of Chicago.

Portes, Alejandro, Luis E. Guarnizo, and Patricia Landolt. 1999. "The Study of Transnationalism: Pitfalls and Promise of an Emergent Research Field." *Ethnic and Racial Studies* 22, no. 2 (March): 224.

Portes, Alejandro, and Robert Manning. 1986. "The Immigrant Enclave: Theory and Empirical Examples." In *Comparative Ethnic Relations*, ed. Joane Nagel and Susan Olzak, 47–68. Orlando, FL: Academic Press.

Portes, Alejandro, and Rubén G. Rumbaut. 1990. *Immigrant America: A Portrait.* Berkeley: University of California Press.

Posadas, Barbara M. 1981. "Cross Boundaries in Interracial Chicago: Filipino American Families since 1925." *Amerasia Journal* 16, no. 2: 31–52.

———. 1990. "Ethnic Life and Labor in Chicago's Pre–World War II Filipino Community." In *Labor Divided: Race and Ethnicity in United States Labor Struggles, 1835–1960*, ed. Robert Asher and Charles Stephenson, 63–80. Albany: State University of New York Press.

Primm, James Neal. 1990. *Lion of the Valley: St. Louis, Missouri.* Boulder, CO: Pruett Publishing.

Ramos-Zayas, Ana Y. 2003. *National Performances: The Politics of Class, Race and Space in Puerto Rican Chicago.* Chicago: University of Chicago Press.

Reimers, David M. 1985. *Still the Golden Door: The Third World Comes to America.* New York: Columbia University Press.

Reynolds, C. N. 1935. "The Chinese Tongs." *American Journal of Sociology* 40 (March): 612–623.

Riggs, Fred W. 1950. *Pressures on Congress: A Study of the Repeal of Chinese Exclusion.* New York: King's Crown Press.

Roediger, David R. 1991. *The Wage of Whiteness: Race and the Making of the American Working Class.* New York: Verso.

———. 2002. *Colored White: Transcending the Racial Past.* Berkeley: University of California Press.

Rohsenow, John S. 2004. "Chinese Language Use in Chicagoland." In *Ethnolinguistic Chicago: Language and Literacy in the City's Neighborhoods,* ed. Marcia Farr, 321–355. Mahwah, NJ: Lawrence Erlbaum Associates.

Rumbaut, Rubén G. 1989. "The Structure of Refugee: Southeast Asian Refugees in the United States, 1975–1985." *International Review of Comparative Public Policy* 1:97–129.

Salyer, Lucy E. 1995. *Laws Harsh as Tigers: Chinese Immigrants and the Shaping of Modern Immigration Law.* Chapel Hill: University of North Carolina Press.

Sanders, James W. 1977. *The Education of an Urban Minority: Catholics in Chicago, 1833–1965.* New York: Oxford University Press.

Sandmeyer, Elmer C. 1973. *The Anti-Chinese Movement.* Urbana: University of Illinois Press.

Saxton, Alexander. 1971. *The Indispensable Enemy: Labor and the Anti-Chinese Movement in California.* Berkeley: University of California Press.

Shah, Nayan. 2001. *Contagious Divides: Epidemics and Race in San Francisco's Chinatown.* Berkeley: University of California Press.

Shaw, Clifford R. 1930 *The Jack-Roller: A Delinquent Boy's Own Story.* Chicago: University of Chicago Press.

Shepard, Charles O. 1921. "Wong Chin Foo—The Story of a Chair." *Publications of Buffalo Historical Society* 25:53–55.

Shum, Lynette. 2003. "Remembering Chinatown: Haining Street of Wellington." In *Unfolding History, Evolving Identity,* ed. Manying Ip, 73–93. Auckland: Auckland University Press.

Sickels, Robert J. 1972. *Race, Marriage, and the Law.* Albuquerque: University of New Mexico Press.

Sinclair, Upton. (1906) 1960. *The Jungle.* Reprint, New York: Signet.

Siu, Paul C. P. 1953. "The Sojourner." *American Journal of Sociology* 58:34–44.

———. 1987. *The Chinese Laundryman: A Study of Social Isolation.* Edited by John Kuo Wei Tchen. New York: New York University Press.

Smith, Carl. 1995. *Urban Disorder and the Shape of Belief: The Great Chicago Fire, the Haymarket Bomb, and the Model Town of Pullman.* Chicago: University of Chicago Press.

So, Larry. 1992. "The Chinese Community in Chicago." Chicago: Chinese American Service League.

Soong, Ruth Joan. 1931. "A Survey of the Education of Chinese Children in Chicago." Master's thesis, University of Chicago.

Spear, Allan H. 1967. *Black Chicago: The Making of Negro Ghetto, 1890–1920.* Chicago: University of Chicago Press.

Spears, Timothy B. 2005. *Chicago Dreaming: Midwesterners and the City, 1871–1919.* Chicago: University of Chicago Press.

Squires, Gregory, Larry Bennett, Kathleen McCourt, and Philip Nyden. 1987. *Chicago: Race, Class, and the Response to Urban Decline.* Philadelphia: Temple University Press.

Strauss, Daniel M. W. 1998. "Chinese Multilingualism in Chicago." PhD diss., Northwestern University.

Sung, Betty Lee. 1967. *Mountain of Gold: The Story of Chinese in America.* New York: Macmillan.

———. 1990. *Chinese American Intermarriage.* New York: Center for Migration Studies.

Suttles, Gerald D. 1968. *The Social Order of the Slum: Ethnicity and Territory in the Inner City.* Chicago: University of Chicago Press.

———. 1972. *The Social Construction of Communities.* Chicago: University of Chicago Press.

Swenson, John F. 1991. "Chicagoua/Chicago: The Origin, Meaning, and Etymology of a Place Name." *Illinois Historical Journal* 84, no. 4 (Winter): 235–248.

Symanski, Richard. 1981. *The Immoral Landscape: Female Prostitution in Western Societies.* Toronto: Butterworths.

Takaki, Ronald. 1989. *Strangers from a Different Shore: A History of Asian Americans.* Boston: Little, Brown.

Tam, Shirley Sui-Ling. 1988. "Police Round-Up of Chinese in Cleveland in 1925: A Case Study in a Racist Measure and the Chinese Response." Master's thesis, Case Western Reserve University.

Tan, Chee-Beng, ed. 2007. *Transnational Chinese Networks.* London: Routledge.

Tang, Vincent. 1980. "Chinese Women Immigrants and the Two-Edged Sword of Habeas Corpus." In *The Chinese American Experience: Papers from the Second National Conference on Chinese American Studies,* ed. Genny Lim, 48–56. Chinese Historical Society of America and the Chinese Cultural Foundation of San Francisco.

Tchen, John Kuo Wei. 1984. *Genthe's Photographs of San Francisco's Old Chinatown.* New York: Dover.

———. 1990. "New York Chinese: The Nineteenth-Century Pre-Chinatown Settlement." In *Chinese America: History and Perspectives, 1990,* Chinese Historical Society of America, 157–192. San Francisco: Chinese Historical Society of America.

————. 1999. *New York before Chinatown: Orientalism and the Shaping of American Culture, 1776–1882*. Baltimore: Johns Hopkins University Press.

Thomas, W. I. 1901. "The Gambling Instinct." *American Journal of Sociology* 6:750–763.

Thompson, Richard H. 1987. *Toronto's Chinatown: The Changing Social Organization of an Ethnic Community*. New York: AMS Press.

Tong, Benson. 1994. *Unsubmissive Women: Chinese Prostitutes in Nineteenth-Century San Francisco*. Norman: University of Oklahoma Press.

Tsai, Shih-shan Henry. 1986. *The Chinese Experience in America*. Bloomington: Indiana University Press.

Tseng, Yen-Fen. 1995. "Beyond 'Little Taipei': The Development of Taiwanese Immigrant Business in Los Angeles." *International Migration Review* 29, no. 1 (Spring): 33–58.

Tu, Wei-ming. 1994. *The Living Tree: The Changing Meaning of Being Chinese Today*. Stanford, CA: Stanford University Press.

Tung, William L. 1974. *The Chinese in America 1820–1973: A Chronology & Fact Book*. Dobbs Ferry, NY: Oceana Publications.

Tuttle, William M., Jr. 1970. *Race Riot: Chicago in the Red Summer of 1919*. New York: Atheneum.

Vialles, Noelie. 1994. *Animal to Edible*. Cambridge: Cambridge University Press.

Võ, Linda Trinh. 2004. *Mobilizing an Asian American Community*. Philadelphia: Temple University Press.

Võ, Linda Trinh, and Rick Bonus, eds. 2002. *Contemporary Asian American Communities: Intersections and Divergences*. Philadelphia: Temple University Press.

Walton, William. 1893. *Art and Architecture*. Philadelphia: G. Barrie.

Wang, Gungwu. 1992. *China and the Chinese Overseas*. Singapore: Times Academic Press.

————. 2000. *The Chinese Overseas: From Earthbound China to the Quest for Autonomy*. Cambridge, MA: Harvard University Press.

Wang, L. Ling-chi. 1994. "Roots and the Changing Identity of the Chinese in the United States." In *The Living Tree: The Changing Meaning of Being Chinese Today*, ed. Tu Wei-ming, 185–212. Stanford, CA: Stanford University Press.

————. 1995. "The Structure of Dual Domination: Toward a Paradigm for the Study of the Chinese Diaspora in the United States." *Amerasia Journal* 12:149–169.

Wang, Laura. 1988. "Vallejo's Chinese Community, 1860–1960." In *Chinese America, History and Perspective*, Chinese Historical Society of America, 153–168. San Francisco: Chinese Historical Society of America.

Wang, Linda Qingling. 1997. "Chinese Immigrant Adaptation in an American Urban Context: Chicago as a Case Study." PhD diss., University of Wisconsin–Madison.

Wang, Xiao-Lei. 1992. "Resilience and Fragility in Language Acquisition: A Comparative Study of the Gestural Communication Systems of Chinese and American Deaf Children." PhD diss., University of Chicago.

Wang, Xinyang. 2001. *Surviving the City: The Chinese Immigrant Experience in New York City, 1890–1970*. Lanham, MD: Rowman & Littlefield.

Wang, Y. C. 1966. *Chinese Intellectuals and the West, 1872–1949*. Chapel Hill: University of North Carolina Press.

Ward, David. 1989. *Poverty, Ethnicity and the American City, 1840–1925: Changing Conceptions of the Slum and Ghetto*. New York: Cambridge University Press.

Warren, Elizabeth. 1979. *Chicago's Uptown: Public Policy, Neighborhood Decay, and Citizen Action in an Urban Community*. Urban Insight Series No. 3. Chicago: Loyola University.

Whyte, William F. 1943. *Street Corner Society: The Social Structure of an Italian Slum*. Chicago: University of Chicago Press.

Wilson, Margaret Gibbons. 1969. "Concentration and Dispersal of the Chinese Population of Chicago: 1870 to the Present." Master's thesis, University of Chicago.

Wilson, William Julius. 1987. *The Truly Disadvantaged: The Inner City, the Underclass, and Public Policy*. Chicago: University of Chicago Press.

Wirth, Louis. (1928) 1956. *The Ghetto*. Chicago: University of Chicago Press.

Wirth, Louis, and Eleanor H. Bernert. 1949. *Local Community Fact Book of Chicago*. Chicago: University of Chicago Press.

Wittman, Timothy N. 1988. "On Leong Merchants Association Building." Report submitted to the Commission on Chicago Landmarks.

Wong, Bernard P. 1988. *Patronage, Brokerage, Entrepreneurship and the Chinese Community of New York*. New York: AMS Press.

Wong, K. Scott. 1996. "'The Eagle Seeks a Helpless Quarry': Chinatown, the Police, and the Press. The 1903 Boston Chinatown Raid Revisited." *Amerasia Journal* 22, no. 3: 81–103.

Wong, K. Scott, and Sucheng Chan, eds. 1998. *Claiming America: Constructing Chinese American Identities during the Exclusion Era*. Philadelphia: Temple University Press.

Wong, Sau-Ling C. 1995. "Denationalization Reconsidered: Asian American Cultural Criticism at a Theoretical Crossroads." *Amerasia Journal* 21:1–27.

Wu, Ching-Chao. 1928. "Chinatowns: A Study of Symbiosis and Assimilation." PhD diss., University of Chicago.

Wu, Yuan-li, ed. 1980. *The Economic Condition of Chinese Americans.* Chicago: Pacific/Asian American Mental Health Research Center.

Yang, C. K. 1959. *The Chinese Family in the Communist Revolution.* Cambridge, MA: Harvard University Press.

Yang, Fenggang. 1999. *Chinese Christians in America: Conversion, Assimilation, and Adhesive Identities.* University Park: Penn State University Press.

Yang, Philip Q. 2006. "Transnationalism as a New Mode of Immigrant Adaptation: Preliminary Evidence from Chinese Transnational Migrants." *Journal of Chinese Overseas* 2, no. 2: 173–192.

Yans-McLaughlin, Virginia. 1982. *Family and Community: Italian Immigrants in Buffalo, 1880–1930.* Urbana: University of Illinois Press.

Yao, Tai-Ti Tsou. 1977. "Solving Communication Problems in Chicago's Chinatown," Master's thesis, University of Illinois at Chicago.

Ye, Weili. 2001. *Seeking Modernity in the United States, 1900–1927.* Stanford, CA: Stanford University Press.

Yeh, Chiou-Ling. 2008. *Making an American Festival: Chinese New Year in San Francisco's Chinatown.* Berkeley: University of California Press.

Yen, Lili Yun-Chien. 1999. "Attitudes and Beliefs about Cervical Cancer Screening among Chinese-American Women in Chicago." Master's thesis, Midwestern University.

Yen, Wendy Wen-yawn. 1990. "Dawn Always Comes after Darkness." Translated by Huping Ling. *World Journal Weekly*, May 8, 9, and 10.

Yin, Xiao-huang, ed. 2002. *The Expanding Roles of Chinese Americans in US-China Relations: Transnational Networks and Trans-Pacific Interactions.* New York: M. E. Sharpe.

Young, Pauline V. 1932. *Pilgrims of Russian Town.* Chicago: University of Chicago Press.

Yu, Henry. 2001. *Thinking Orientals: Migration, Contact, and Exoticism in Modern America.* Oxford: Oxford University Press.

Yu, Renqiu. 1983. "Chinese American Contributions to the Educational Development of Toisan 1910–1940." *Amerasia* 10, no. 1: 47–72.

———. 1987. "Chop Suey: From Chinese Food to Chinese American Food." *Chinese America: History and Perspectives.* 87–99.

———. 1992. *To Save China, to Save Ourselves: The Chinese Hand Laundry Alliance of New York.* Philadelphia: Temple University Press.

Yung, Judy. 1986. *Chinese Women of America, A Pictorial History.* Seattle: University of Washington Press.

———. 1995. *Unbound Feet: A Social History of Chinese Women in San Francisco.* Berkeley: University of California Press.

Yung, Judy, Gordon H. Chang, and Him Mark Lai. 2006. *Chinese American Voices: From the Gold Rush to the Present.* Berkeley: University of California Press.

Yung, Wing. 1909. *My Life in China and America.* New York: Henry Holt & Company.

Zhang, Qingsong. 1998. "The Origins of the Chinese Americanization Movement: Wong Chin Foo and the Chinese Equal Rights League." In *Claiming America: Constructing Chinese American Identity during the Exclusion Era*, ed. K. Scott Wong and Sucheng Chan, 41–63. Philadelphia: Temple University Press.

Zhang, Tingwei, et al. 1994. *Open Space Needs in Chicago's Chinatown Area.* Chicago: Center for Urban Economic Development, University of Illinois at Chicago.

Zhao, Jianli. 2002. *Strangers in the City: The Atlanta Chinese, Their Community, and Stories of Their Lives.* New York: Routledge.

Zhao, Xiaojian. 2002. *Remaking Chinese America: Immigration, Family, and Community, 1940–1965.* New Brunswick, NJ: Rutgers University Press.

Zhou, Min. 1992. *Chinatown: The Socioeconomic Potential of an Urban Enclave.* Philadelphia: Temple University Press.

Zhou, Yu. 1996. "Ethnic Networks as Transactional Networks: Chinese Networks in the Producer Service Sectors of Los Angeles." PhD diss., University of Minnesota.

Index

Strassburger, John B., 37
"street of Shanghai" (Shanghai Village), at the 1933–34 World's Fair: A Century of Progress, 77–78, 165–166
Stridiron, H. H., 41, 141
students and intellectuals: academic fields, 175, 185; connecting China, 175–177, 186; connecting Chinatown, 175–178, 187–203; contemporary period, 180–187; extracurricular activities, 175; motives to study in America, 181–183; government-sponsored, 183; pioneer period, 173–176; population in America, 183; from PRC 182–186; relationship with Chinatown, 187–189; return to China, 178–179; self-supporting, 183; sex ratio, 183–185; socioeconomic background, 181, 185; from Taiwan, 180–182, 186–187; wartime and postwar period, 176–180; writings of Chinatown, 189–203
suburbanization, of Chinese Americans in Chicago, 216, 226–229
Sun Leung, 50. *See also* Chinatown Trunk Mystery in New York; Elsie Sigel murder
Sun Life Assurance Company of Canada, 123
Sun Yat-sen, 149, 153, 163, 166–167
Sunday schools, 32–33, 51, 159–161. *See also* Baptist Chinese Mission; racial contacts

Tael, 250n5
Tai Wah and Company, 60, 63–64. *See also* grocery stores
Taishan, 13, 19–21. *See also* Siyi
Taishanese, 20–22: in Chicago, 32, 60–96, 127; remittance to China, 21–22, 84–87, 239–241, 245; to the United States, 245. See also Duanfen Township; Moy brothers; Moys; transnational economic activities
Tchen, John Kuo Wei, 10, 198, 250n3
Thai, Stanley, Dato' Seri, 215
Three People's Principles, 153
Tiananmen Incident, 186
Tom Lok, 73–74. *See also* restaurants, Chinese
Tom, T., 125
Toy, Charlie, 169
Toy Chow, 128
Toy, F., 101
Toy Hung Chuck, 66
Toy Shee, 88–91. *See also* Hong Sling
Transcontinental Railroad, 16–17, 30. *See also* Chinese immigrants

transnational migration, 5–6, 12–20: and businessmen, 60–96; and connection to China, 163–169; 187–207, 237–241; and economic activities, 8–9, 59–96, 239–241, 245; and ethnic networks, 59–91, 237–237; and family lives, 100–130; forces of, 12–20; future of, 242–245; and *qiaokan*, 239–241; and remittances to China, 21–22, 84–87, 239–241, 245. *See also* Chinese niche businesses; Hong Sling; merchants; migration; Moy Dong Chow; Moy Dong Hoy; Moy Dong Yee; Taishanese
transnationalism, definition of, 6
tripartite division, 229–231
Tun, Charles W., 169

Ung Yok, 37
Union Stockyards, 54
University of Chicago, 2, 3, 47, 172, 190, 226, 230
University of Illinois at Chicago, 230–231

Viet My, 224. *See also* restaurants, Vietnamese
Vietnamese Association of Illinois, 235
Vietnamese refugees, 222–225. *See also* Southeast Asian refugees
Vietnamese restaurants. *See* restaurants, Vietnamese
Vietnamese Thai Binh Restaurant, 224. *See also* restaurants, Vietnamese

Wah Kee, 69
Wah Mee Corporation, 76–77, 87–88. *See also* Chinese Village at the 1893 World's Columbian Exposition
Wah Mei Drum and Bugle Corp, 210
Wah Yung Company, 87–88. *See also* Chinese Village at the 1893 World's Columbian Exposition
Wang, Chi Che, Dr., 175–176
Wang, Gung-Hsing, 145, 217
Wang, H. F., 162
Wang, Laura, 99
Wang, Linda Qingling, 189, 201
Wang, Y. C., 174
Wang Yuanlin, 22
War Bride Act of 1945, 206
war efforts, Chinese American, 167–169; enrollment in the armed forces, 169
Wee Ying Lo, 73. *See also* restaurants, Chinese
Weng Songping, 242–243

CPSIA information can be obtained
at www.ICGtesting.com
Printed in the USA
LVOW08s1040190517

535146LV00001B/85/P